KAMISAMA KAZOKU

Translation – Christine Schilling
Adaptation – Brynne Chandler
Editorial Assistant – Mallory Reaves
Lettering and Design – Team Pokopen
Production Assistant – Suzy Wells
Production Manager – James Dashiell
Editor – Brynne Chandler

A Go! Comi manga

Published by Go! Media Entertainment, LLC

Kamisama Kazoku vol. 1
© 2006 Yoshikazu Kuwashima, MEDIA FACTORY Inc.
© 2006 TaPari, DAIWON C.I. Inc.
 First published in Japan in 2006 by MEDIA FACTORY, Inc.
And in Korea by DAIWON C. I. Inc.
English translation rights reserved by Go! Media Entertainment LLC.
Under the license from MEDIA FACTORY, Inc., and DAIWON C. I. Inc.
Through TOHAN CORPORATION, Tokyo

English Text © 2008 Go! Media Entertainment, LLC. All rights reserved.

This book is a work of fiction. Names, places and incidents are either a
product of the author's imagination or are used fictitiously.

No part of this book may be reproduced or transmitted in any form or by any
means physical or digital without permission in writing from the publisher.

Visit us online at www.gocomi.com
e-mail: info@gocomi.com

ISBN 978-1-933617-99-2

First printed in June 2008

1   2   3   4   5   6   7   8   9

Manufactured in the United States of America

KAMISAMA KAZOKU

by
Tapari &
Yoshikazu Kuwashima

Volume 1

go!comi

contents

THIS WORK IS PURELY FICTION. ANY RELATION TO ACTUAL PERSONS, ORGANIZATIONS, ETC. IS STRICTLY COINCIDENCE. ♥

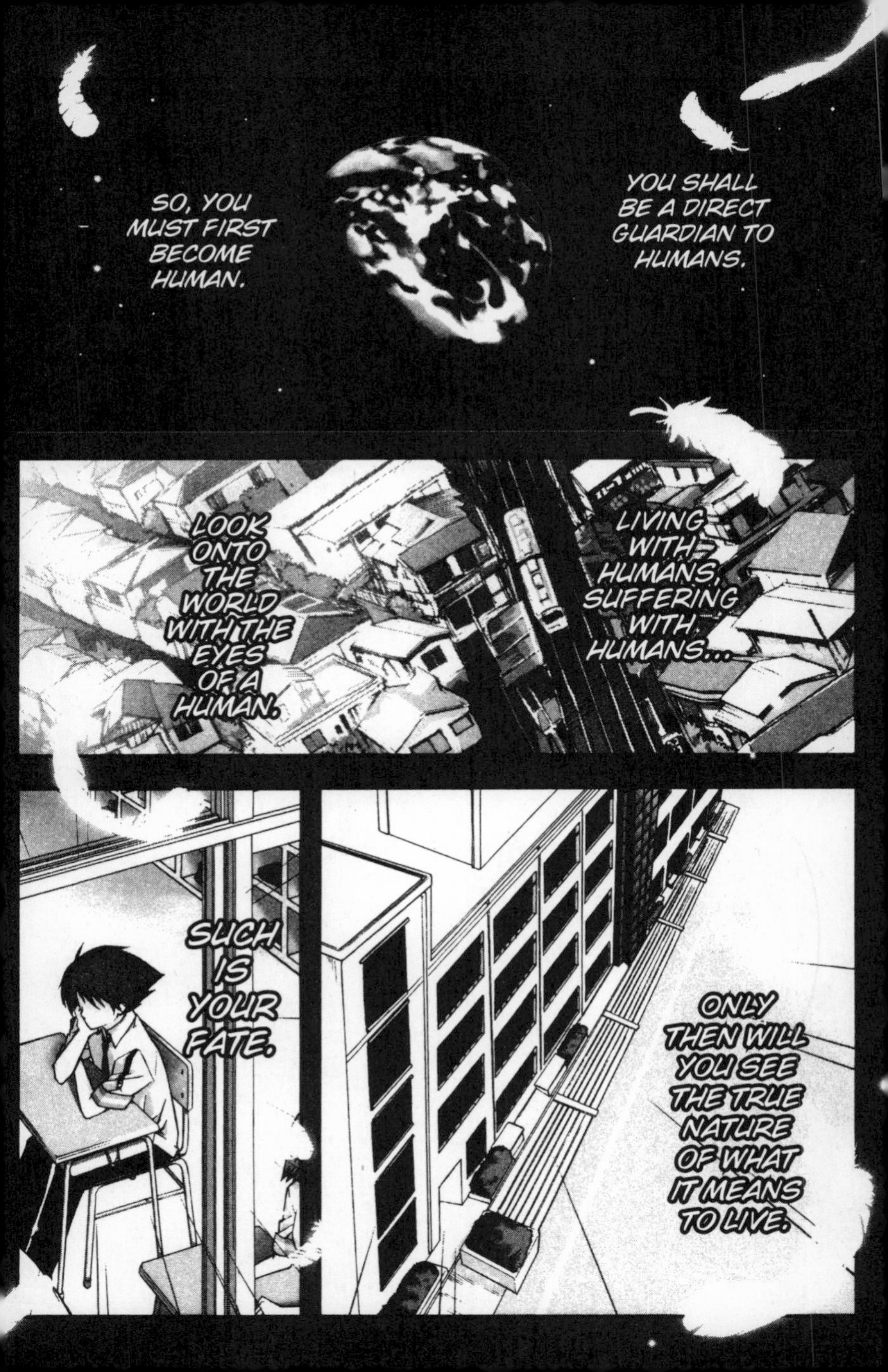
YOU SHALL BE A DIRECT GUARDIAN TO HUMANS.
SO, YOU MUST FIRST BECOME HUMAN.
LIVING WITH HUMANS, SUFFERING WITH HUMANS...
LOOK ONTO THE WORLD WITH THE EYES OF A HUMAN.
ONLY THEN WILL YOU SEE THE TRUE NATURE OF WHAT IT MEANS TO LIVE.
SUCH IS YOUR FATE.

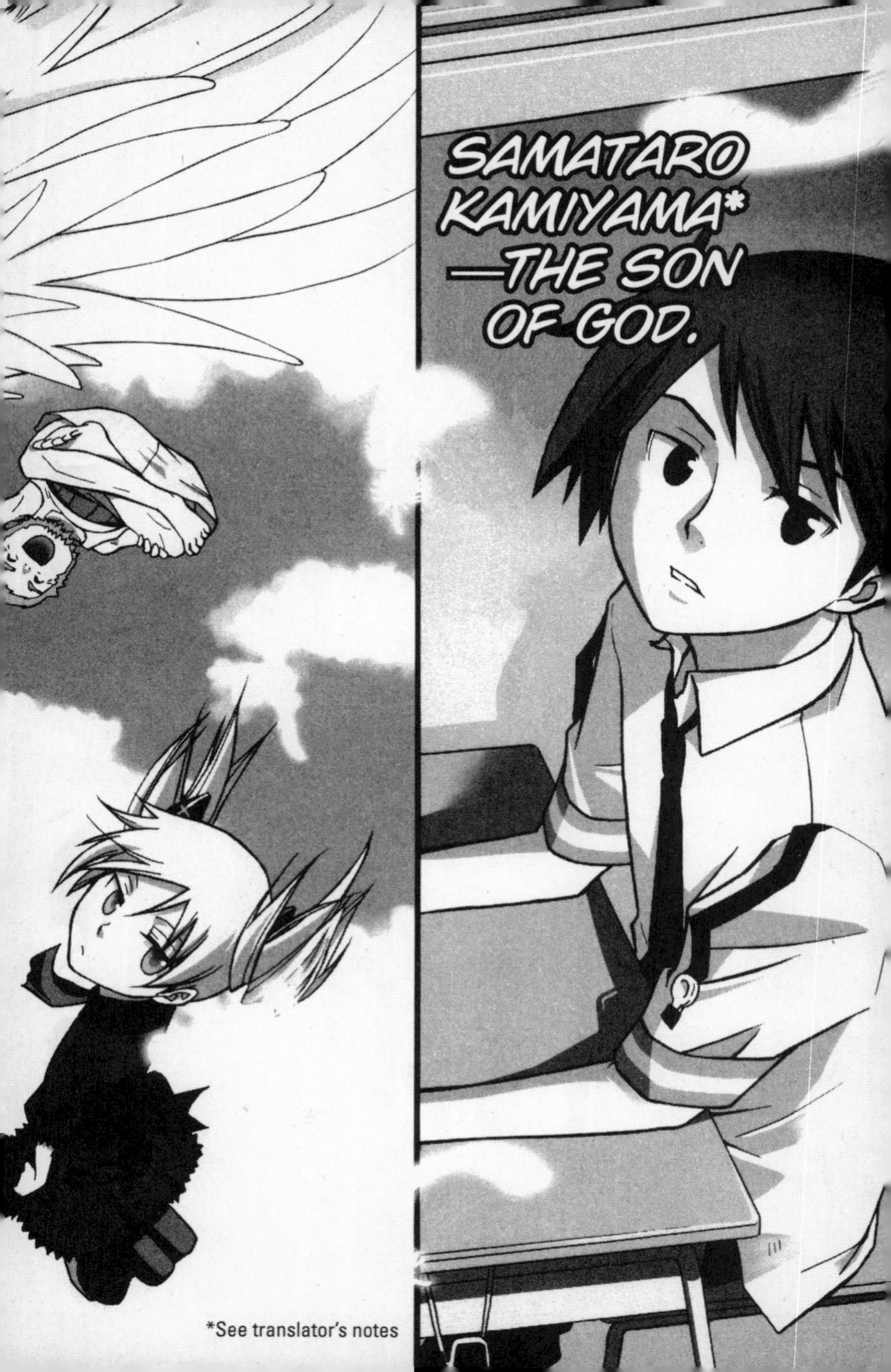
SAMATARO KAMIYAMA* —THE SON OF GOD.

*See translator's notes

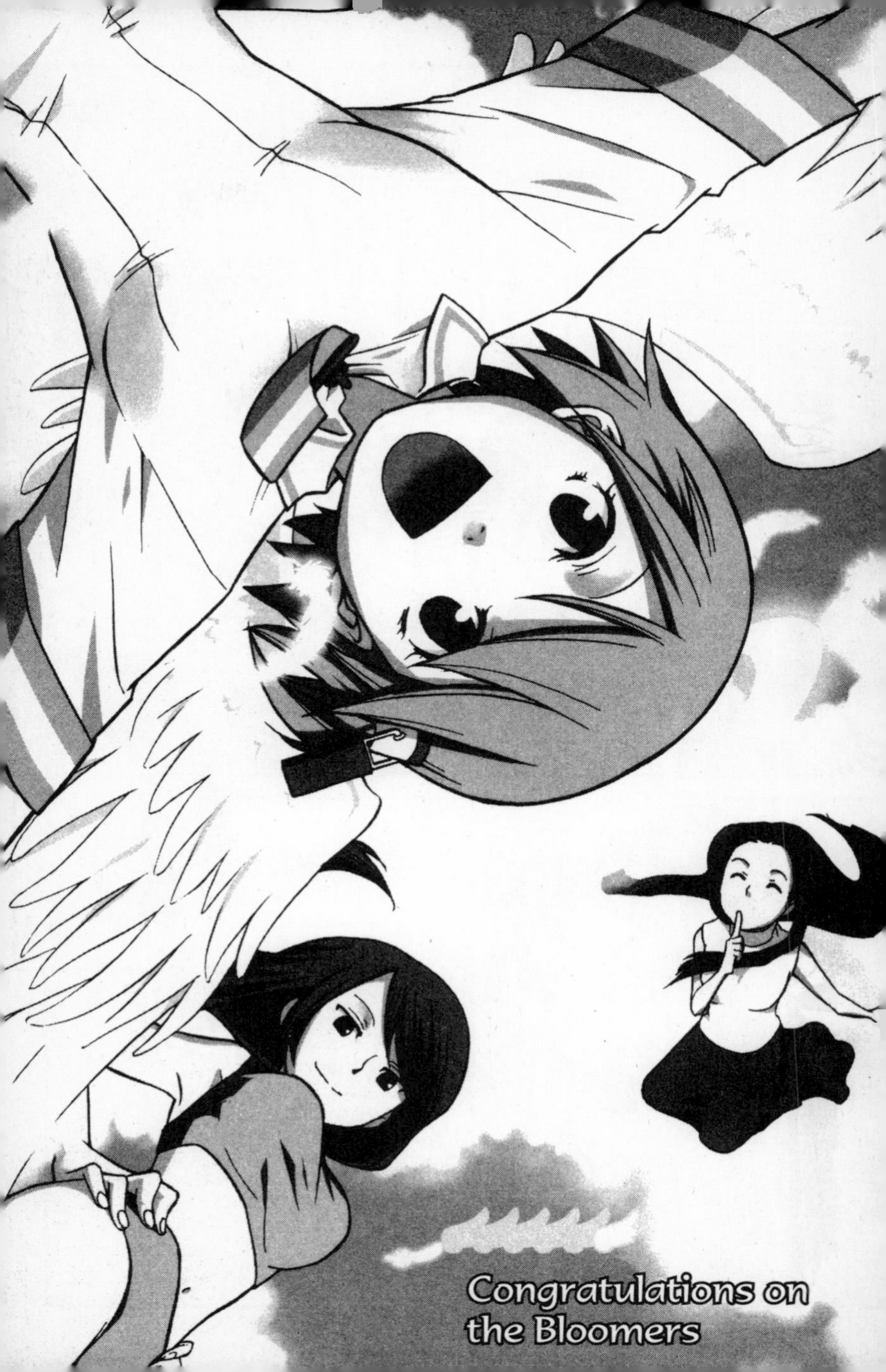
Congratulations on the Bloomers

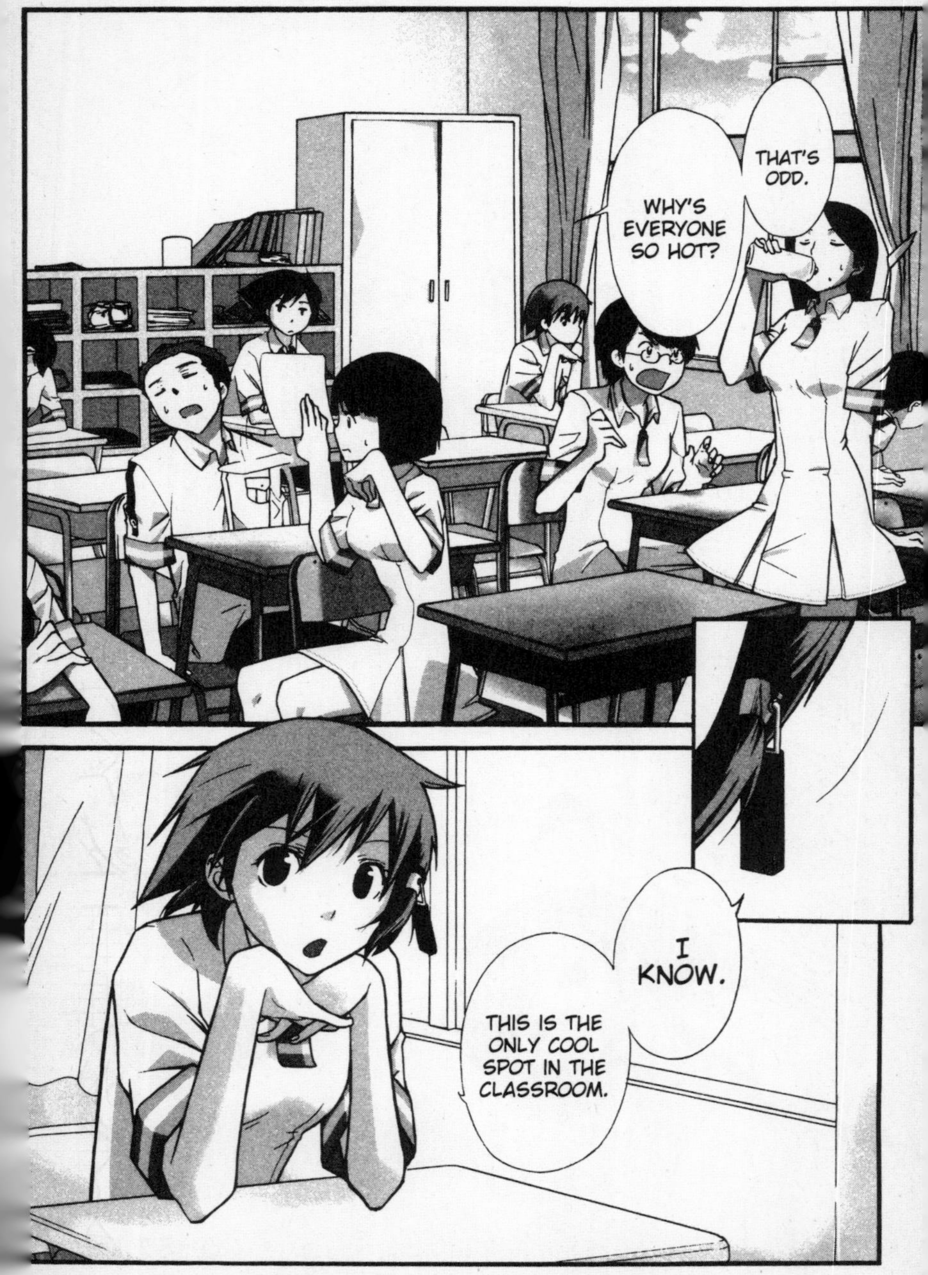
THAT'S ODD.
WHY'S EVERYONE SO HOT?
I KNOW.
THIS IS THE ONLY COOL SPOT IN THE CLASSROOM.

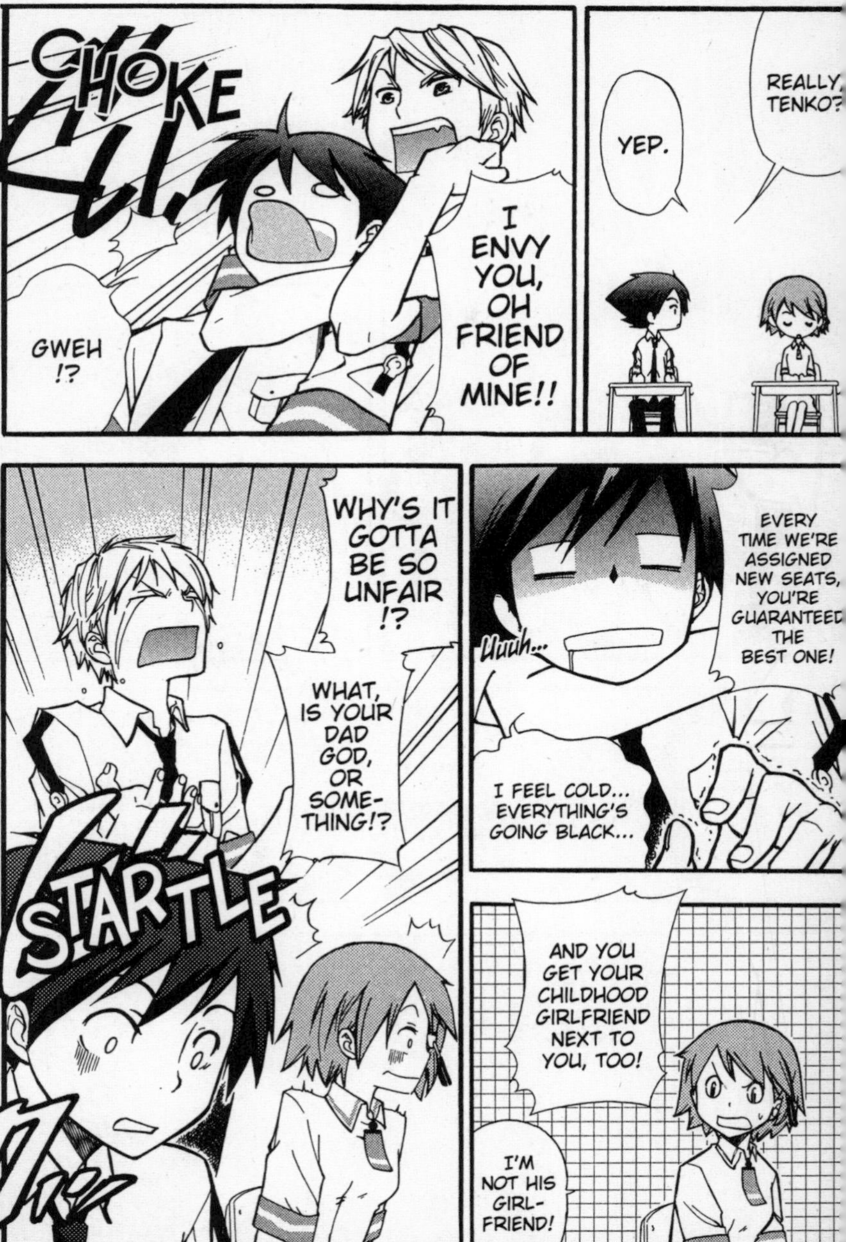
REALLY, TENKO?
YEP.
CHOKE
I ENVY YOU, OH FRIEND OF MINE!!
GWEH !?
EVERY TIME WE'RE ASSIGNED NEW SEATS, YOU'RE GUARANTEED THE BEST ONE!
Uuuh...
I FEEL COLD... EVERYTHING'S GOING BLACK...
AND YOU GET YOUR CHILDHOOD GIRLFRIEND NEXT TO YOU, TOO!
I'M NOT HIS GIRL-FRIEND!
WHY'S IT GOTTA BE SO UNFAIR !?
WHAT, IS YOUR DAD GOD, OR SOME-THING!?
STARTLE

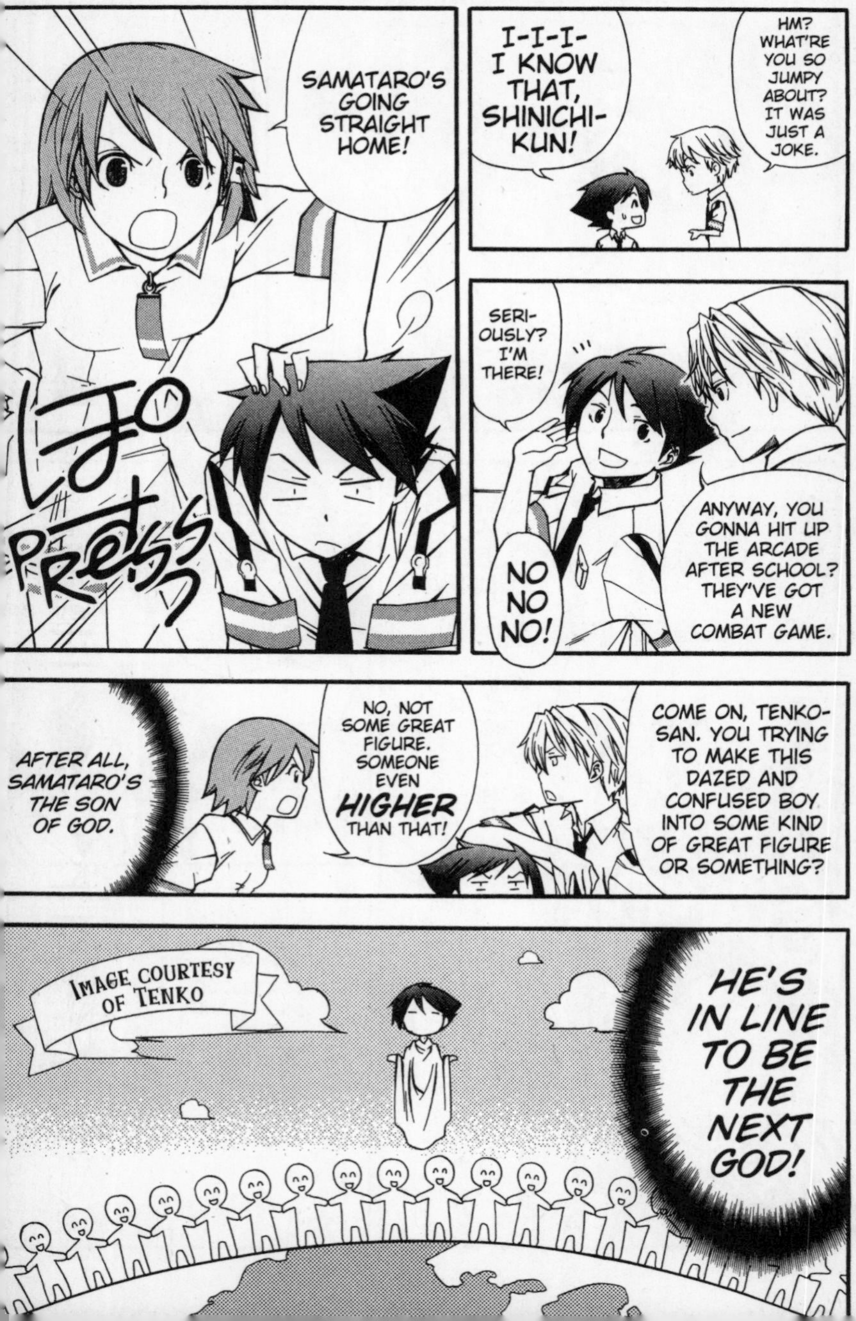
HM? WHAT'RE YOU SO JUMPY ABOUT? IT WAS JUST A JOKE.
I-I-I- I KNOW THAT, SHINICHI-KUN!
ANYWAY, YOU GONNA HIT UP THE ARCADE AFTER SCHOOL? THEY'VE GOT A NEW COMBAT GAME.
SERI-OUSLY? I'M THERE!
NO NO NO!
SAMATARO'S GOING STRAIGHT HOME!
PRESS
COME ON, TENKO-SAN. YOU TRYING TO MAKE THIS DAZED AND CONFUSED BOY INTO SOME KIND OF GREAT FIGURE OR SOMETHING?
NO, NOT SOME GREAT FIGURE. SOMEONE EVEN HIGHER THAN THAT!
AFTER ALL, SAMATARO'S THE SON OF GOD.
HE'S IN LINE TO BE THE NEXT GOD!
IMAGE COURTESY OF TENKO

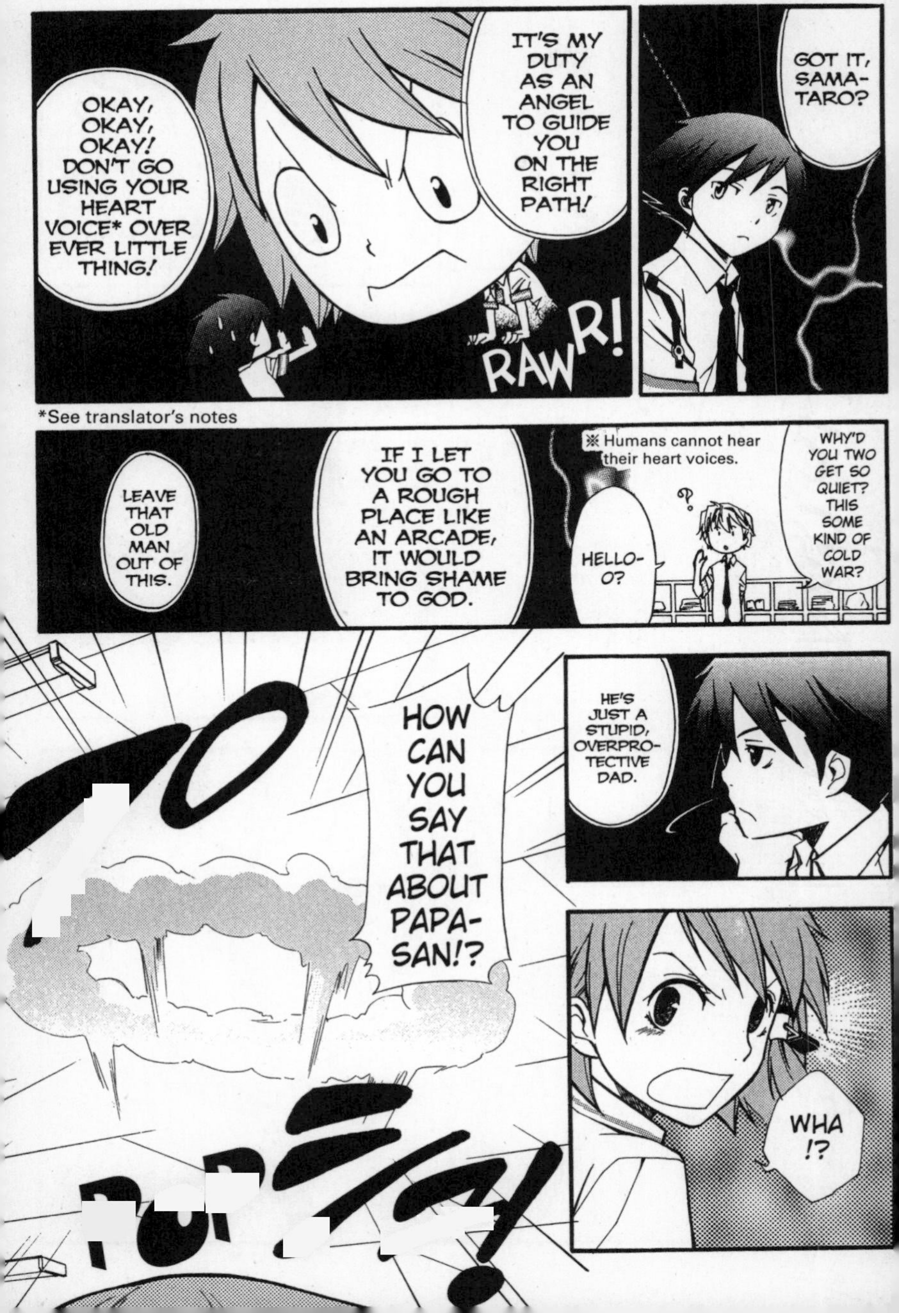
GOT IT, SAMA-TARO?
IT'S MY DUTY AS AN ANGEL TO GUIDE YOU ON THE RIGHT PATH!
OKAY, OKAY, OKAY! DON'T GO USING YOUR HEART VOICE* OVER EVER LITTLE THING!
RAWR!
WHY'D YOU TWO GET SO QUIET? THIS SOME KIND OF COLD WAR?
※ Humans cannot hear their heart voices.
HELLO-O?
IF I LET YOU GO TO A ROUGH PLACE LIKE AN ARCADE, IT WOULD BRING SHAME TO GOD.
LEAVE THAT OLD MAN OUT OF THIS.
HE'S JUST A STUPID, OVERPROTECTIVE DAD.
WHA!?
HOW CAN YOU SAY THAT ABOUT PAPA-SAN!?

*See translator's notes

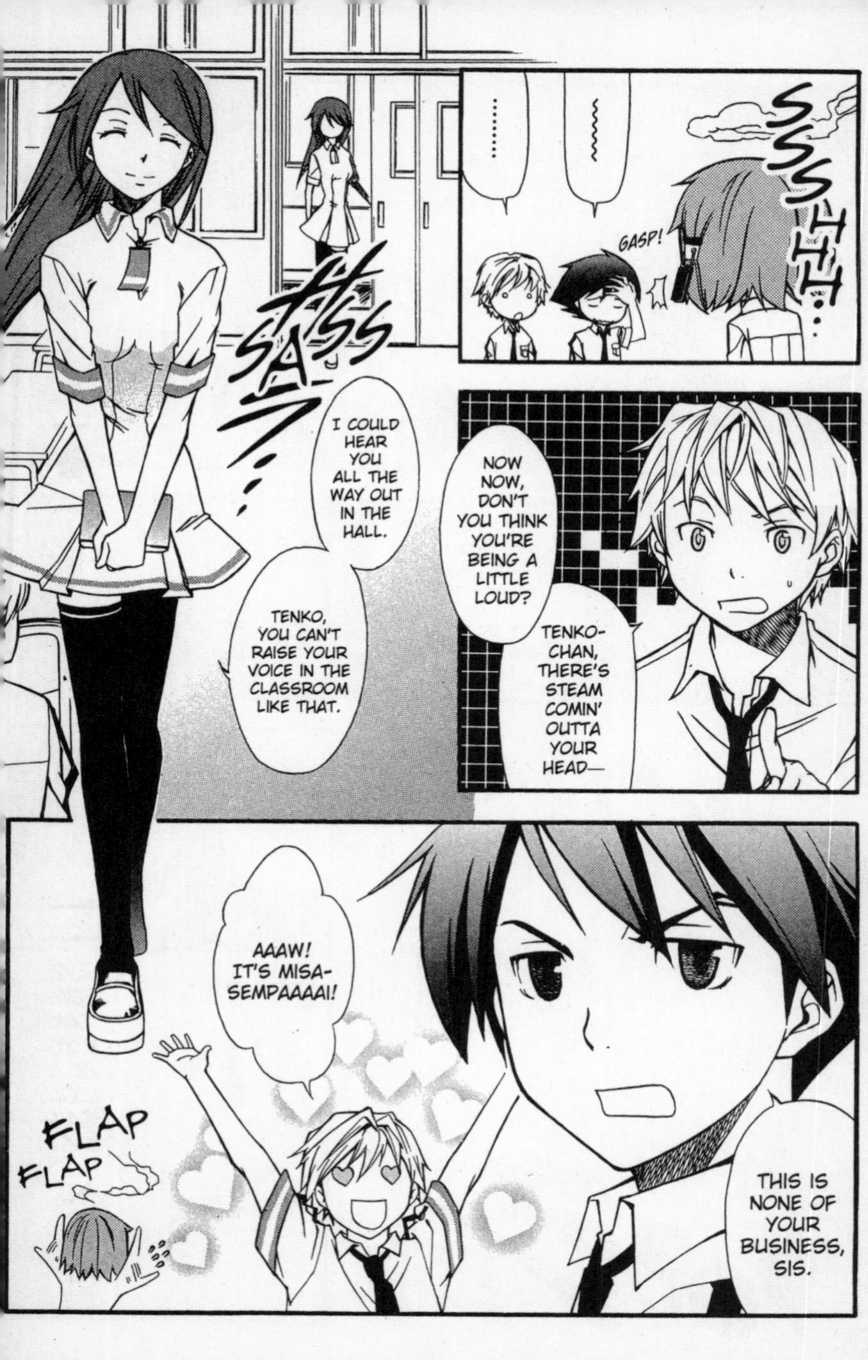
SSSHHH...
GASP!
……
TENKO-CHAN, THERE'S STEAM COMIN' OUTTA YOUR HEAD—
NOW NOW, DON'T YOU THINK YOU'RE BEING A LITTLE LOUD?
HISSS
SA
I COULD HEAR YOU ALL THE WAY OUT IN THE HALL.
TENKO, YOU CAN'T RAISE YOUR VOICE IN THE CLASSROOM LIKE THAT.
THIS IS NONE OF YOUR BUSINESS, SIS.
AAAW! IT'S MISA-SEMPAAAAI!
FLAP
FLAP

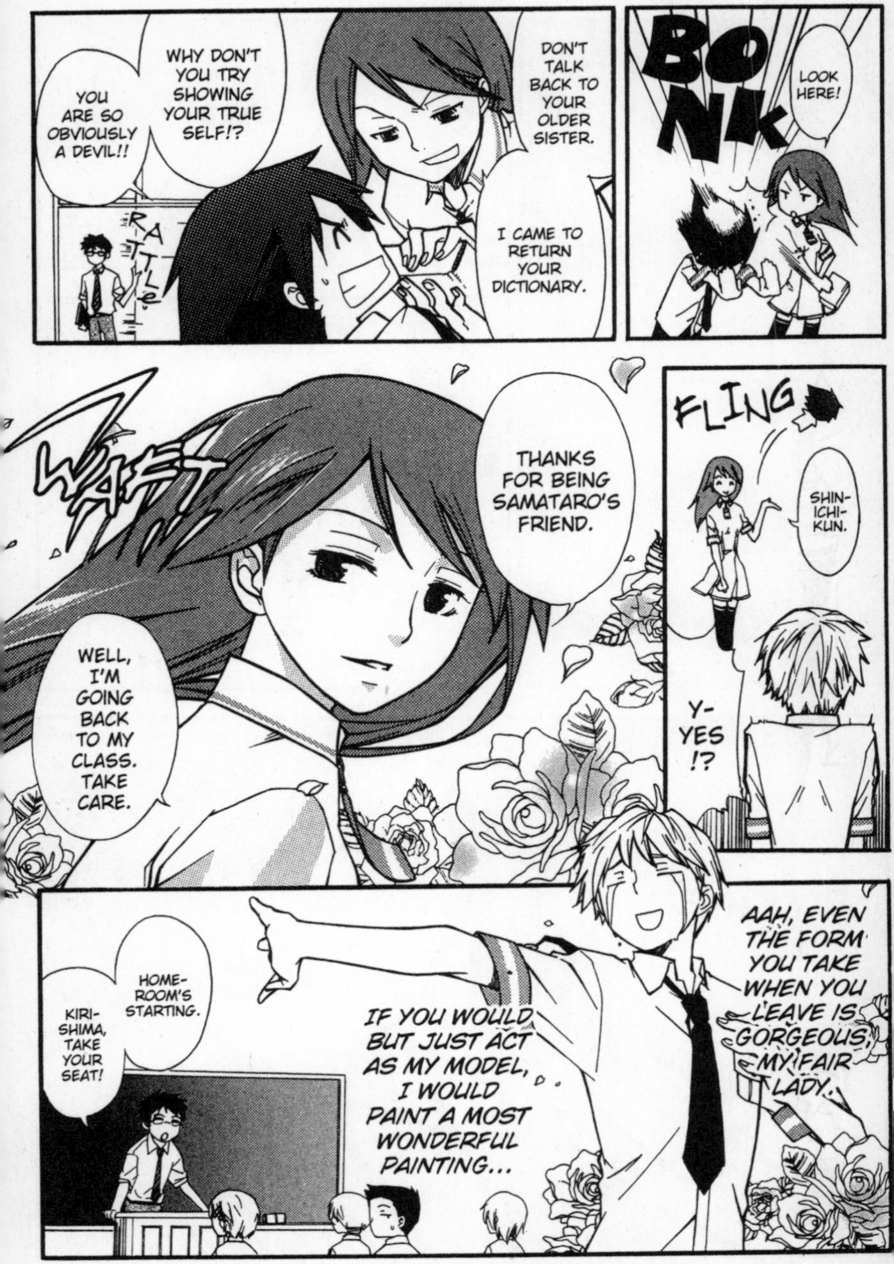
BONK
LOOK HERE!
I CAME TO RETURN YOUR DICTIONARY.
DON'T TALK BACK TO YOUR OLDER SISTER.
WHY DON'T YOU TRY SHOWING YOUR TRUE SELF!?
YOU ARE SO OBVIOUSLY A DEVIL!!
RATTLE
FLING
SHIN-ICHI-KUN.
Y-YES!?
THANKS FOR BEING SAMATARO'S FRIEND.
WAFT
WELL, I'M GOING BACK TO MY CLASS. TAKE CARE.
AAH, EVEN THE FORM YOU TAKE WHEN YOU LEAVE IS GORGEOUS, MY FAIR LADY.
IF YOU WOULD BUT JUST ACT AS MY MODEL, I WOULD PAINT A MOST WONDERFUL PAINTING...
HOME-ROOM'S STARTING.
KIRI-SHIMA, TAKE YOUR SEAT!

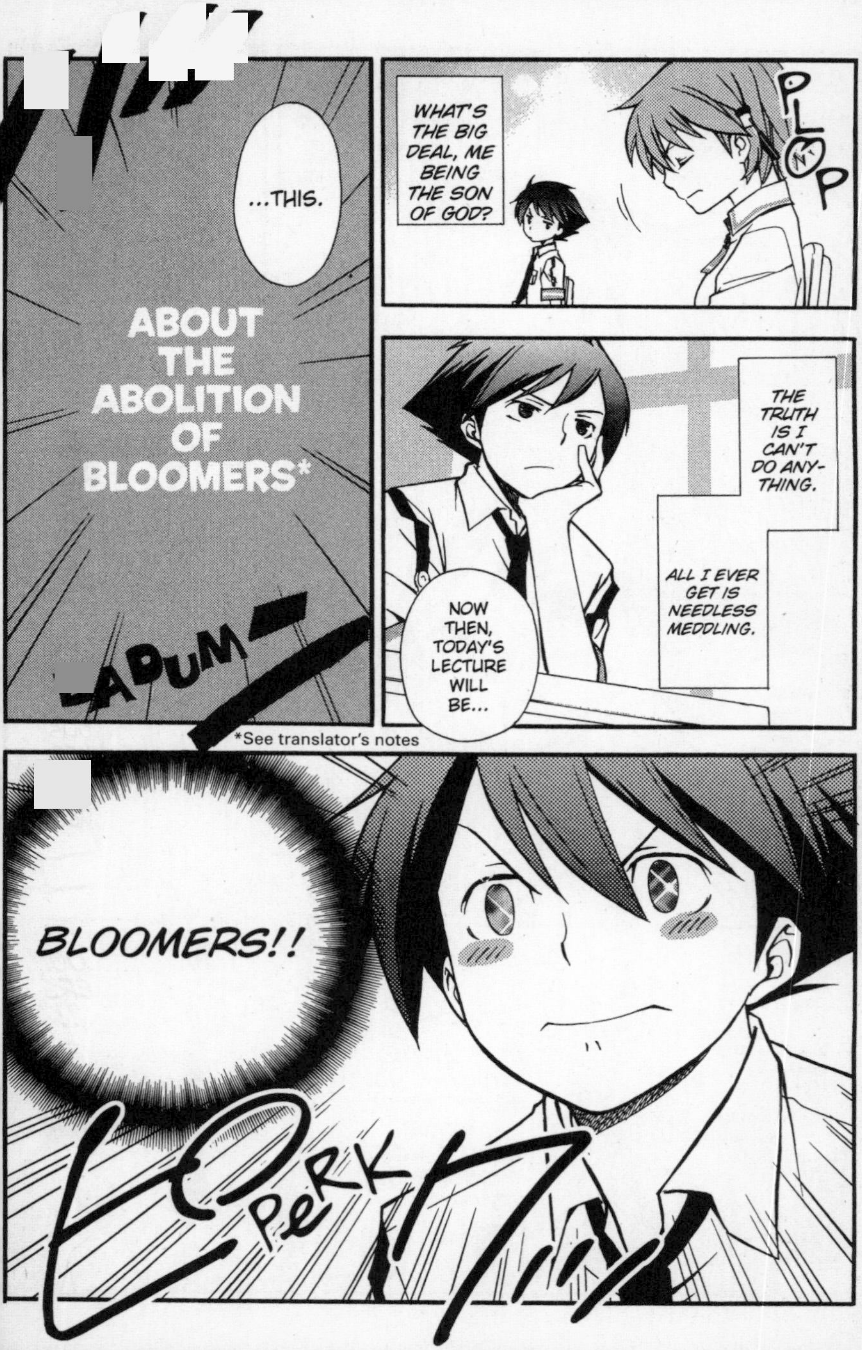
WHAT'S THE BIG DEAL, ME BEING THE SON OF GOD?
PLOP
THE TRUTH IS I CAN'T DO ANYTHING.
ALL I EVER GET IS NEEDLESS MEDDLING.
NOW THEN, TODAY'S LECTURE WILL BE...
...THIS.
ABOUT THE ABOLITION OF BLOOMERS*
BLOOMERS!!
PERK
*See translator's notes

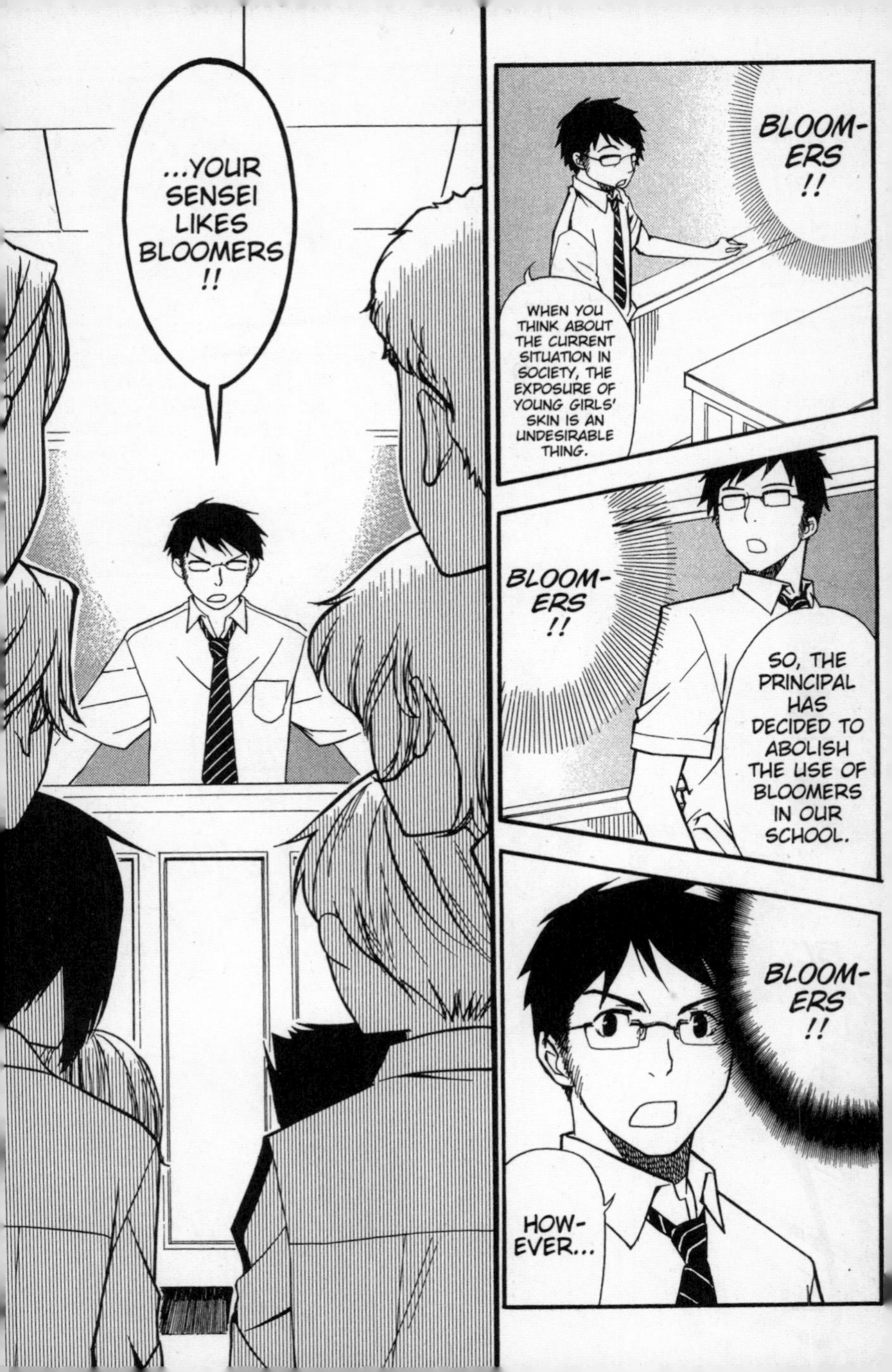
BLOOM-ERS!!
WHEN YOU THINK ABOUT THE CURRENT SITUATION IN SOCIETY, THE EXPOSURE OF YOUNG GIRLS' SKIN IS AN UNDESIRABLE THING.
SO, THE PRINCIPAL HAS DECIDED TO ABOLISH THE USE OF BLOOMERS IN OUR SCHOOL.
BLOOM-ERS!!
BLOOM-ERS!!
HOW-EVER...
...YOUR SENSEI LIKES BLOOMERS!!

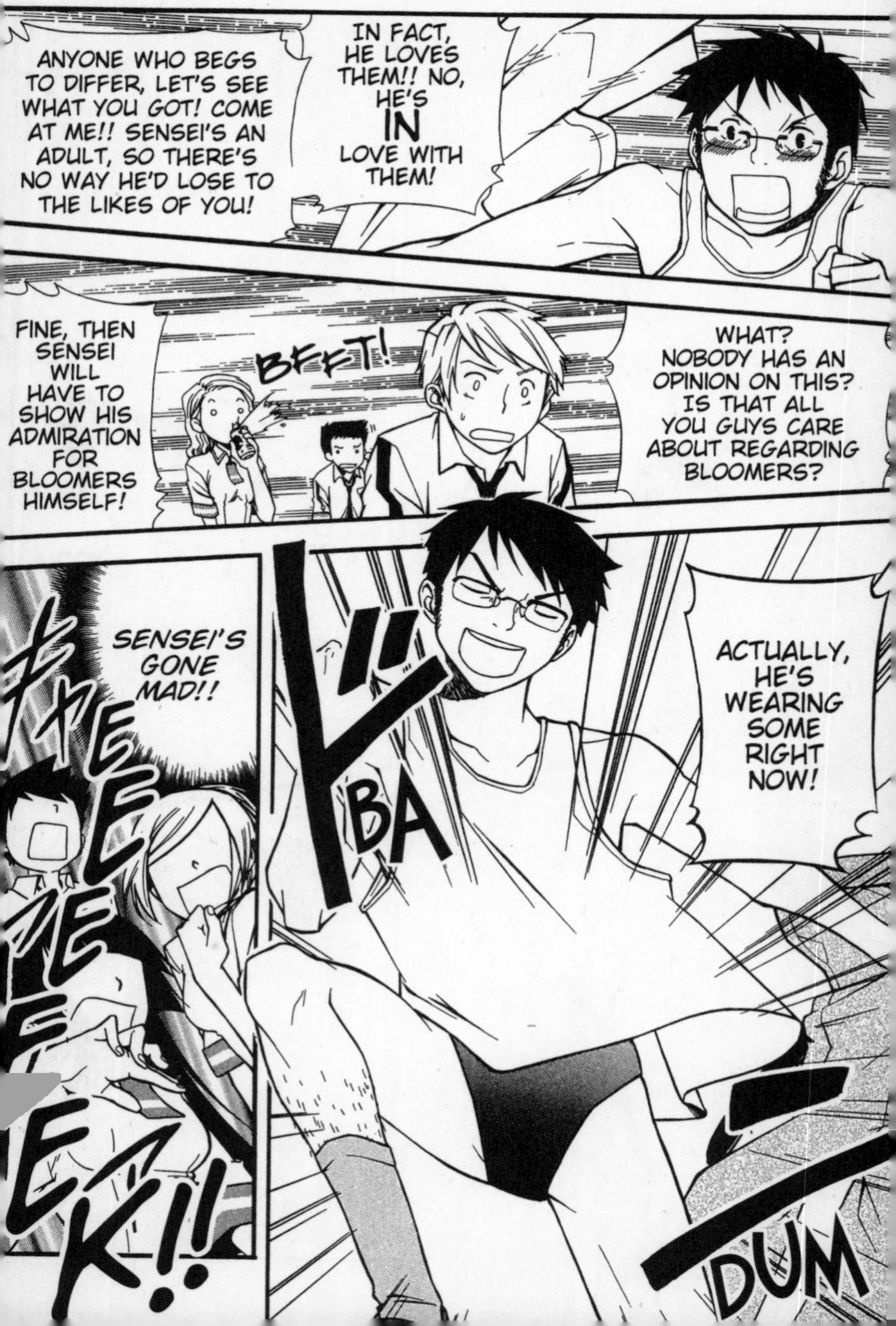
IN FACT, HE LOVES THEM!! NO, HE'S IN LOVE WITH THEM!
ANYONE WHO BEGS TO DIFFER, LET'S SEE WHAT YOU GOT! COME AT ME!! SENSEI'S AN ADULT, SO THERE'S NO WAY HE'D LOSE TO THE LIKES OF YOU!
WHAT? NOBODY HAS AN OPINION ON THIS? IS THAT ALL YOU GUYS CARE ABOUT REGARDING BLOOMERS?
BFFT!
FINE, THEN SENSEI WILL HAVE TO SHOW HIS ADMIRATION FOR BLOOMERS HIMSELF!
ACTUALLY, HE'S WEARING SOME RIGHT NOW!
BA
DUM
SENSEI'S GONE MAD!!
EEEEEEK!!

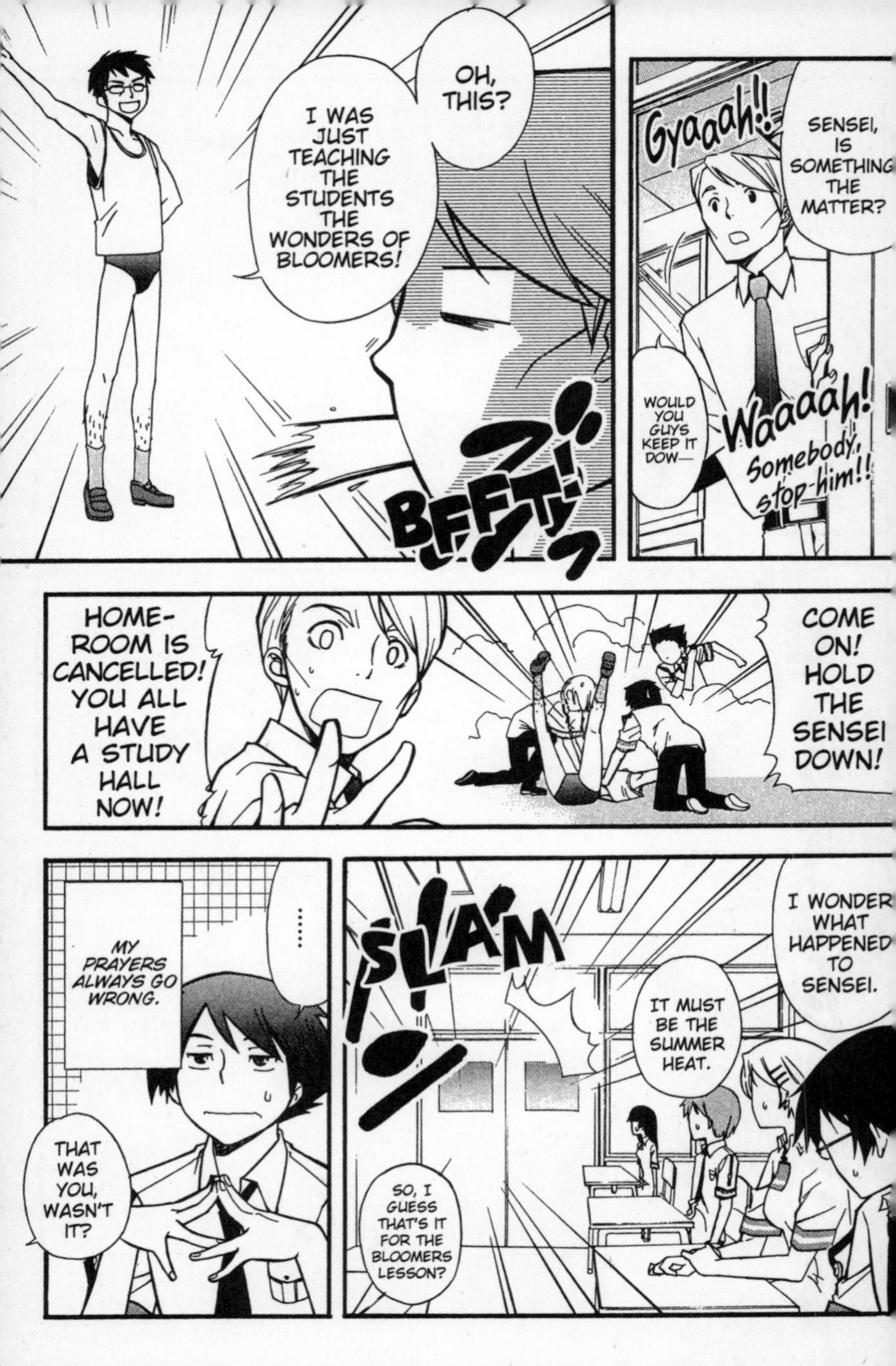
SENSEI, IS SOMETHING THE MATTER?
Gyaaah!!
WOULD YOU GUYS KEEP IT DOW—
Waaaah!
Somebody stop-him!!
OH, THIS?
I WAS JUST TEACHING THE STUDENTS THE WONDERS OF BLOOMERS!
BFFT!
COME ON! HOLD THE SENSEI DOWN!
HOME-ROOM IS CANCELLED! YOU ALL HAVE A STUDY HALL NOW!
I WONDER WHAT HAPPENED TO SENSEI.
IT MUST BE THE SUMMER HEAT.
SLAM
SO, I GUESS THAT'S IT FOR THE BLOOMERS LESSON?
......
MY PRAYERS ALWAYS GO WRONG.
THAT WAS YOU, WASN'T IT?

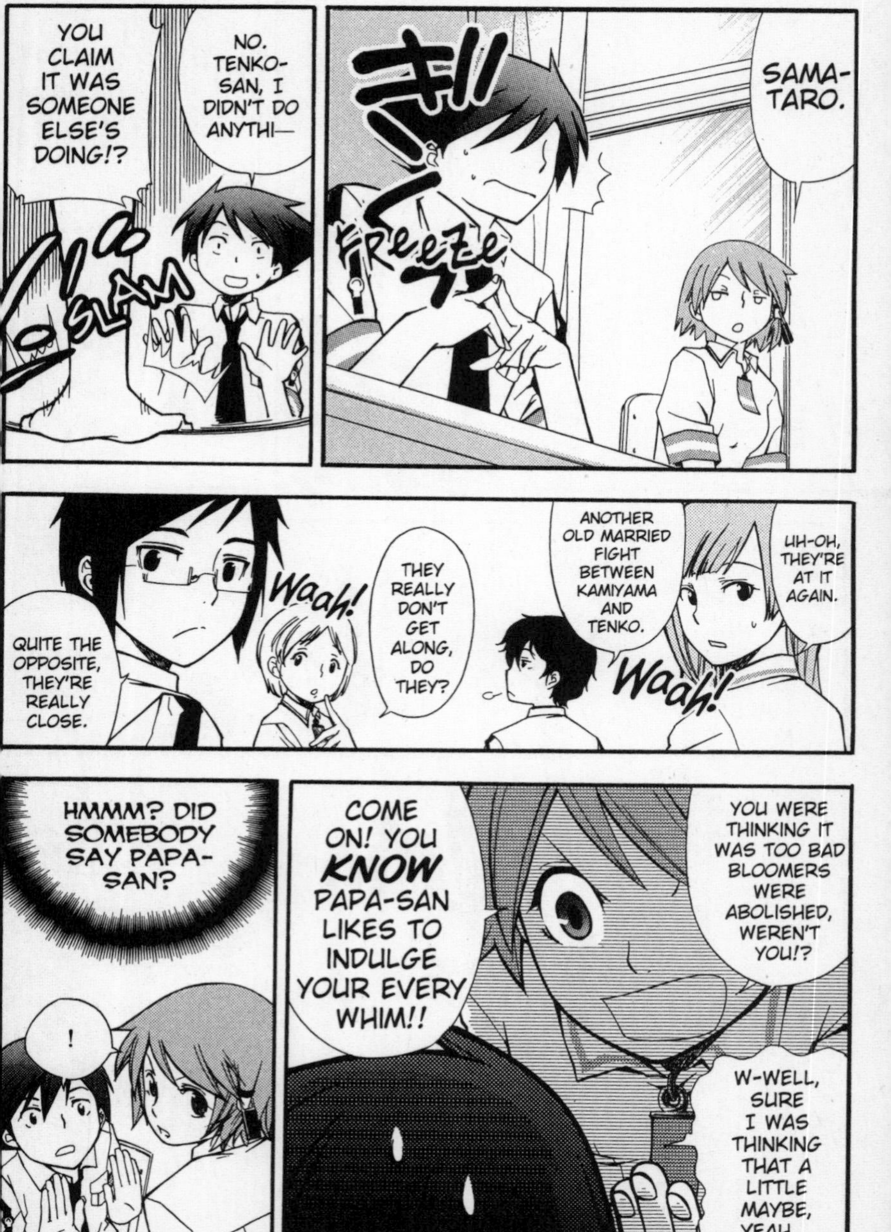
SAMA-TARO.
FREEZE
NO. TENKO-SAN, I DIDN'T DO ANYTHI—
YOU CLAIM IT WAS SOMEONE ELSE'S DOING!?
SLAM
UH-OH, THEY'RE AT IT AGAIN.
ANOTHER OLD MARRIED FIGHT BETWEEN KAMIYAMA AND TENKO.
Waah!
THEY REALLY DON'T GET ALONG, DO THEY?
Waah!
QUITE THE OPPOSITE, THEY'RE REALLY CLOSE.
YOU WERE THINKING IT WAS TOO BAD BLOOMERS WERE ABOLISHED, WEREN'T YOU!?
COME ON! YOU ***KNOW*** PAPA-SAN LIKES TO INDULGE YOUR EVERY WHIM!!
W-WELL, SURE I WAS THINKING THAT A LITTLE MAYBE, YEAH...
HMMM? DID SOMEBODY SAY PAPA-SAN?
!

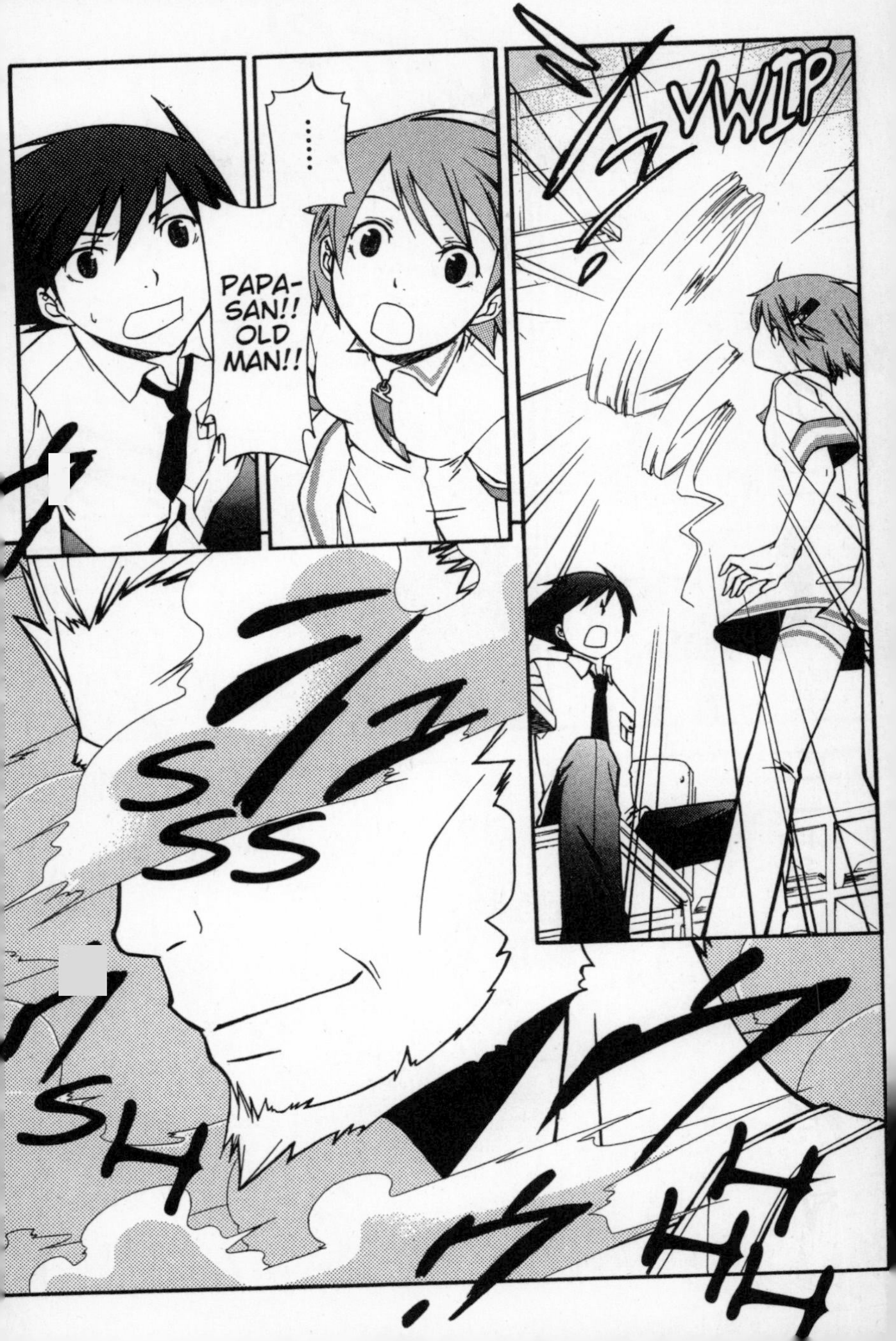
YWIP
......
PAPA-SAN!! OLD MAN!!
SSS
SH
HHHH

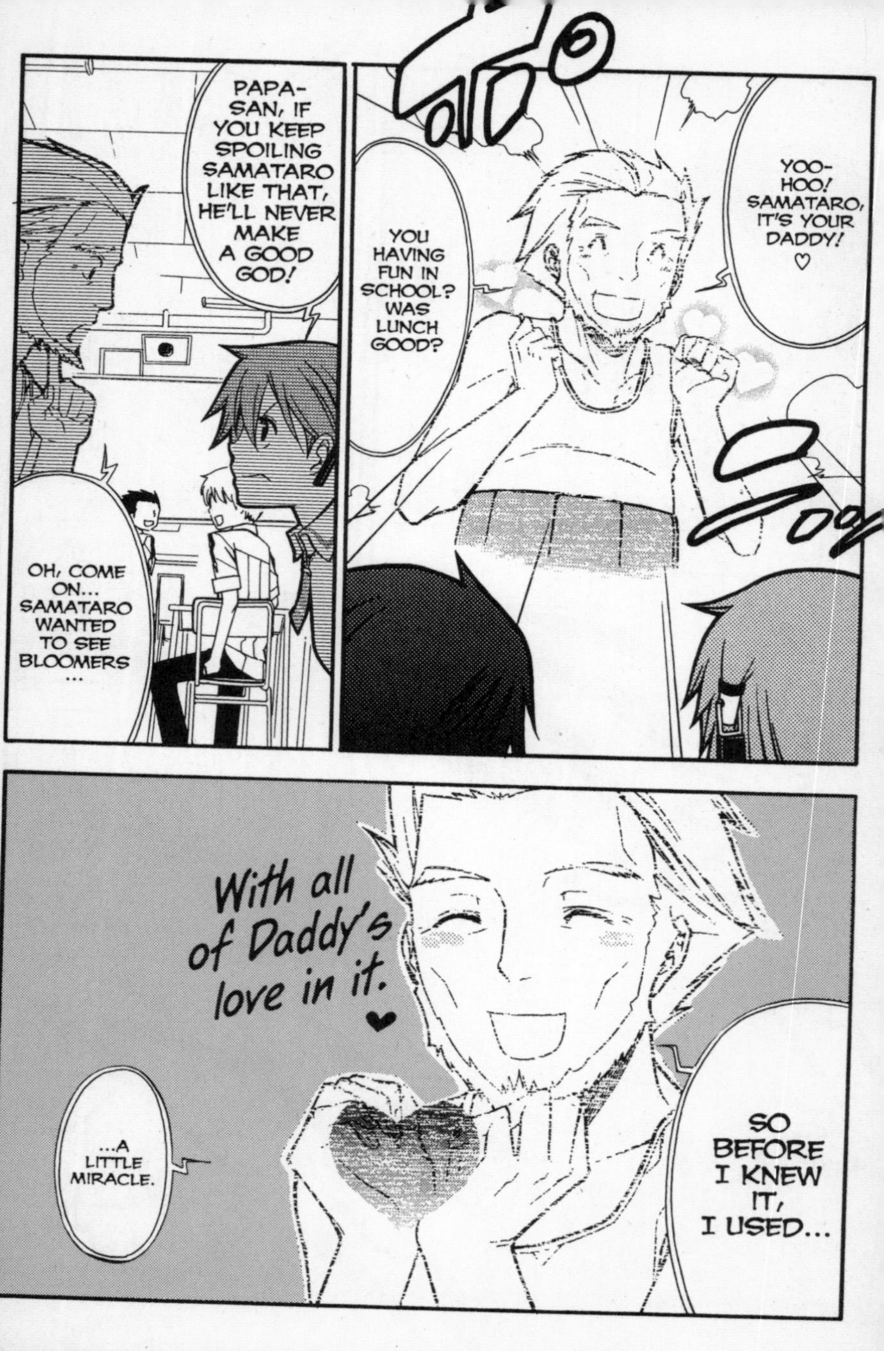
YOO-HOO! SAMATARO, IT'S YOUR DADDY! ♡
YOU HAVING FUN IN SCHOOL? WAS LUNCH GOOD?
PAPA-SAN, IF YOU KEEP SPOILING SAMATARO LIKE THAT, HE'LL NEVER MAKE A GOOD GOD!
OH, COME ON... SAMATARO WANTED TO SEE BLOOMERS...
SO BEFORE I KNEW IT, I USED...
With all of Daddy's love in it.
...A LITTLE MIRACLE.

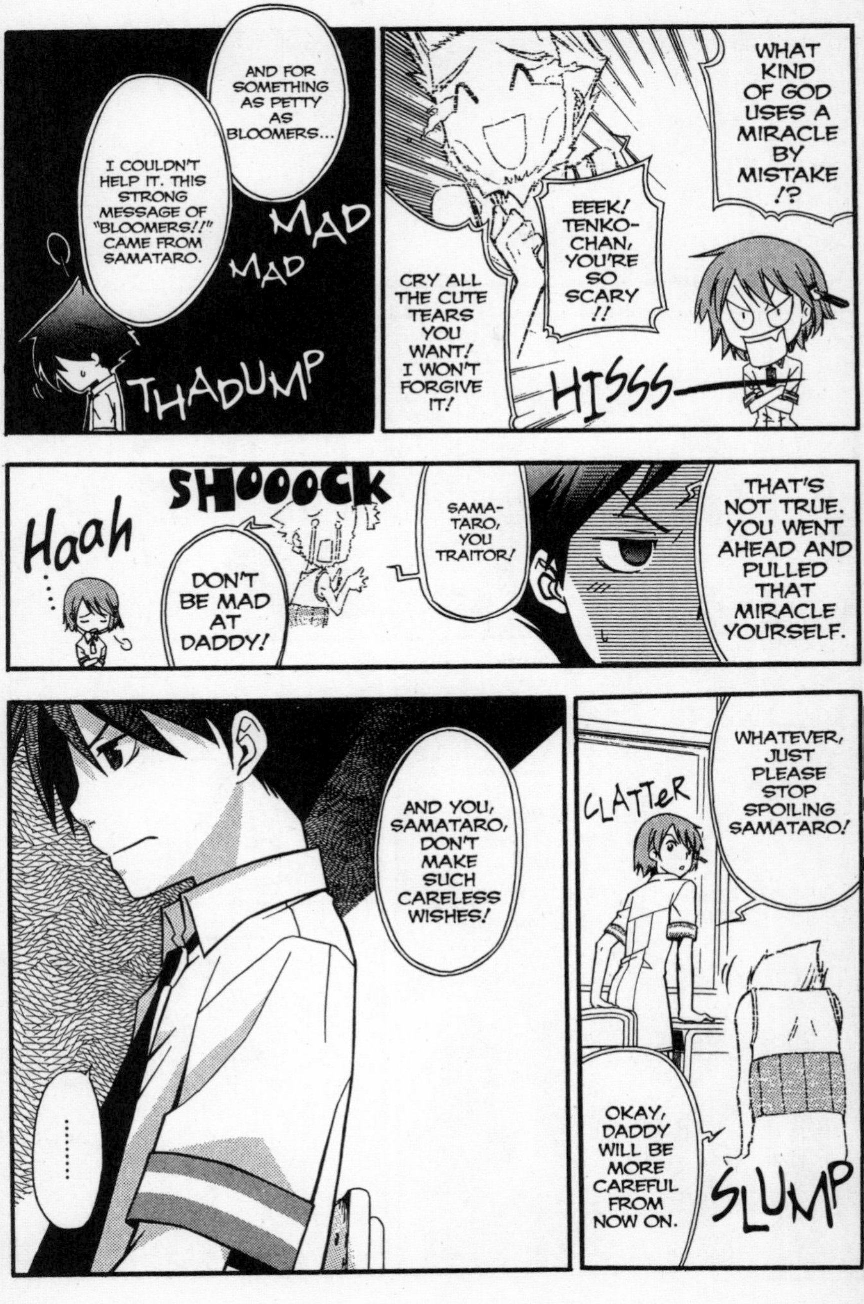
WHAT KIND OF GOD USES A MIRACLE BY MISTAKE!?
EEEK! TENKO-CHAN, YOU'RE SO SCARY!!
CRY ALL THE CUTE TEARS YOU WANT! I WON'T FORGIVE IT!
HISSS
AND FOR SOMETHING AS PETTY AS BLOOMERS...
I COULDN'T HELP IT. THIS STRONG MESSAGE OF "BLOOMERS!!" CAME FROM SAMATARO.
MAD
MAD
THADUMP
THAT'S NOT TRUE. YOU WENT AHEAD AND PULLED THAT MIRACLE YOURSELF.
SAMA-TARO, YOU TRAITOR!
SHOOOCK
DON'T BE MAD AT DADDY!
Haah
WHATEVER, JUST PLEASE STOP SPOILING SAMATARO!
CLATTER
OKAY, DADDY WILL BE MORE CAREFUL FROM NOW ON.
SLUMP
AND YOU, SAMATARO, DON'T MAKE SUCH CARELESS WISHES!
......

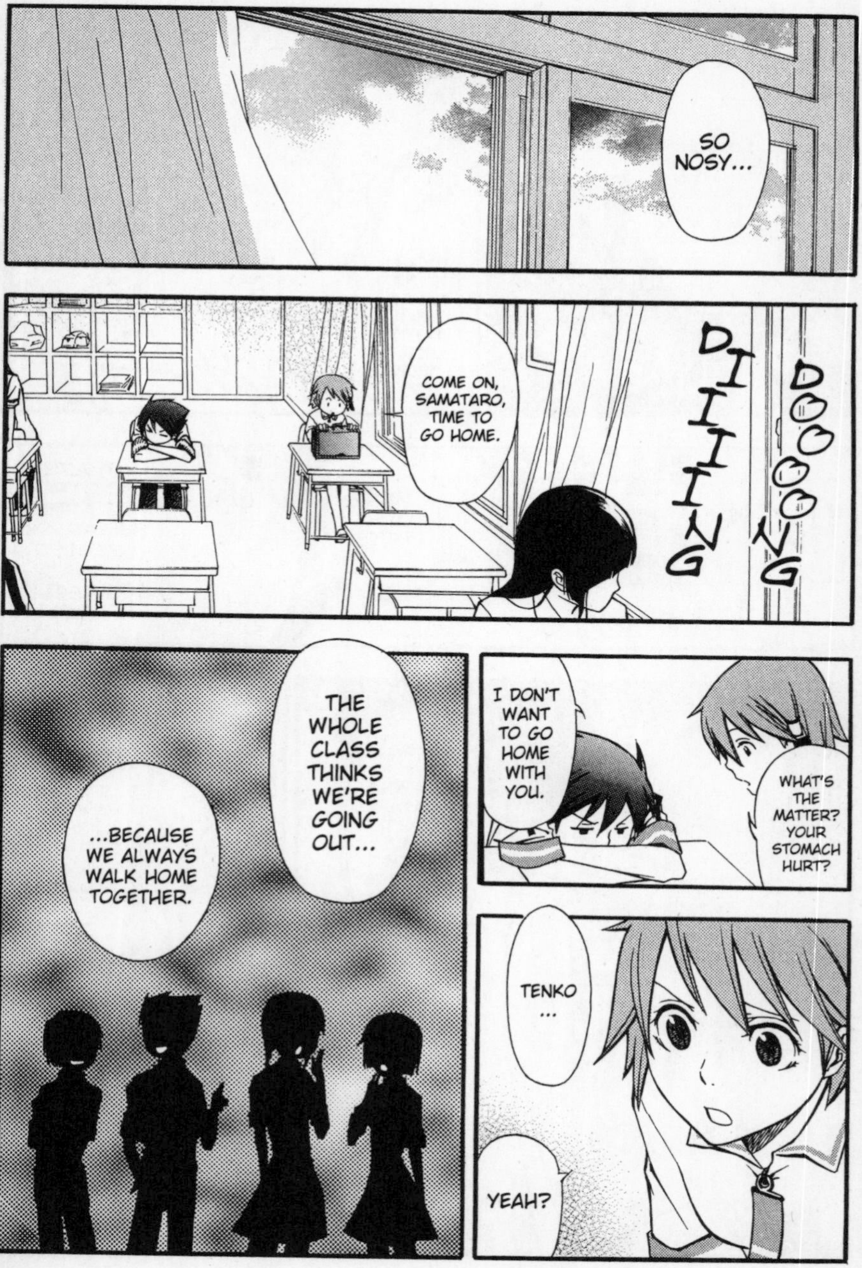
SO NOSY...
DIIIING
DOOOOONG
COME ON, SAMATARO, TIME TO GO HOME.
WHAT'S THE MATTER? YOUR STOMACH HURT?
I DON'T WANT TO GO HOME WITH YOU.
TENKO ...
YEAH?
THE WHOLE CLASS THINKS WE'RE GOING OUT...
...BECAUSE WE ALWAYS WALK HOME TOGETHER.

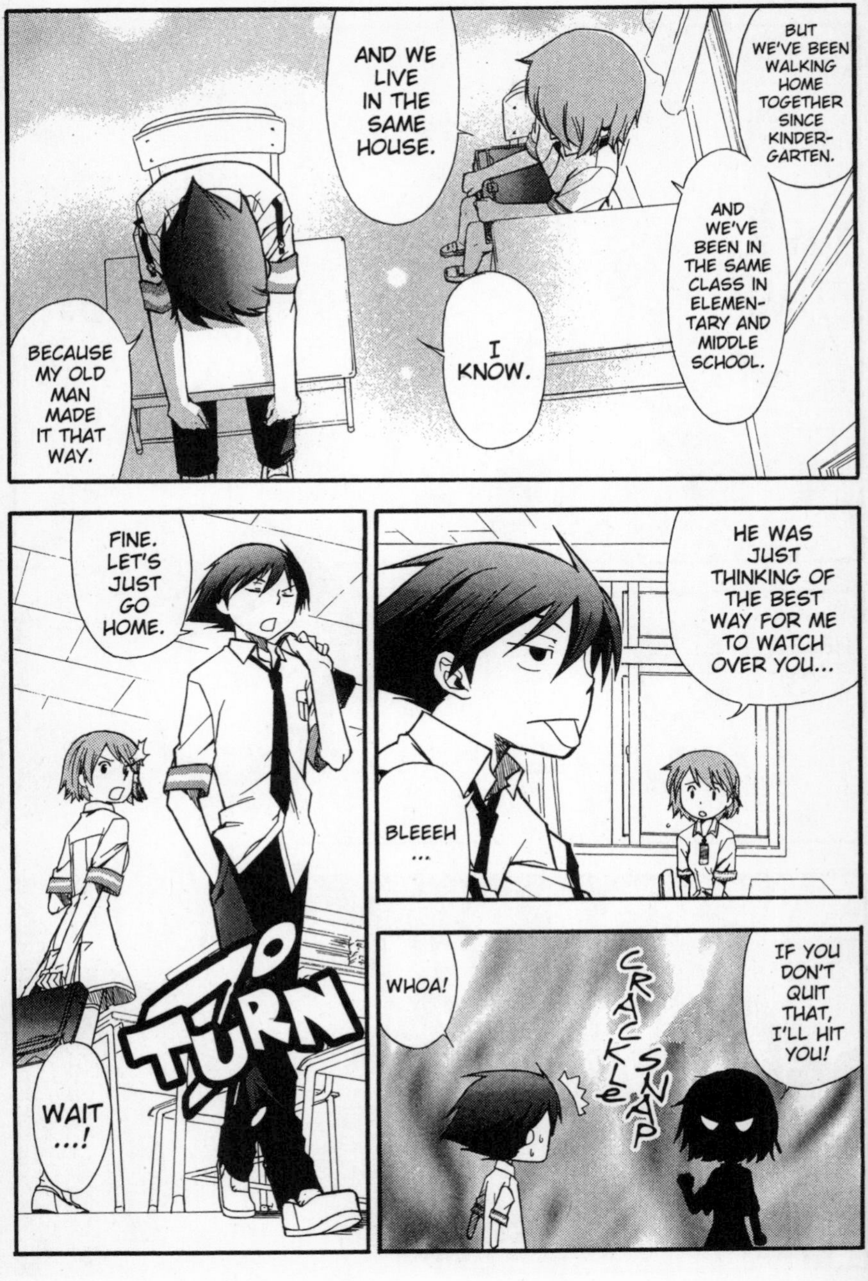

BUT WE'VE BEEN WALKING HOME TOGETHER SINCE KINDER-GARTEN.
AND WE'VE BEEN IN THE SAME CLASS IN ELEMEN-TARY AND MIDDLE SCHOOL.
AND WE LIVE IN THE SAME HOUSE.
I KNOW.
BECAUSE MY OLD MAN MADE IT THAT WAY.
HE WAS JUST THINKING OF THE BEST WAY FOR ME TO WATCH OVER YOU...
BLEEEH ...
IF YOU DON'T QUIT THAT, I'LL HIT YOU!
CRACKLE SNAP
WHOA!
FINE. LET'S JUST GO HOME.
TURN
WAIT ...!

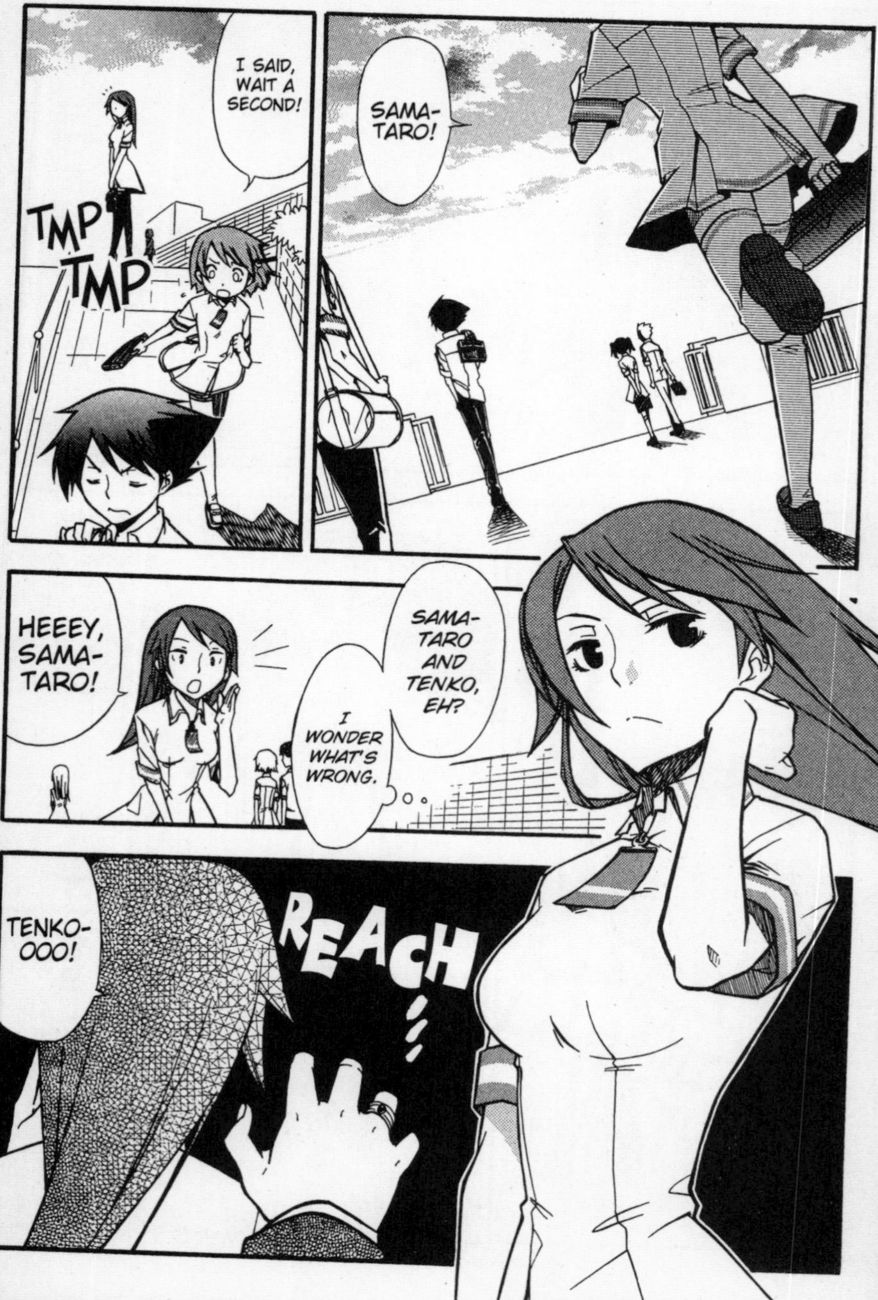
SAMA-TARO!
I SAID, WAIT A SECOND!
TMP TMP
SAMA-TARO AND TENKO, EH?
I WONDER WHAT'S WRONG.
HEEEY, SAMA-TARO!
REACH
TENKO-OOO!

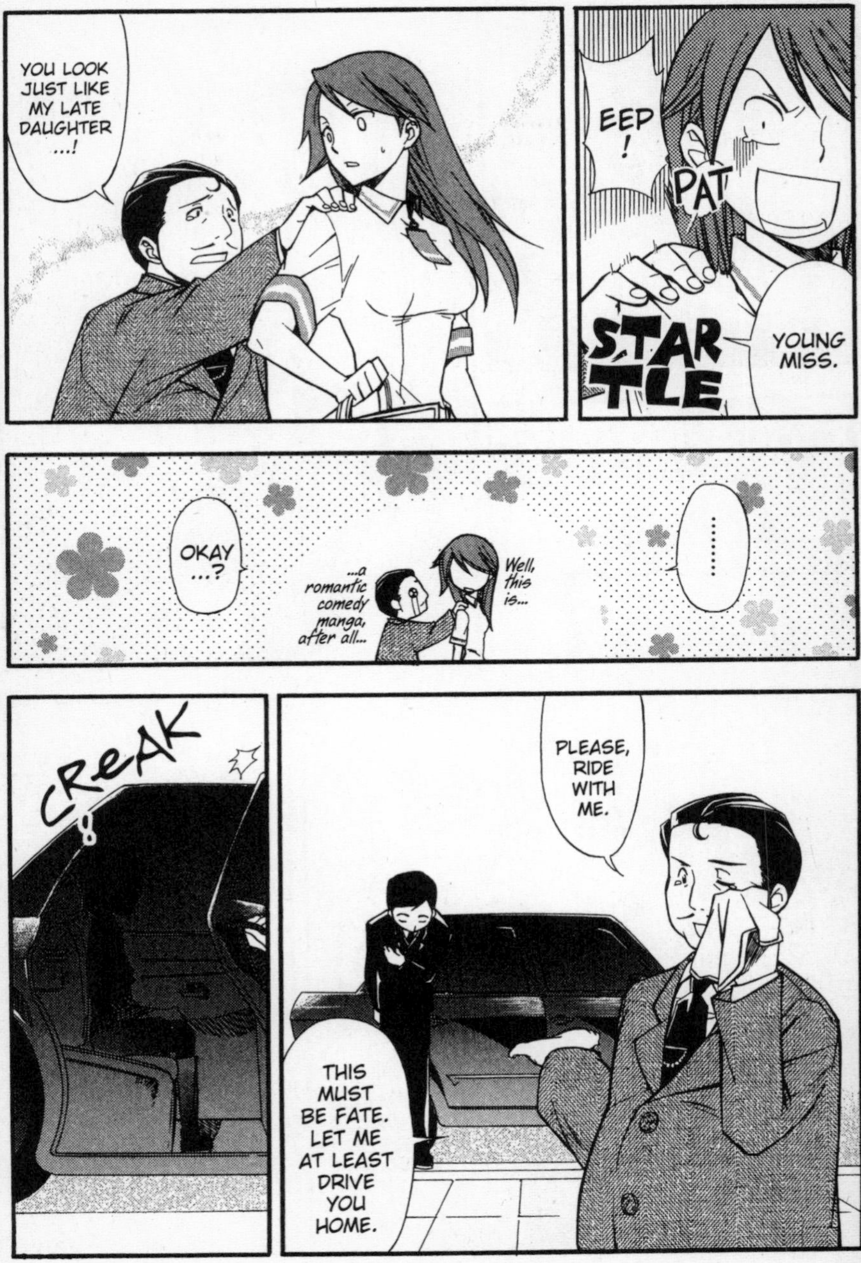
EEP!
PAT
STARTLE
YOUNG MISS.
YOU LOOK JUST LIKE MY LATE DAUGHTER ...!
......
Well, this is...
...a romantic comedy manga, after all...
OKAY ...?
PLEASE, RIDE WITH ME.
THIS MUST BE FATE. LET ME AT LEAST DRIVE YOU HOME.
CREAK

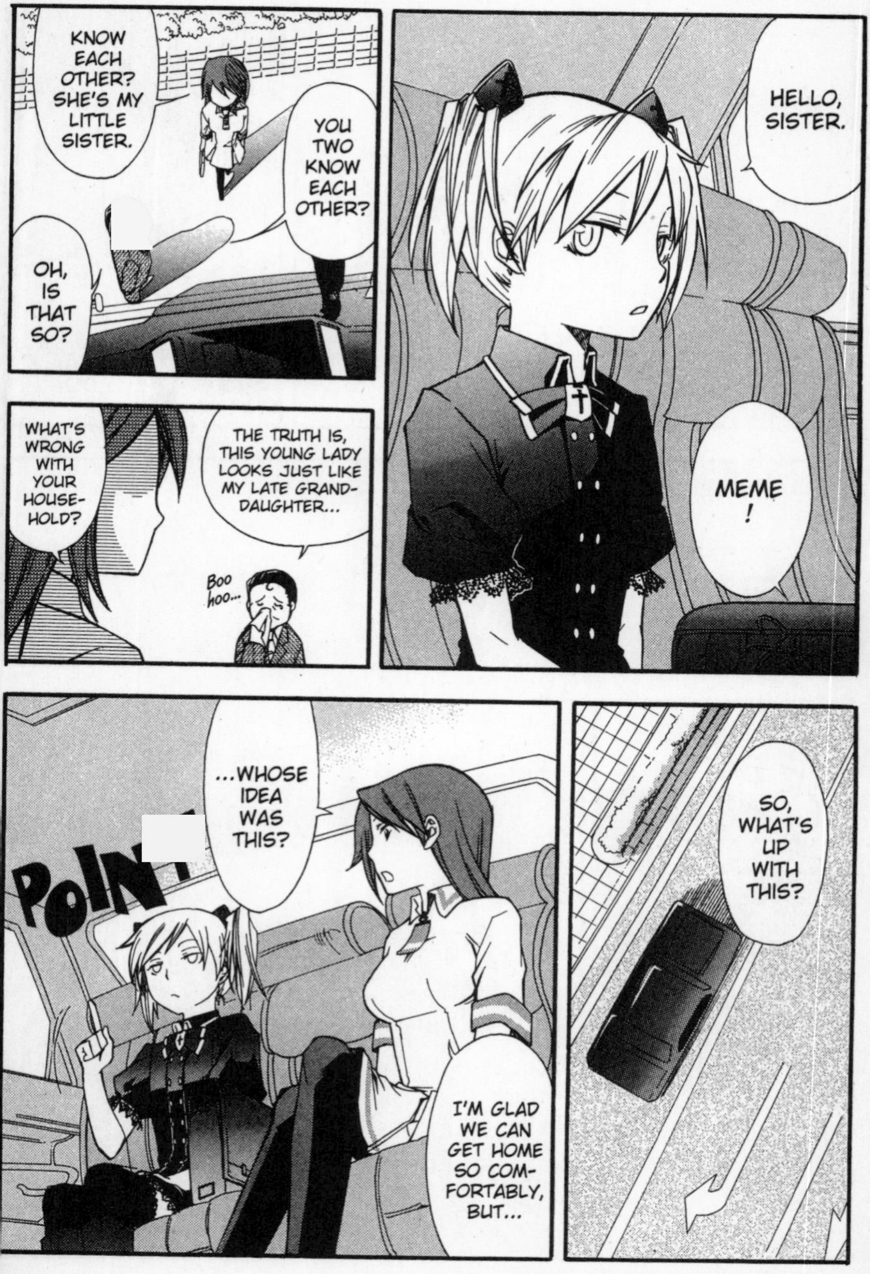
HELLO, SISTER.
MEME!
YOU TWO KNOW EACH OTHER?
KNOW EACH OTHER? SHE'S MY LITTLE SISTER.
OH, IS THAT SO?
THE TRUTH IS, THIS YOUNG LADY LOOKS JUST LIKE MY LATE GRAND-DAUGHTER...
WHAT'S WRONG WITH YOUR HOUSE-HOLD?
Boo hoo...
SO, WHAT'S UP WITH THIS?
I'M GLAD WE CAN GET HOME SO COM-FORTABLY, BUT...
...WHOSE IDEA WAS THIS?
POINT

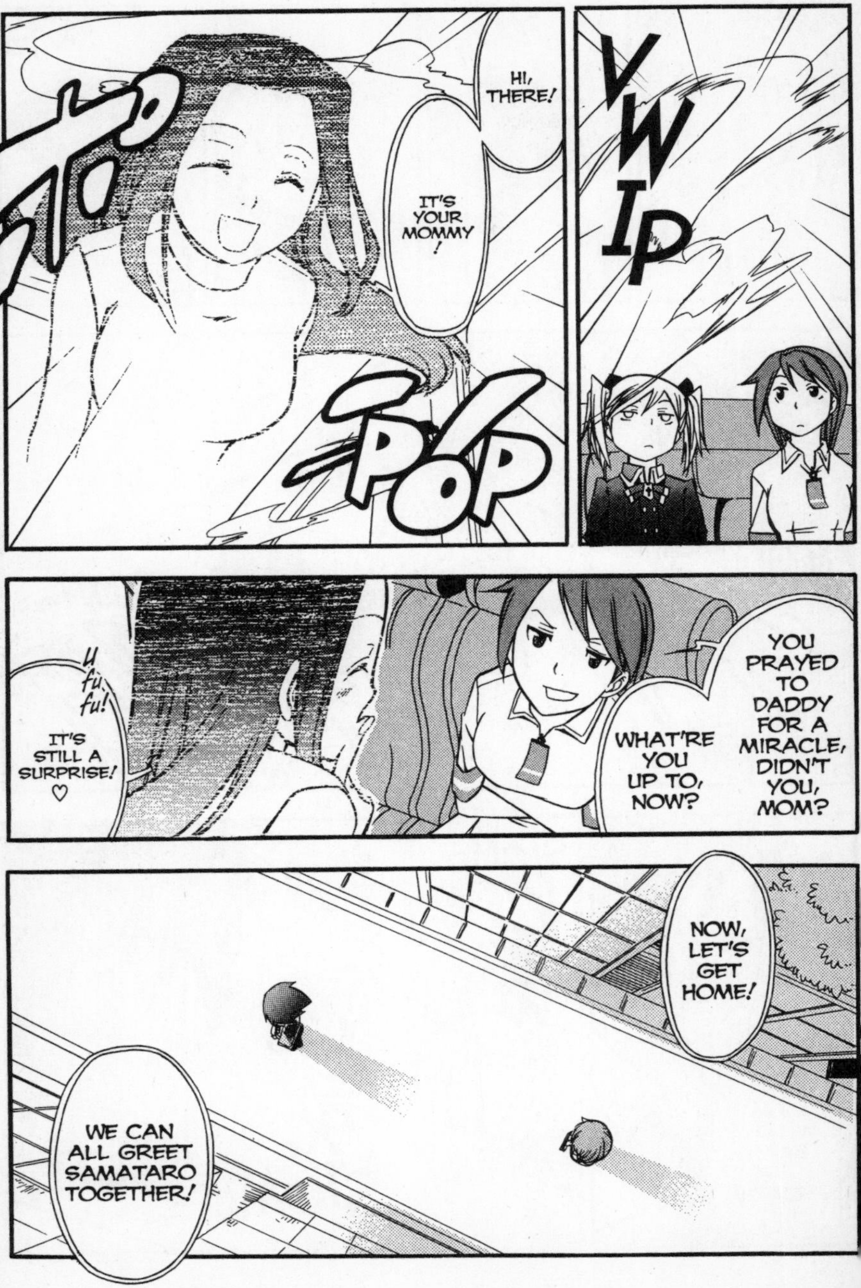
VWIP
HI, THERE!
IT'S YOUR MOMMY!
POP POP
YOU PRAYED TO DADDY FOR A MIRACLE, DIDN'T YOU, MOM?
WHAT'RE YOU UP TO, NOW?
U fu fu!
IT'S STILL A SURPRISE! ♡
NOW, LET'S GET HOME!
WE CAN ALL GREET SAMATARO TOGETHER!

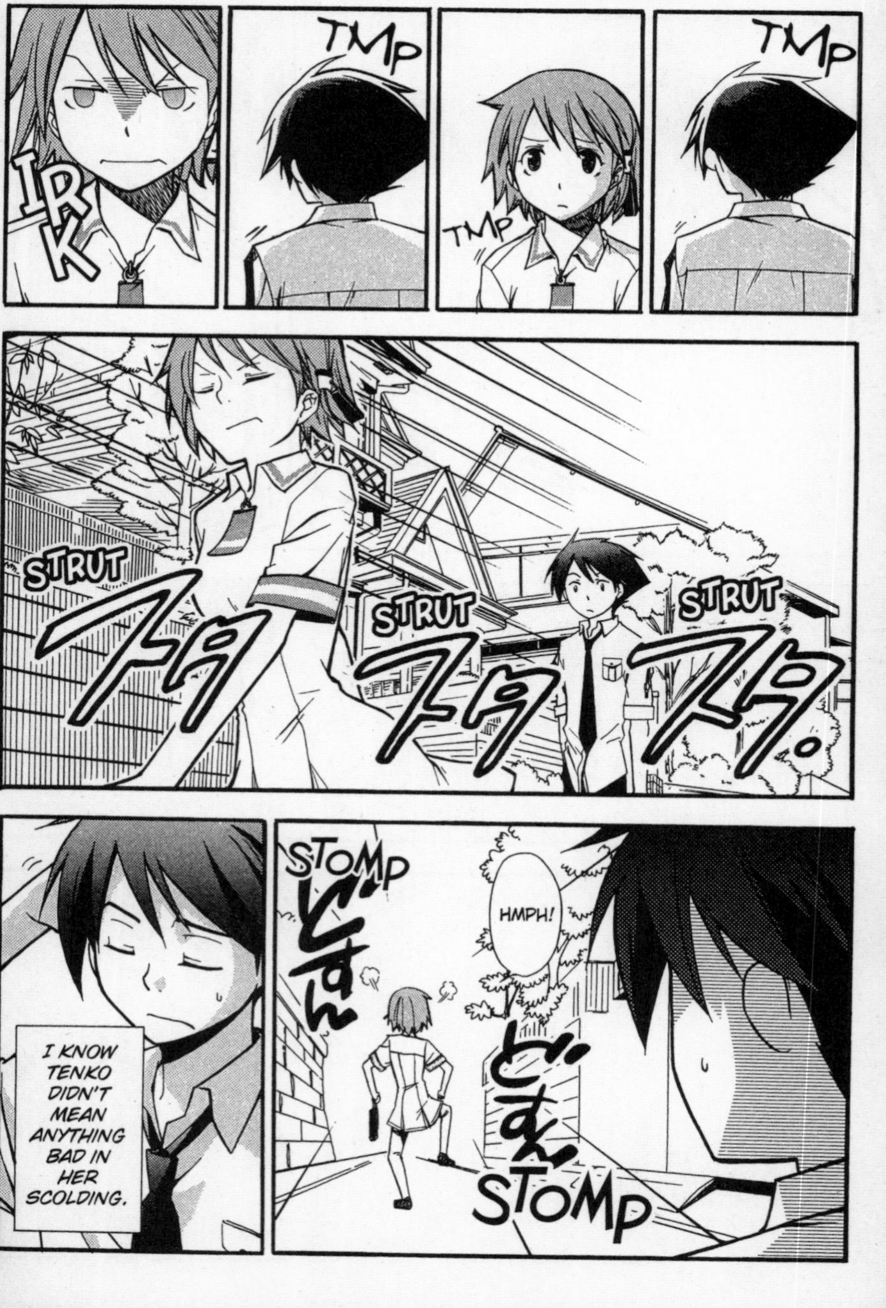

TMP
TMP
TMP
IRK
STRUT
スタ
STRUT
スタ
STRUT
スタ。
HMPH!
STOMP
どすん
どすん
STOMP
I KNOW TENKO DIDN'T MEAN ANYTHING BAD IN HER SCOLDING.

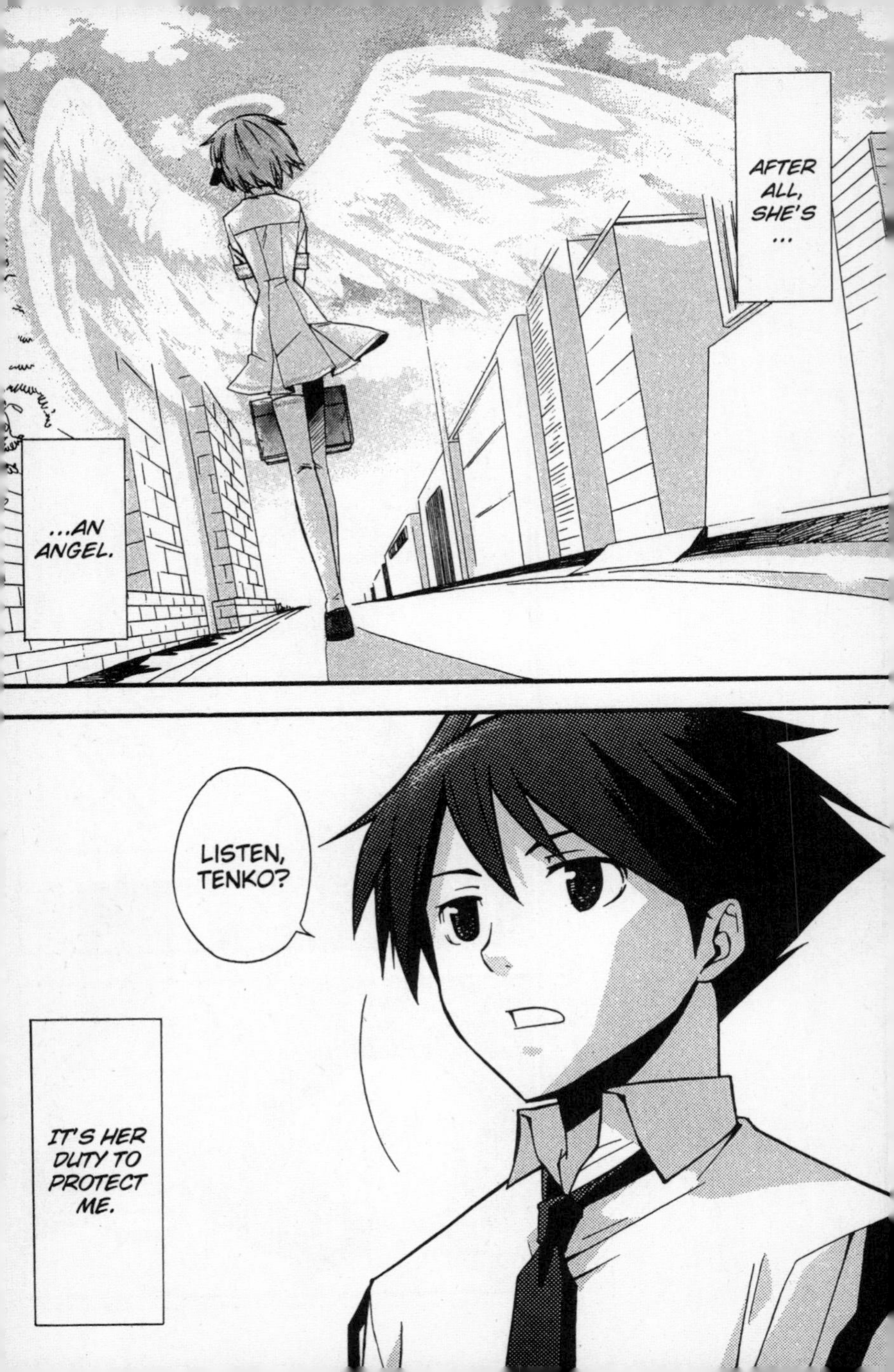
AFTER ALL, SHE'S ...
...AN ANGEL.
LISTEN, TENKO?
IT'S HER DUTY TO PROTECT ME.

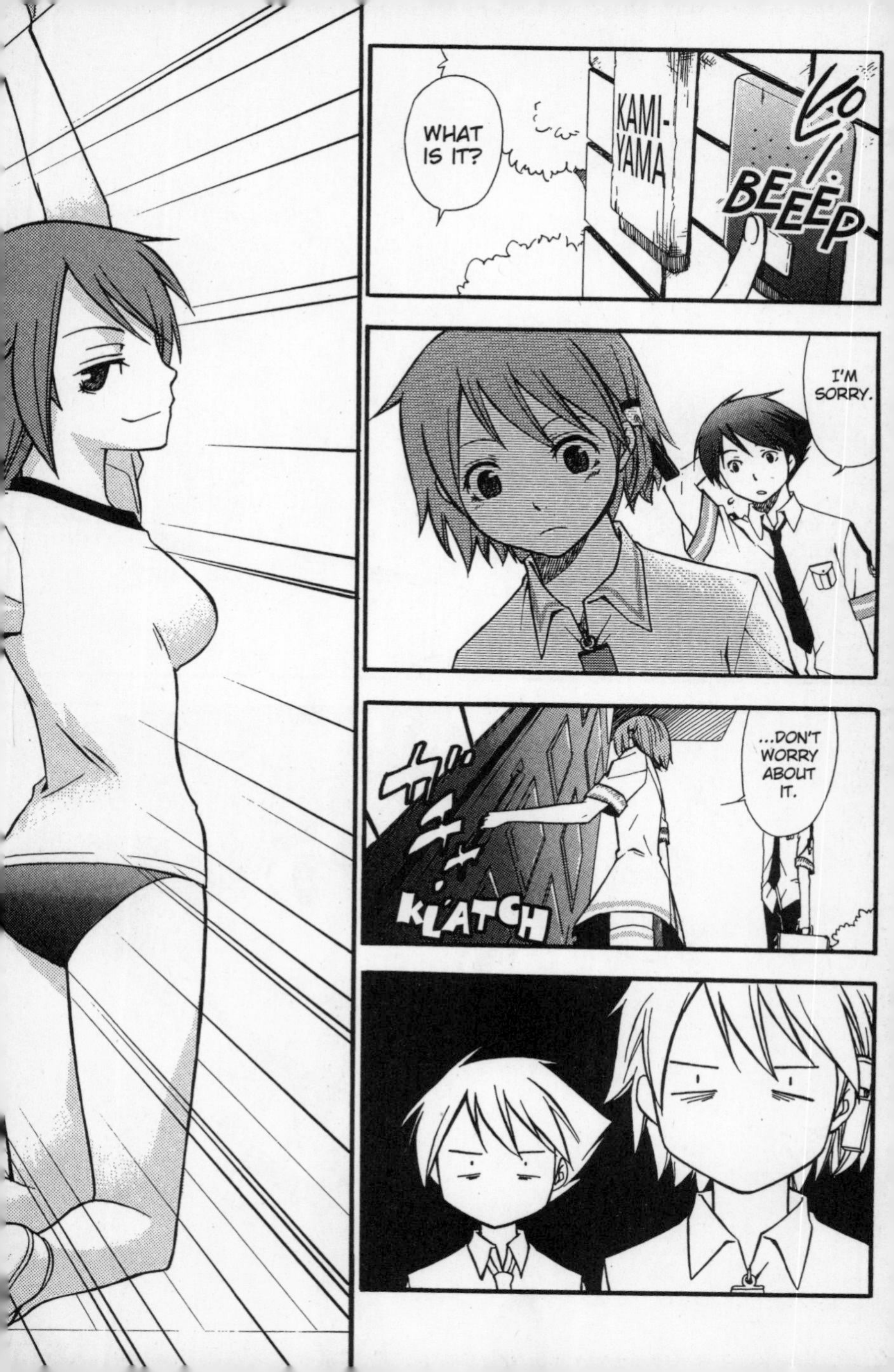
BEEEP
KAMI-YAMA
WHAT IS IT?
I'M SORRY.
...DON'T WORRY ABOUT IT.
KLATCH

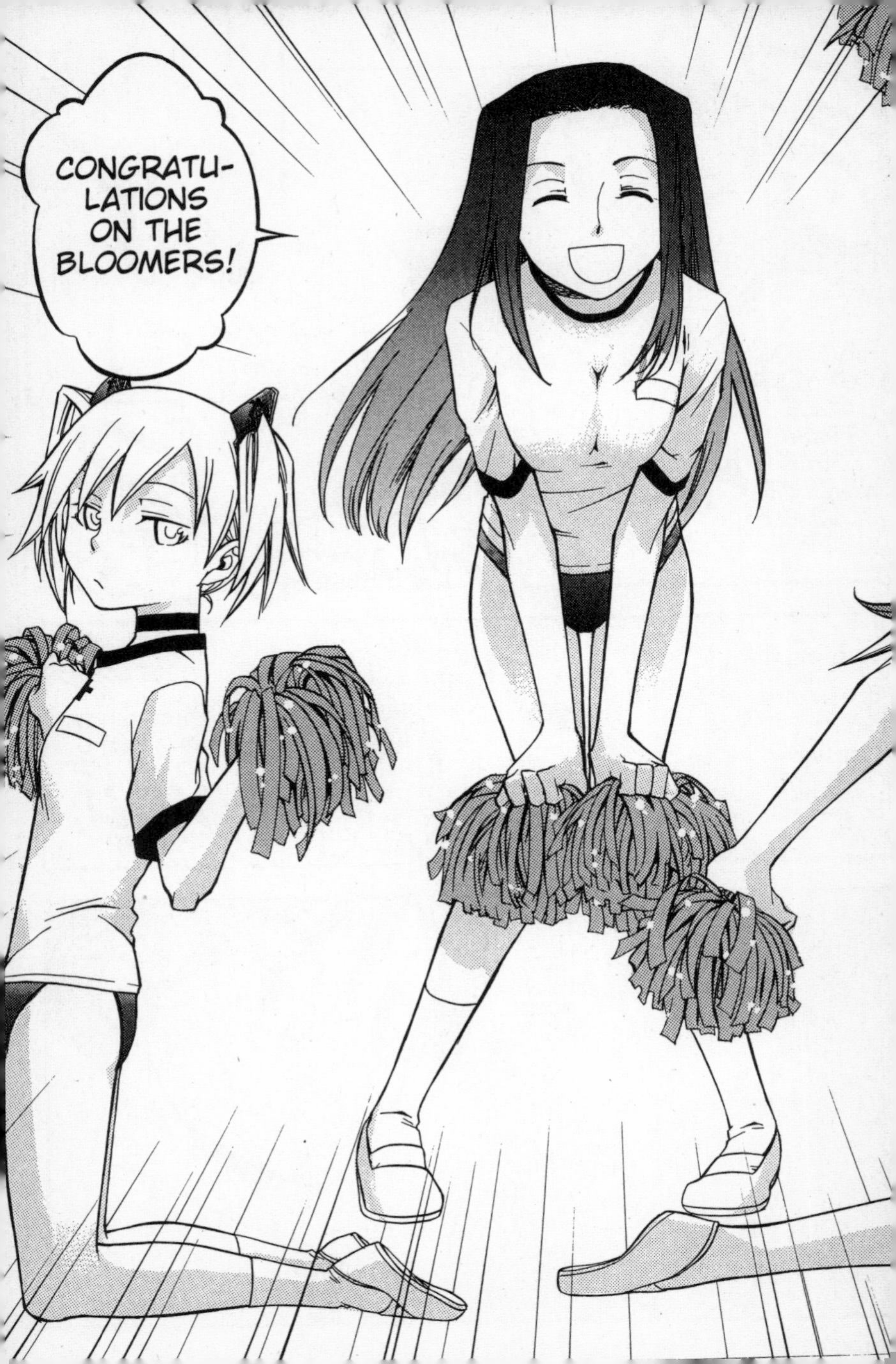
CONGRATULATIONS ON THE BLOOMERS!

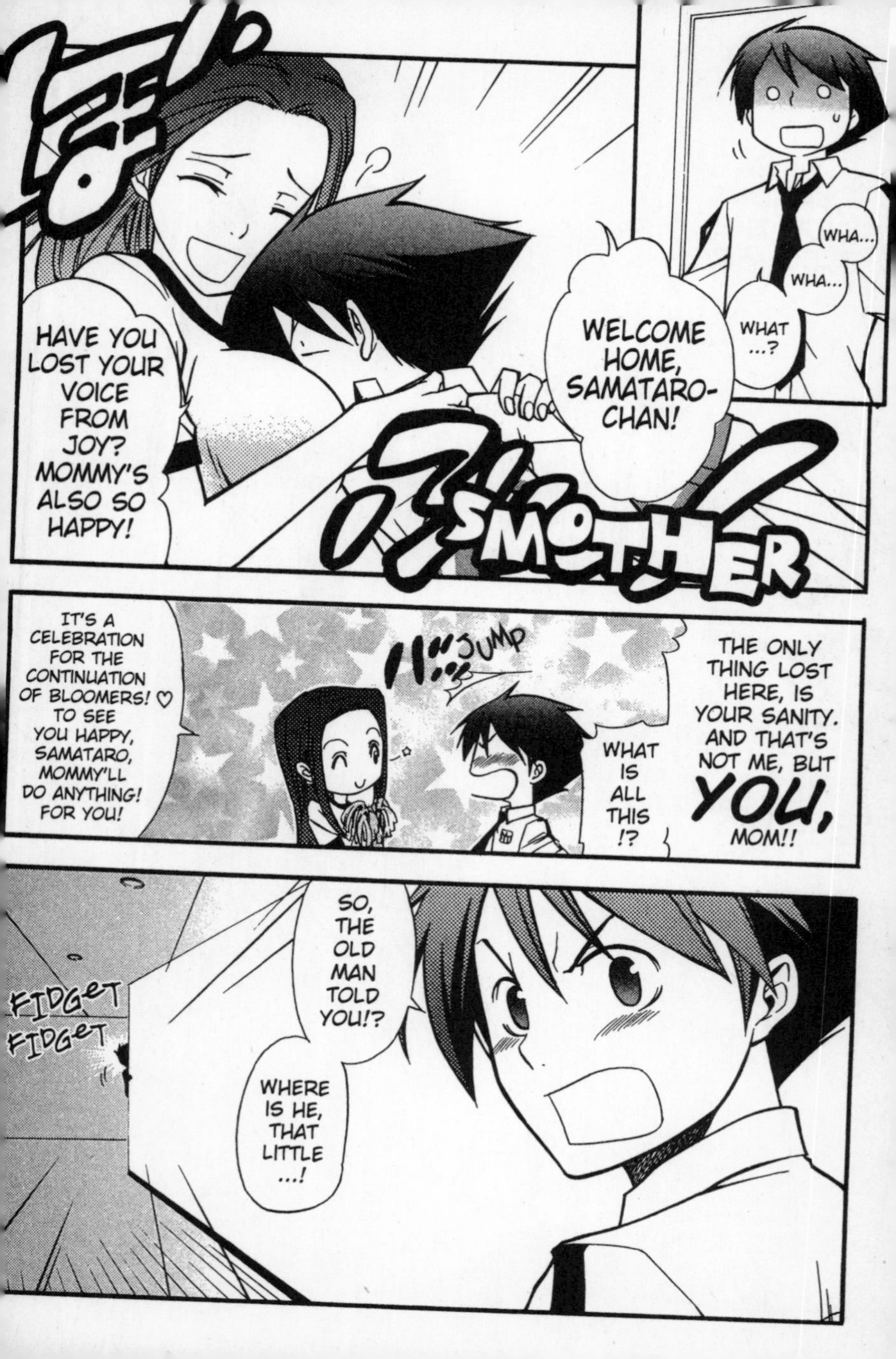
WHA...
WHA...
WHAT ...?
WELCOME HOME, SAMATARO-CHAN!
HAVE YOU LOST YOUR VOICE FROM JOY? MOMMY'S ALSO SO HAPPY!
SMOTHER
THE ONLY THING LOST HERE, IS YOUR SANITY. AND THAT'S NOT ME, BUT YOU, MOM!!
WHAT IS ALL THIS !?
JUMP
IT'S A CELEBRATION FOR THE CONTINUATION OF BLOOMERS! ♡ TO SEE YOU HAPPY, SAMATARO, MOMMY'LL DO ANYTHING! FOR YOU!
SO, THE OLD MAN TOLD YOU!?
WHERE IS HE, THAT LITTLE ...!
FIDGET FIDGET

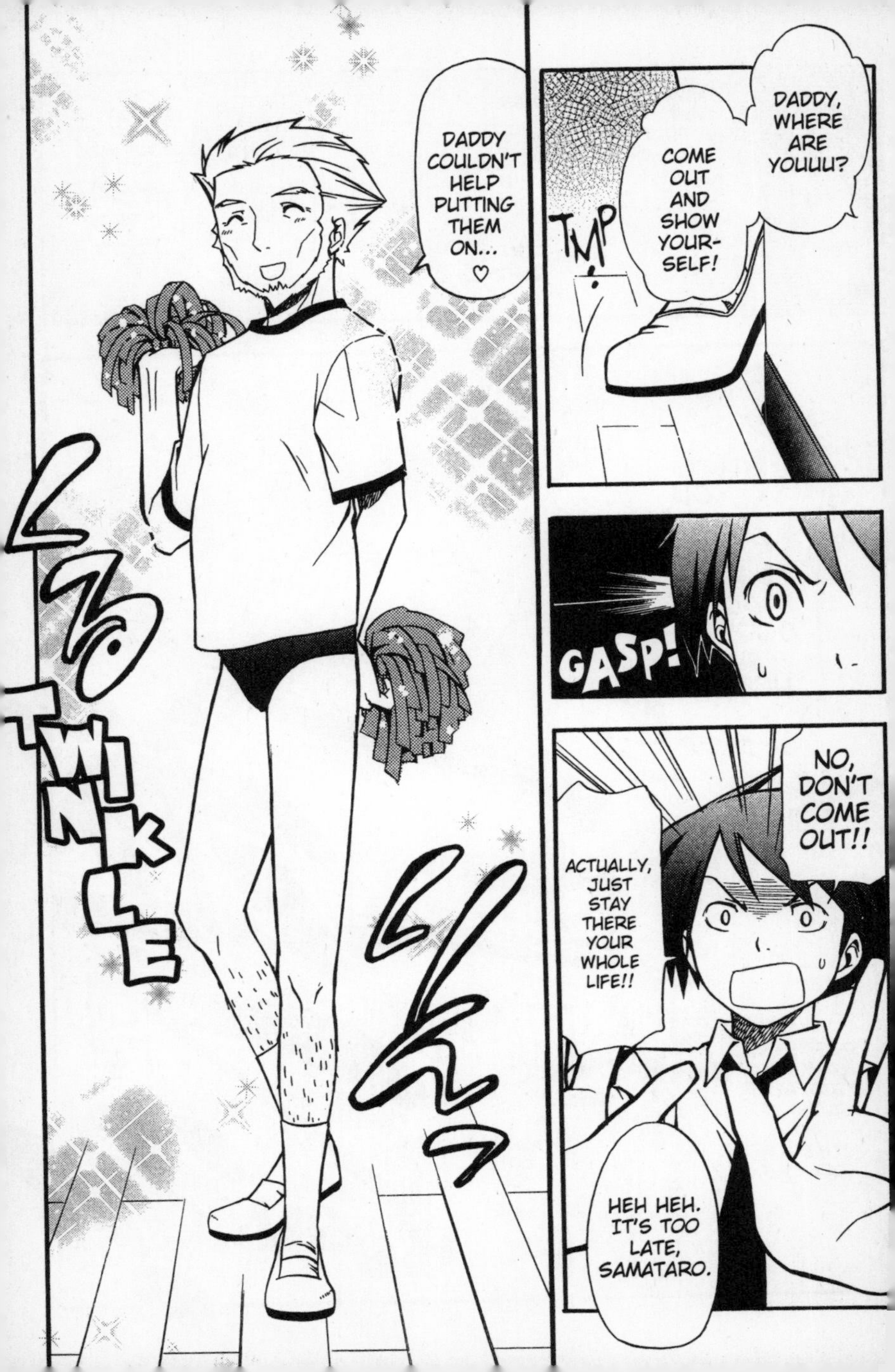
DADDY, WHERE ARE YOUUU?
COME OUT AND SHOW YOUR-SELF!
TMP
GASP!
NO, DON'T COME OUT!!
ACTUALLY, JUST STAY THERE YOUR WHOLE LIFE!!
HEH HEH. IT'S TOO LATE, SAMATARO.
DADDY COULDN'T HELP PUTTING THEM ON... ♡
TWINKLE

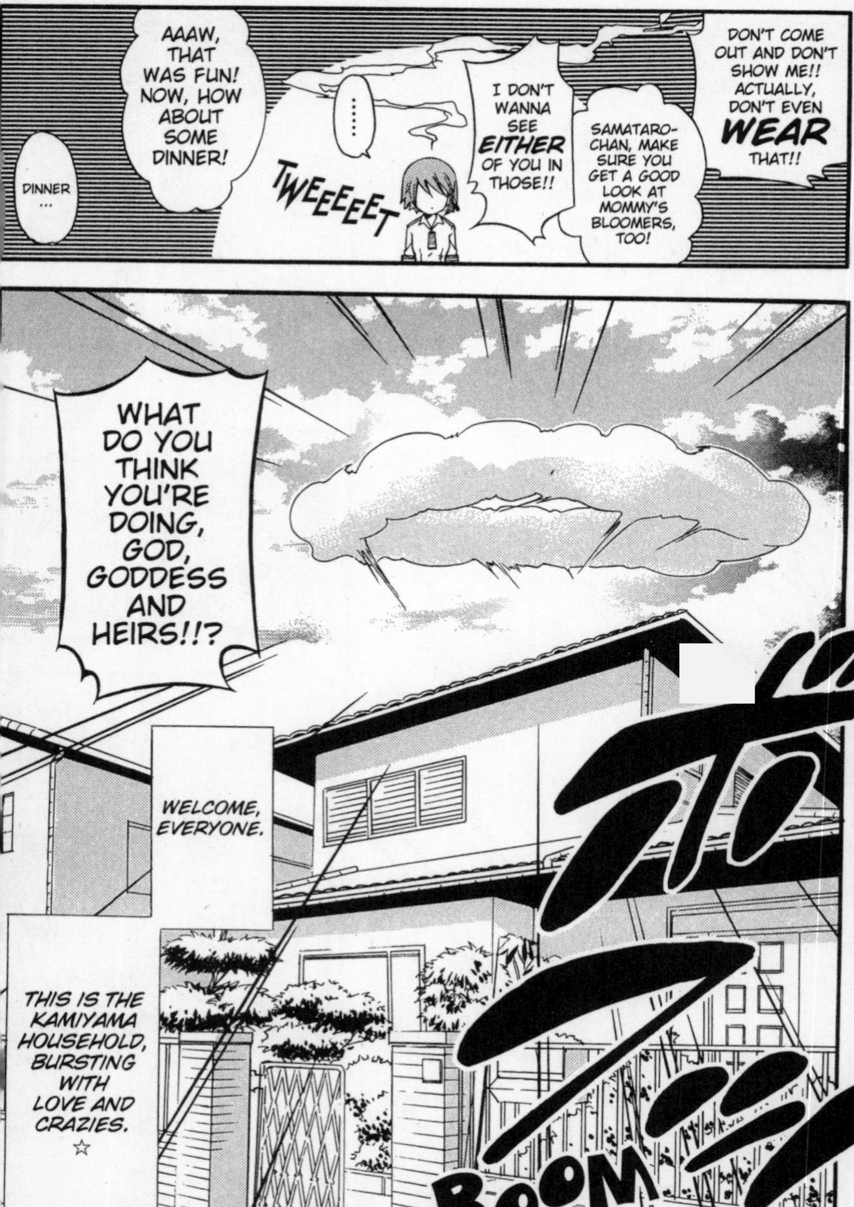
DON'T COME OUT AND DON'T SHOW ME!! ACTUALLY, DON'T EVEN **WEAR** THAT!!
SAMATARO-CHAN, MAKE SURE YOU GET A GOOD LOOK AT MOMMY'S BLOOMERS, TOO!
I DON'T WANNA SEE **EITHER** OF YOU IN THOSE!!
......
TWEEEEET
AAAW, THAT WAS FUN! NOW, HOW ABOUT SOME DINNER!
DINNER ...
WHAT DO YOU THINK YOU'RE DOING, GOD, GODDESS AND HEIRS!!?
BOOM
WELCOME, EVERYONE.
THIS IS THE KAMIYAMA HOUSEHOLD, BURSTING WITH LOVE AND CRAZIES. ☆

KAMISAMA KAZOKU

The Transfer Student

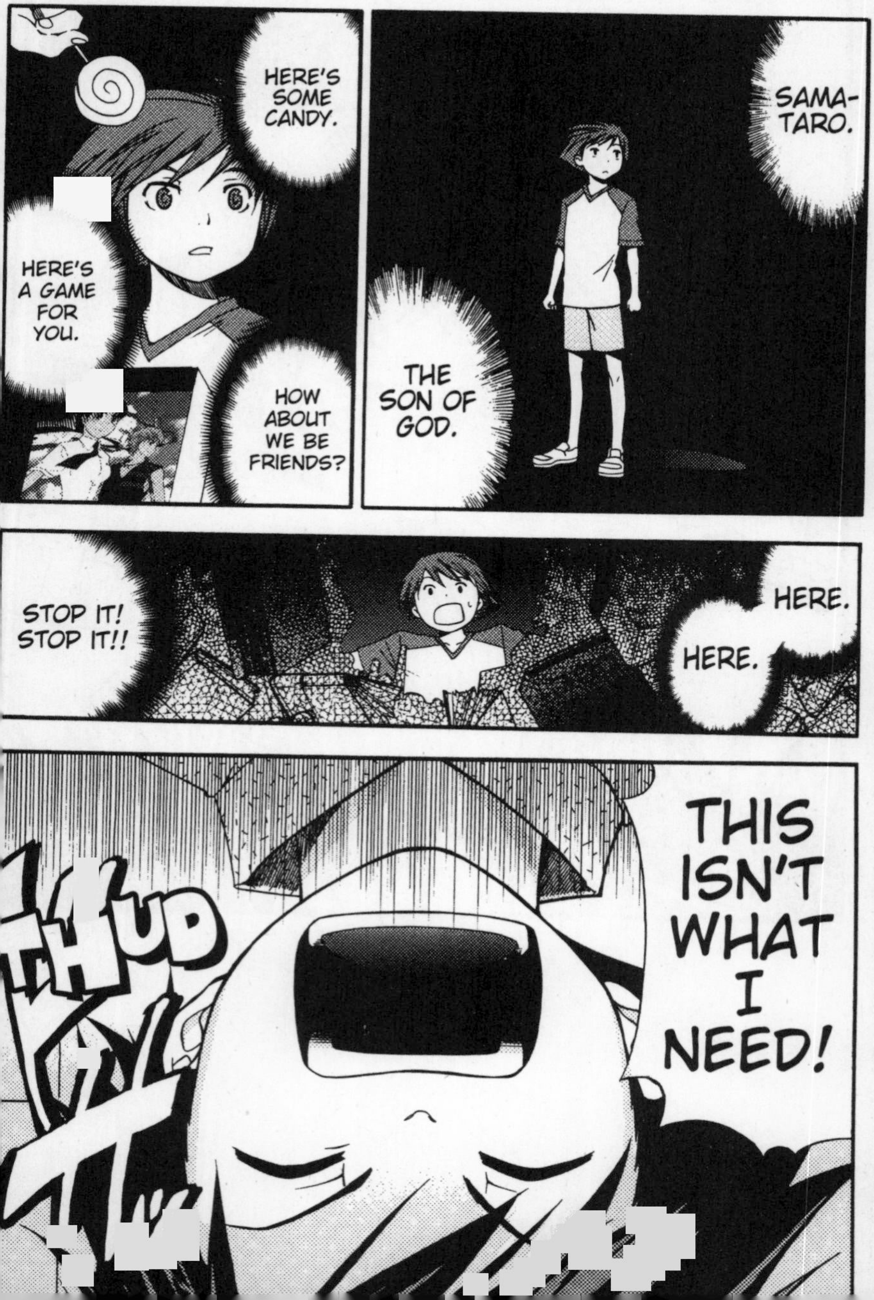
SAMA-TARO.
THE SON OF GOD.
HERE'S SOME CANDY.
HERE'S A GAME FOR YOU.
HOW ABOUT WE BE FRIENDS?
HERE.
HERE.
STOP IT! STOP IT!!
THIS ISN'T WHAT I NEED!
THUD

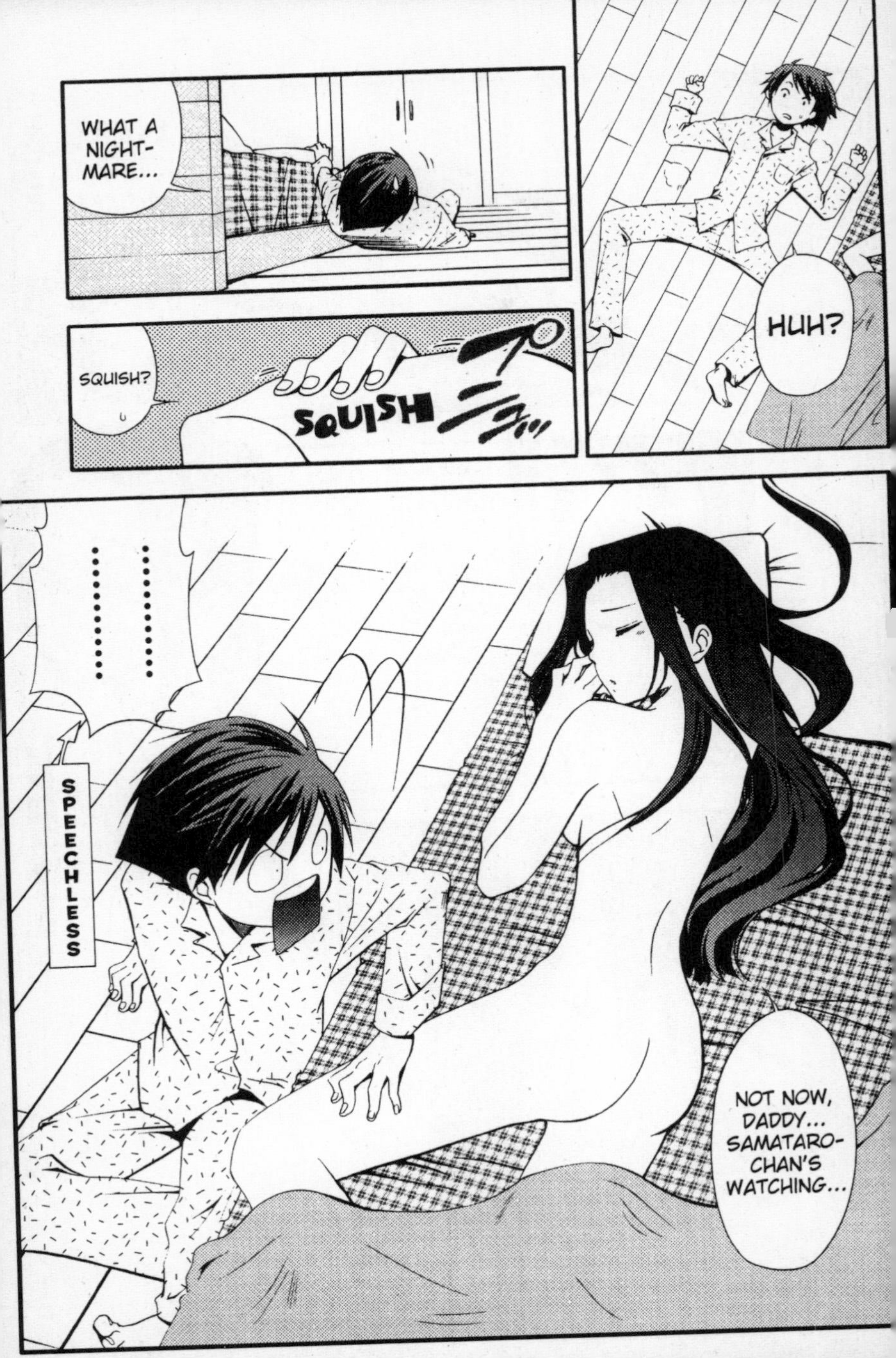
HUH?
WHAT A NIGHT-MARE...
SQUISH
SQUISH?
NOT NOW, DADDY... SAMATARO-CHAN'S WATCHING...
......
......
SPEECHLESS

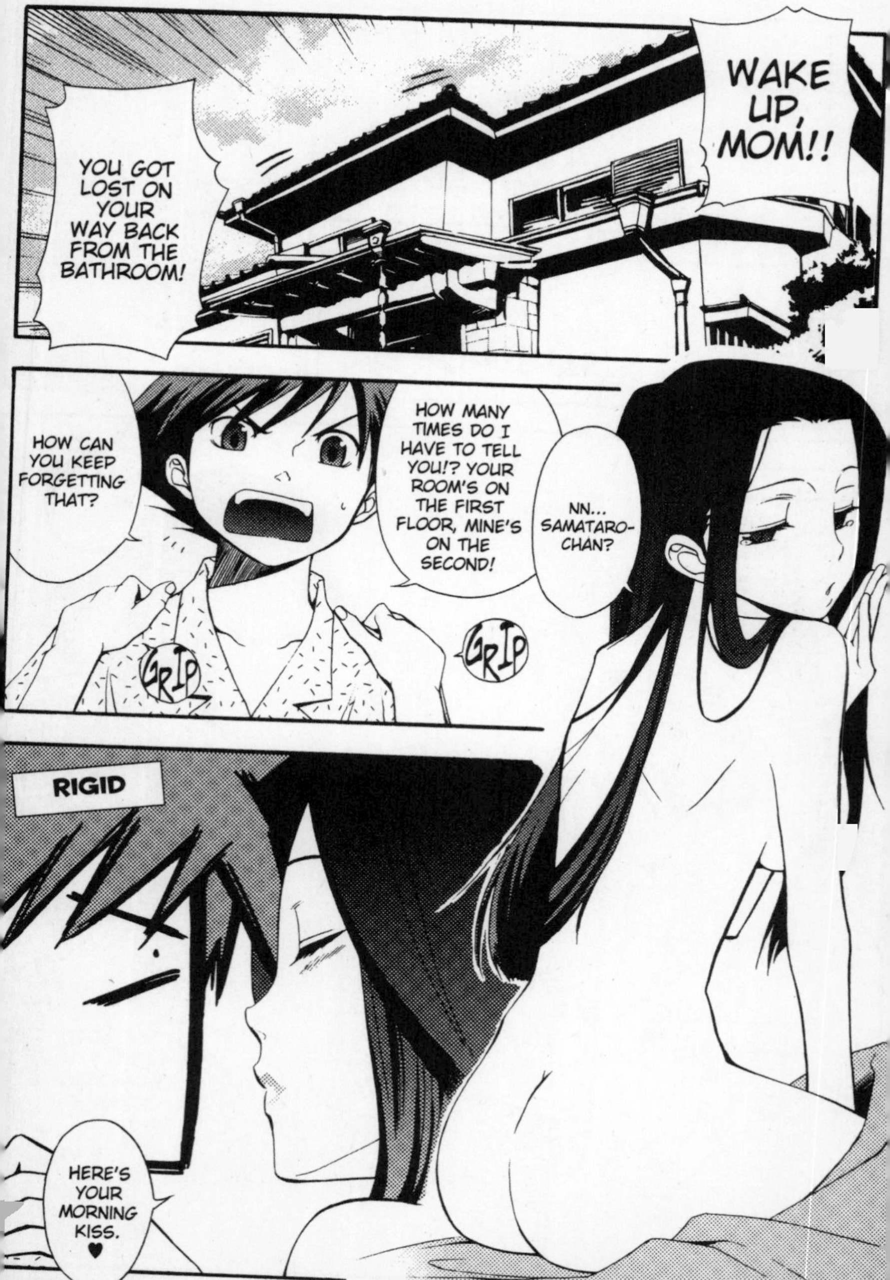
WAKE UP, MOM!!
YOU GOT LOST ON YOUR WAY BACK FROM THE BATHROOM!
NN... SAMATARO-CHAN?
HOW MANY TIMES DO I HAVE TO TELL YOU!? YOUR ROOM'S ON THE FIRST FLOOR, MINE'S ON THE SECOND!
HOW CAN YOU KEEP FORGETTING THAT?
GRIP
GRIP
RIGID
HERE'S YOUR MORNING KISS. ♥

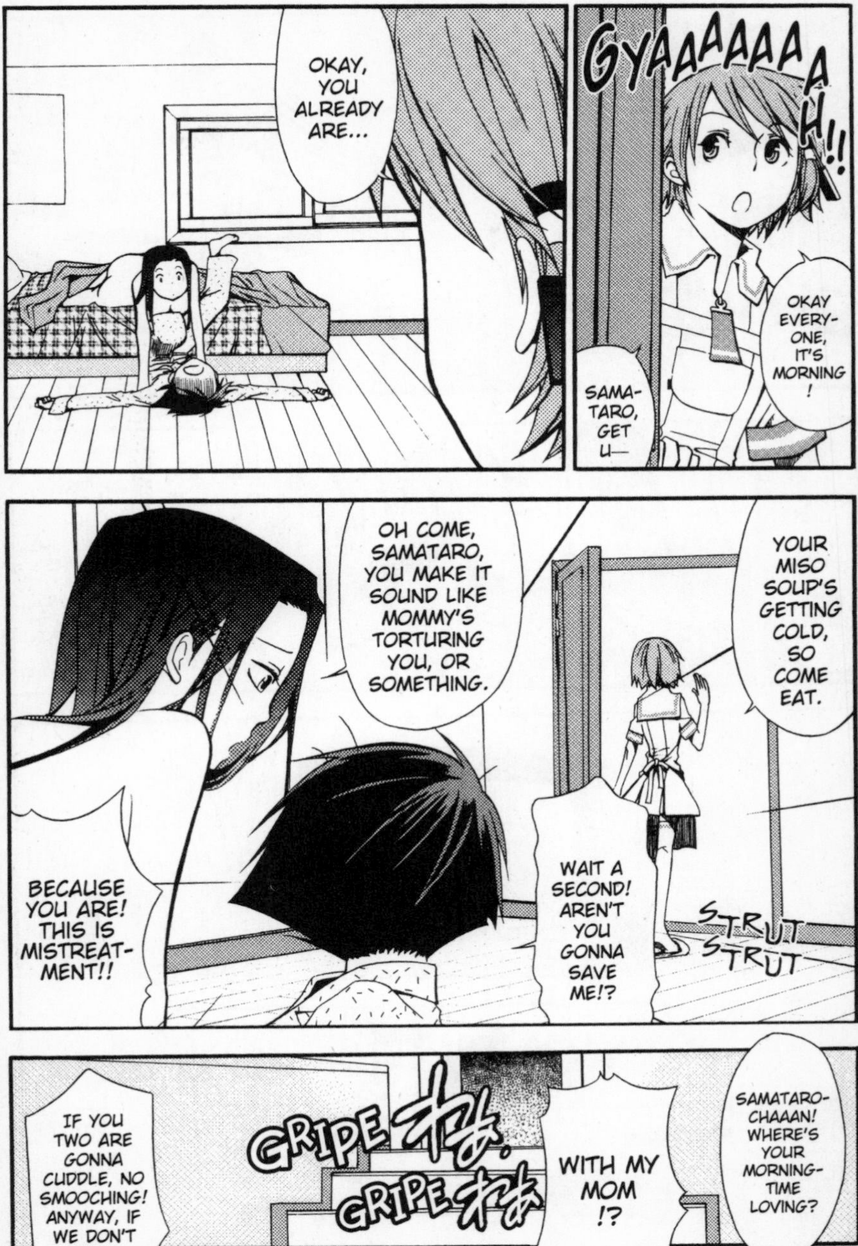
GYAAAAAAAH!!
OKAY EVERYONE, IT'S MORNING!
SAMATARO, GET U—
OKAY, YOU ALREADY ARE...
YOUR MISO SOUP'S GETTING COLD, SO COME EAT.
OH COME, SAMATARO, YOU MAKE IT SOUND LIKE MOMMY'S TORTURING YOU, OR SOMETHING.
STRUT STRUT
WAIT A SECOND! AREN'T YOU GONNA SAVE ME!?
BECAUSE YOU ARE! THIS IS MISTREAT-MENT!!
SAMATARO-CHAAAN! WHERE'S YOUR MORNING-TIME LOVING?
WITH MY MOM!?
GRIPE
GRIPE
IF YOU TWO ARE GONNA CUDDLE, NO SMOOCHING! ANYWAY, IF WE DON'T HURRY...

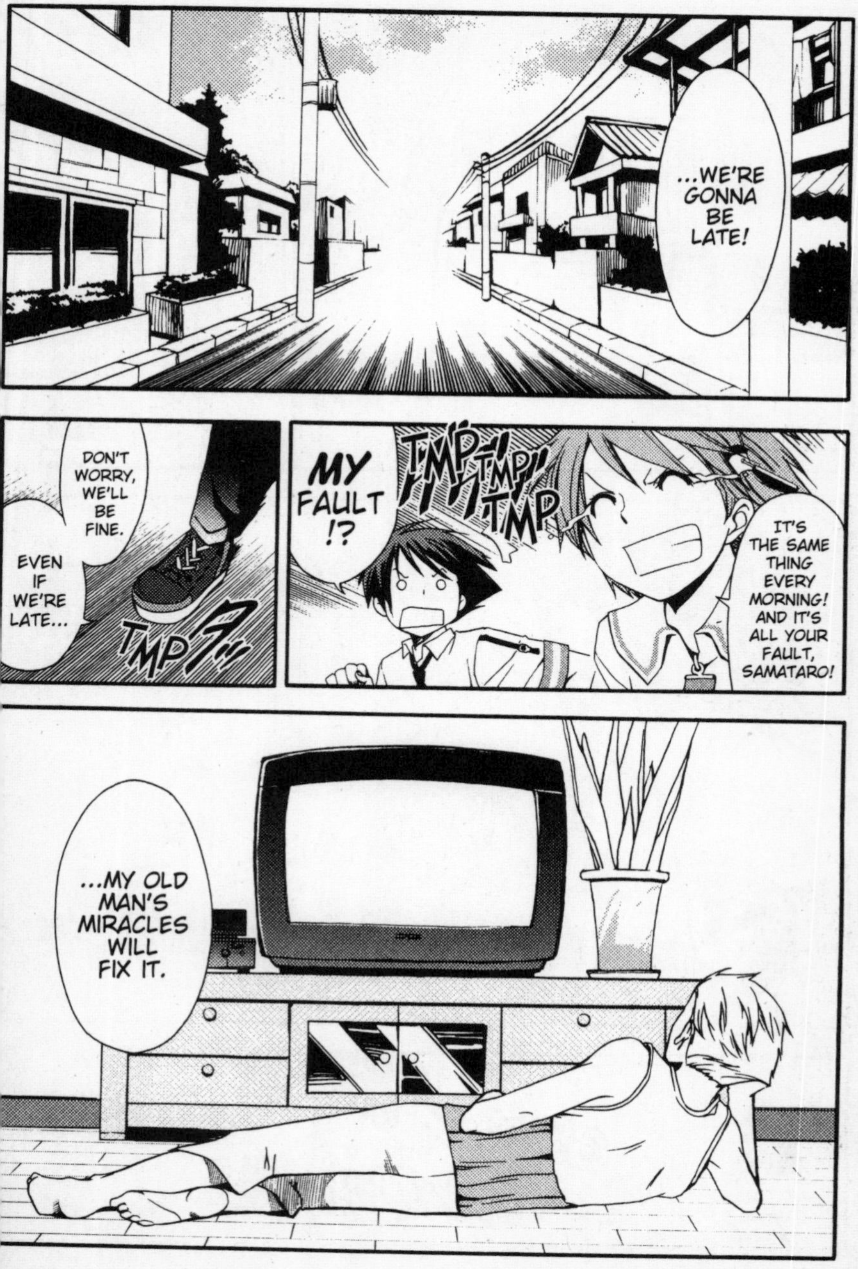
...WE'RE GONNA BE LATE!
IT'S THE SAME THING EVERY MORNING! AND IT'S ALL YOUR FAULT, SAMATARO!
TMP TMP TMP
MY FAULT!?
DON'T WORRY, WE'LL BE FINE.
EVEN IF WE'RE LATE...
TMP
...MY OLD MAN'S MIRACLES WILL FIX IT.

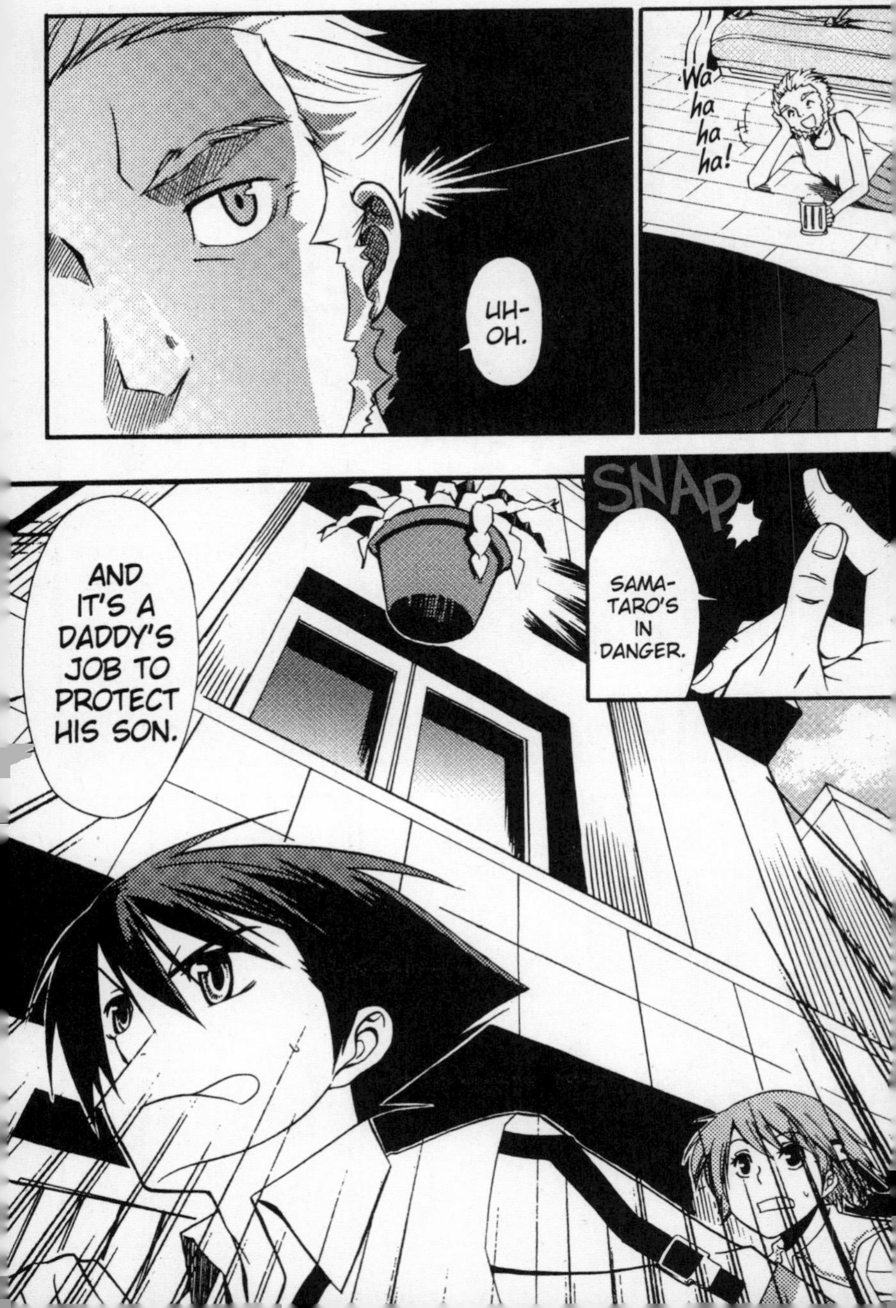
Wa ha ha ha!
UH-OH.
SNAP
SAMA-TARO'S IN DANGER.
AND IT'S A DADDY'S JOB TO PROTECT HIS SON.

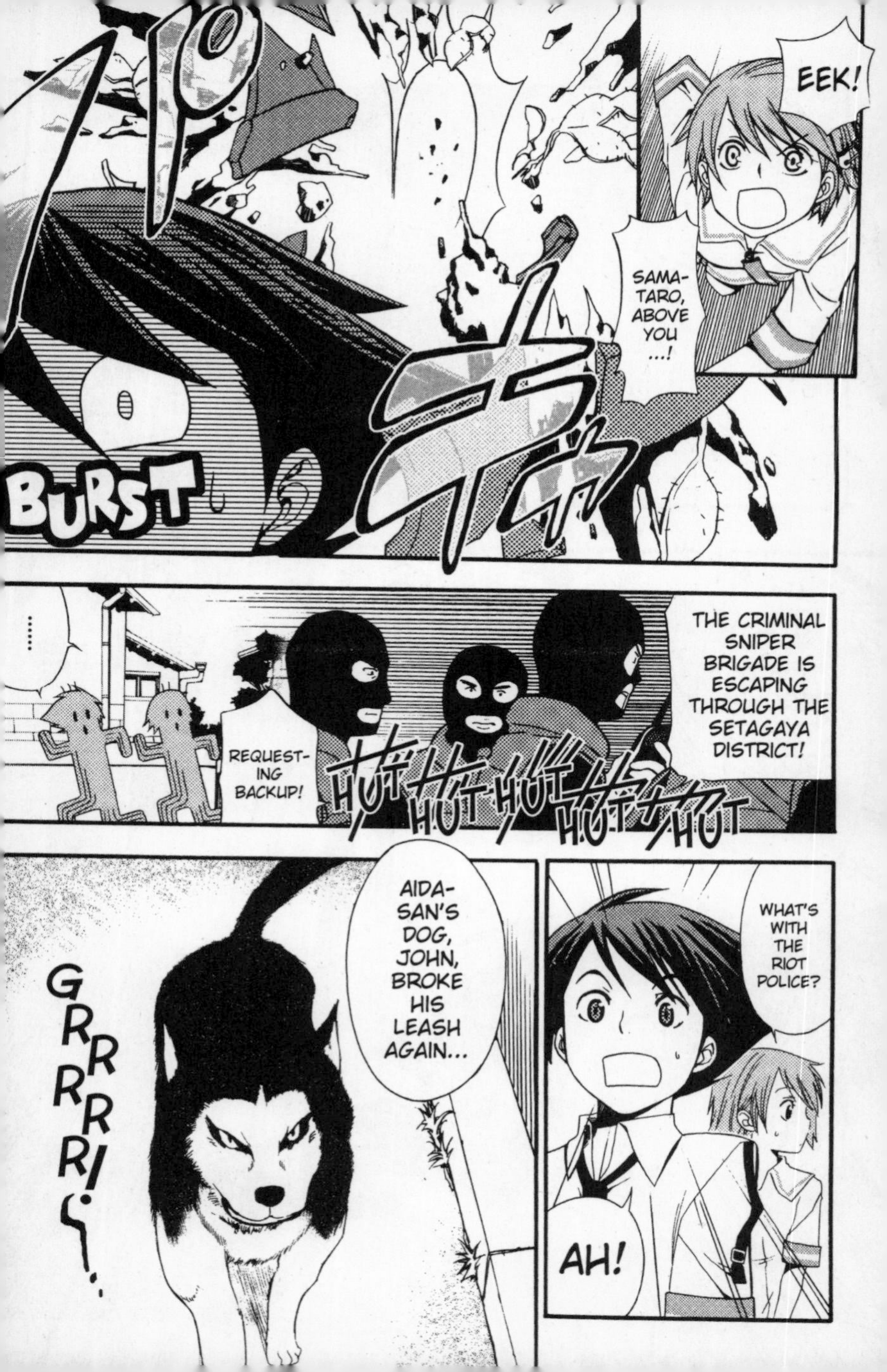
EEK!
SAMA-TARO, ABOVE YOU ...!
BURST
THE CRIMINAL SNIPER BRIGADE IS ESCAPING THROUGH THE SETAGAYA DISTRICT!
HUT HUT HUT HUT HUT HUT
REQUESTING BACKUP!
......
WHAT'S WITH THE RIOT POLICE?
AH!
AIDA-SAN'S DOG, JOHN, BROKE HIS LEASH AGAIN...
GRRRRR!

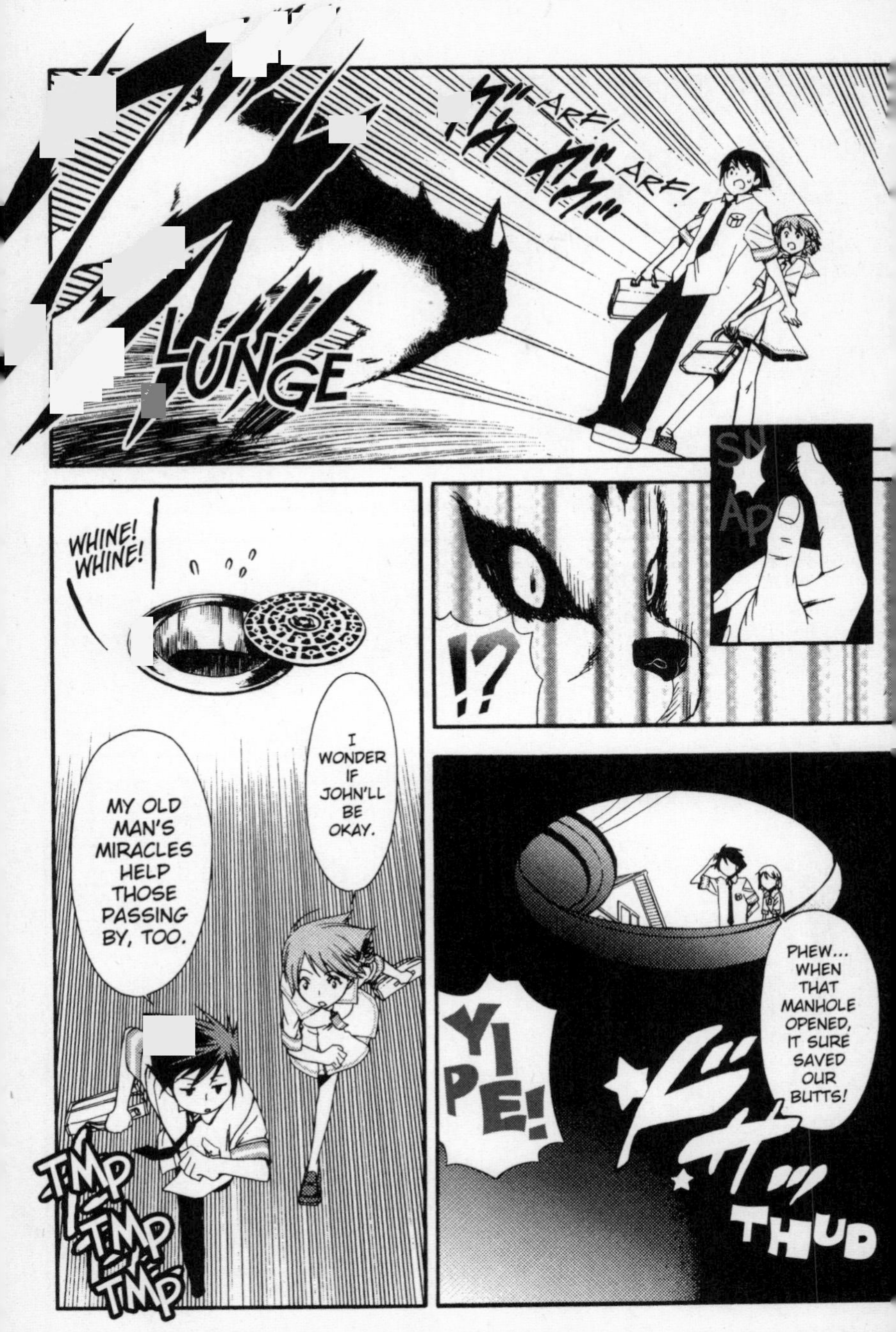
ARF!
ARF!
LUNGE
SNAP
!?
PHEW... WHEN THAT MANHOLE OPENED, IT SURE SAVED OUR BUTTS!
THUD
YIPE!
WHINE! WHINE!
I WONDER IF JOHN'LL BE OKAY.
MY OLD MAN'S MIRACLES HELP THOSE PASSING BY, TOO.
TMP-TMP-TMP

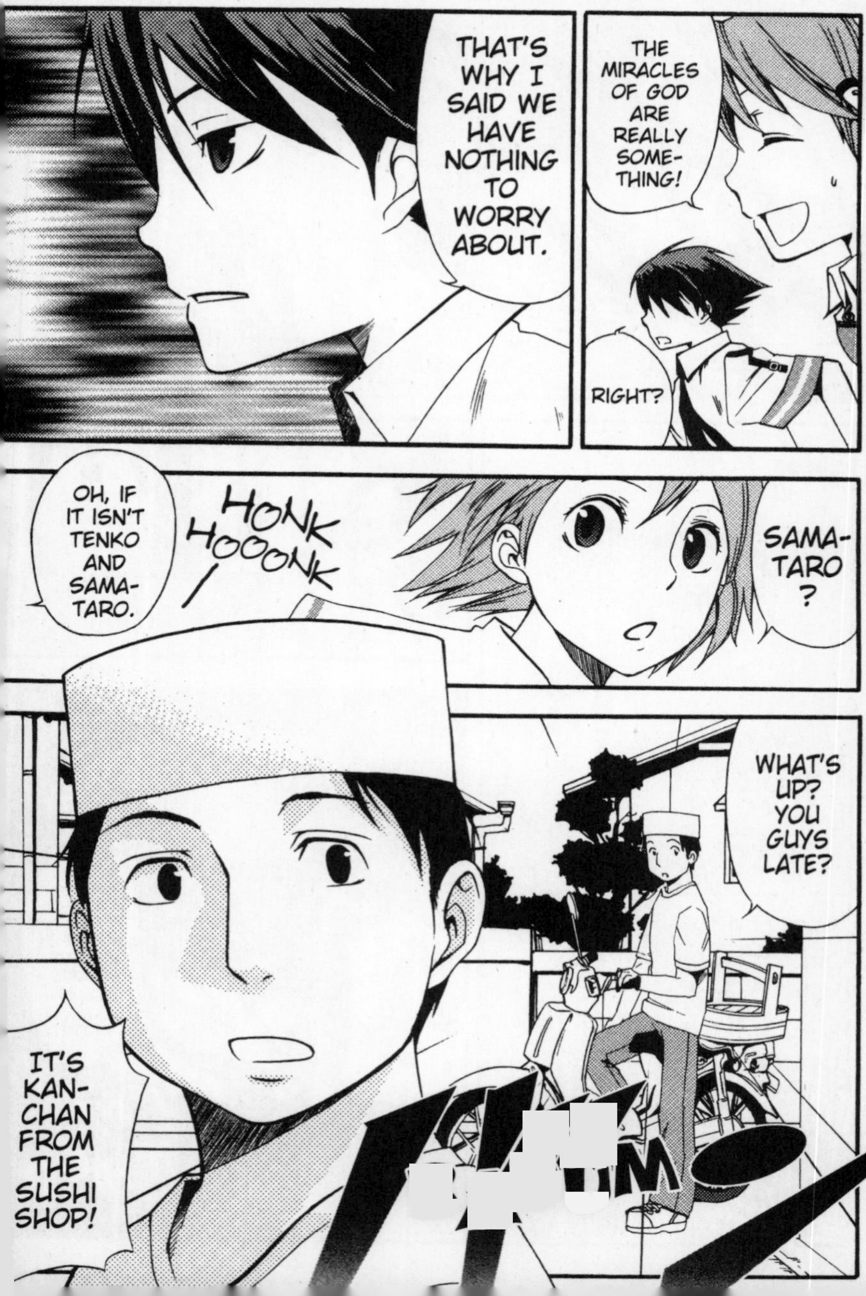
THE MIRACLES OF GOD ARE REALLY SOME-THING!
RIGHT?
THAT'S WHY I SAID WE HAVE NOTHING TO WORRY ABOUT.
SAMA-TARO?
HONK HOOOONK
OH, IF IT ISN'T TENKO AND SAMA-TARO.
WHAT'S UP? YOU GUYS LATE?
IT'S KAN-CHAN FROM THE SUSHI SHOP!

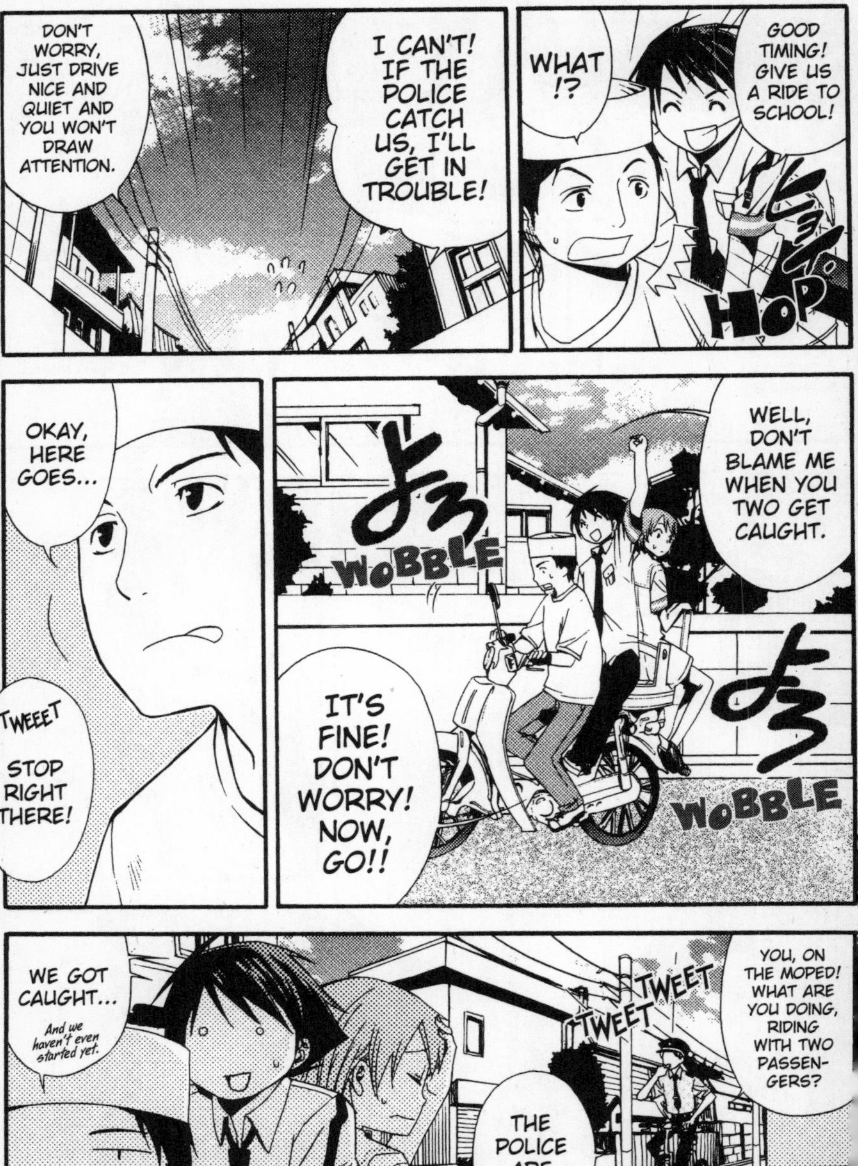
GOOD TIMING! GIVE US A RIDE TO SCHOOL!
WHAT!?
HOP
I CAN'T! IF THE POLICE CATCH US, I'LL GET IN TROUBLE!
DON'T WORRY, JUST DRIVE NICE AND QUIET AND YOU WON'T DRAW ATTENTION.
WELL, DON'T BLAME ME WHEN YOU TWO GET CAUGHT.
よろ
WOBBLE
よろ
WOBBLE
IT'S FINE! DON'T WORRY! NOW, GO!!
OKAY, HERE GOES...
TWEEET
STOP RIGHT THERE!
YOU, ON THE MOPED! WHAT ARE YOU DOING, RIDING WITH TWO PASSENGERS?
TWEET TWEET
THE POLICE ARE AFTER US.
WE GOT CAUGHT...
And we haven't even started yet.

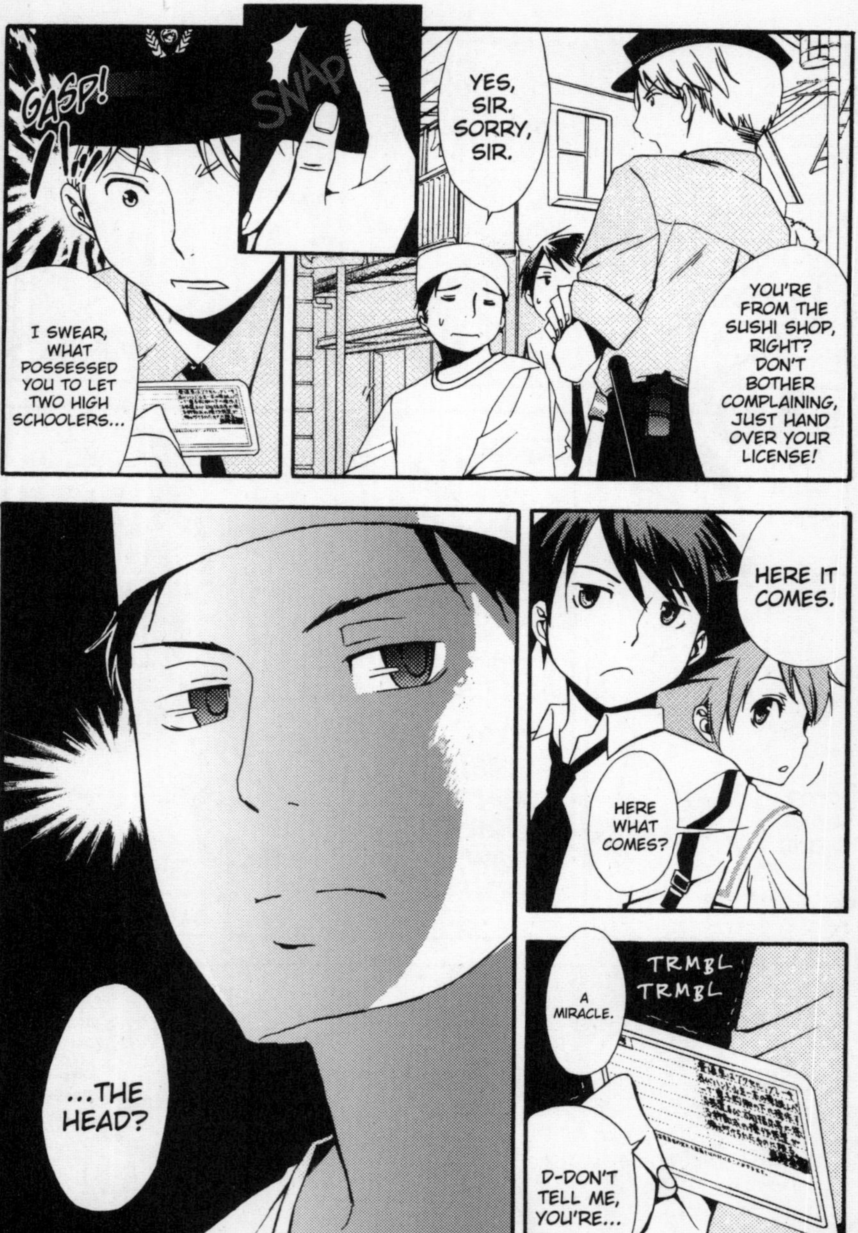
YOU'RE FROM THE SUSHI SHOP, RIGHT? DON'T BOTHER COMPLAINING, JUST HAND OVER YOUR LICENSE!
YES, SIR. SORRY, SIR.
SNAP
GASP!
I SWEAR, WHAT POSSESSED YOU TO LET TWO HIGH SCHOOLERS...
HERE IT COMES.
HERE WHAT COMES?
TRMBL TRMBL
A MIRACLE.
D-DON'T TELL ME, YOU'RE...
...THE HEAD?

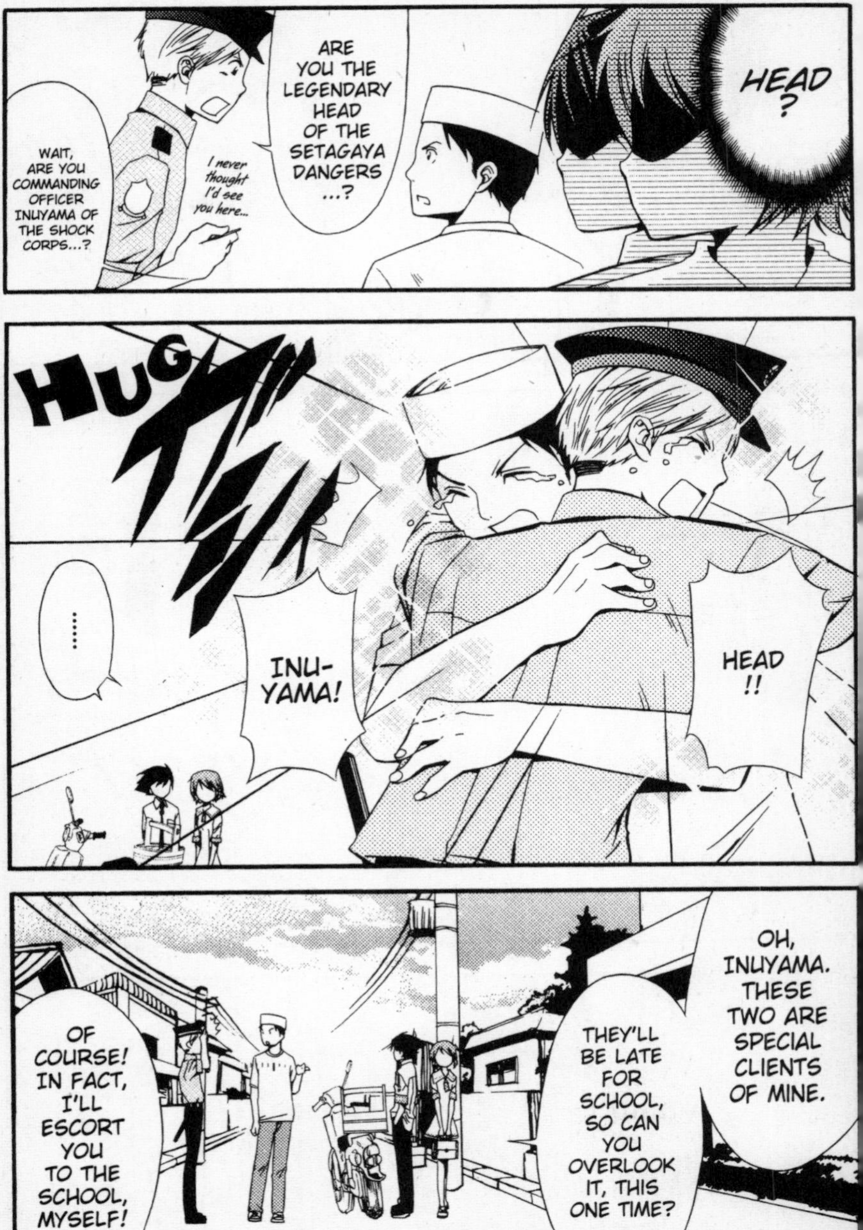
HEAD?
ARE YOU THE LEGENDARY HEAD OF THE SETAGAYA DANGERS ...?
I never thought I'd see you here...
WAIT, ARE YOU COMMANDING OFFICER INUYAMA OF THE SHOCK CORPS...?
HUG
HEAD!!
INU-YAMA!
......
OH, INUYAMA. THESE TWO ARE SPECIAL CLIENTS OF MINE.
THEY'LL BE LATE FOR SCHOOL, SO CAN YOU OVERLOOK IT, THIS ONE TIME?
OF COURSE! IN FACT, I'LL ESCORT YOU TO THE SCHOOL, MYSELF!

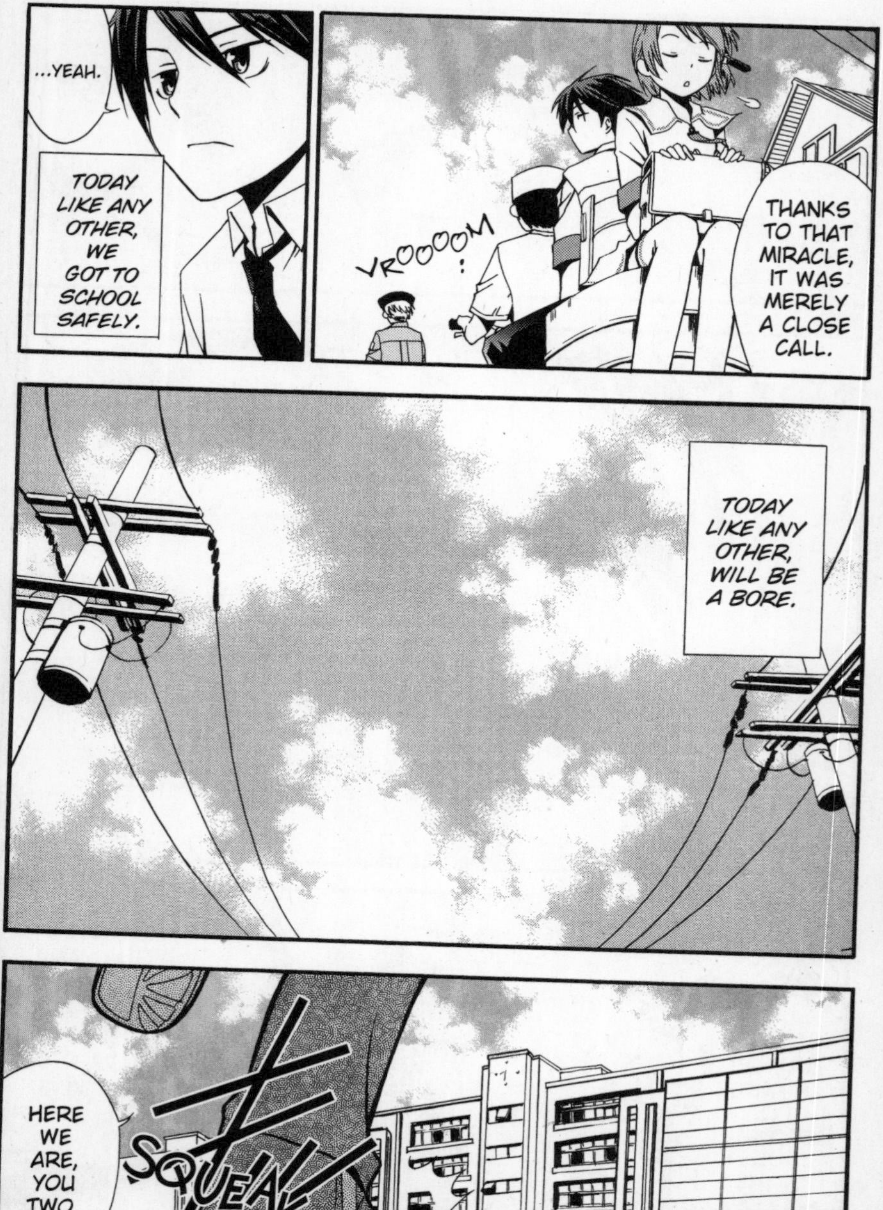
THANKS TO THAT MIRACLE, IT WAS MERELY A CLOSE CALL.
VROOOOM
...YEAH.
TODAY LIKE ANY OTHER, WE GOT TO SCHOOL SAFELY.
TODAY LIKE ANY OTHER, WILL BE A BORE.
SQUEAK
HERE WE ARE, YOU TWO.

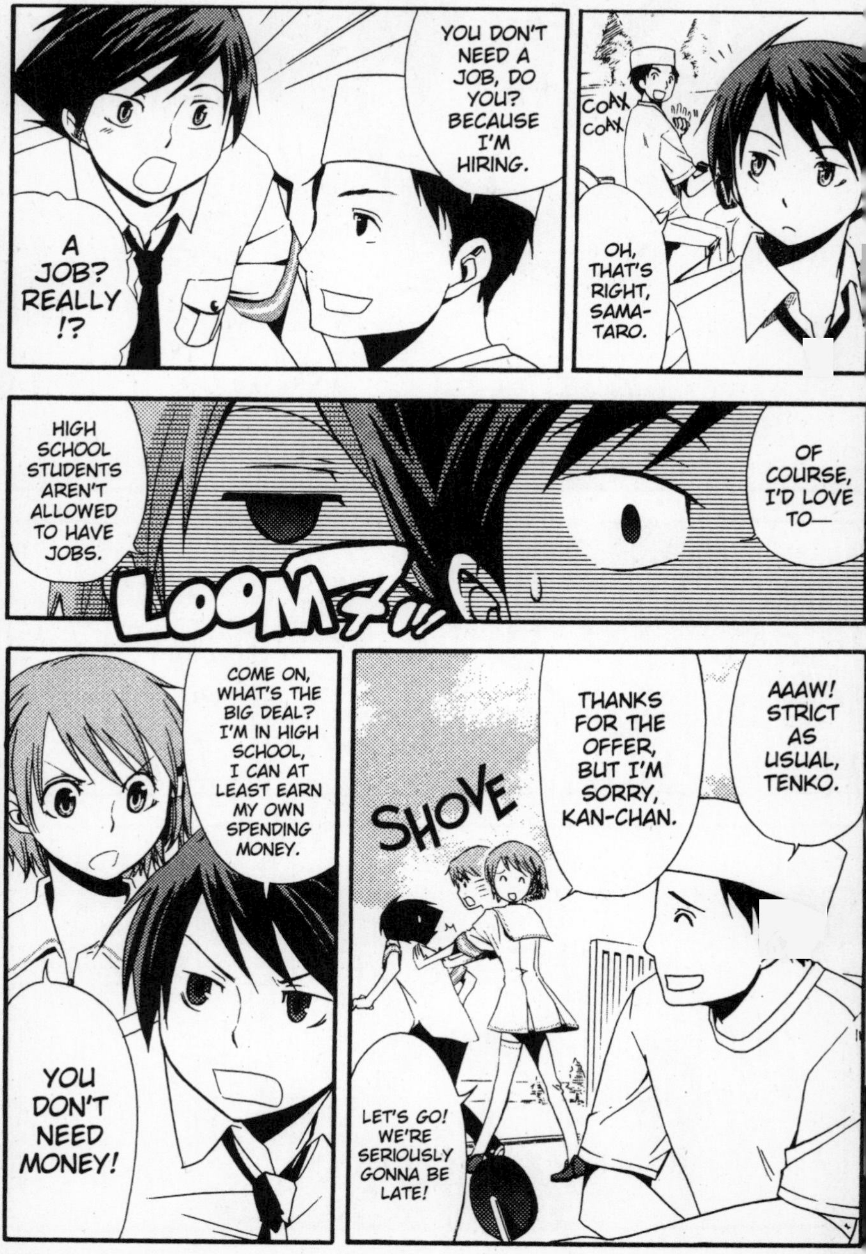
COAX COAX
OH, THAT'S RIGHT, SAMATARO.
YOU DON'T NEED A JOB, DO YOU? BECAUSE I'M HIRING.
A JOB? REALLY!?
OF COURSE, I'D LOVE TO—
HIGH SCHOOL STUDENTS AREN'T ALLOWED TO HAVE JOBS.
LOOM
AAAW! STRICT AS USUAL, TENKO.
THANKS FOR THE OFFER, BUT I'M SORRY, KAN-CHAN.
SHOVE
LET'S GO! WE'RE SERIOUSLY GONNA BE LATE!
COME ON, WHAT'S THE BIG DEAL? I'M IN HIGH SCHOOL, I CAN AT LEAST EARN MY OWN SPENDING MONEY.
YOU DON'T NEED MONEY!

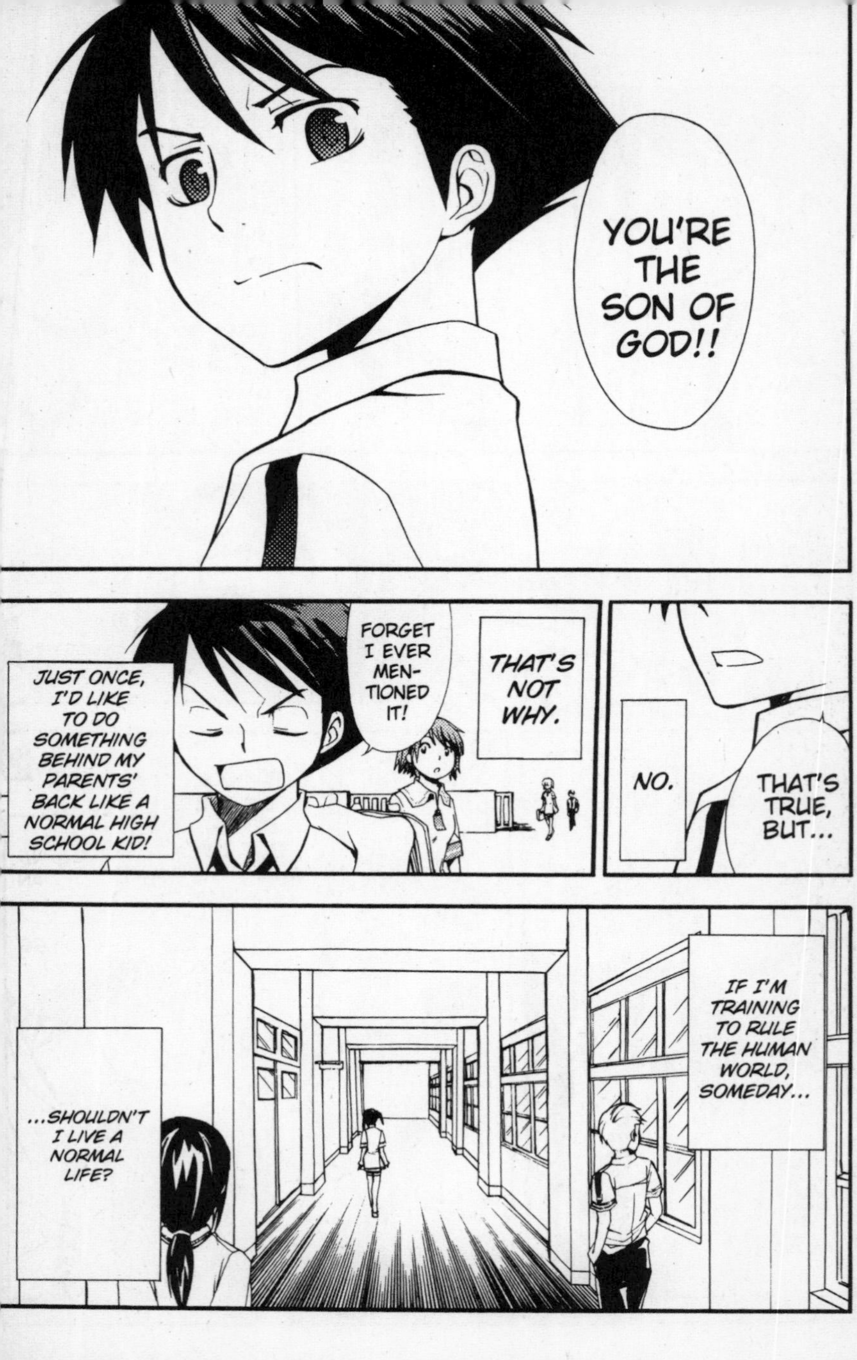
YOU'RE THE SON OF GOD!!
THAT'S TRUE, BUT...
NO.
THAT'S NOT WHY.
FORGET I EVER MEN- TIONED IT!
JUST ONCE, I'D LIKE TO DO SOMETHING BEHIND MY PARENTS' BACK LIKE A NORMAL HIGH SCHOOL KID!
IF I'M TRAINING TO RULE THE HUMAN WORLD, SOMEDAY...
...SHOULDN'T I LIVE A NORMAL LIFE?

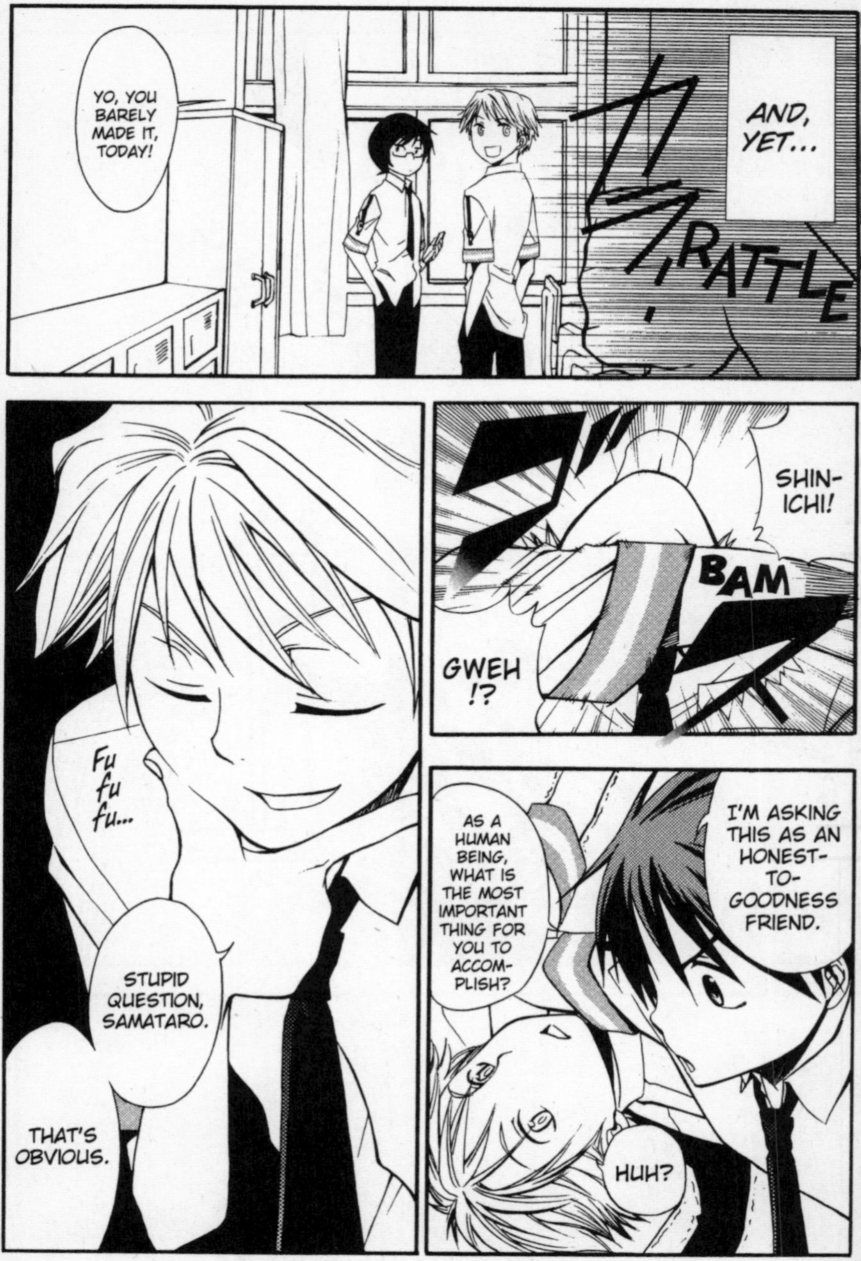
AND, YET...
RATTLE
YO, YOU BARELY MADE IT, TODAY!
SHIN-ICHI!
BAM
GWEH !?
I'M ASKING THIS AS AN HONEST-TO-GOODNESS FRIEND.
AS A HUMAN BEING, WHAT IS THE MOST IMPORTANT THING FOR YOU TO ACCOMPLISH?
HUH?
Fu fu fu...
STUPID QUESTION, SAMATARO.
THAT'S OBVIOUS.

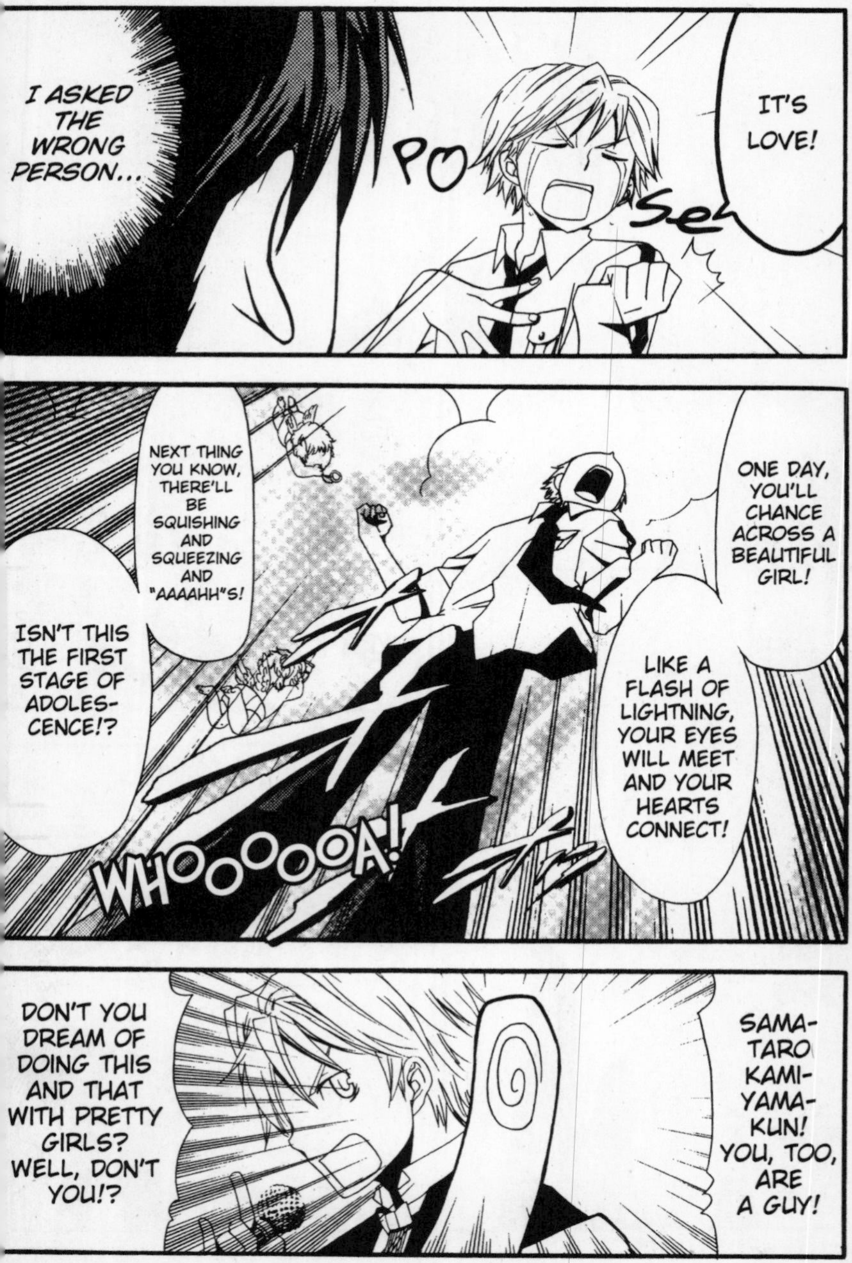
IT'S LOVE!
PO
SE
I ASKED THE WRONG PERSON...
ONE DAY, YOU'LL CHANCE ACROSS A BEAUTIFUL GIRL!
LIKE A FLASH OF LIGHTNING, YOUR EYES WILL MEET AND YOUR HEARTS CONNECT!
NEXT THING YOU KNOW, THERE'LL BE SQUISHING AND SQUEEZING AND "AAAAHH"S!
ISN'T THIS THE FIRST STAGE OF ADOLES-CENCE!?
WHOOOOOOA!
SAMA-TARO KAMI-YAMA-KUN! YOU, TOO, ARE A GUY!
DON'T YOU DREAM OF DOING THIS AND THAT WITH PRETTY GIRLS? WELL, DON'T YOU!?

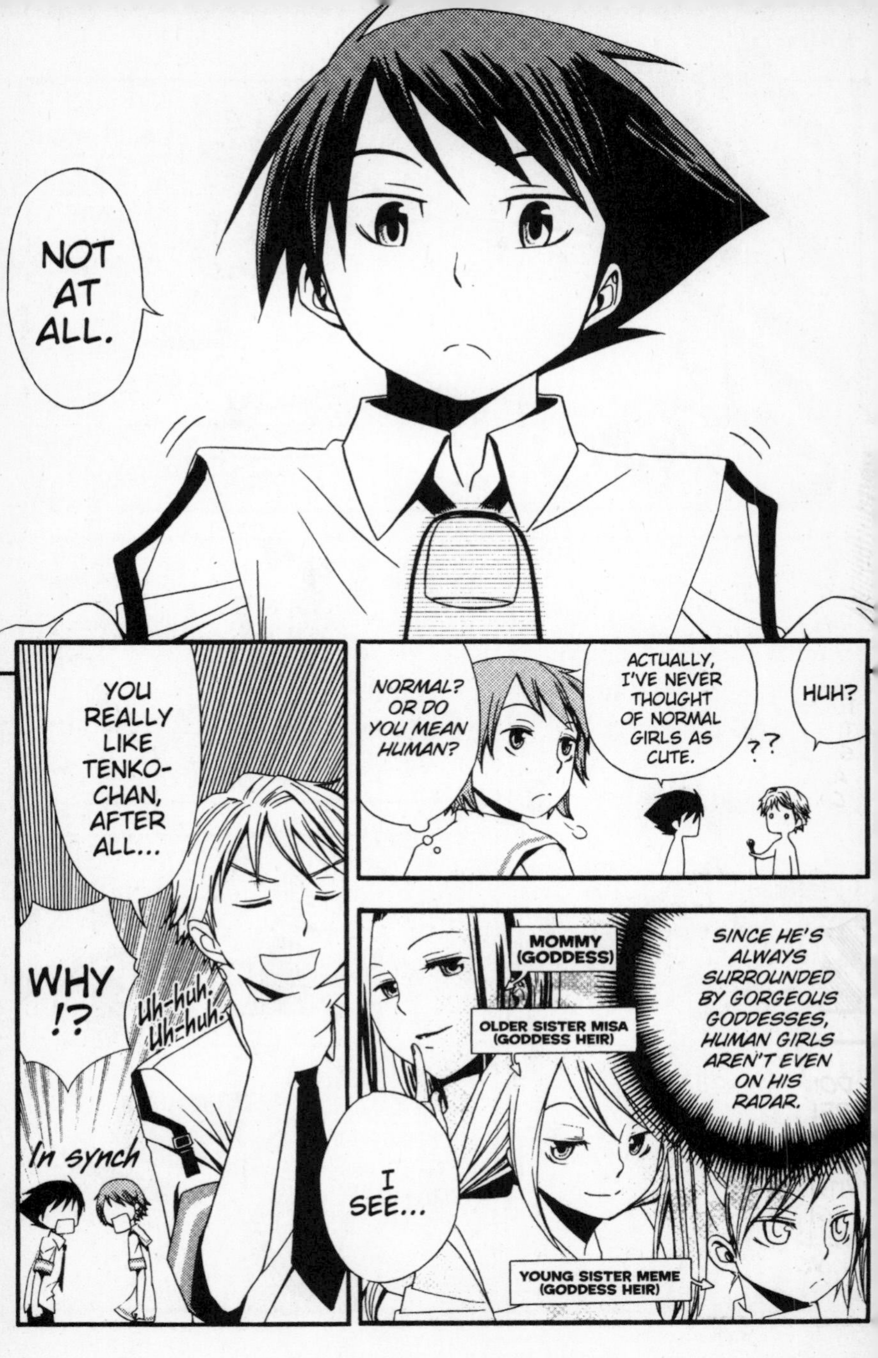
NOT AT ALL.
HUH?
ACTUALLY, I'VE NEVER THOUGHT OF NORMAL GIRLS AS CUTE.
??
NORMAL? OR DO YOU MEAN HUMAN?
SINCE HE'S ALWAYS SURROUNDED BY GORGEOUS GODDESSES, HUMAN GIRLS AREN'T EVEN ON HIS RADAR.
MOMMY (GODDESS)
OLDER SISTER MISA (GODDESS HEIR)
YOUNG SISTER MEME (GODDESS HEIR)
I SEE...
YOU REALLY LIKE TENKO-CHAN, AFTER ALL...
Uh-huh. Uh-huh.
WHY !?
In synch

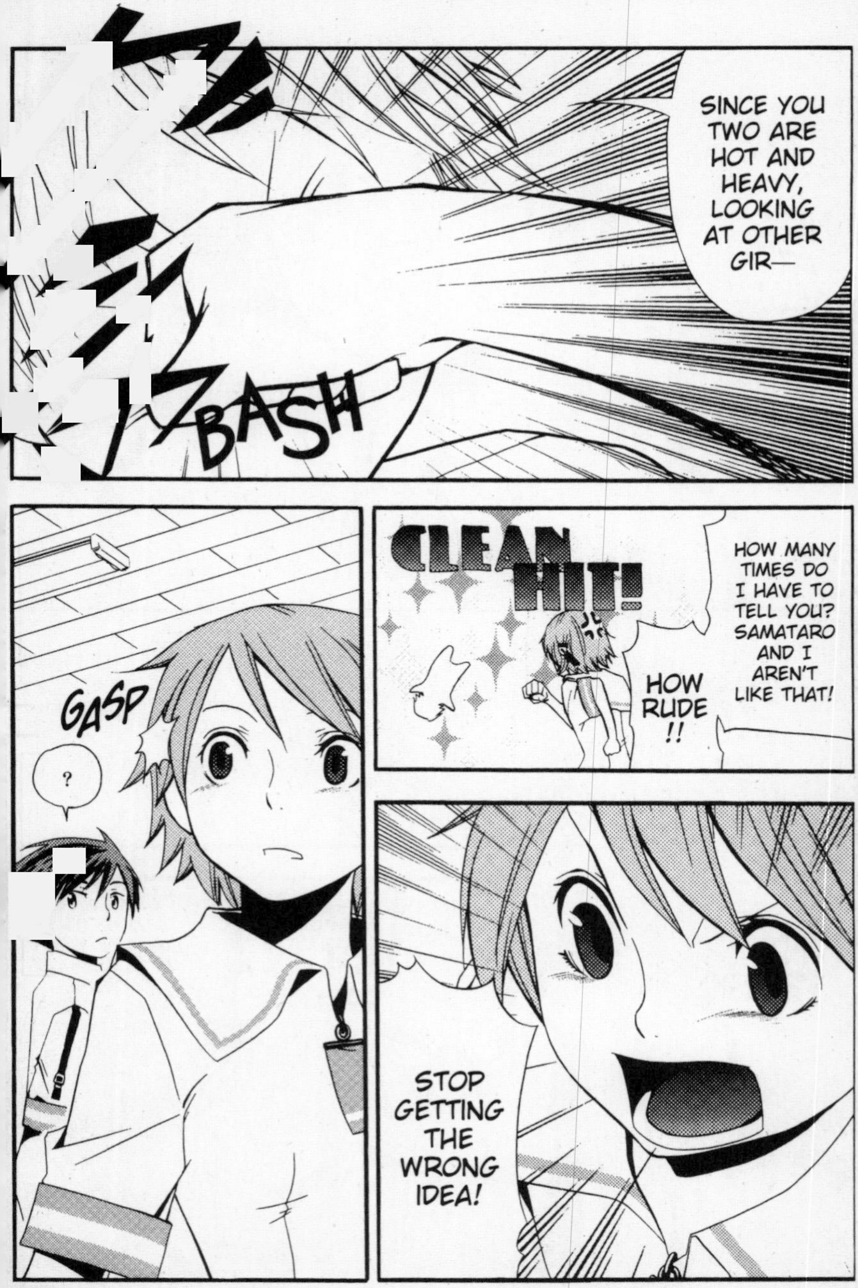
SINCE YOU TWO ARE HOT AND HEAVY, LOOKING AT OTHER GIR—
BASH
HOW MANY TIMES DO I HAVE TO TELL YOU? SAMATARO AND I AREN'T LIKE THAT!
CLEAN HIT!
HOW RUDE !!
STOP GETTING THE WRONG IDEA!
GASP
?

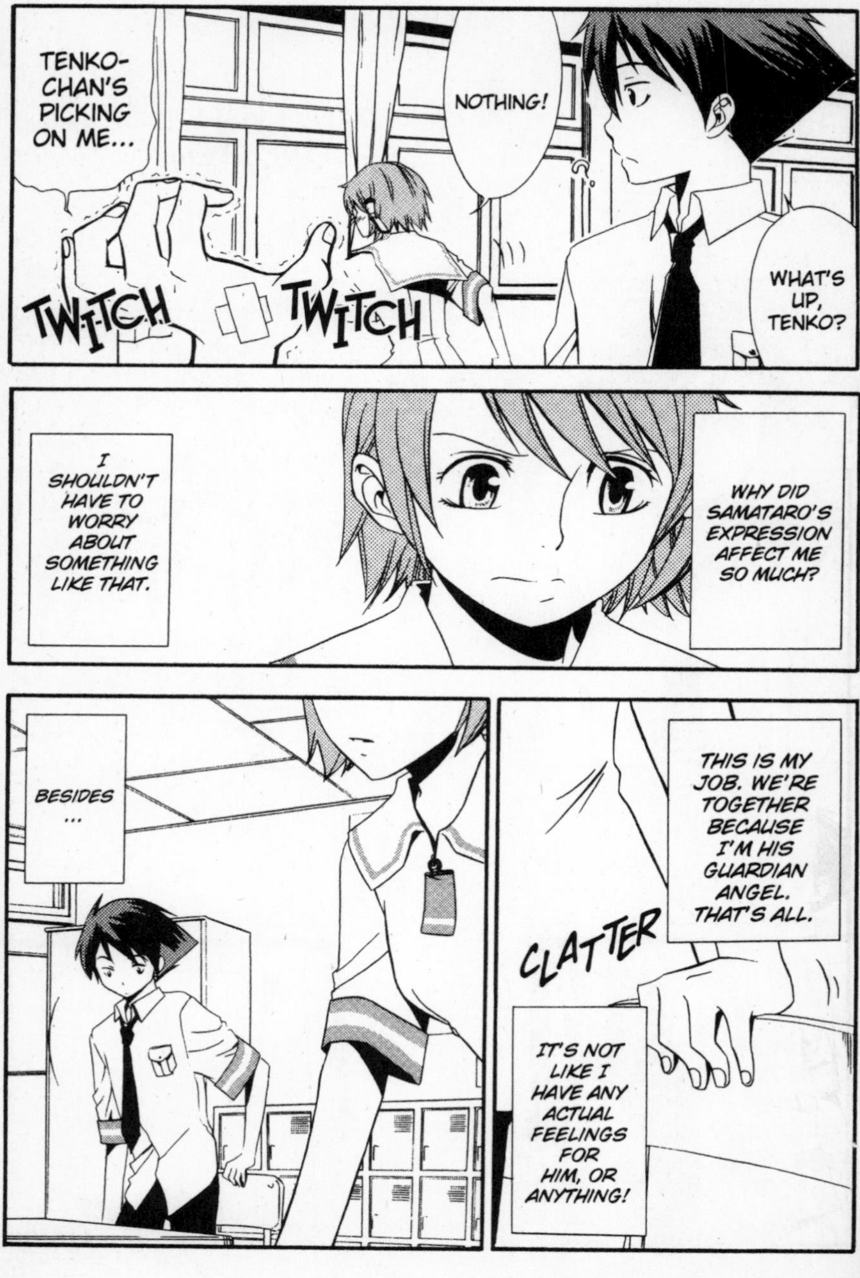

WHAT'S UP, TENKO?
NOTHING!
TENKO-CHAN'S PICKING ON ME...
TWITCH
TWITCH
WHY DID SAMATARO'S EXPRESSION AFFECT ME SO MUCH?
I SHOULDN'T HAVE TO WORRY ABOUT SOMETHING LIKE THAT.
THIS IS MY JOB. WE'RE TOGETHER BECAUSE I'M HIS GUARDIAN ANGEL. THAT'S ALL.
CLATTER
IT'S NOT LIKE I HAVE ANY ACTUAL FEELINGS FOR HIM, OR ANYTHING!
BESIDES ...

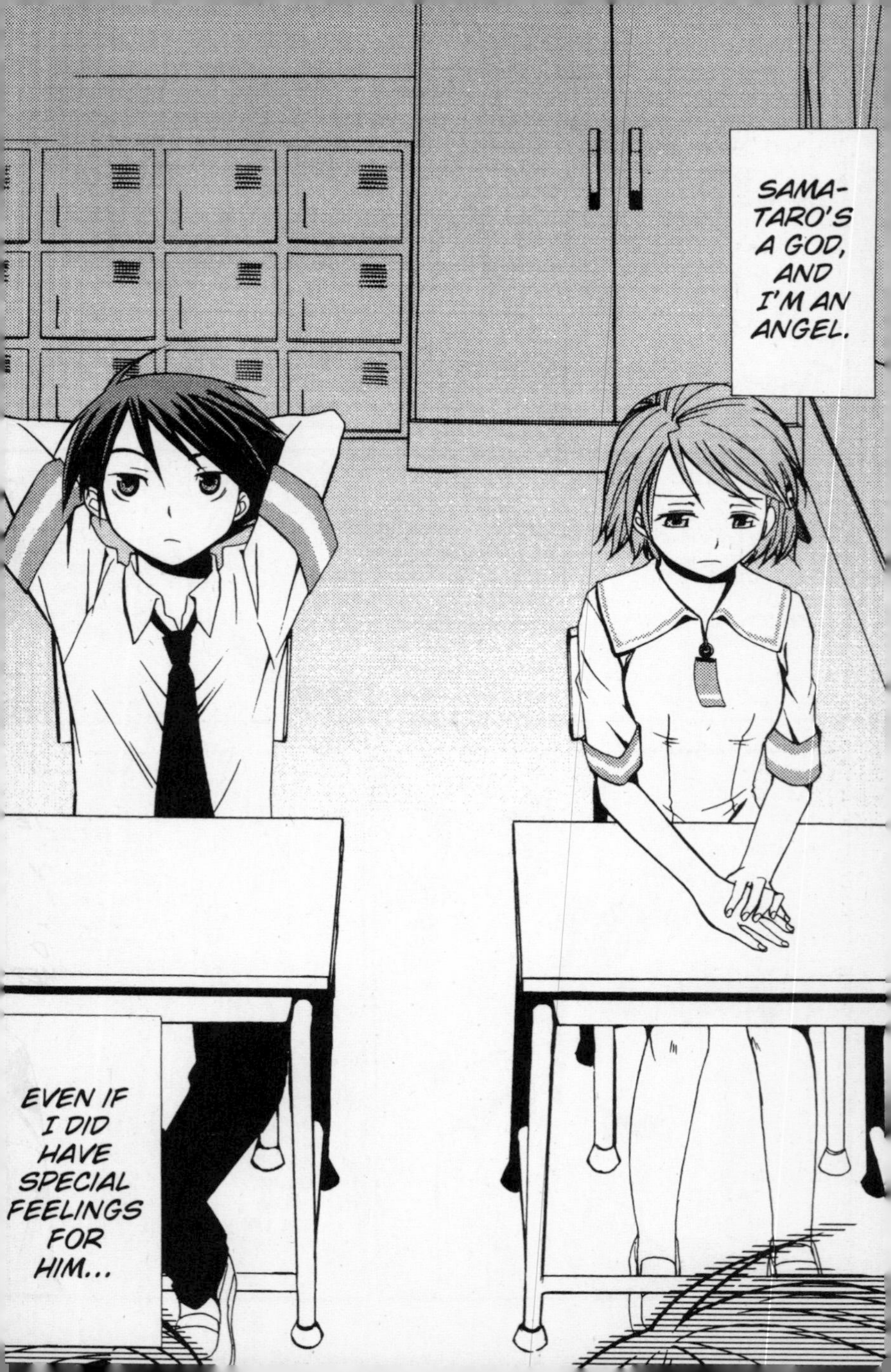
SAMA-TARO'S A GOD, AND I'M AN ANGEL.
EVEN IF I DID HAVE SPECIAL FEELINGS FOR HIM...

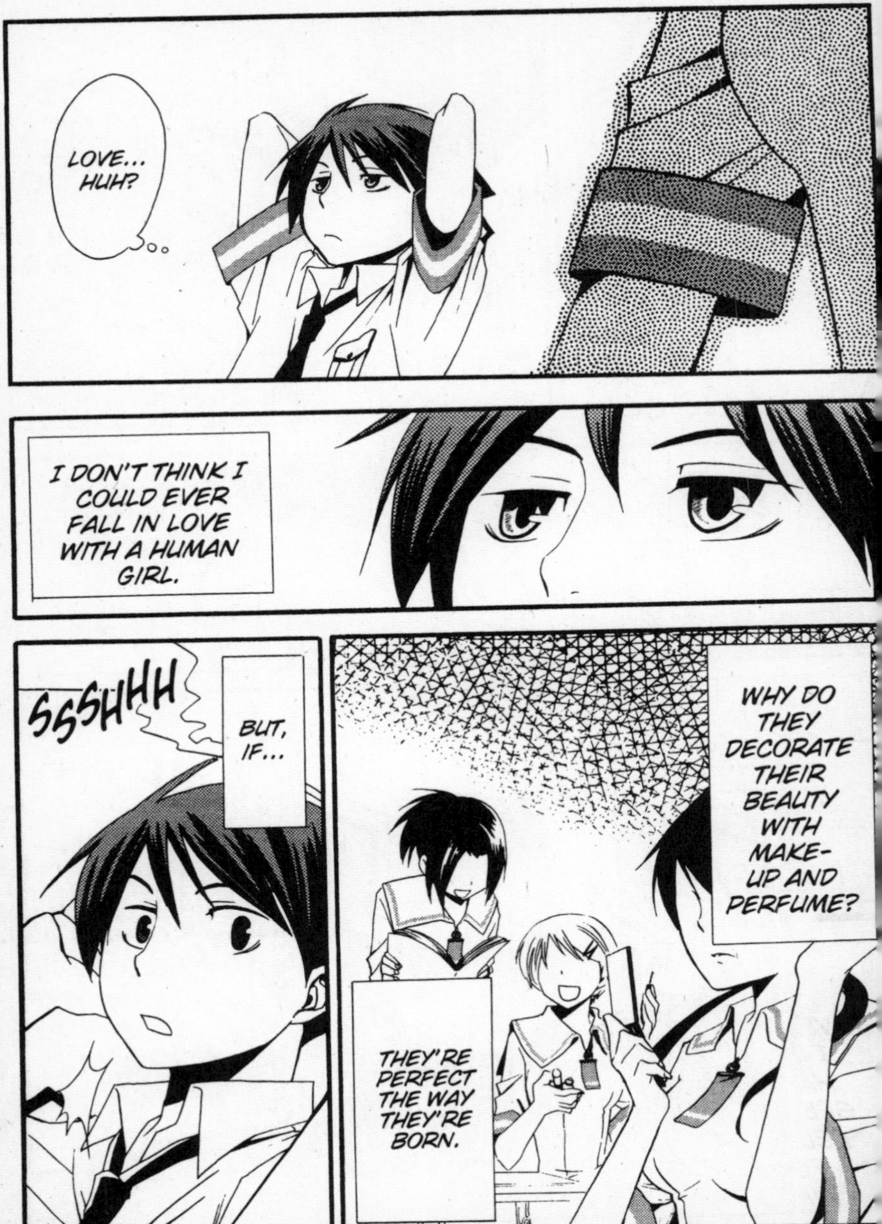
LOVE... HUH?
I DON'T THINK I COULD EVER FALL IN LOVE WITH A HUMAN GIRL.
WHY DO THEY DECORATE THEIR BEAUTY WITH MAKE-UP AND PERFUME?
THEY'RE PERFECT THE WAY THEY'RE BORN.
BUT, IF...
SSSHHH

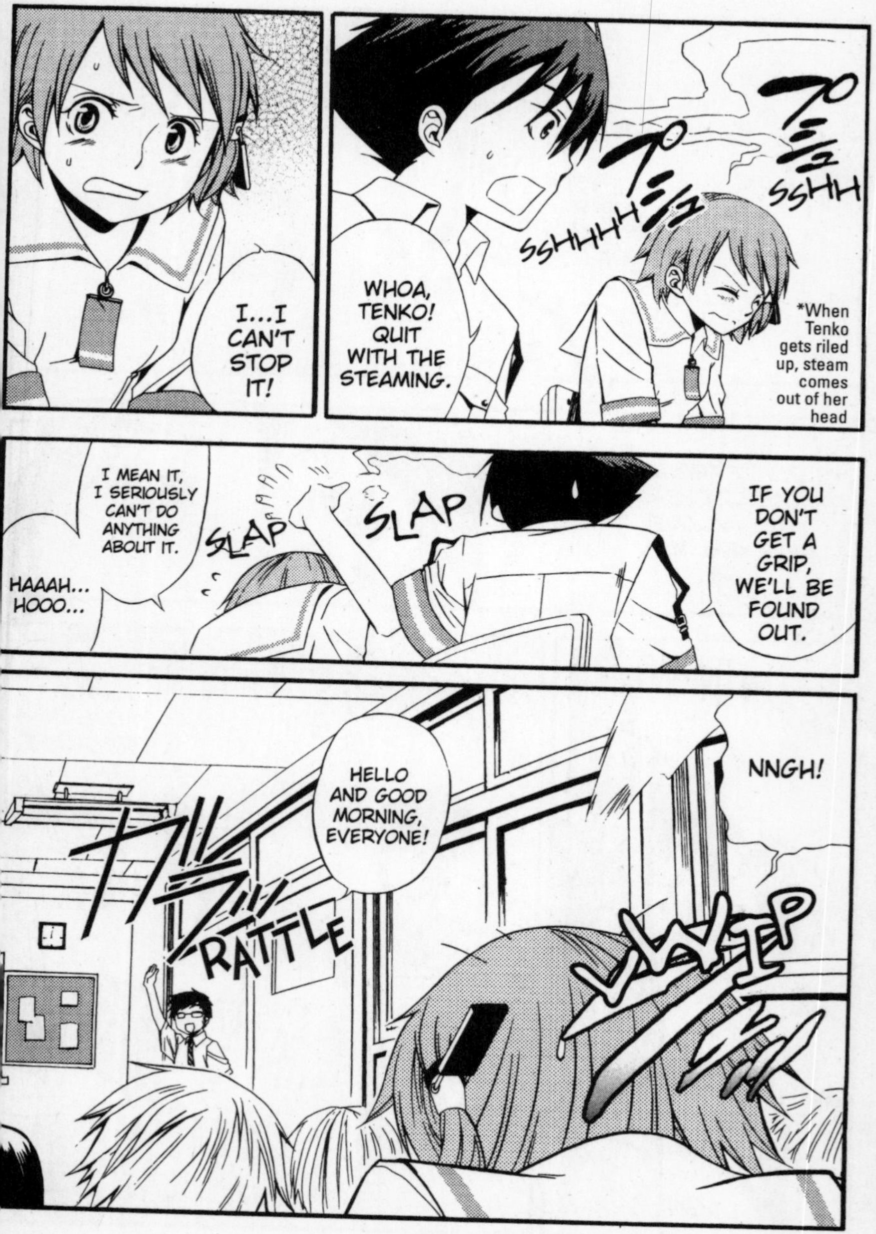
プシュ
SSHH
プシュ
SSHHHH
WHOA, TENKO! QUIT WITH THE STEAMING.
*When Tenko gets riled up, steam comes out of her head
I...I CAN'T STOP IT!
IF YOU DON'T GET A GRIP, WE'LL BE FOUND OUT.
SLAP
SLAP
I MEAN IT, I SERIOUSLY CAN'T DO ANYTHING ABOUT IT.
HAAAH... HOOO...
NNGH!
WHIP
HELLO AND GOOD MORNING, EVERYONE!
ガラッ
RATTLE

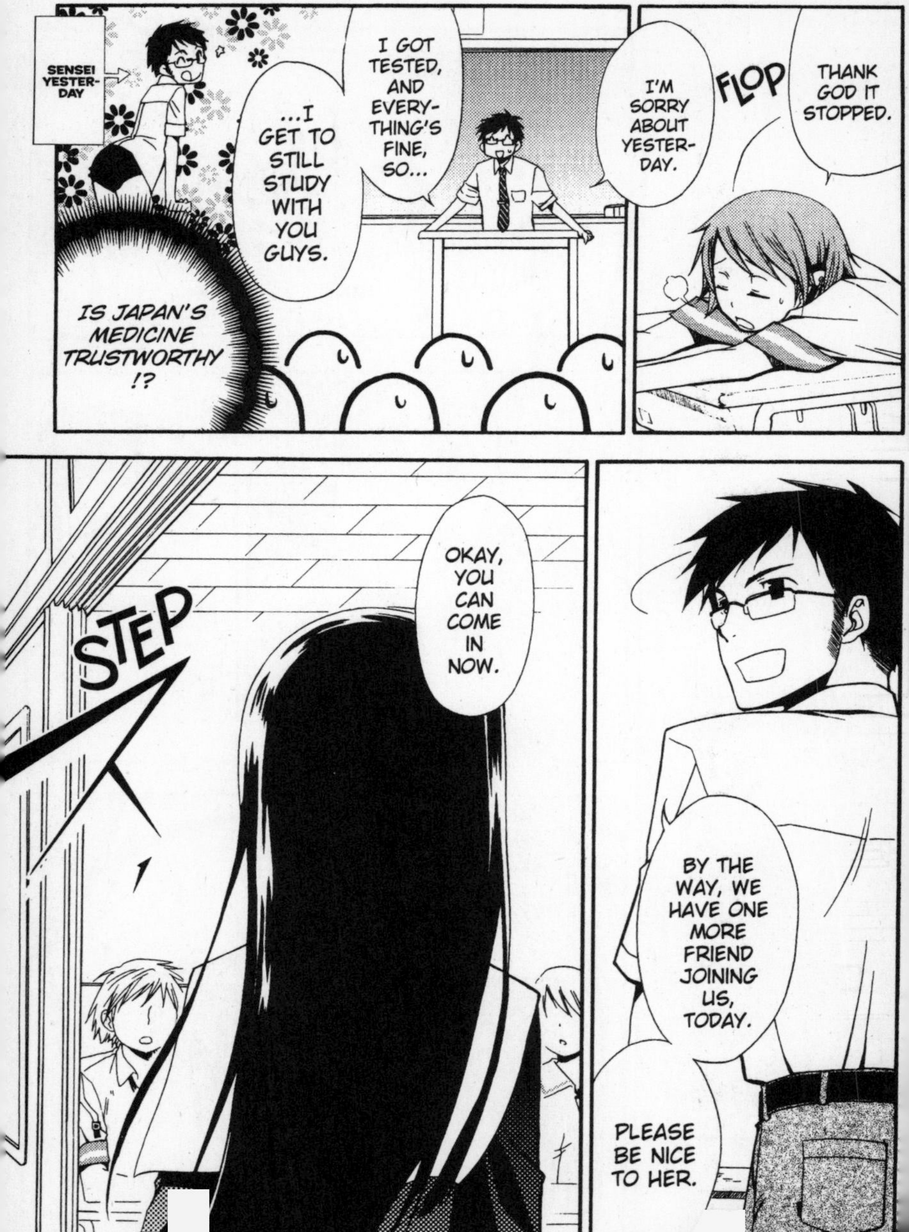
THANK GOD IT STOPPED.
FLOP
I'M SORRY ABOUT YESTER-DAY.
I GOT TESTED, AND EVERY-THING'S FINE, SO...
...I GET TO STILL STUDY WITH YOU GUYS.
SENSEI YESTER-DAY
IS JAPAN'S MEDICINE TRUSTWORTHY !?
BY THE WAY, WE HAVE ONE MORE FRIEND JOINING US, TODAY.
PLEASE BE NICE TO HER.
OKAY, YOU CAN COME IN NOW.
STEP

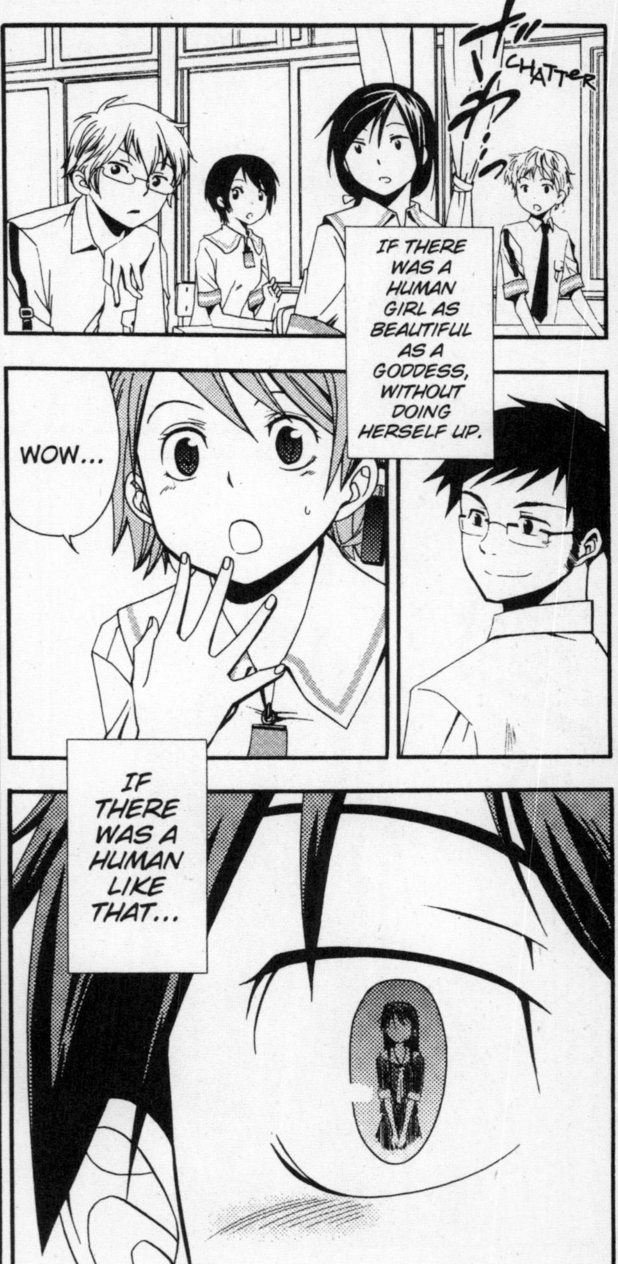
CHATTER
IF THERE WAS A HUMAN GIRL AS BEAUTIFUL AS A GODDESS, WITHOUT DOING HERSELF UP.
WOW...
IF THERE WAS A HUMAN LIKE THAT...

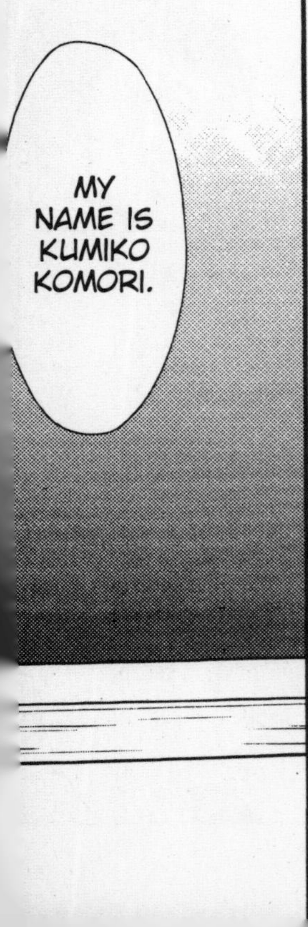
MY NAME IS KUMIKO KOMORI.

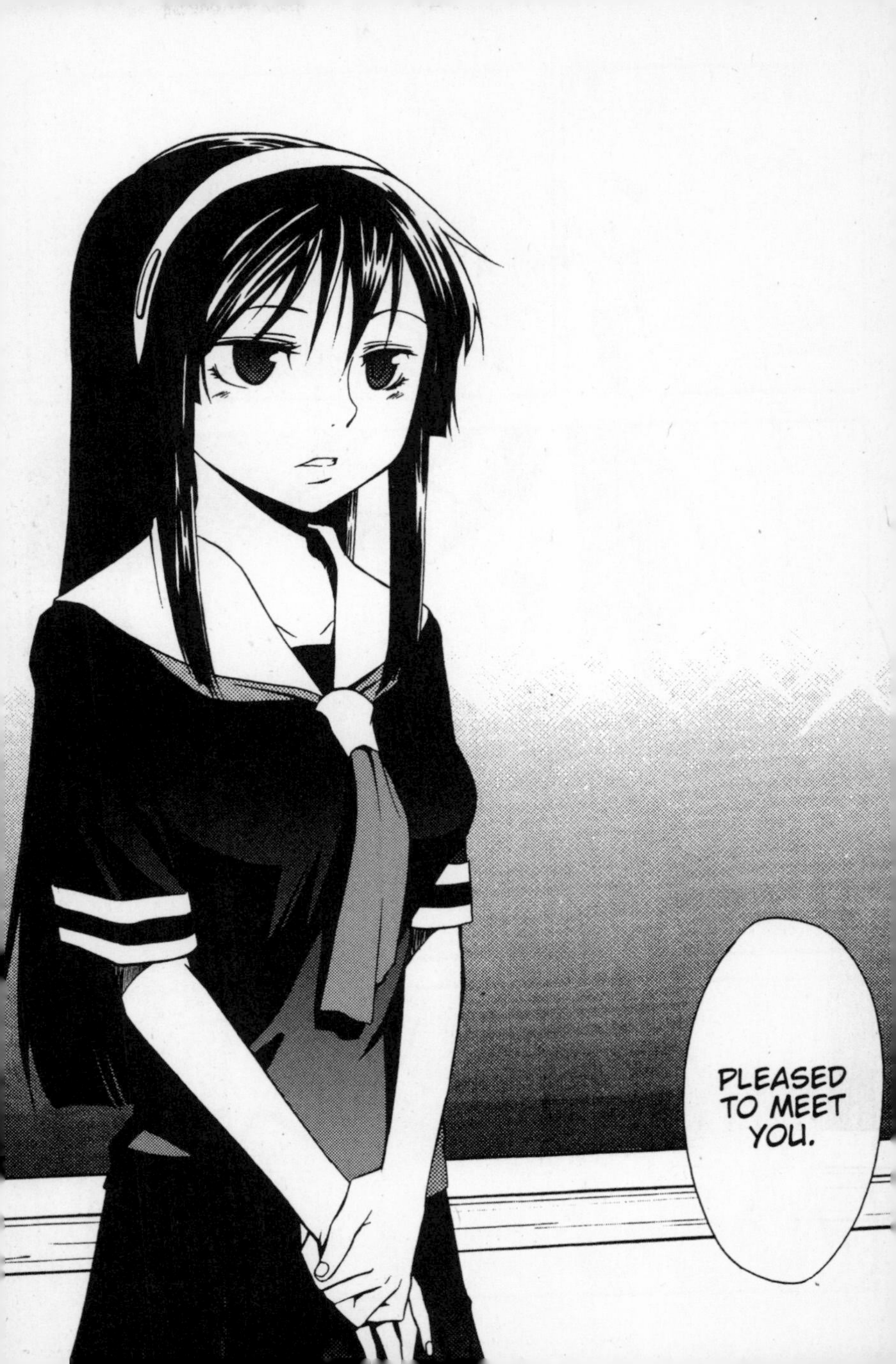
PLEASED TO MEET YOU.

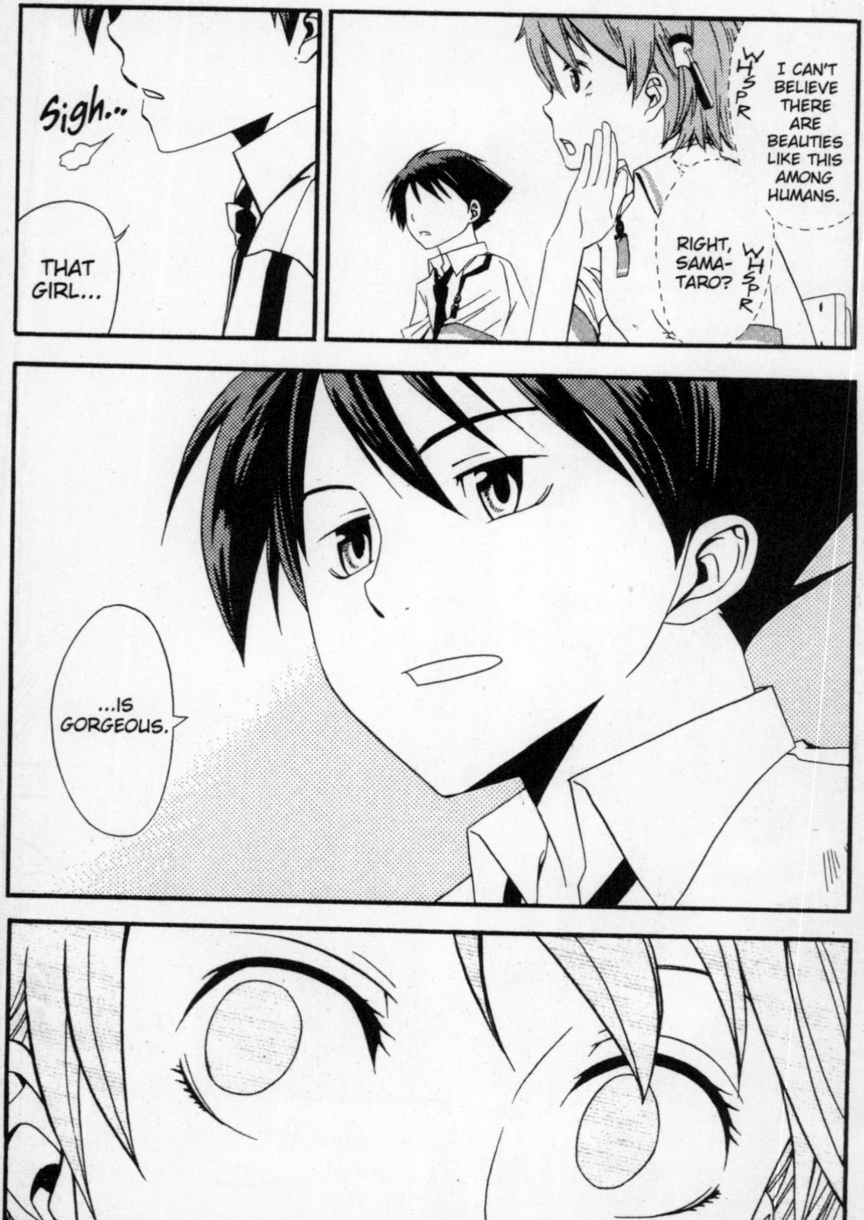
WHSPR
I CAN'T BELIEVE THERE ARE BEAUTIES LIKE THIS AMONG HUMANS.
RIGHT, SAMATARO?
WHSPR
Sigh...
THAT GIRL...
...IS GORGEOUS.

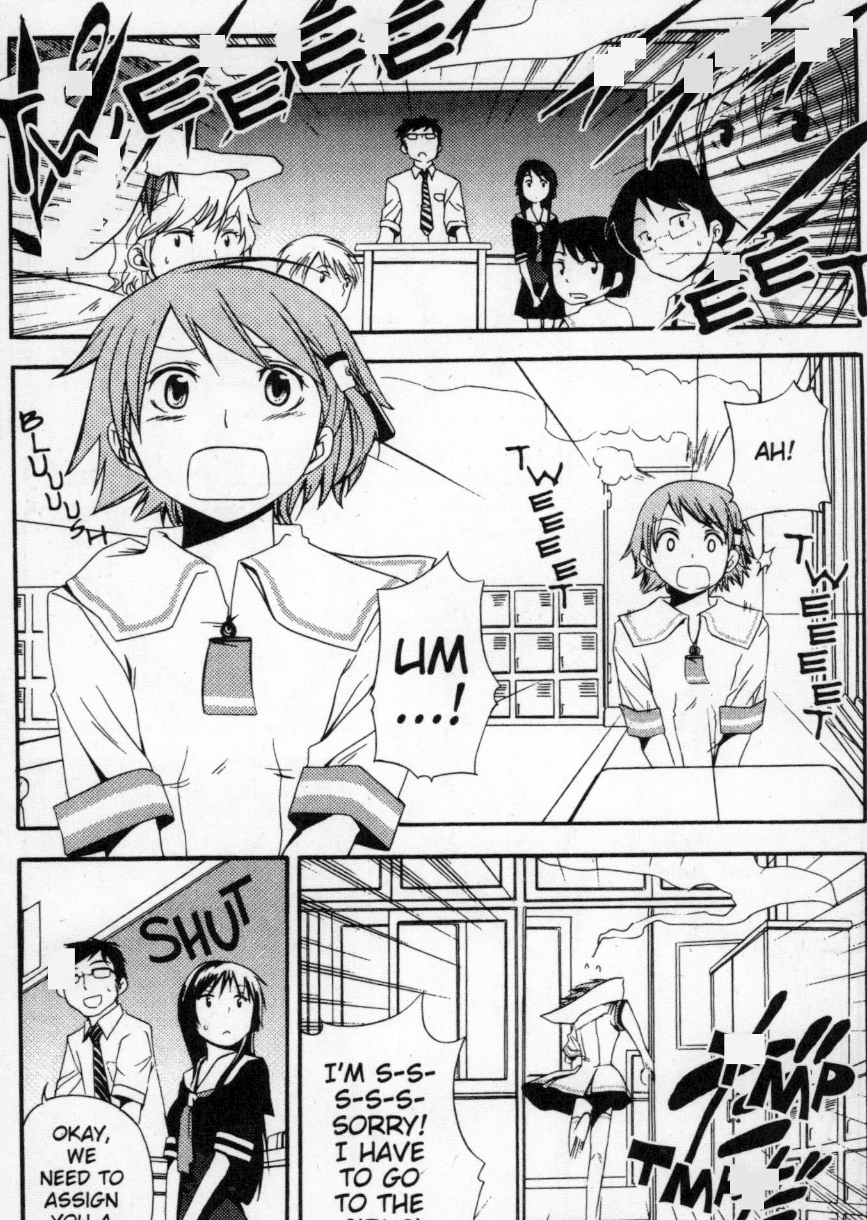
EEET
AH!
TWEEEEET
TWEEEET
BLUUUUUSH
UM ...!
I'M S-S-S-S-S-SORRY! I HAVE TO GO TO THE GIRLS' ROOM!
SHUT
OKAY, WE NEED TO ASSIGN YOU A SEAT, KOMORI.

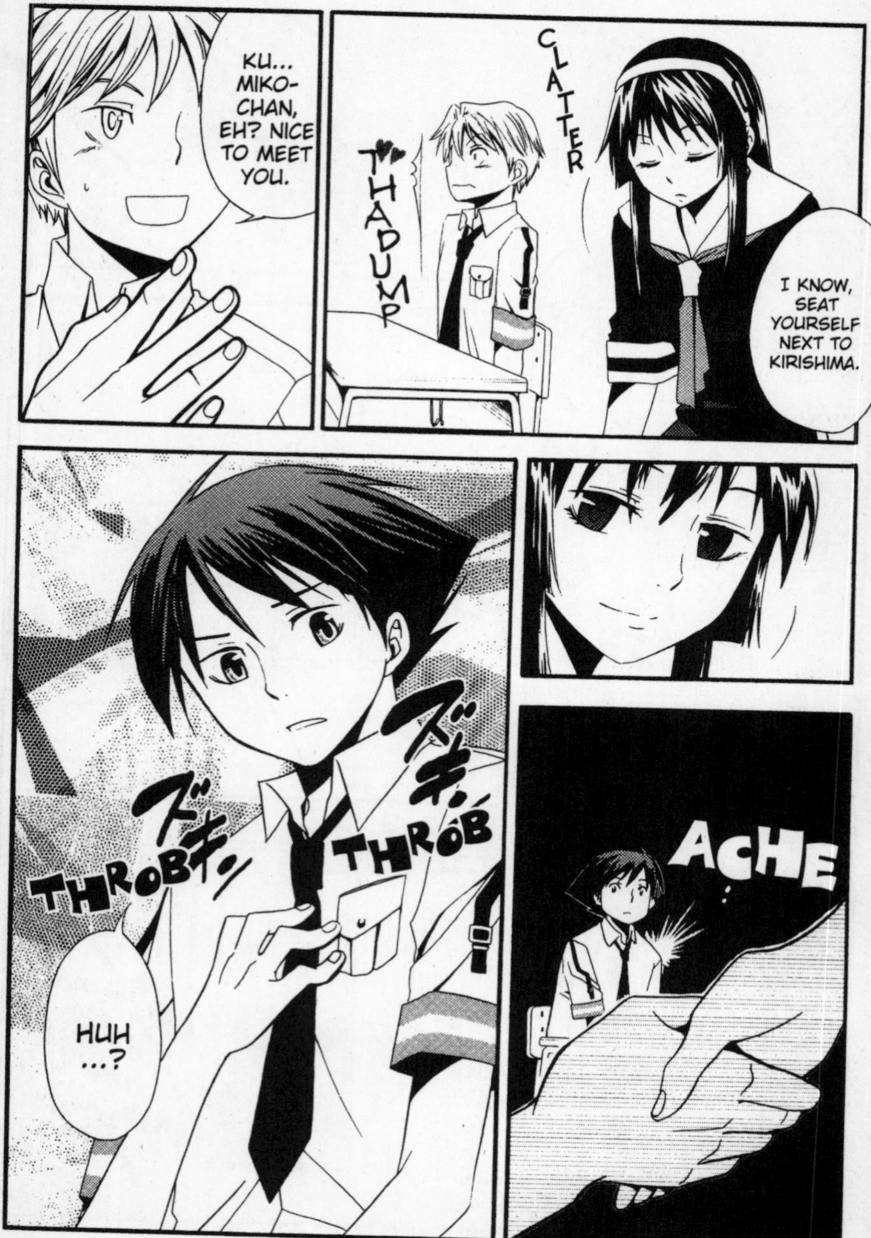
I KNOW, SEAT YOURSELF NEXT TO KIRISHIMA.
CLATTER
THADUMP
KU... MIKO-CHAN, EH? NICE TO MEET YOU.
ACHE
ズキッ
THROB
ズキッ
THROB
HUH ...?

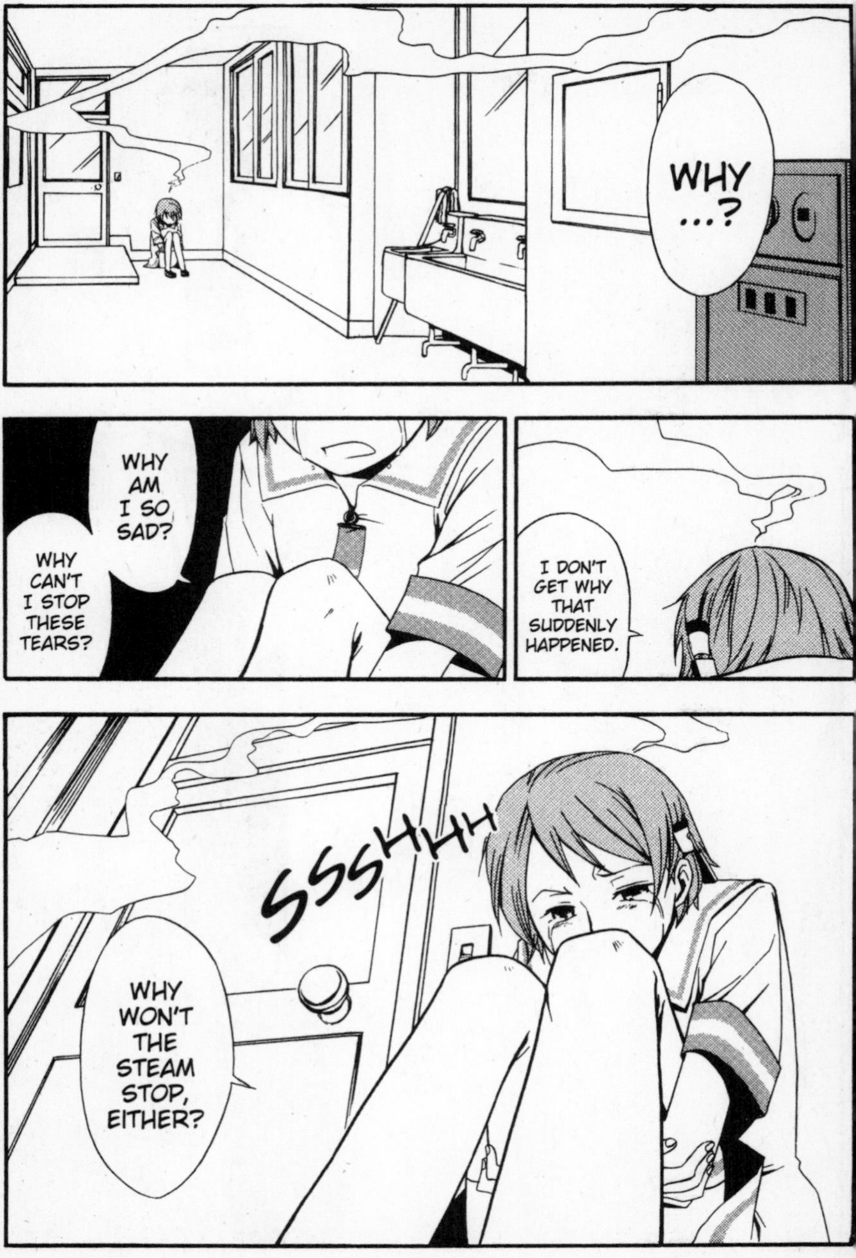
WHY ...?
I DON'T GET WHY THAT SUDDENLY HAPPENED.
WHY AM I SO SAD?
WHY CAN'T I STOP THESE TEARS?
SSSHHH
WHY WON'T THE STEAM STOP, EITHER?

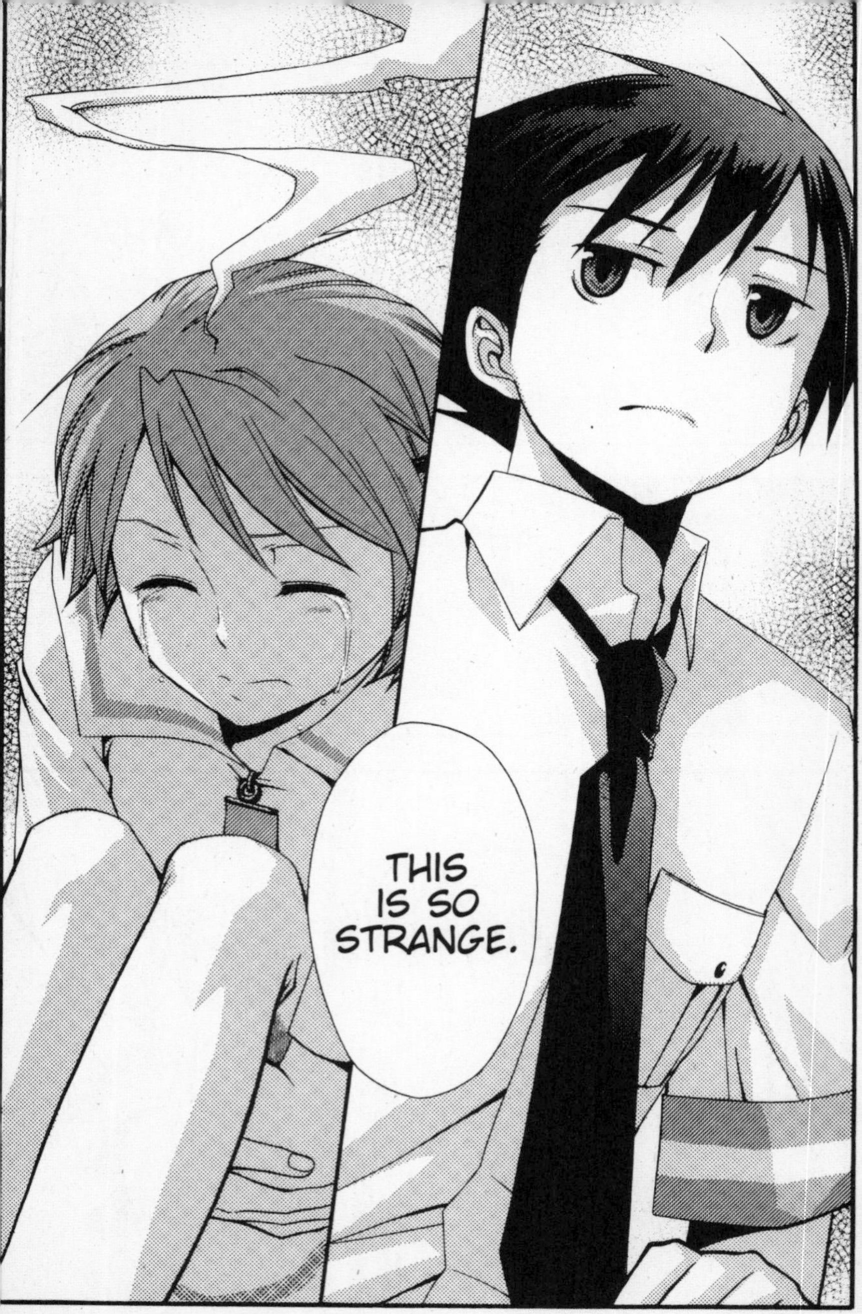
THIS IS SO STRANGE.

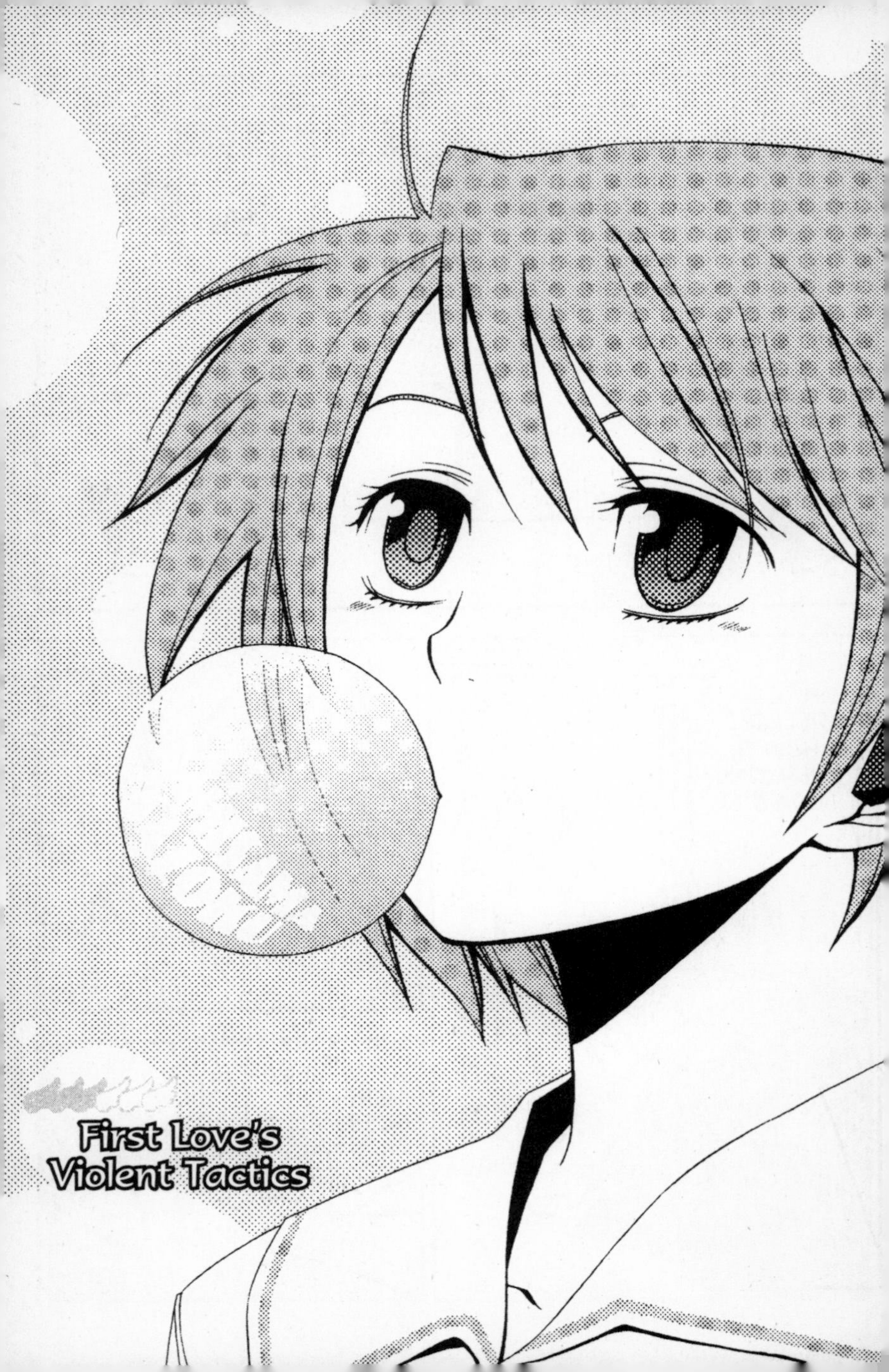
First Love's
Violent Tactics

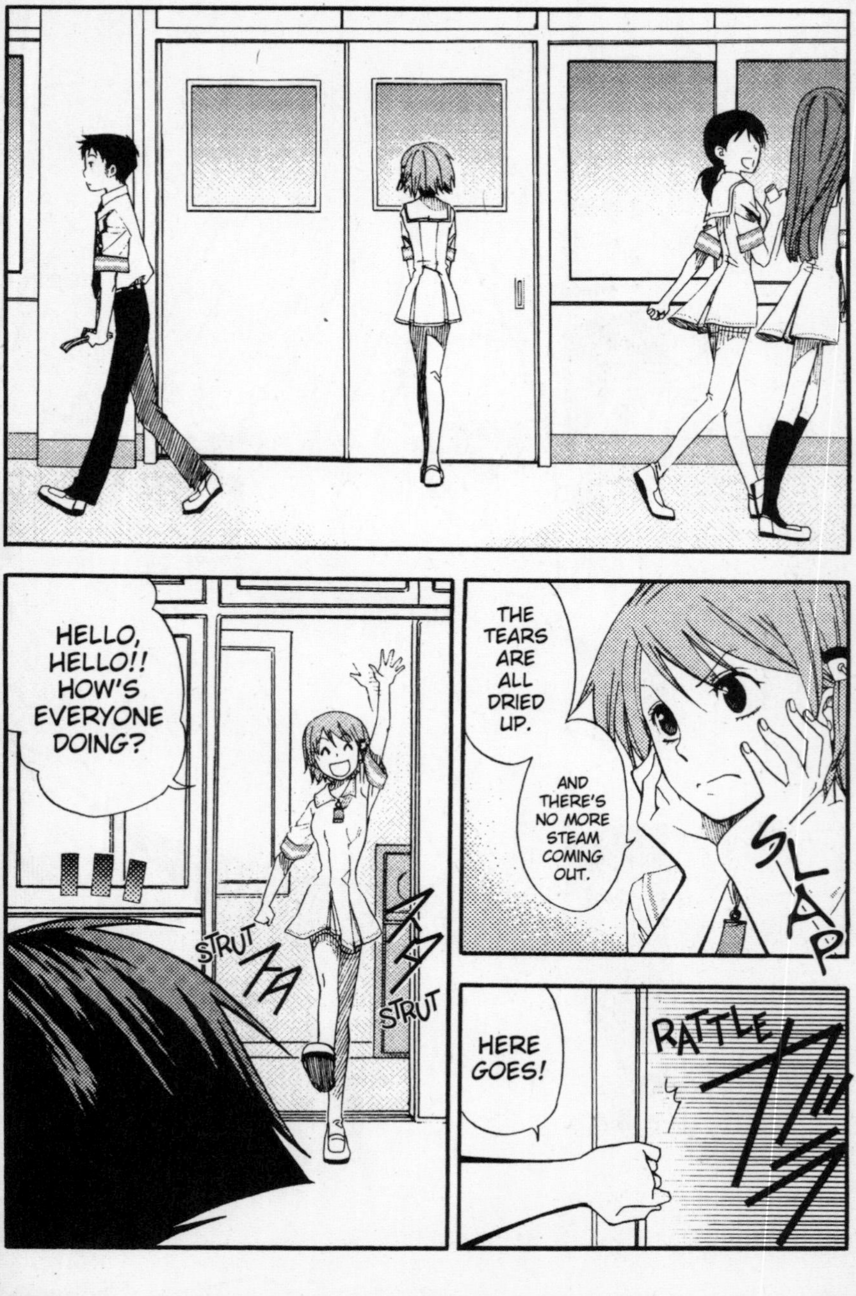
THE TEARS ARE ALL DRIED UP.
AND THERE'S NO MORE STEAM COMING OUT.
SLAP
HERE GOES!
RATTLE
HELLO, HELLO!! HOW'S EVERYONE DOING?
STRUT
STRUT

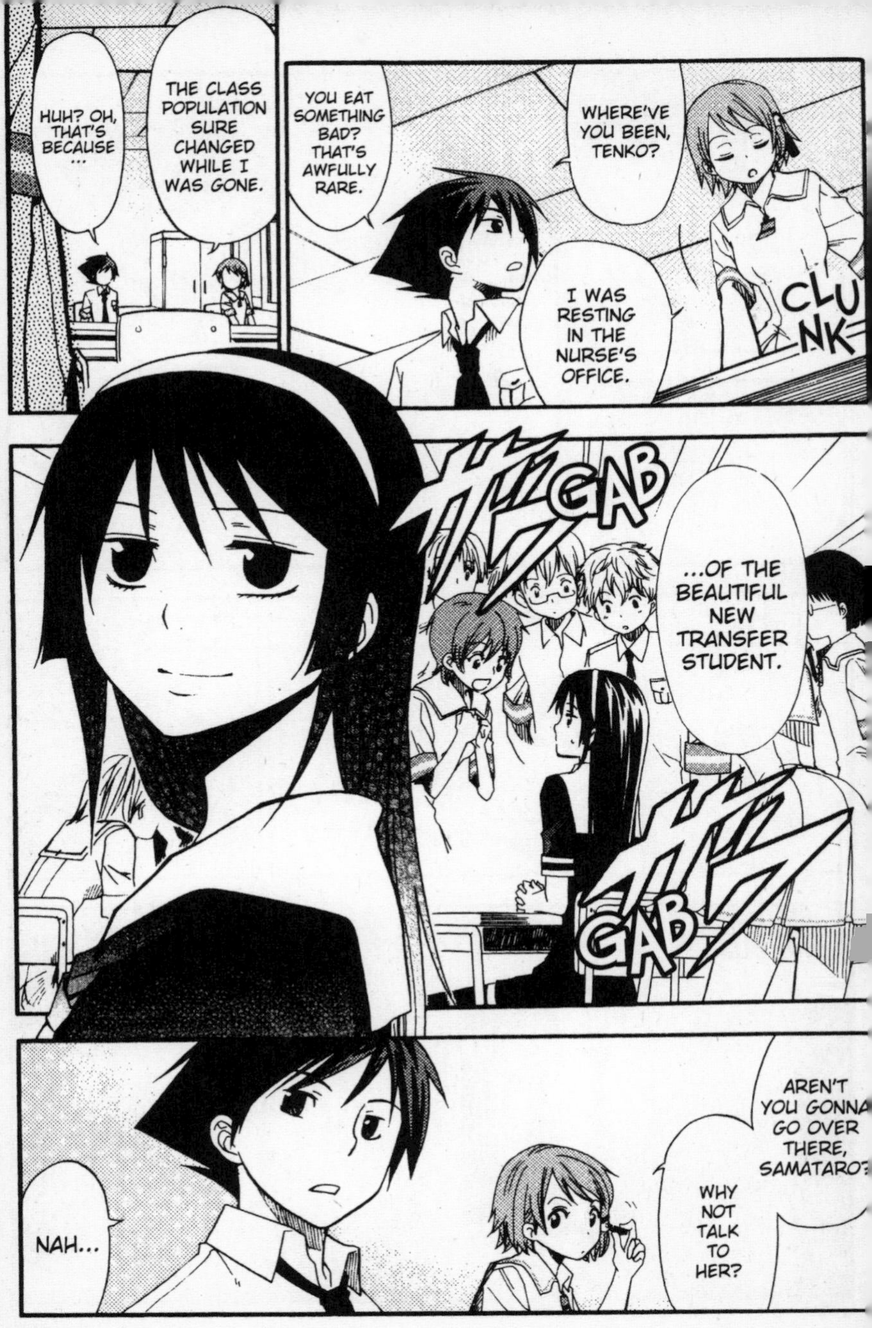
CLUNK
WHERE'VE YOU BEEN, TENKO?
I WAS RESTING IN THE NURSE'S OFFICE.
YOU EAT SOMETHING BAD? THAT'S AWFULLY RARE.
THE CLASS POPULATION SURE CHANGED WHILE I WAS GONE.
HUH? OH, THAT'S BECAUSE ...
GAB
...OF THE BEAUTIFUL NEW TRANSFER STUDENT.
GAB
AREN'T YOU GONNA GO OVER THERE, SAMATARO?
WHY NOT TALK TO HER?
NAH...

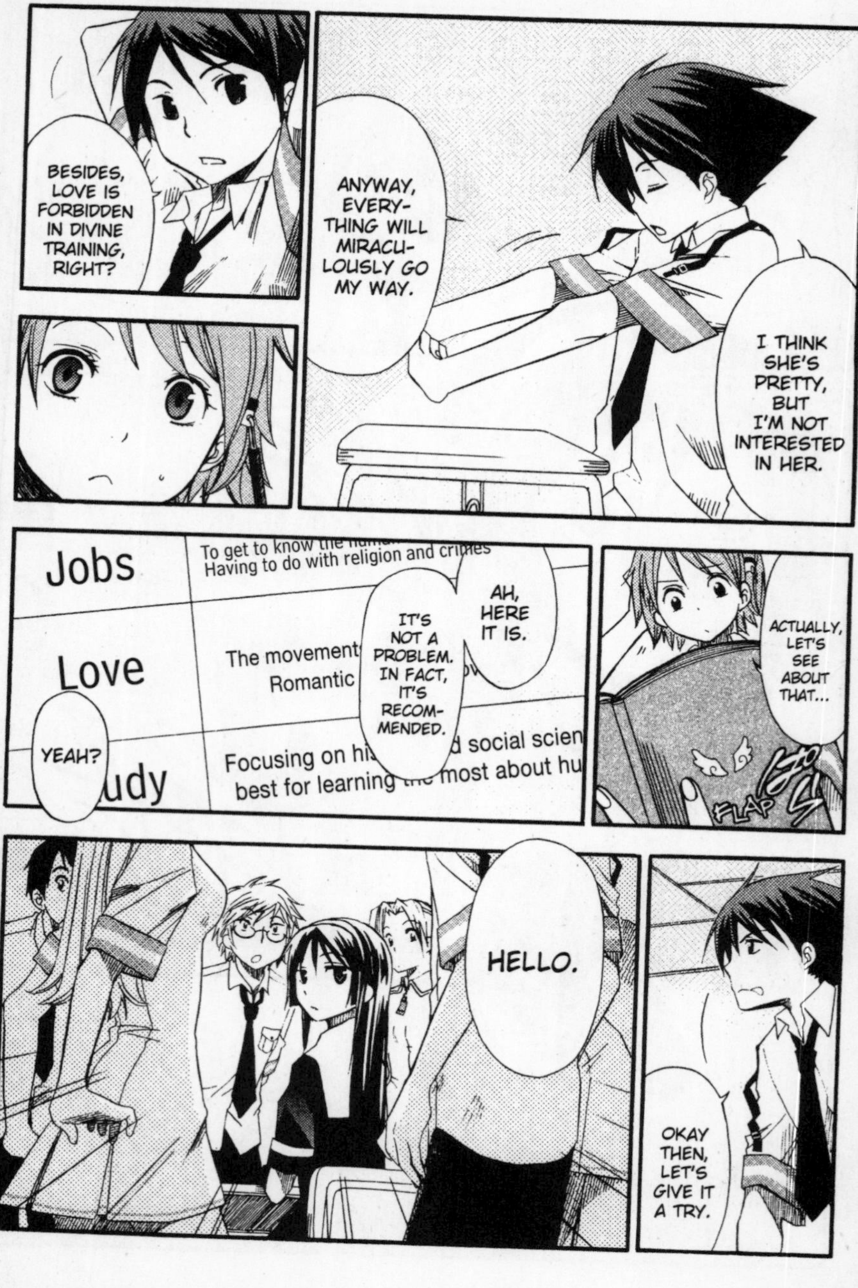

I THINK SHE'S PRETTY, BUT I'M NOT INTERESTED IN HER.
ANYWAY, EVERY-THING WILL MIRACU-LOUSLY GO MY WAY.
BESIDES, LOVE IS FORBIDDEN IN DIVINE TRAINING, RIGHT?
ACTUALLY, LET'S SEE ABOUT THAT...
FLAP
Jobs
Having to do with religion and crimes
AH, HERE IT IS.
IT'S NOT A PROBLEM. IN FACT, IT'S RECOMMENDED.
Love
The movement
Romantic
YEAH?
udy
Focusing on his
d social scien
best for learning
most about hu
OKAY THEN, LET'S GIVE IT A TRY.
HELLO.

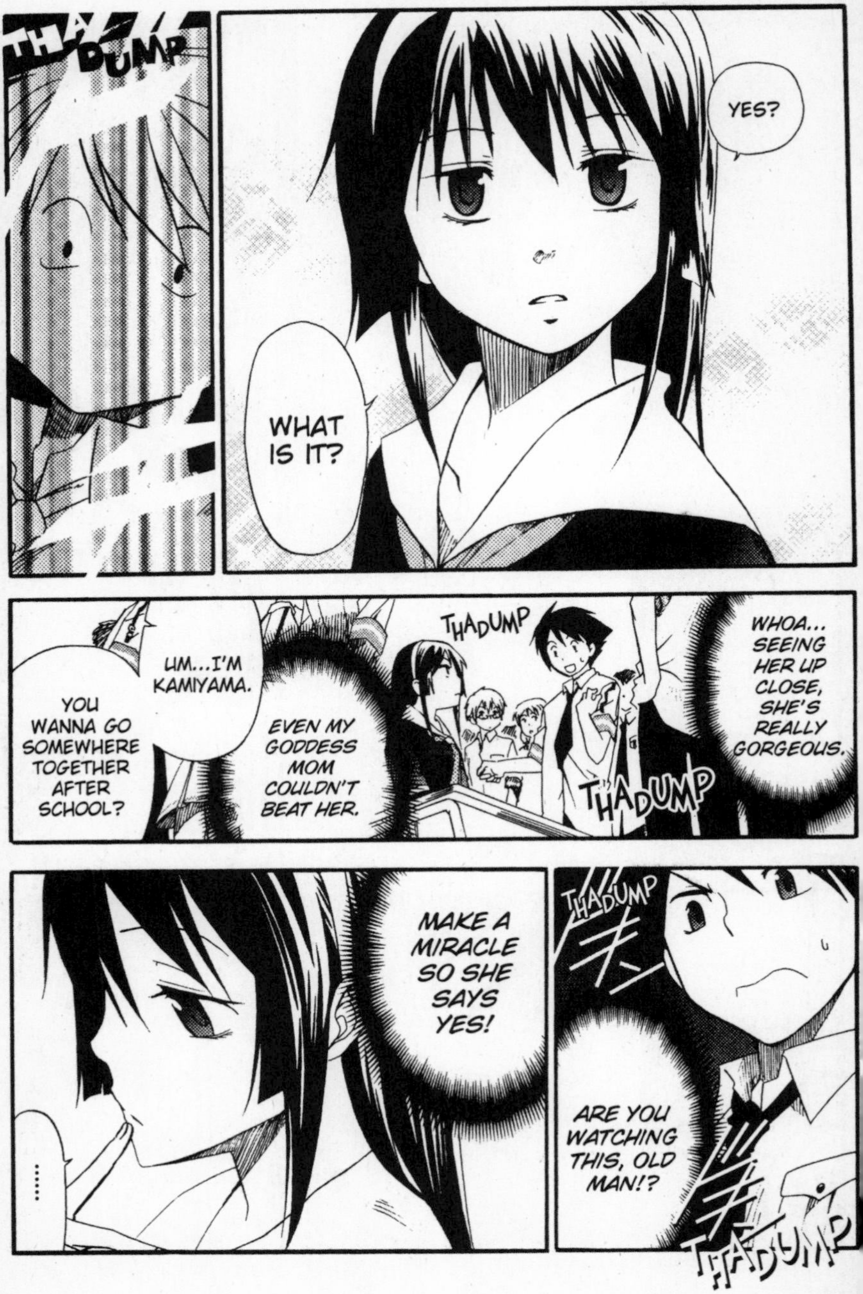
YES?
WHAT IS IT?
THADUMP
WHOA... SEEING HER UP CLOSE, SHE'S REALLY GORGEOUS.
THADUMP
THADUMP
EVEN MY GODDESS MOM COULDN'T BEAT HER.
UM...I'M KAMIYAMA.
YOU WANNA GO SOMEWHERE TOGETHER AFTER SCHOOL?
THADUMP
ARE YOU WATCHING THIS, OLD MAN!?
THADUMP
MAKE A MIRACLE SO SHE SAYS YES!
......

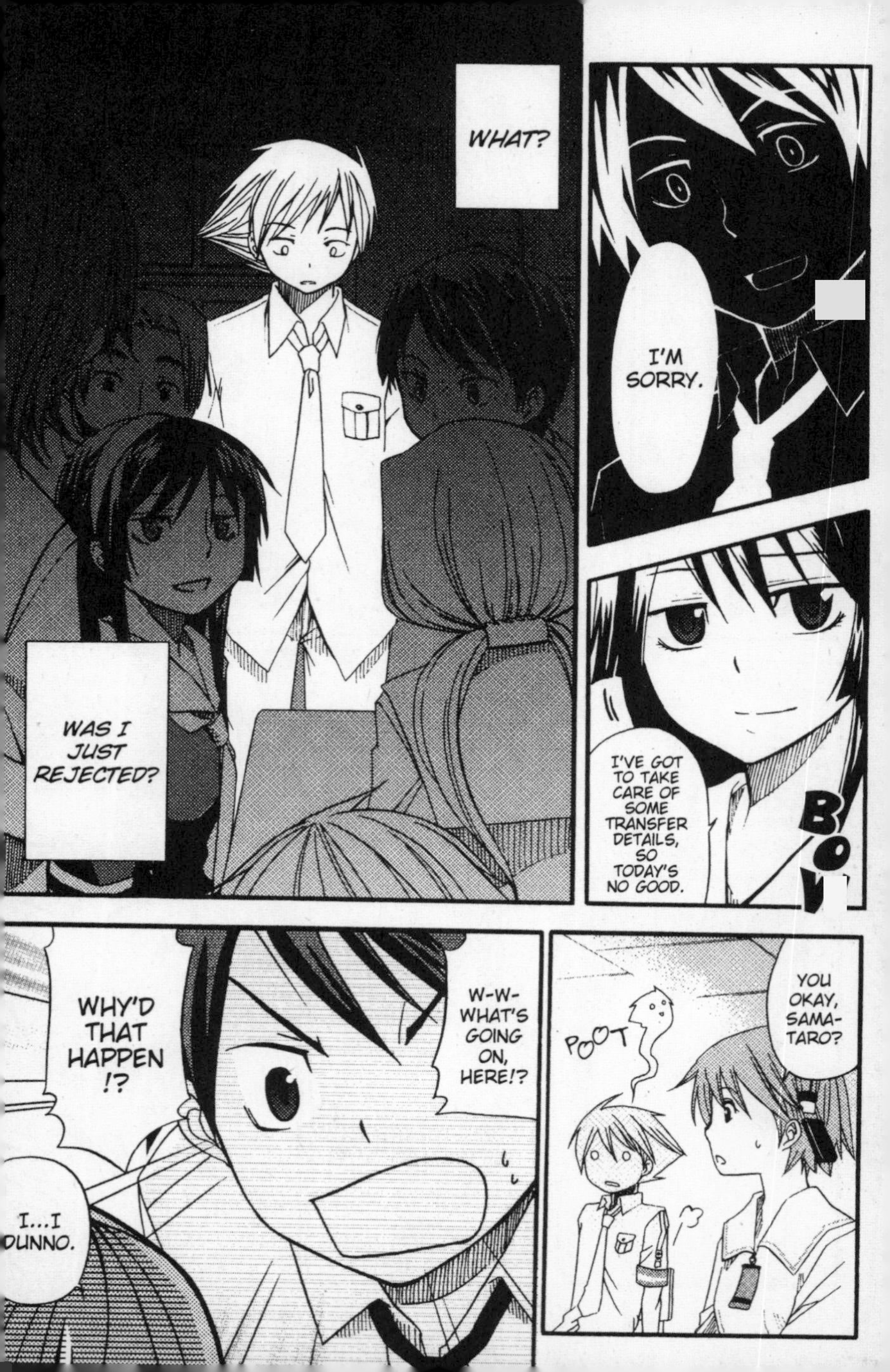
I'M SORRY.
I'VE GOT TO TAKE CARE OF SOME TRANSFER DETAILS, SO TODAY'S NO GOOD.
BOW
WHAT?
WAS I JUST REJECTED?
YOU OKAY, SAMATARO?
POOT
W-W-WHAT'S GOING ON, HERE!?
WHY'D THAT HAPPEN!?
I...I DUNNO.

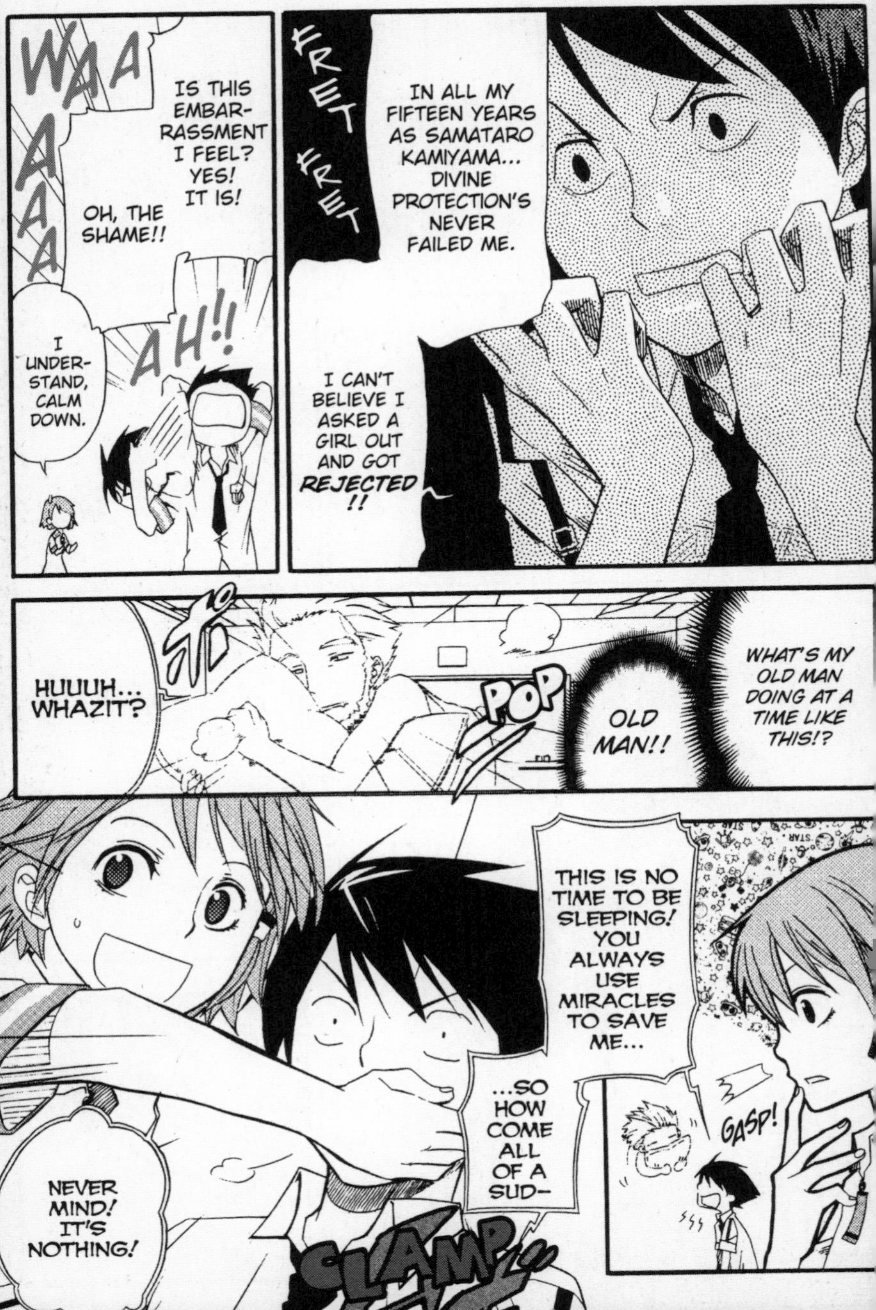
FRET FRET
IN ALL MY FIFTEEN YEARS AS SAMATARO KAMIYAMA... DIVINE PROTECTION'S NEVER FAILED ME.
I CAN'T BELIEVE I ASKED A GIRL OUT AND GOT REJECTED!!
WAAAAAA
IS THIS EMBARRASSMENT I FEEL? YES! IT IS!
OH, THE SHAME!!
AH!!
I UNDERSTAND, CALM DOWN.
WHAT'S MY OLD MAN DOING AT A TIME LIKE THIS!?
OLD MAN!!
POP
HUUUH... WHAZIT?
GASP!
THIS IS NO TIME TO BE SLEEPING! YOU ALWAYS USE MIRACLES TO SAVE ME...
...SO HOW COME ALL OF A SUD-
CLAMP
NEVER MIND! IT'S NOTHING!

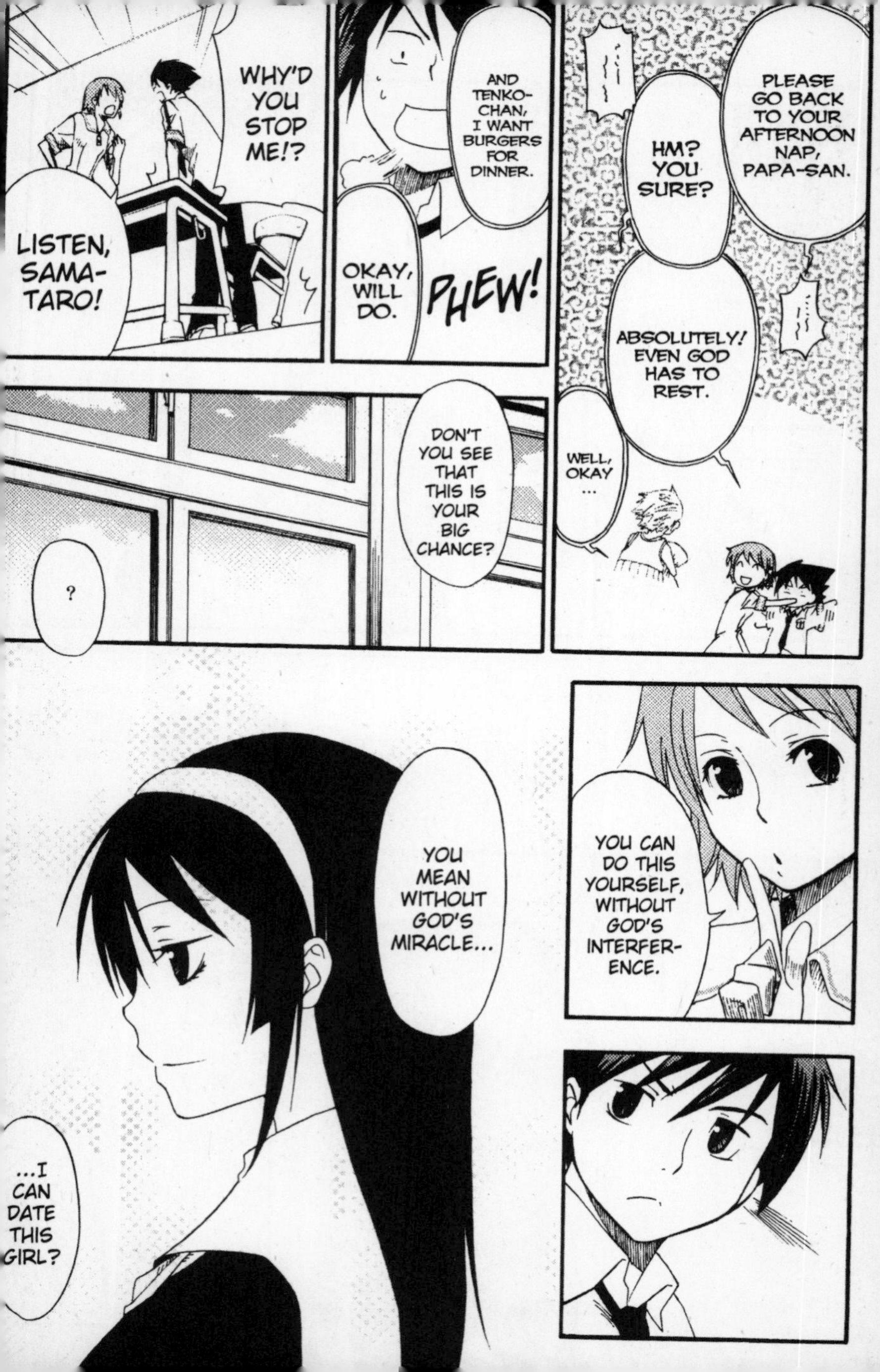
PLEASE GO BACK TO YOUR AFTERNOON NAP, PAPA-SAN.
HM? YOU SURE?
ABSOLUTELY! EVEN GOD HAS TO REST.
WELL, OKAY...
AND TENKO-CHAN, I WANT BURGERS FOR DINNER.
OKAY, WILL DO.
PHEW!
WHY'D YOU STOP ME!?
LISTEN, SAMA-TARO!
DON'T YOU SEE THAT THIS IS YOUR BIG CHANCE?
?
YOU CAN DO THIS YOURSELF, WITHOUT GOD'S INTERFERENCE.
YOU MEAN WITHOUT GOD'S MIRACLE...
...I CAN DATE THIS GIRL?

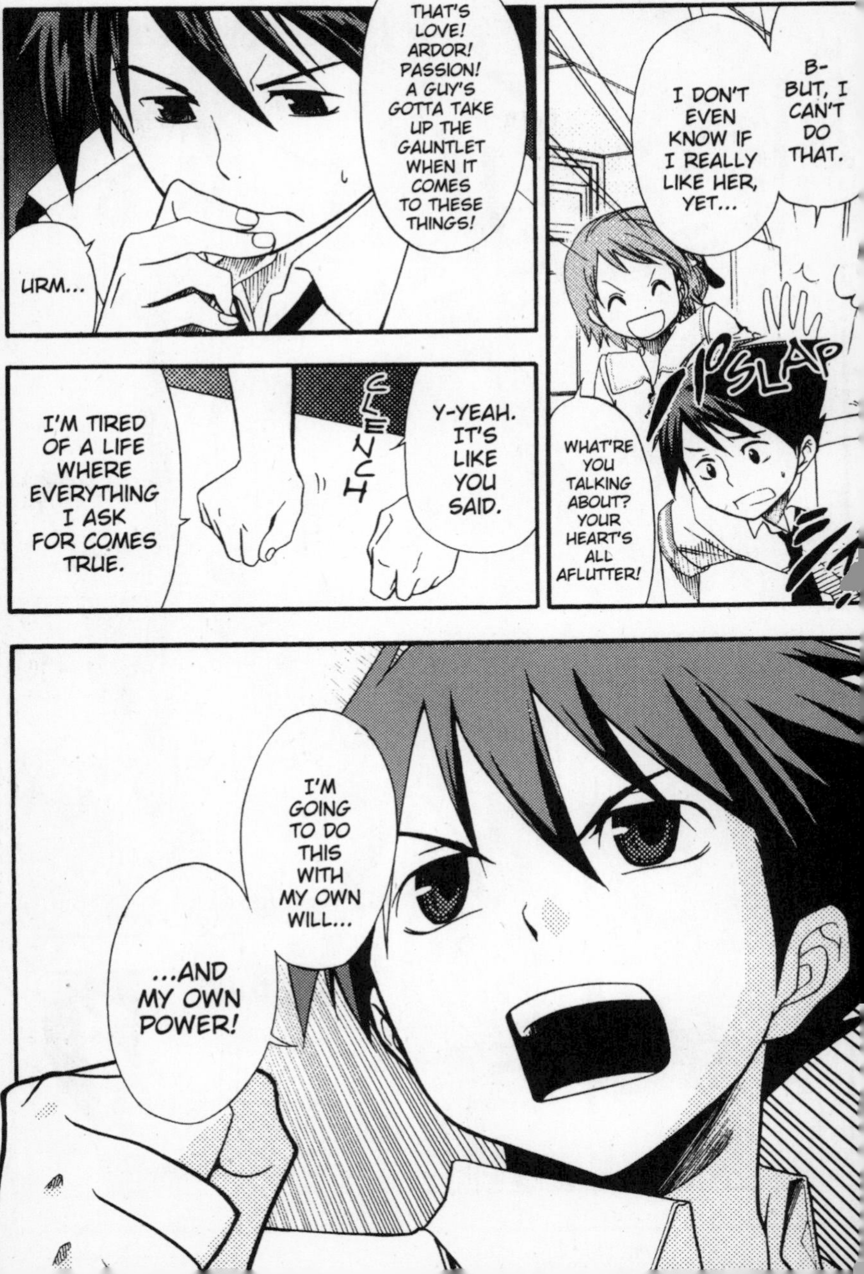
B-BUT, I CAN'T DO THAT.
I DON'T EVEN KNOW IF I REALLY LIKE HER, YET...
SLAP
WHAT'RE YOU TALKING ABOUT? YOUR HEART'S ALL AFLUTTER!
THAT'S LOVE! ARDOR! PASSION! A GUY'S GOTTA TAKE UP THE GAUNTLET WHEN IT COMES TO THESE THINGS!
URM...
Y-YEAH. IT'S LIKE YOU SAID.
CLENCH
I'M TIRED OF A LIFE WHERE EVERYTHING I ASK FOR COMES TRUE.
I'M GOING TO DO THIS WITH MY OWN WILL...
...AND MY OWN POWER!

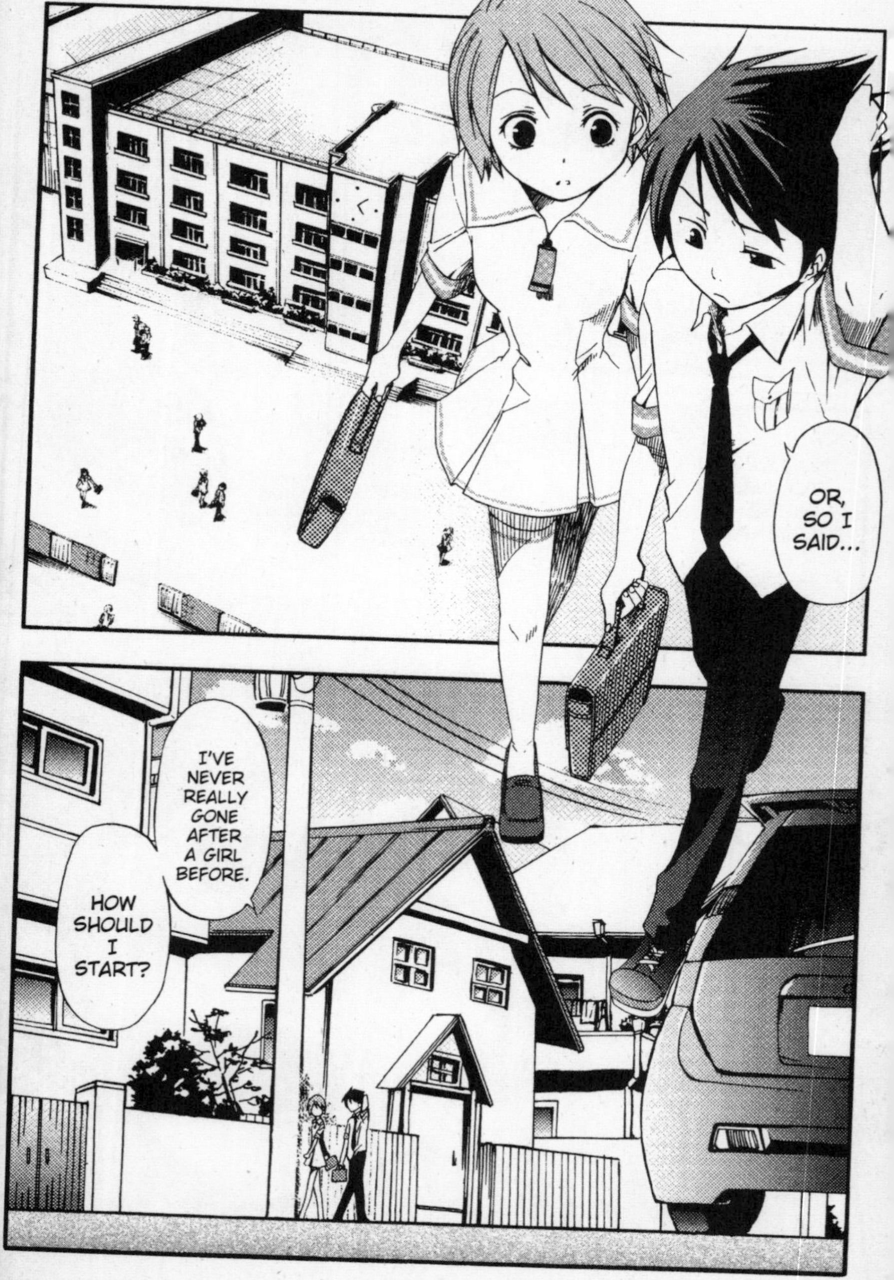
OR, SO I SAID...
I'VE NEVER REALLY GONE AFTER A GIRL BEFORE.
HOW SHOULD I START?

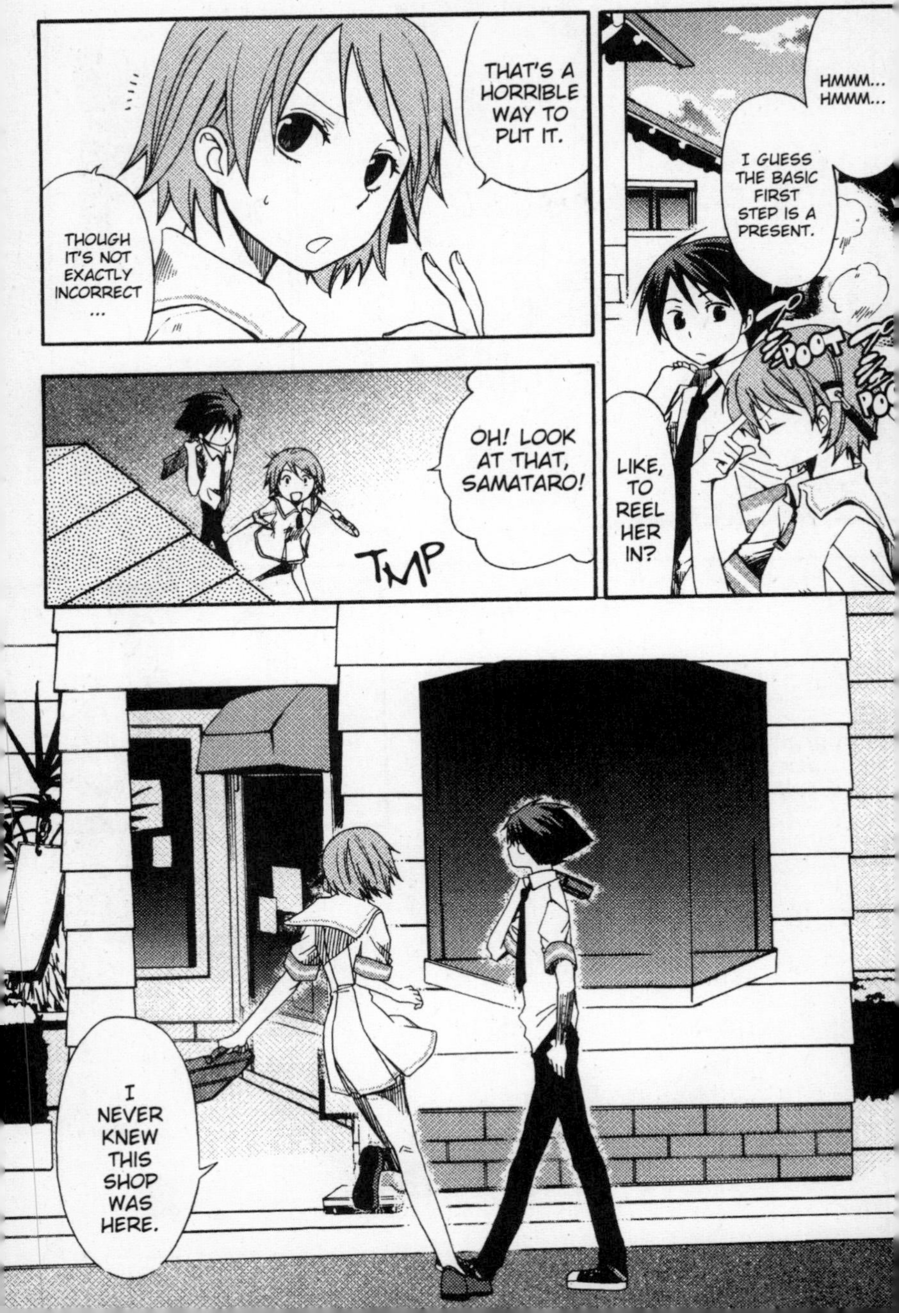
HMMM... HMMM...
I GUESS THE BASIC FIRST STEP IS A PRESENT.
POOT
LIKE, TO REEL HER IN?
THAT'S A HORRIBLE WAY TO PUT IT.
THOUGH IT'S NOT EXACTLY INCORRECT ...
OH! LOOK AT THAT, SAMATARO!
TMP
I NEVER KNEW THIS SHOP WAS HERE.

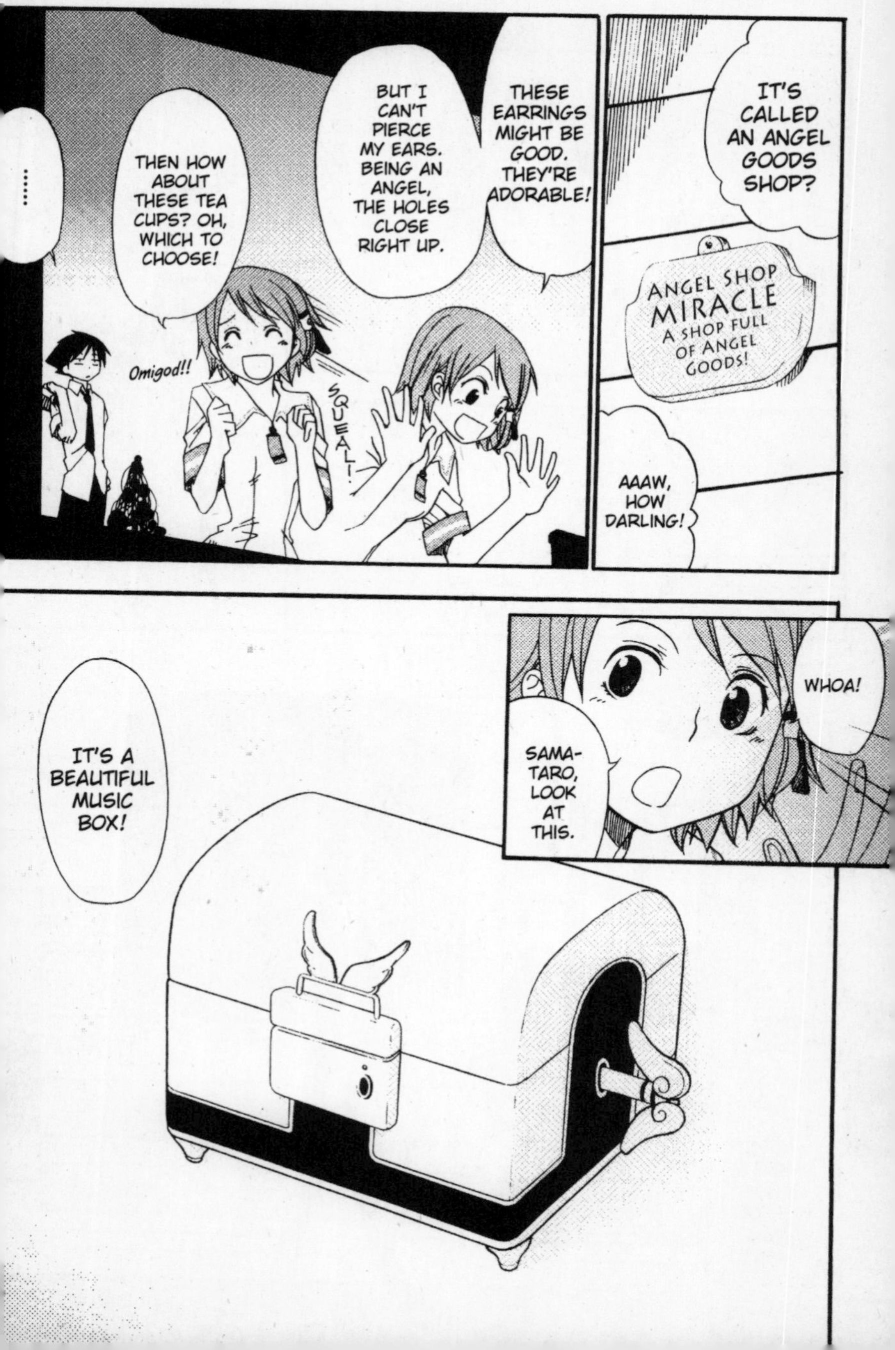
IT'S CALLED AN ANGEL GOODS SHOP?
ANGEL SHOP MIRACLE A SHOP FULL OF ANGEL GOODS!
AAAW, HOW DARLING!
THESE EARRINGS MIGHT BE GOOD. THEY'RE ADORABLE!
BUT I CAN'T PIERCE MY EARS. BEING AN ANGEL, THE HOLES CLOSE RIGHT UP.
SQUEAL!
THEN HOW ABOUT THESE TEA CUPS? OH, WHICH TO CHOOSE!
Omigod!!
......
WHOA!
SAMA-TARO, LOOK AT THIS.
IT'S A BEAUTIFUL MUSIC BOX!

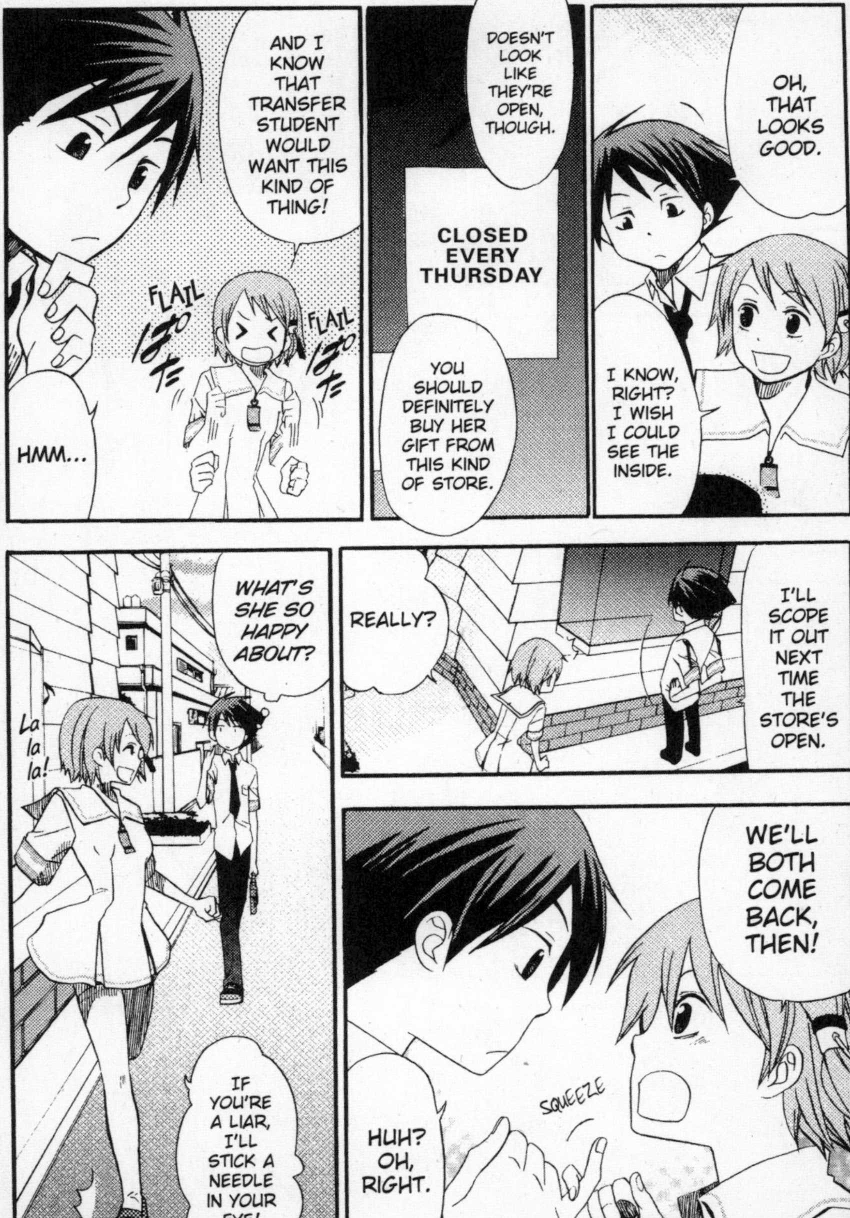
OH, THAT LOOKS GOOD.
I KNOW, RIGHT? I WISH I COULD SEE THE INSIDE.
DOESN'T LOOK LIKE THEY'RE OPEN, THOUGH.
CLOSED EVERY THURSDAY
YOU SHOULD DEFINITELY BUY HER GIFT FROM THIS KIND OF STORE.
AND I KNOW THAT TRANSFER STUDENT WOULD WANT THIS KIND OF THING!
FLAIL
FLAIL
HMM...
I'LL SCOPE IT OUT NEXT TIME THE STORE'S OPEN.
REALLY?
WE'LL BOTH COME BACK, THEN!
SQUEEZE
HUH? OH, RIGHT.
WHAT'S SHE SO HAPPY ABOUT?
La la la!
IF YOU'RE A LIAR, I'LL STICK A NEEDLE IN YOUR EYE!

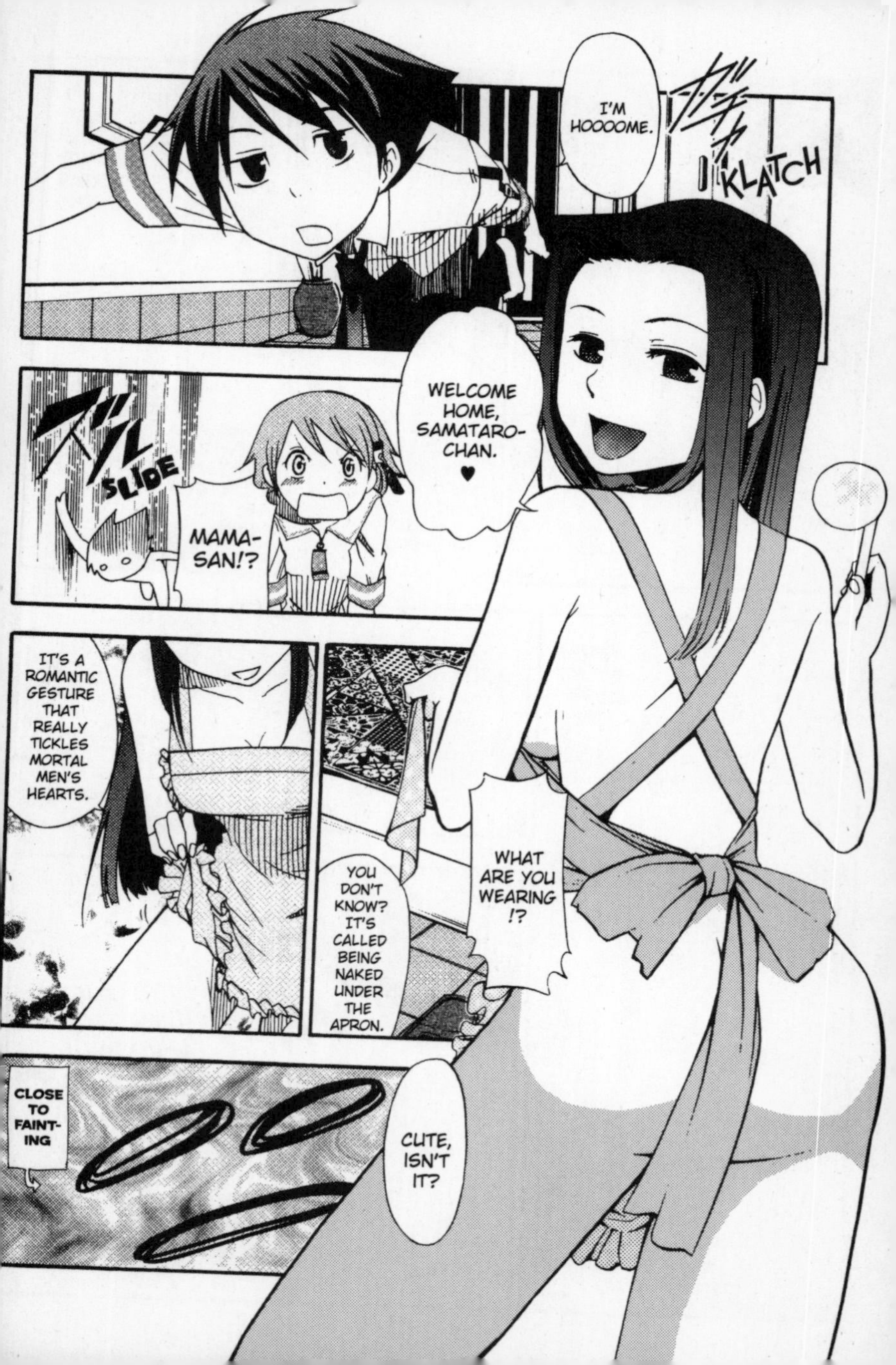
KLATCH
I'M HOOOOME.
WELCOME HOME, SAMATARO-CHAN. ♥
SLIDE
MAMA-SAN!?
WHAT ARE YOU WEARING!?
YOU DON'T KNOW? IT'S CALLED BEING NAKED UNDER THE APRON.
IT'S A ROMANTIC GESTURE THAT REALLY TICKLES MORTAL MEN'S HEARTS.
CUTE, ISN'T IT?
CLOSE TO FAINTING

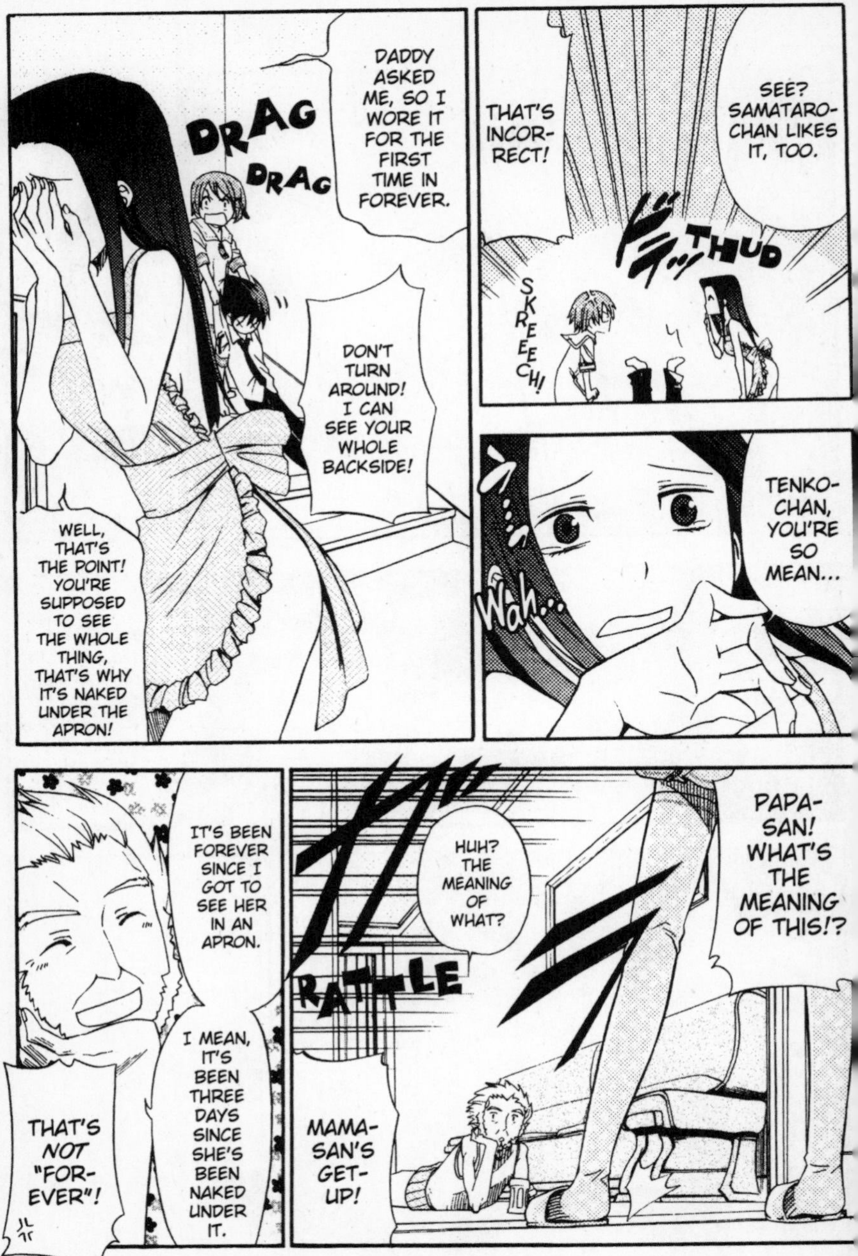
SEE? SAMATARO-CHAN LIKES IT, TOO.
THAT'S INCOR-RECT!
THUD
SKREEECH!
TENKO-CHAN, YOU'RE SO MEAN...
Wah...
DADDY ASKED ME, SO I WORE IT FOR THE FIRST TIME IN FOREVER.
DRAG
DRAG
DON'T TURN AROUND! I CAN SEE YOUR WHOLE BACKSIDE!
WELL, THAT'S THE POINT! YOU'RE SUPPOSED TO SEE THE WHOLE THING, THAT'S WHY IT'S NAKED UNDER THE APRON!
PAPA-SAN! WHAT'S THE MEANING OF THIS!?
HUH? THE MEANING OF WHAT?
RATTLE
MAMA-SAN'S GET-UP!
IT'S BEEN FOREVER SINCE I GOT TO SEE HER IN AN APRON.
I MEAN, IT'S BEEN THREE DAYS SINCE SHE'S BEEN NAKED UNDER IT.
THAT'S *NOT* "FOR-EVER"!

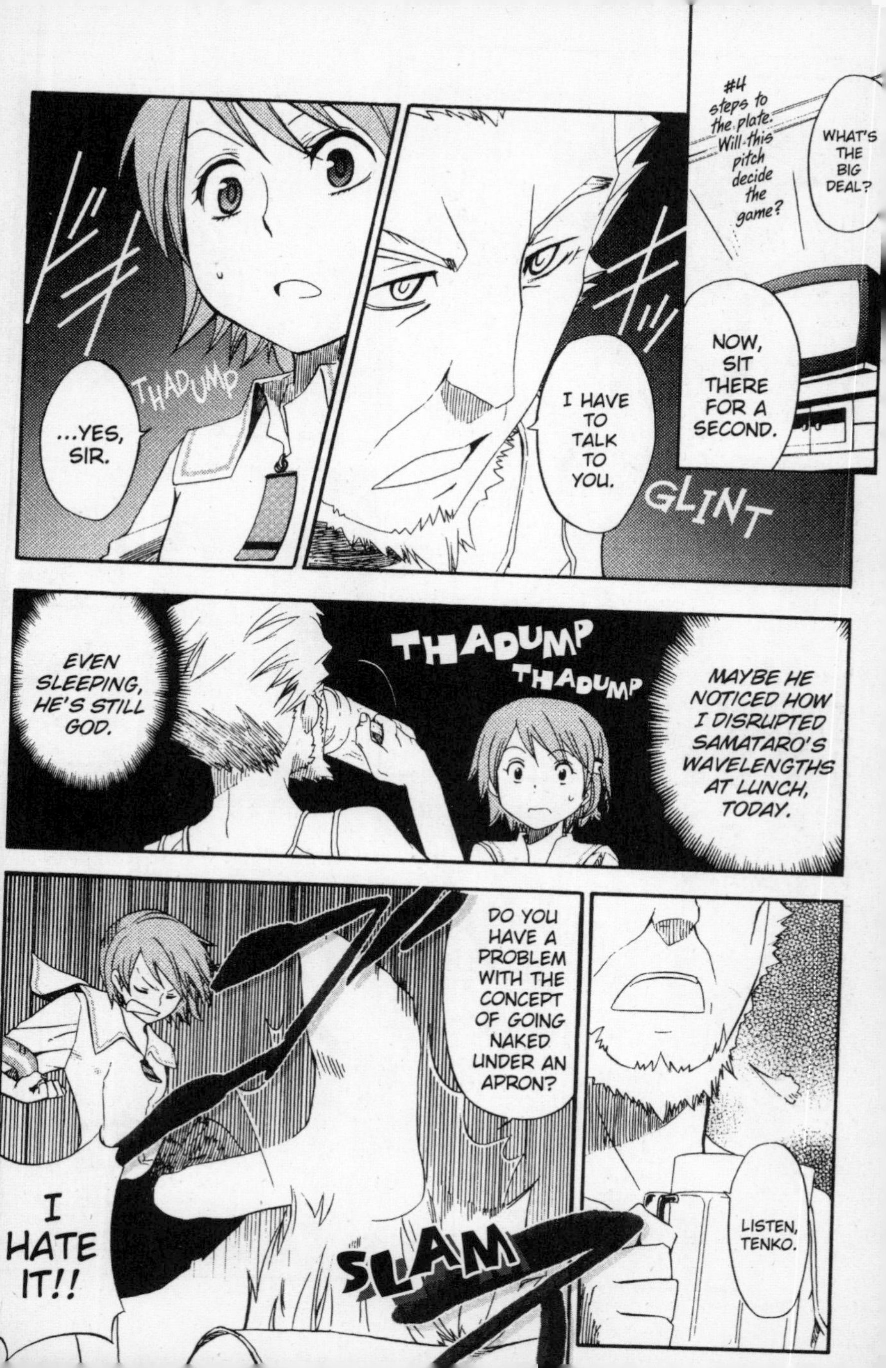
WHAT'S THE BIG DEAL?
#4 steps to the plate. Will this pitch decide the game?
NOW, SIT THERE FOR A SECOND.
GLINT
I HAVE TO TALK TO YOU.
THADUMP
...YES, SIR.
MAYBE HE NOTICED HOW I DISRUPTED SAMATARO'S WAVELENGTHS AT LUNCH, TODAY.
THADUMP THADUMP
EVEN SLEEPING, HE'S STILL GOD.
LISTEN, TENKO.
DO YOU HAVE A PROBLEM WITH THE CONCEPT OF GOING NAKED UNDER AN APRON?
SLAM
I HATE IT!!

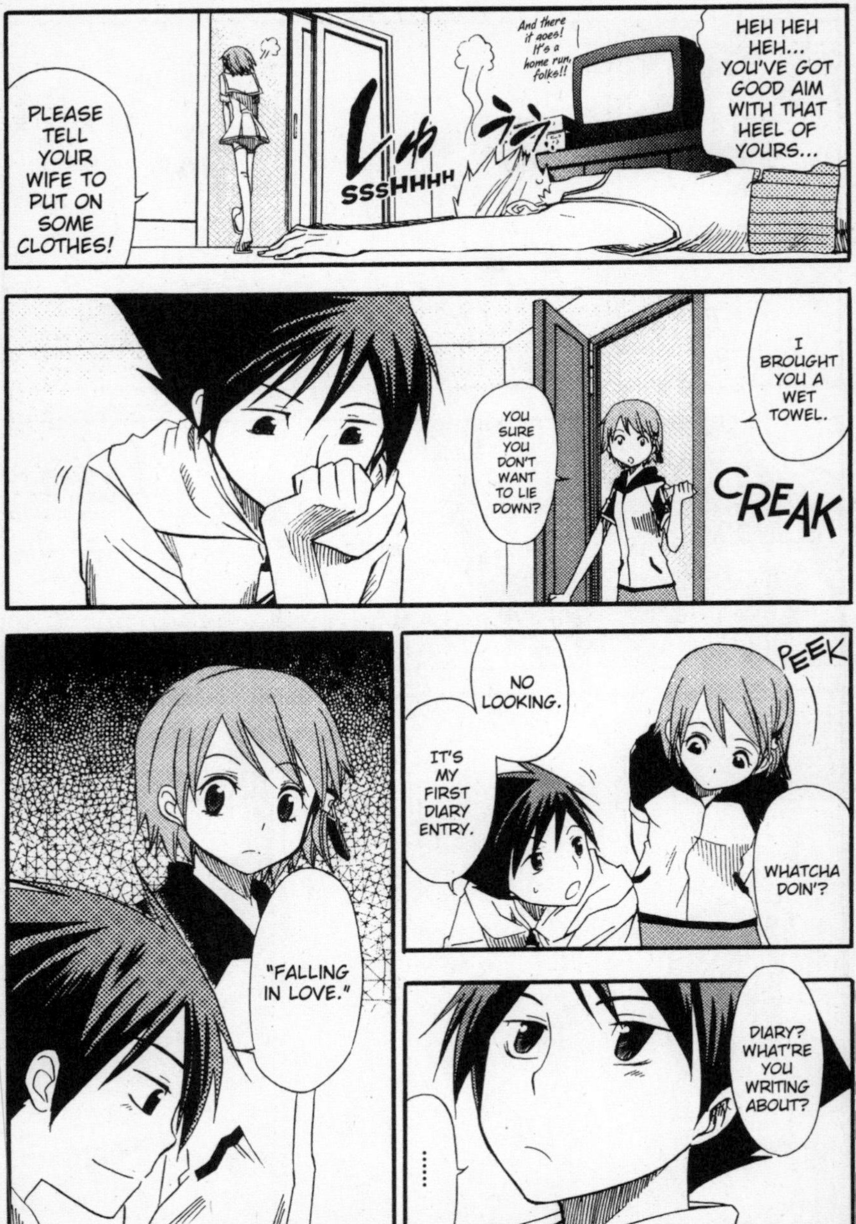
HEH HEH HEH... YOU'VE GOT GOOD AIM WITH THAT HEEL OF YOURS...
And there it goes! It's a home run, folks!!
SSSHHHH
PLEASE TELL YOUR WIFE TO PUT ON SOME CLOTHES!
I BROUGHT YOU A WET TOWEL.
CREAK
YOU SURE YOU DON'T WANT TO LIE DOWN?
PEEK
WHATCHA DOIN'?
NO LOOKING.
IT'S MY FIRST DIARY ENTRY.
DIARY? WHAT'RE YOU WRITING ABOUT?
......
"FALLING IN LOVE."

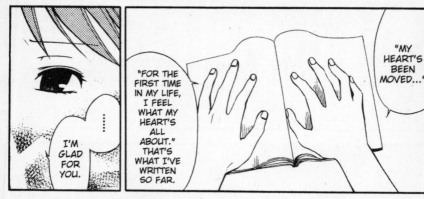

"MY HEART'S BEEN MOVED..."

"FOR THE FIRST TIME IN MY LIFE, I FEEL WHAT MY HEART'S ALL ABOUT." THAT'S WHAT I'VE WRITTEN SO FAR.

.....

I'M GLAD FOR YOU.

I KNOW.

BECAUSE TOMORROW STARTS YOUR BIG PLAN OF ATTACK!

GOOD LUCK!

I'M GLAD I HAVE YOU.

HUH?

TENKO...

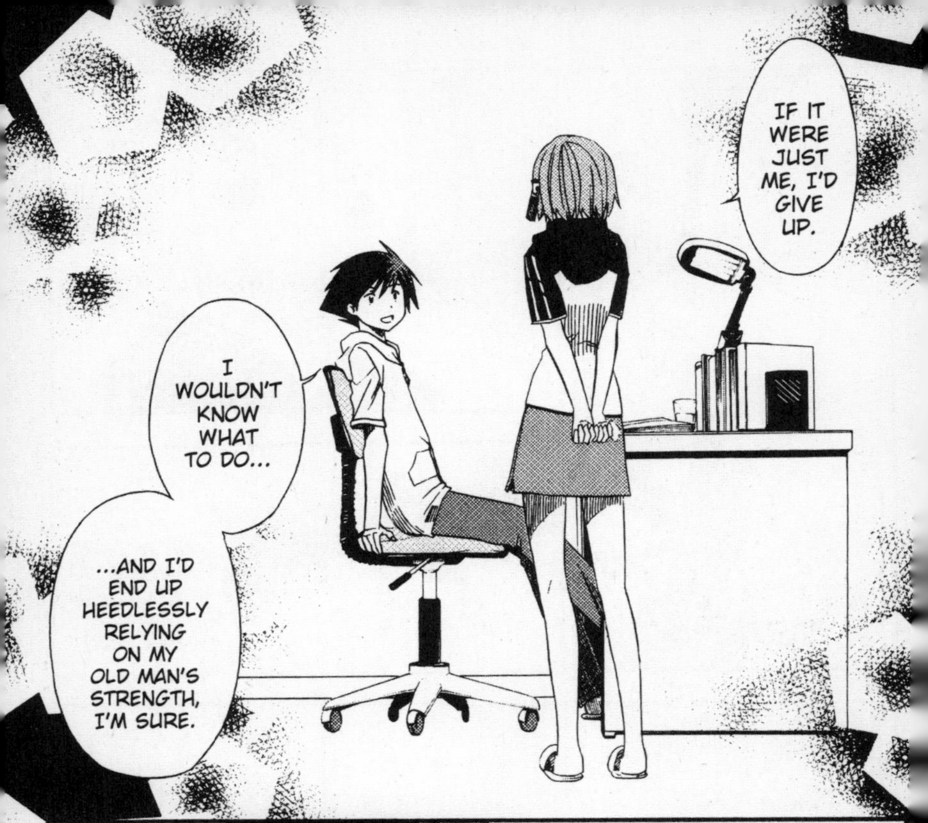
IF IT WERE JUST ME, I'D GIVE UP.
I WOULDN'T KNOW WHAT TO DO...
...AND I'D END UP HEEDLESSLY RELYING ON MY OLD MAN'S STRENGTH, I'M SURE.

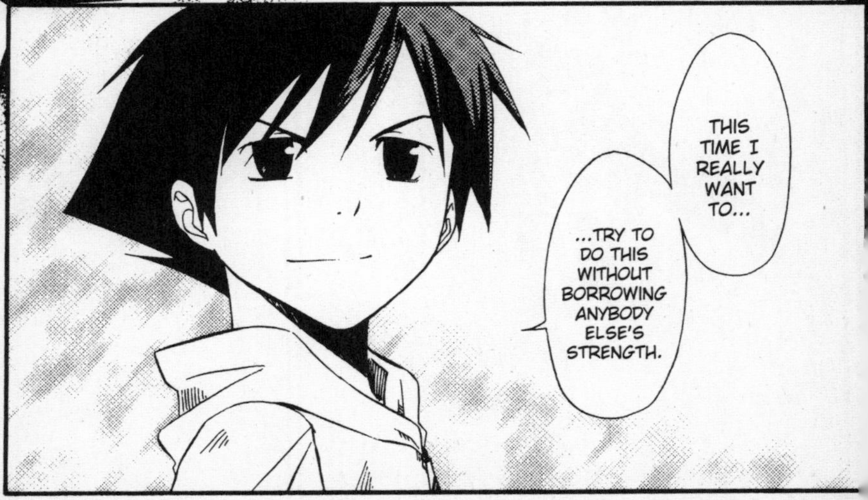
THIS TIME I REALLY WANT TO...
...TRY TO DO THIS WITHOUT BORROWING ANYBODY ELSE'S STRENGTH.

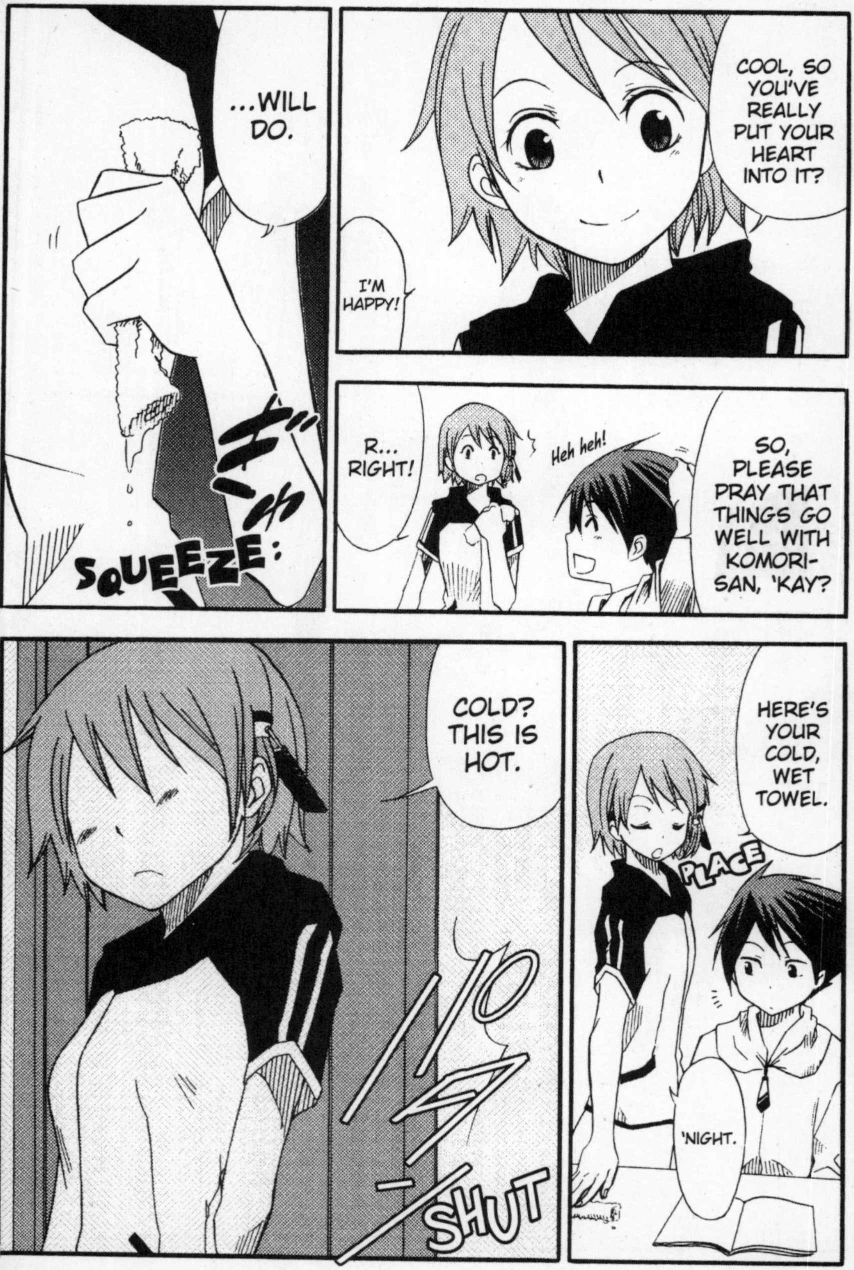
COOL, SO YOU'VE REALLY PUT YOUR HEART INTO IT?
I'M HAPPY!
SO, PLEASE PRAY THAT THINGS GO WELL WITH KOMORI-SAN, 'KAY?
Heh heh!
R... RIGHT!
...WILL DO.
SQUEEZE
HERE'S YOUR COLD, WET TOWEL.
PLACE
'NIGHT.
COLD? THIS IS HOT.
SHUT

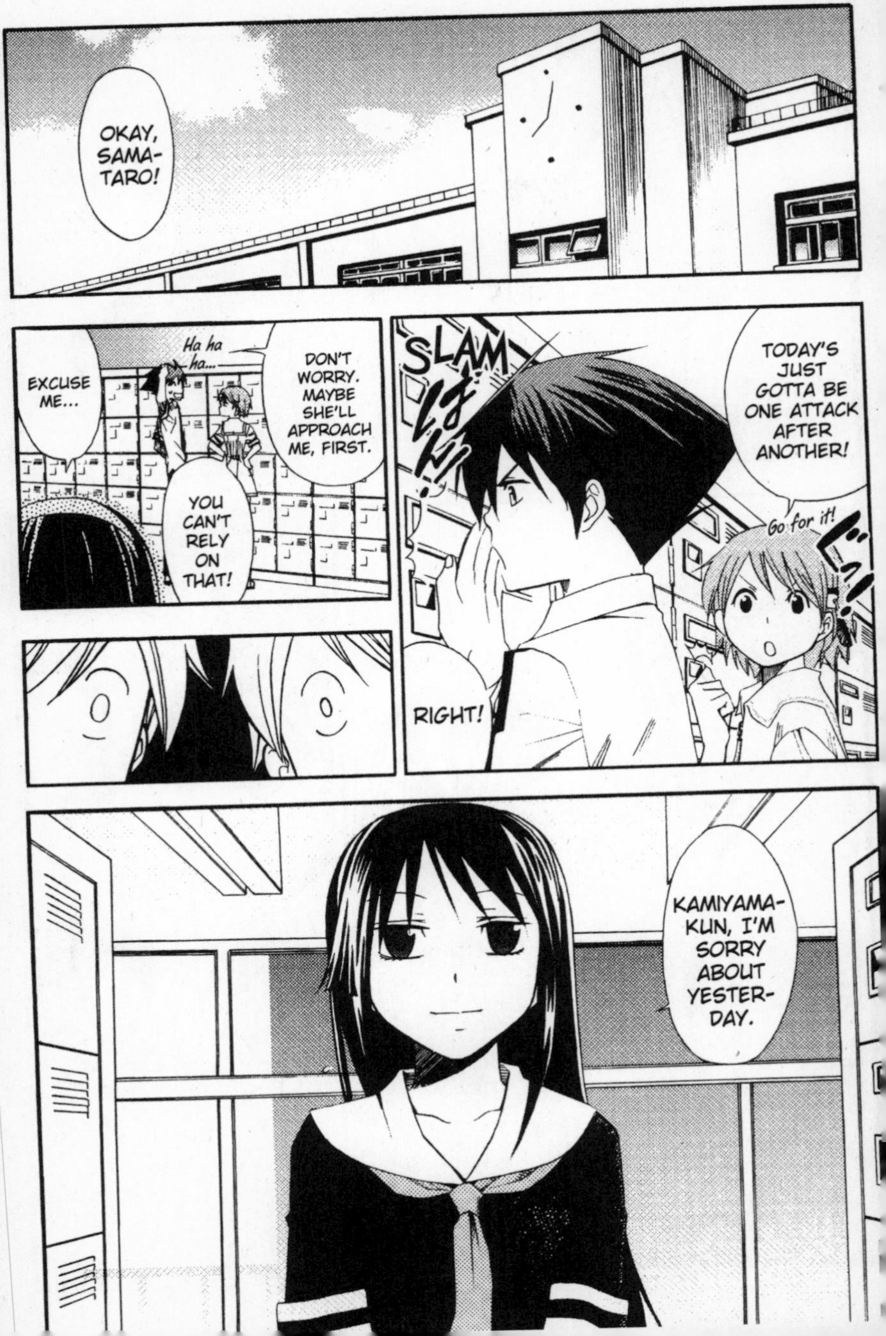
OKAY, SAMA-TARO!
TODAY'S JUST GOTTA BE ONE ATTACK AFTER ANOTHER!
Go for it!
SLAM
RIGHT!
DON'T WORRY. MAYBE SHE'LL APPROACH ME, FIRST.
Ha ha ha...
YOU CAN'T RELY ON THAT!
EXCUSE ME...
KAMIYAMA-KUN, I'M SORRY ABOUT YESTER-DAY.

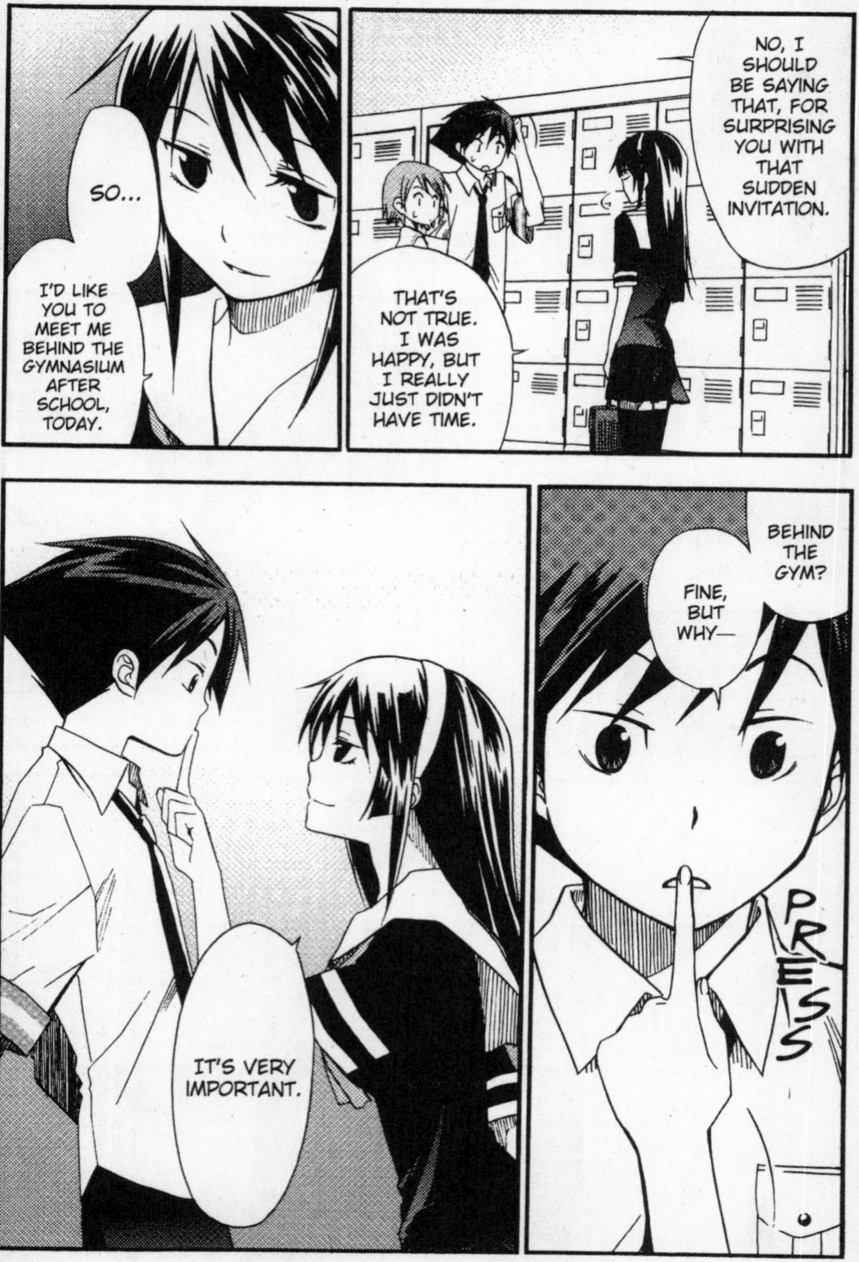
NO, I SHOULD BE SAYING THAT, FOR SURPRISING YOU WITH THAT SUDDEN INVITATION.
THAT'S NOT TRUE. I WAS HAPPY, BUT I REALLY JUST DIDN'T HAVE TIME.
SO...
I'D LIKE YOU TO MEET ME BEHIND THE GYMNASIUM AFTER SCHOOL, TODAY.
BEHIND THE GYM?
FINE, BUT WHY—
PRESS
IT'S VERY IMPORTANT.

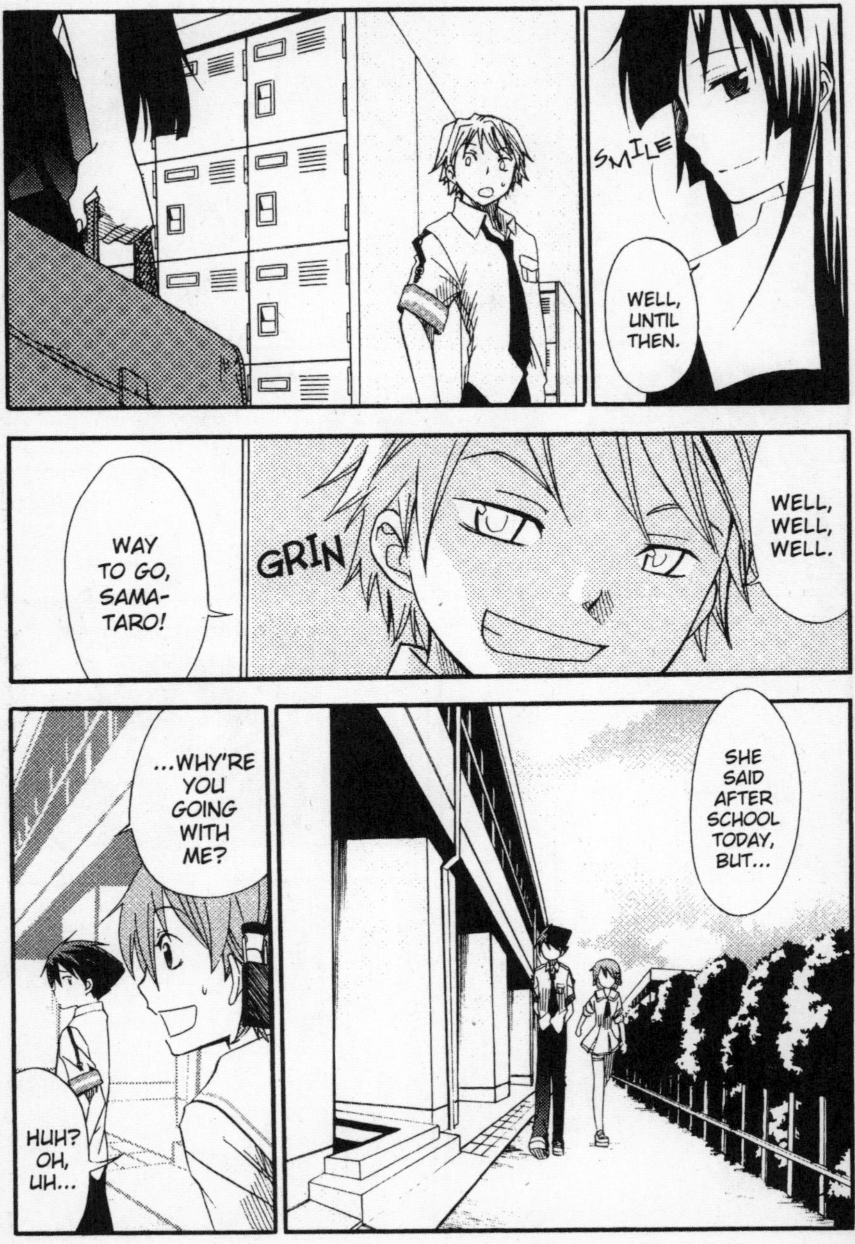
SMILE
WELL, UNTIL THEN.
WELL, WELL, WELL.
GRIN
WAY TO GO, SAMA-TARO!
SHE SAID AFTER SCHOOL TODAY, BUT...
...WHY'RE YOU GOING WITH ME?
HUH? OH, UH...

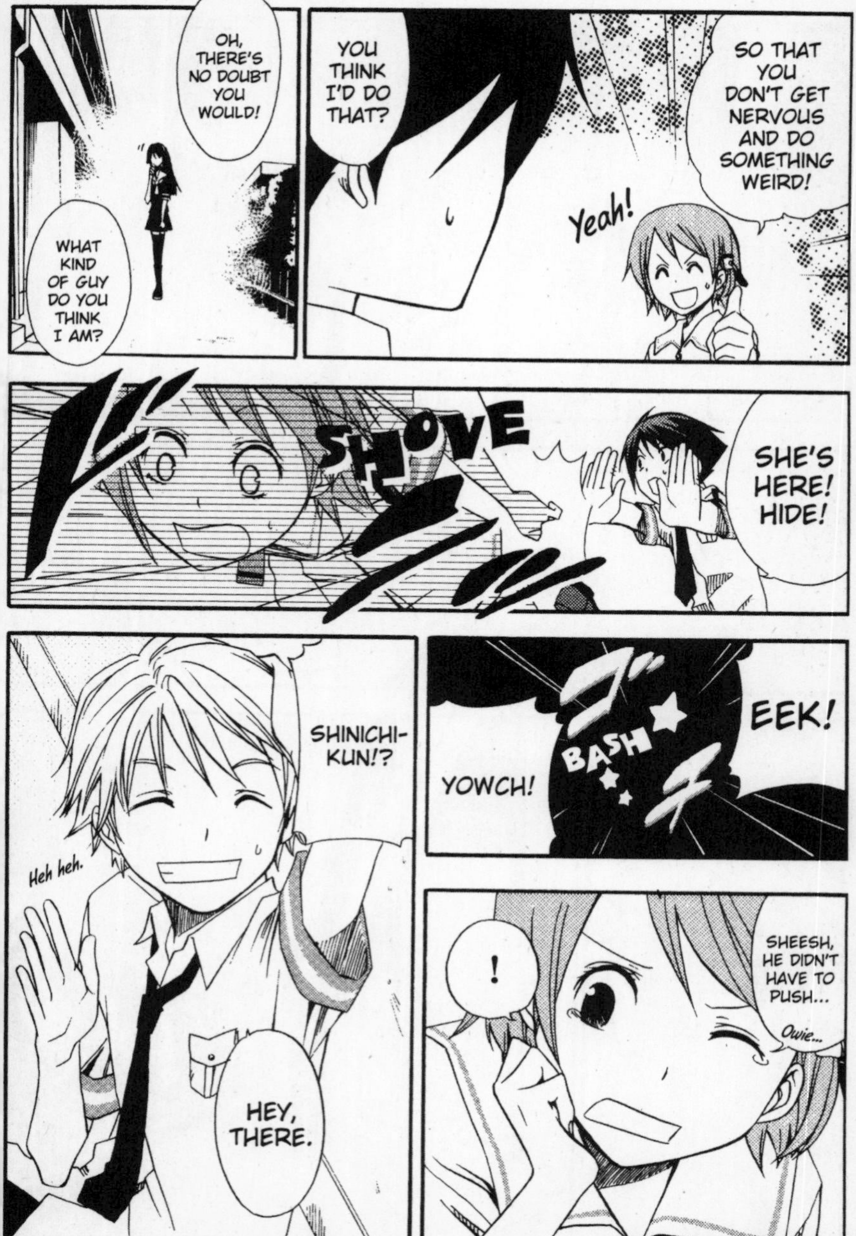
SO THAT YOU DON'T GET NERVOUS AND DO SOMETHING WEIRD!
Yeah!
YOU THINK I'D DO THAT?
OH, THERE'S NO DOUBT YOU WOULD!
WHAT KIND OF GUY DO YOU THINK I AM?
SHE'S HERE! HIDE!
SHOVE
EEK!
BASH
YOWCH!
SHEESH, HE DIDN'T HAVE TO PUSH...
!
Owie...
SHINICHI-KUN!?
Heh heh.
HEY, THERE.

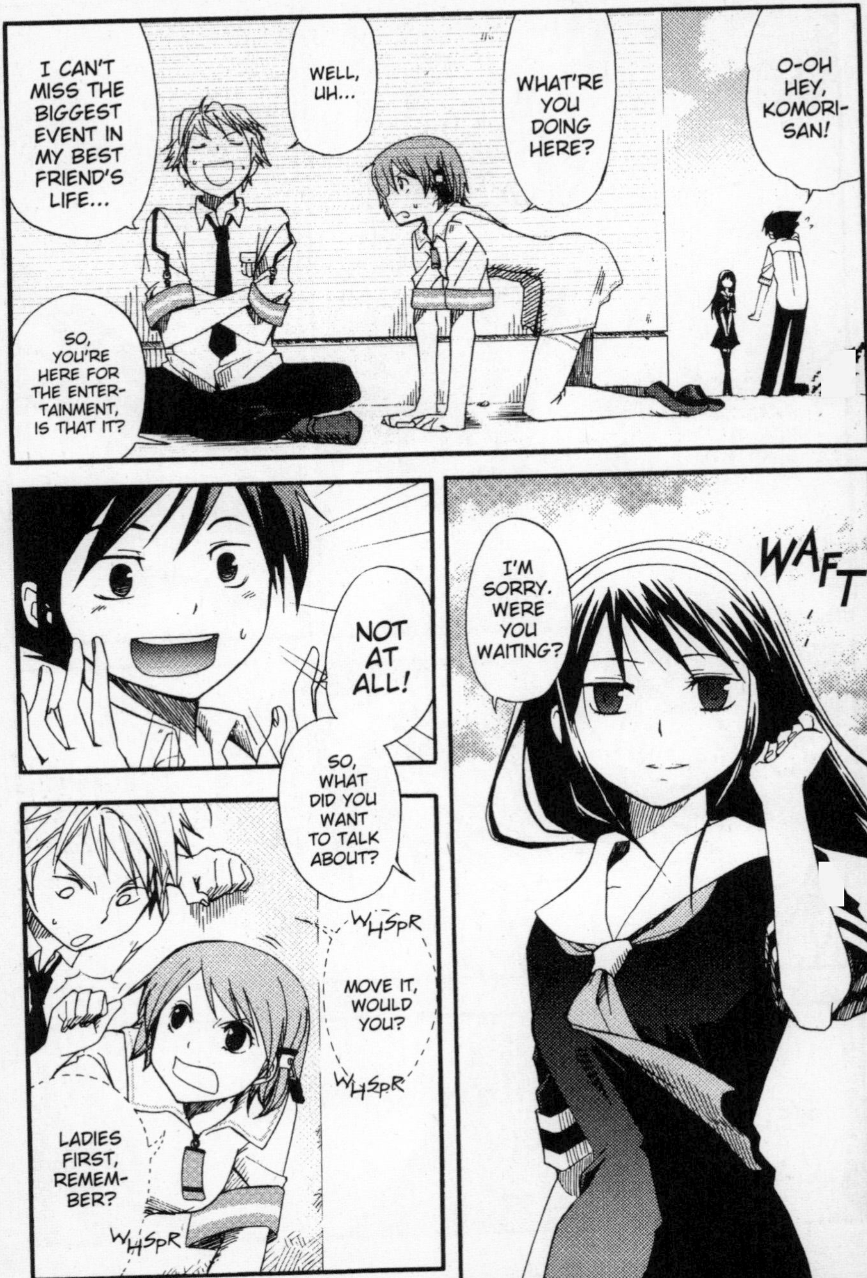

O-OH HEY, KOMORI-SAN!
WHAT'RE YOU DOING HERE?
WELL, UH...
I CAN'T MISS THE BIGGEST EVENT IN MY BEST FRIEND'S LIFE...
SO, YOU'RE HERE FOR THE ENTER-TAINMENT, IS THAT IT?
WAFT
I'M SORRY. WERE YOU WAITING?
NOT AT ALL!
SO, WHAT DID YOU WANT TO TALK ABOUT?
WHSPR
MOVE IT, WOULD YOU?
WHSPR
LADIES FIRST, REMEM-BER?
WHSPR

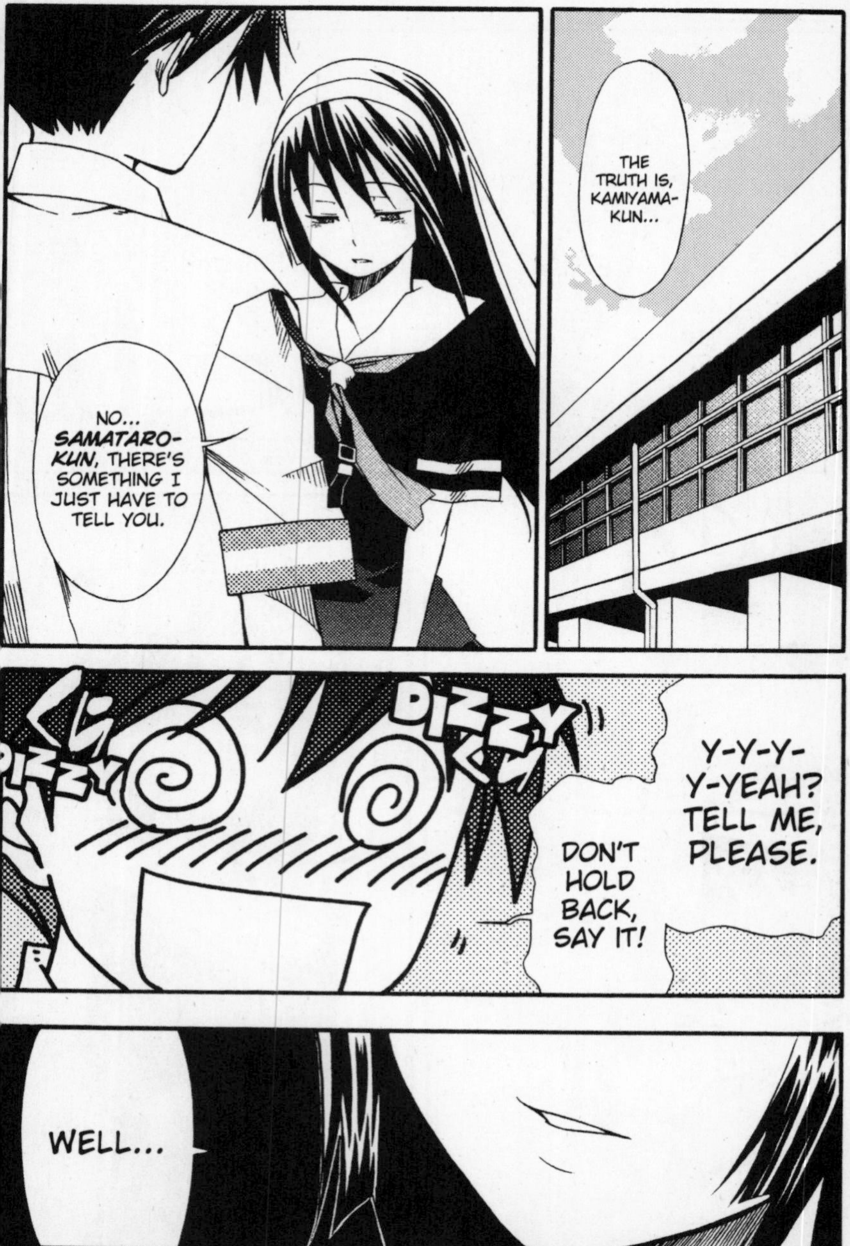
THE TRUTH IS, KAMIYAMA-KUN...
NO... *SAMATARO-KUN*, THERE'S SOMETHING I JUST HAVE TO TELL YOU.
Y-Y-Y-Y-YEAH? TELL ME, PLEASE.
DON'T HOLD BACK, SAY IT!
DIZZY
DIZZY
WELL...

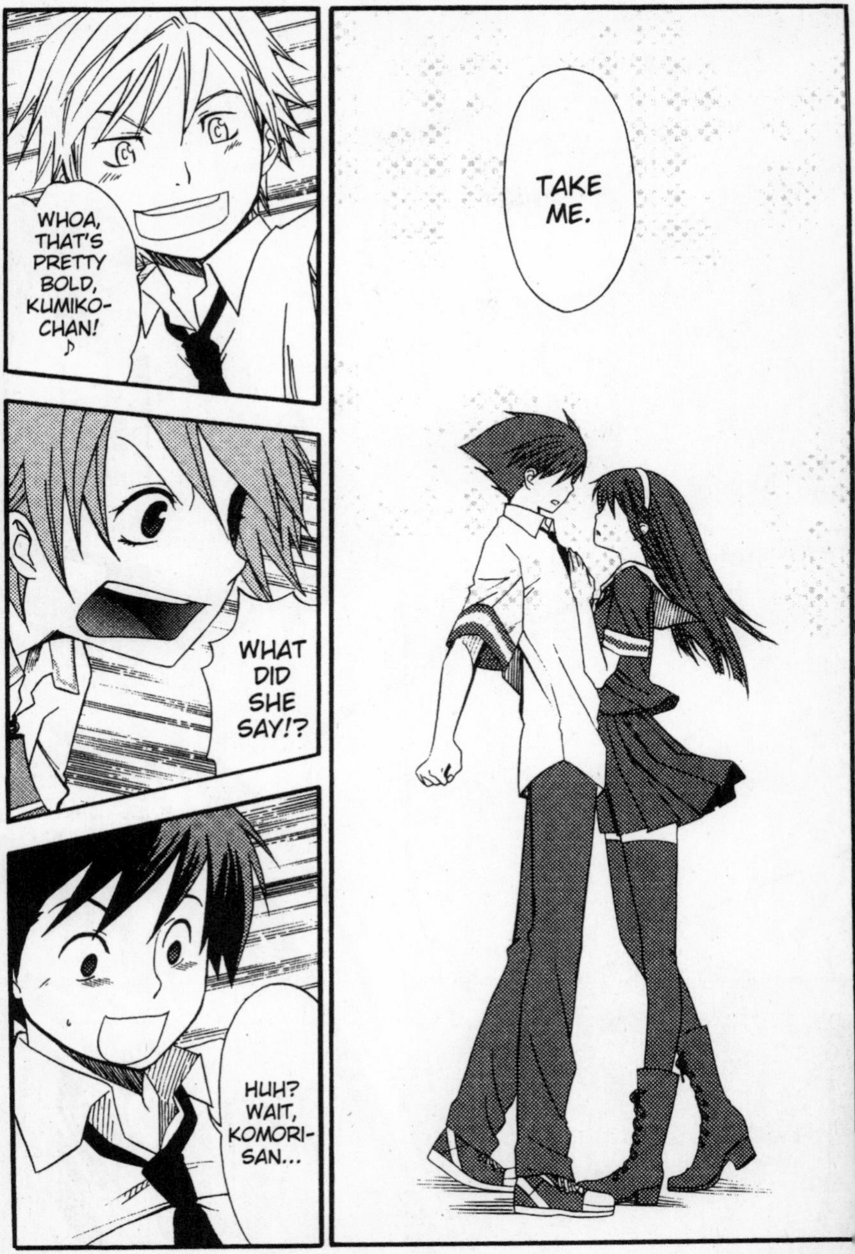
TAKE ME.
WHOA, THAT'S PRETTY BOLD, KUMIKO-CHAN! ♪
WHAT DID SHE SAY!?
HUH? WAIT, KOMORI-SAN...

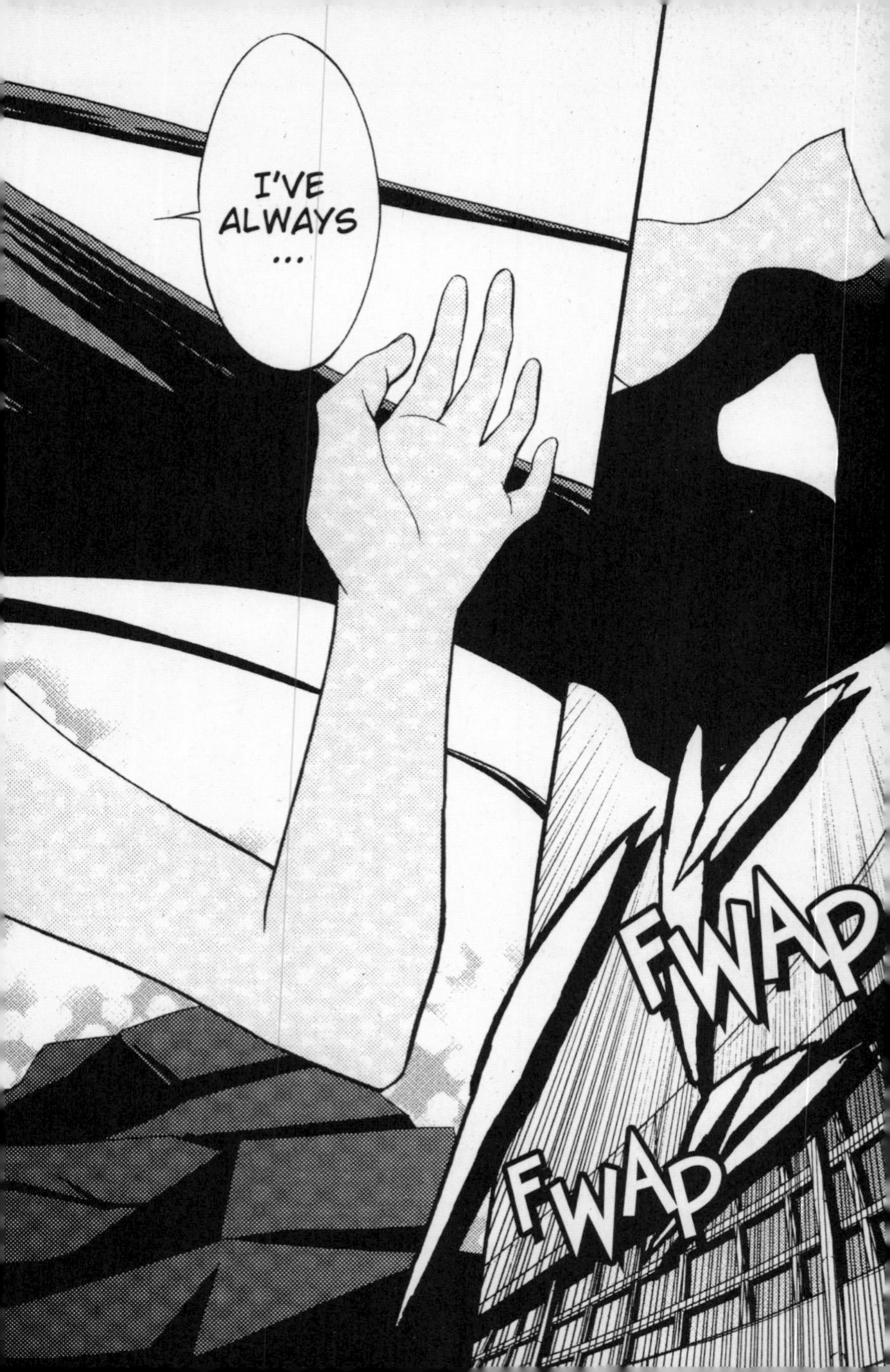
I'VE ALWAYS ...
FWAP
FWAP

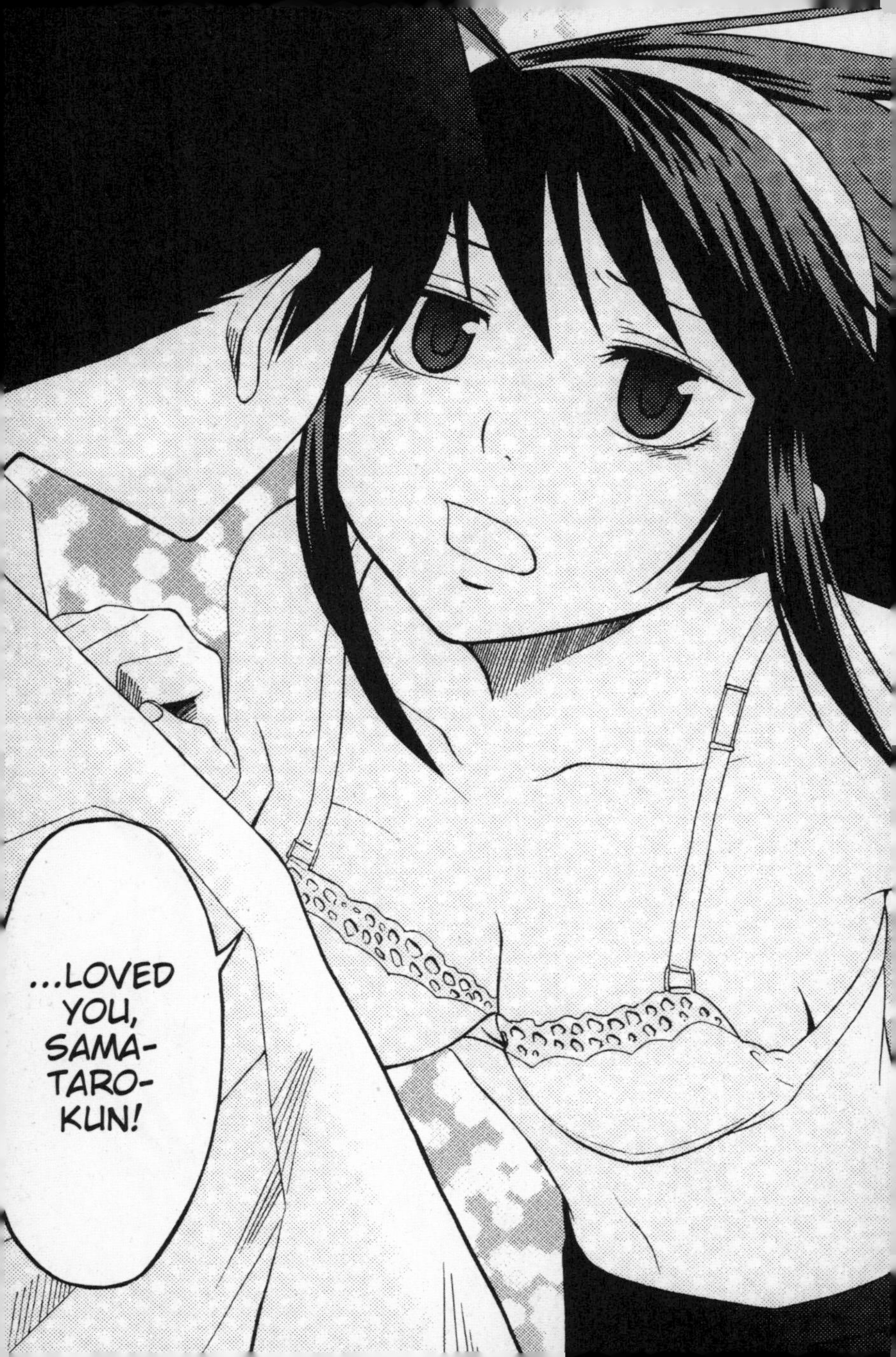
...LOVED YOU, SAMA-TARO-KUN!

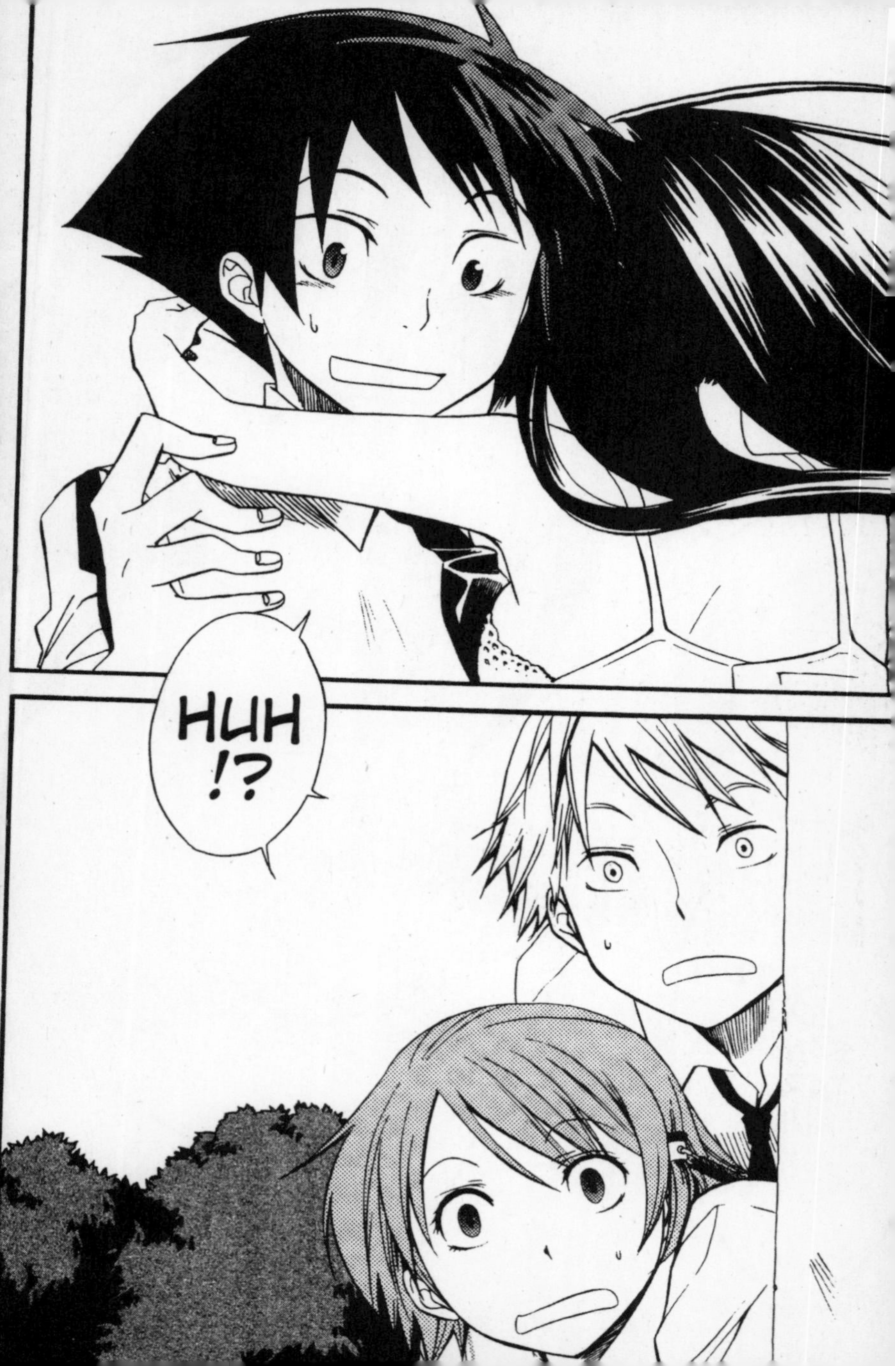
HUH !?

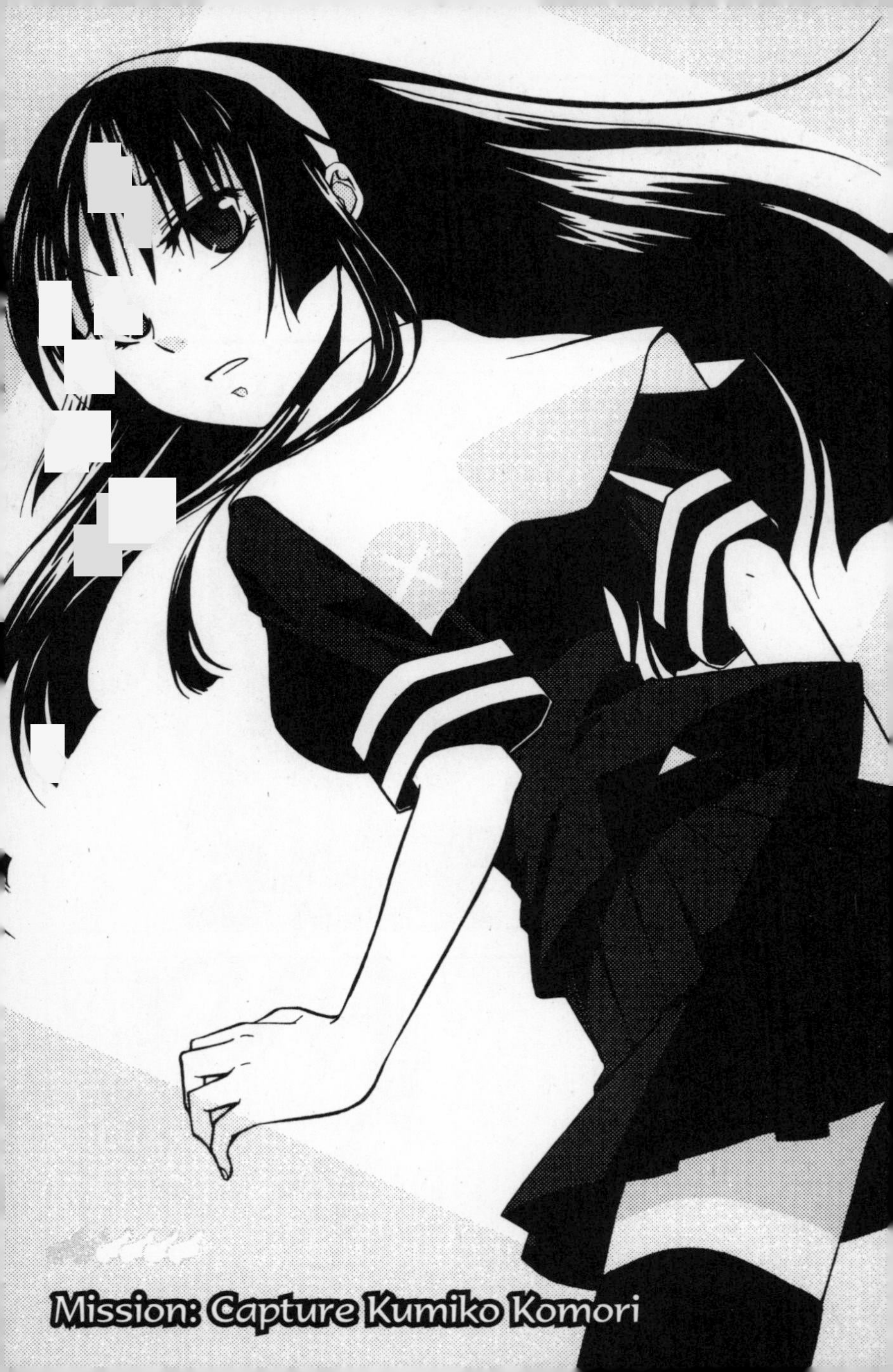
Mission: Capture Kumiko Komori

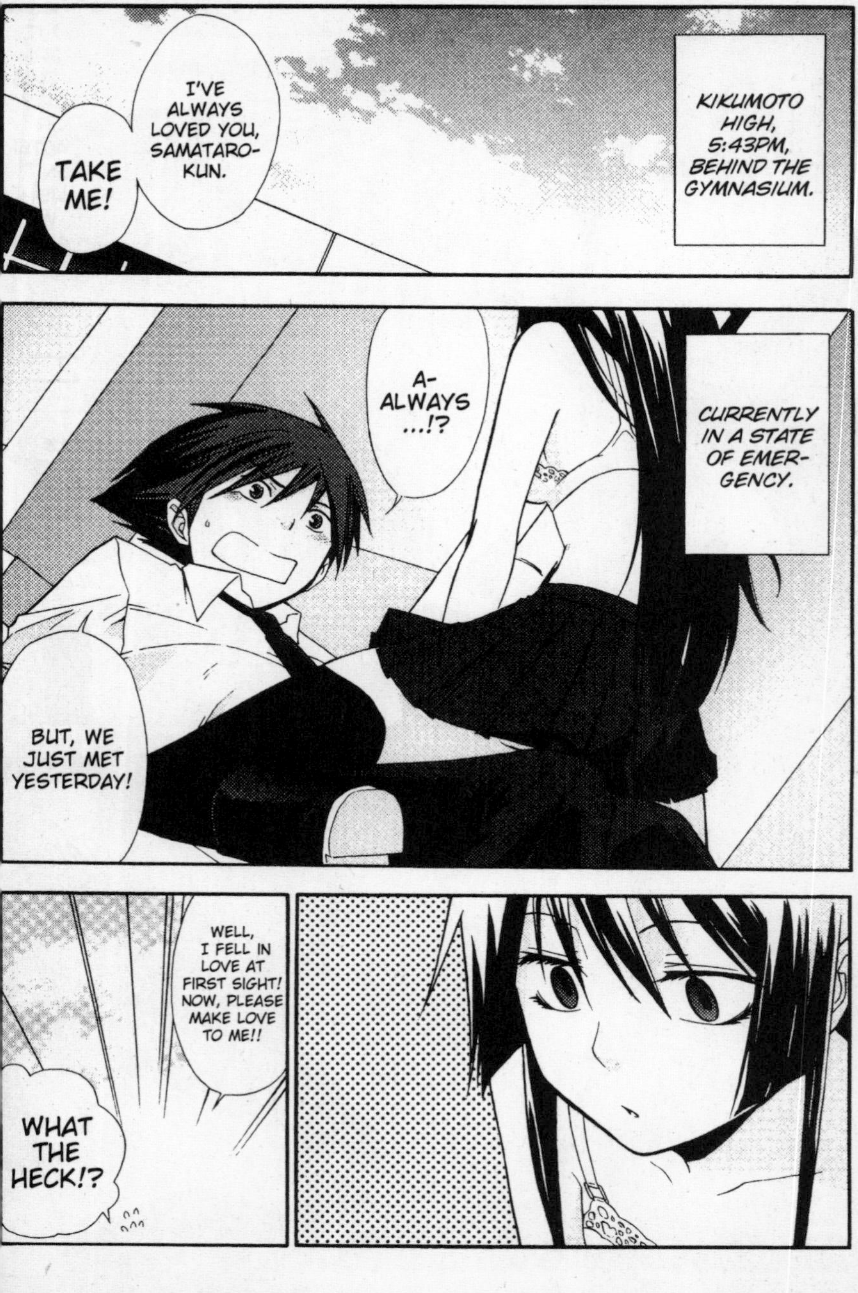
KIKUMOTO HIGH, 5:43PM, BEHIND THE GYMNASIUM.
I'VE ALWAYS LOVED YOU, SAMATARO-KUN.
TAKE ME!
CURRENTLY IN A STATE OF EMERGENCY.
A-ALWAYS ...!?
BUT, WE JUST MET YESTERDAY!
WELL, I FELL IN LOVE AT FIRST SIGHT! NOW, PLEASE MAKE LOVE TO ME!!
WHAT THE HECK!?

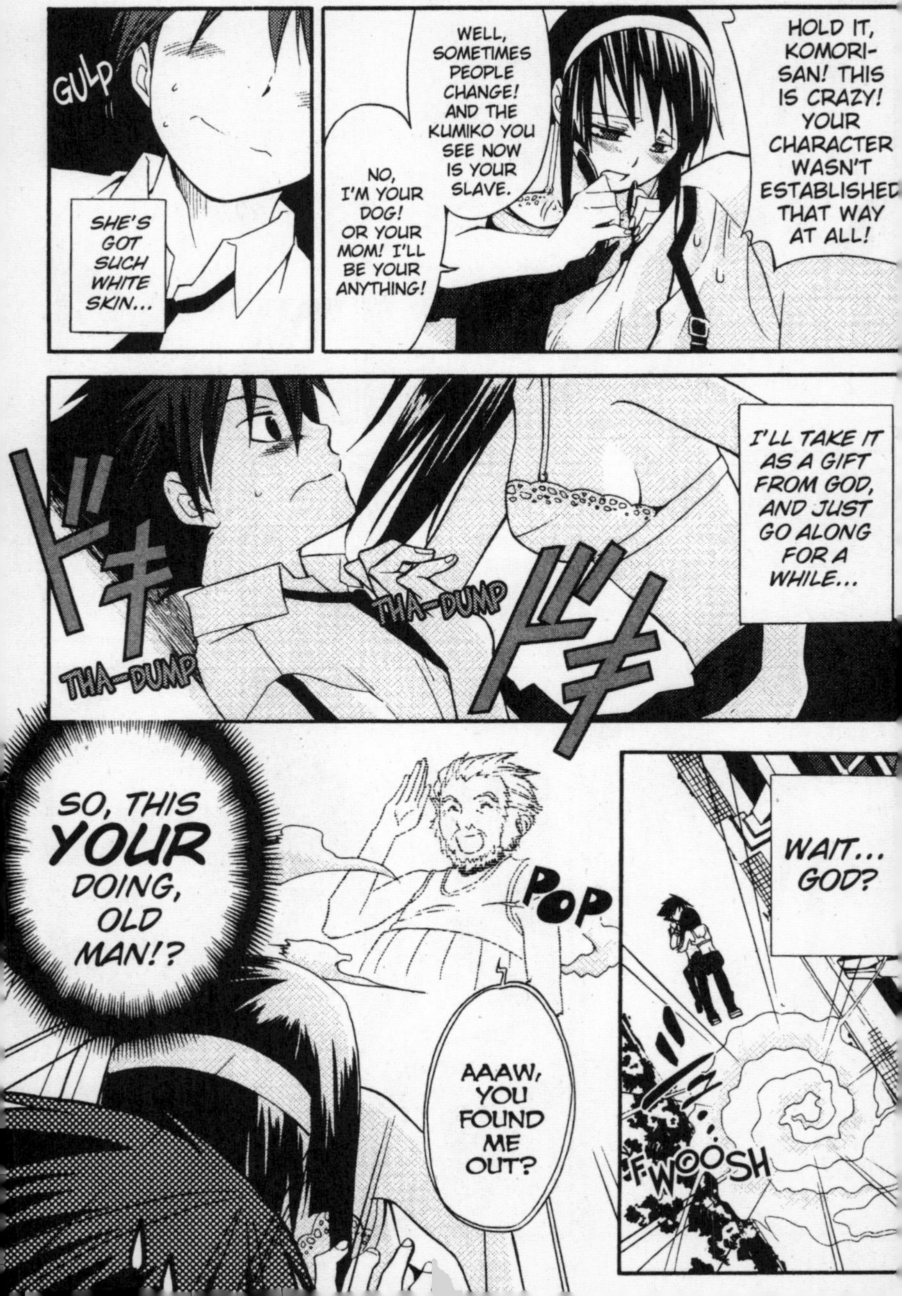
HOLD IT, KOMORI-SAN! THIS IS CRAZY! YOUR CHARACTER WASN'T ESTABLISHED THAT WAY AT ALL!
WELL, SOMETIMES PEOPLE CHANGE! AND THE KUMIKO YOU SEE NOW IS YOUR SLAVE.
NO, I'M YOUR DOG! OR YOUR MOM! I'LL BE YOUR ANYTHING!
GULP
SHE'S GOT SUCH WHITE SKIN...
I'LL TAKE IT AS A GIFT FROM GOD, AND JUST GO ALONG FOR A WHILE...
ドキ
THA-DUMP
ドキ
THA-DUMP
WAIT... GOD?
FWOOSH
SO, THIS YOUR DOING, OLD MAN!?
POP
AAAW, YOU FOUND ME OUT?

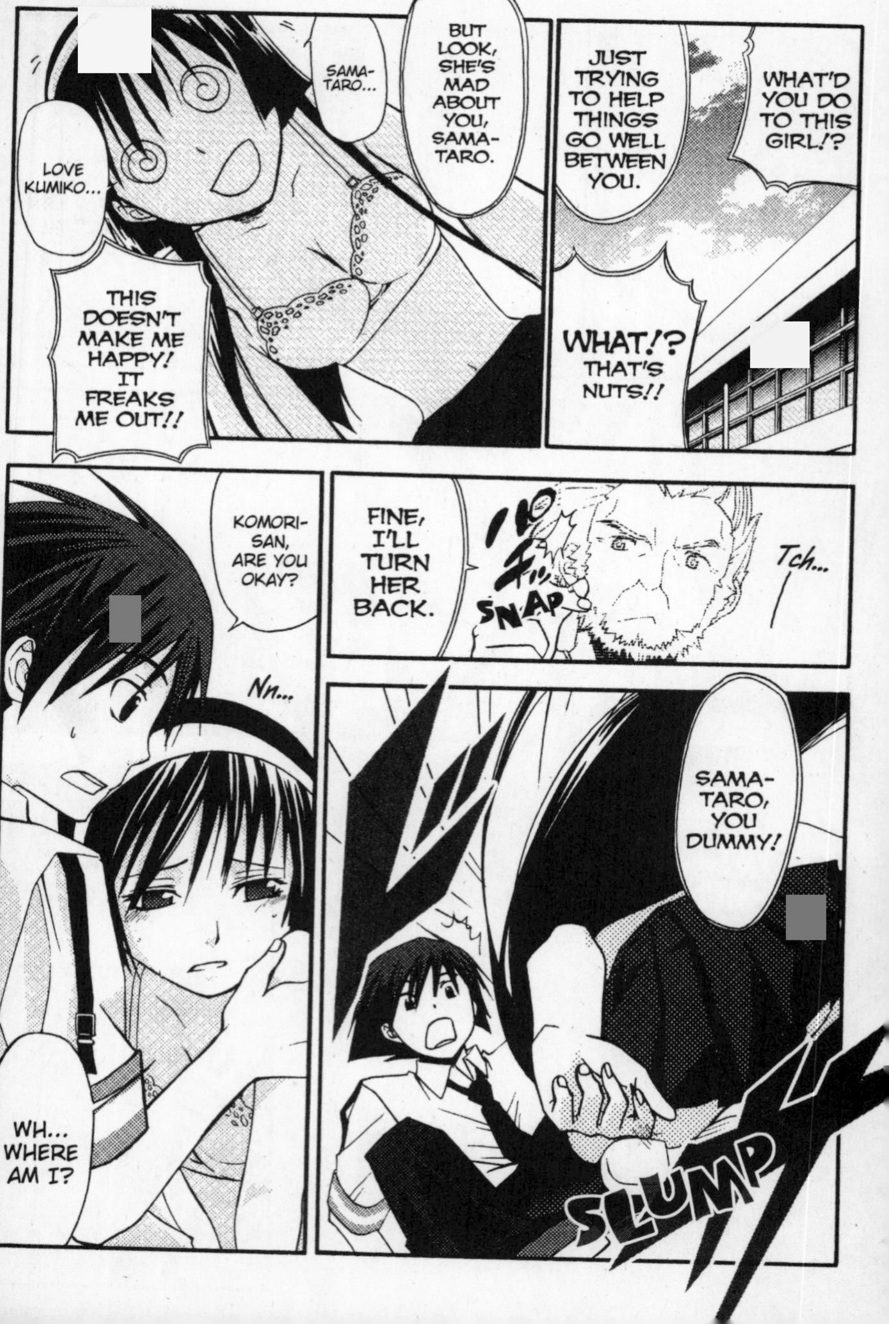
WHAT'D YOU DO TO THIS GIRL!?
JUST TRYING TO HELP THINGS GO WELL BETWEEN YOU.
WHAT!? THAT'S NUTS!!
BUT LOOK, SHE'S MAD ABOUT YOU, SAMA-TARO.
SAMA-TARO...
LOVE KUMIKO...
THIS DOESN'T MAKE ME HAPPY! IT FREAKS ME OUT!!
Tch...
パチッ
SNAP
FINE, I'LL TURN HER BACK.
SAMA-TARO, YOU DUMMY!
SLUMP
KOMORI-SAN, ARE YOU OKAY?
Nn...
WH... WHERE AM I?

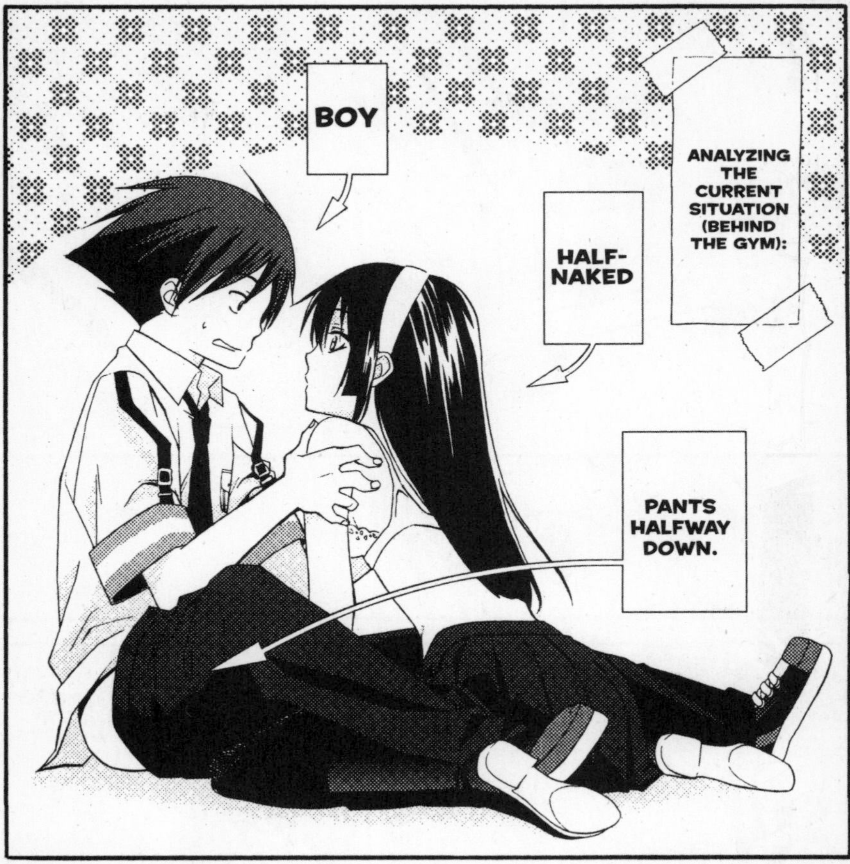
ANALYZING THE CURRENT SITUATION (BEHIND THE GYM):
BOY
HALF-NAKED
PANTS HALFWAY DOWN.

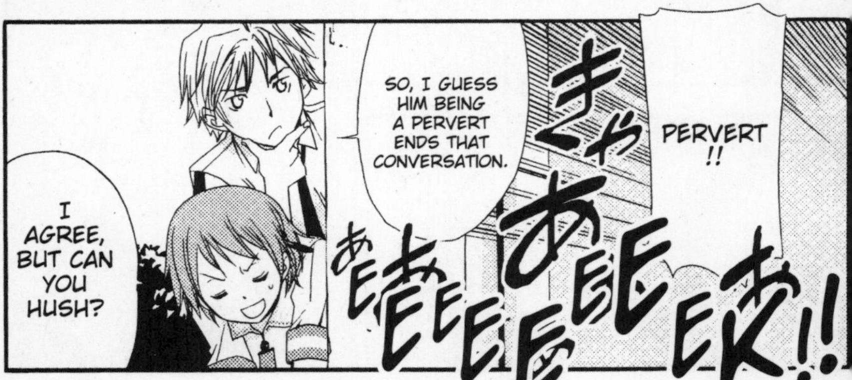
PERVERT !!
きゃあああ
EEEEEEEEEK!!
SO, I GUESS HIM BEING A PERVERT ENDS THAT CONVERSATION.
I AGREE, BUT CAN YOU HUSH?

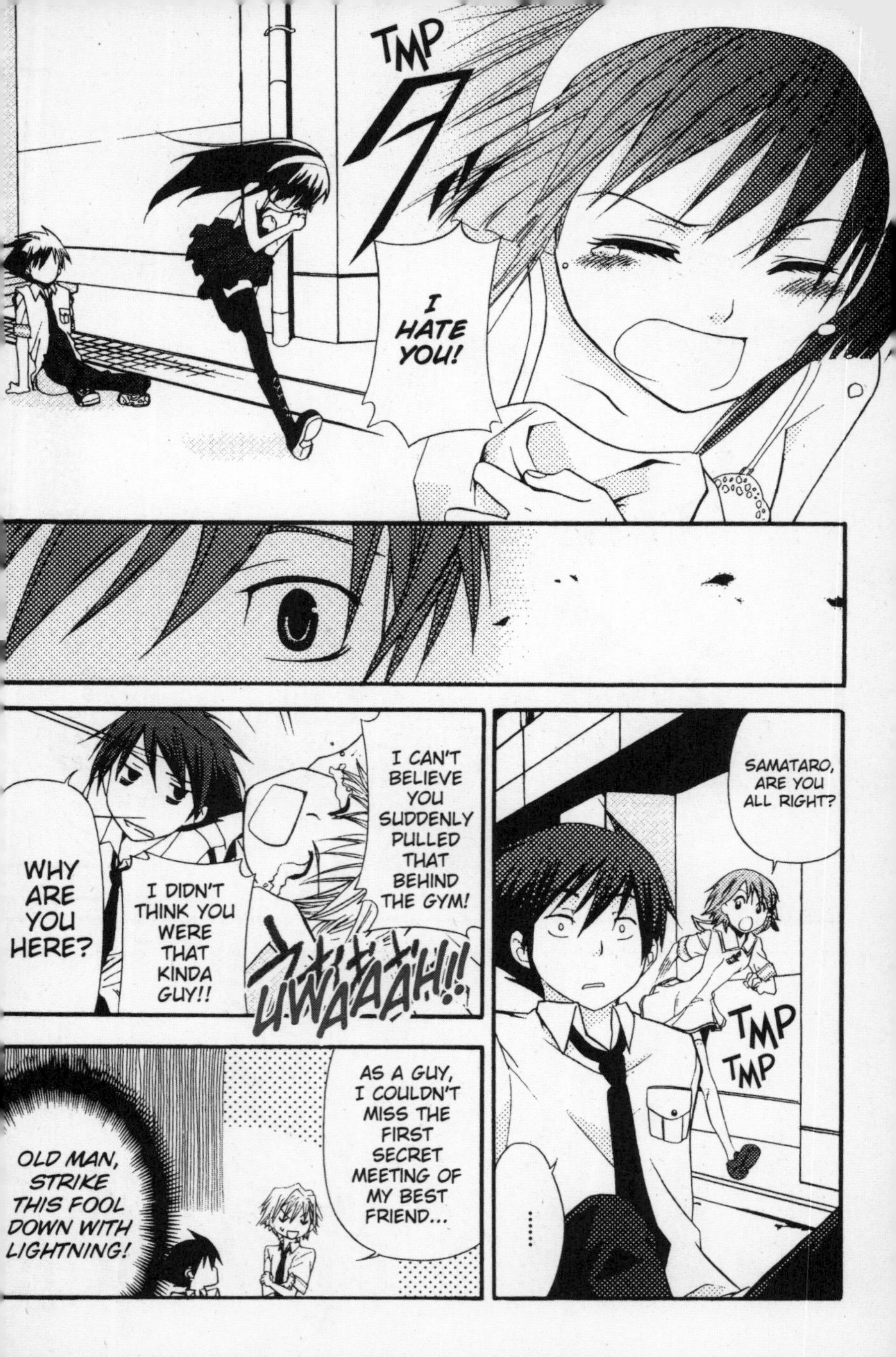
TMP
I HATE YOU!
SAMATARO, ARE YOU ALL RIGHT?
TMP TMP
......
I CAN'T BELIEVE YOU SUDDENLY PULLED THAT BEHIND THE GYM!
UWAAAH!!
I DIDN'T THINK YOU WERE THAT KINDA GUY!!
WHY ARE YOU HERE?
AS A GUY, I COULDN'T MISS THE FIRST SECRET MEETING OF MY BEST FRIEND...
OLD MAN, STRIKE THIS FOOL DOWN WITH LIGHTNING!

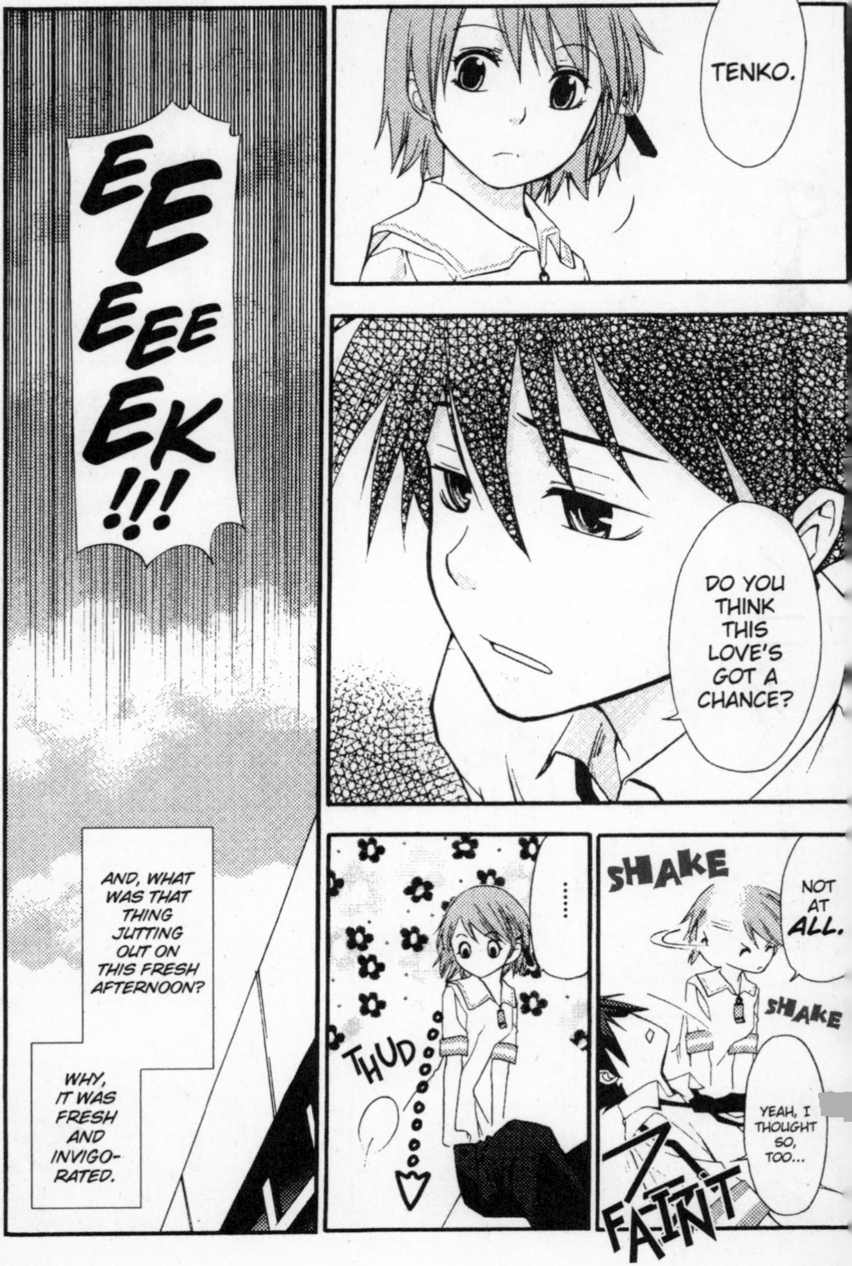
TENKO.
DO YOU THINK THIS LOVE'S GOT A CHANCE?
SHAKE
NOT AT ALL.
SHAKE
YEAH, I THOUGHT SO, TOO...
FAINT
......
THUD
EEEEEEK!!!
AND, WHAT WAS THAT THING JUTTING OUT ON THIS FRESH AFTERNOON?
WHY, IT WAS FRESH AND INVIGO-RATED.

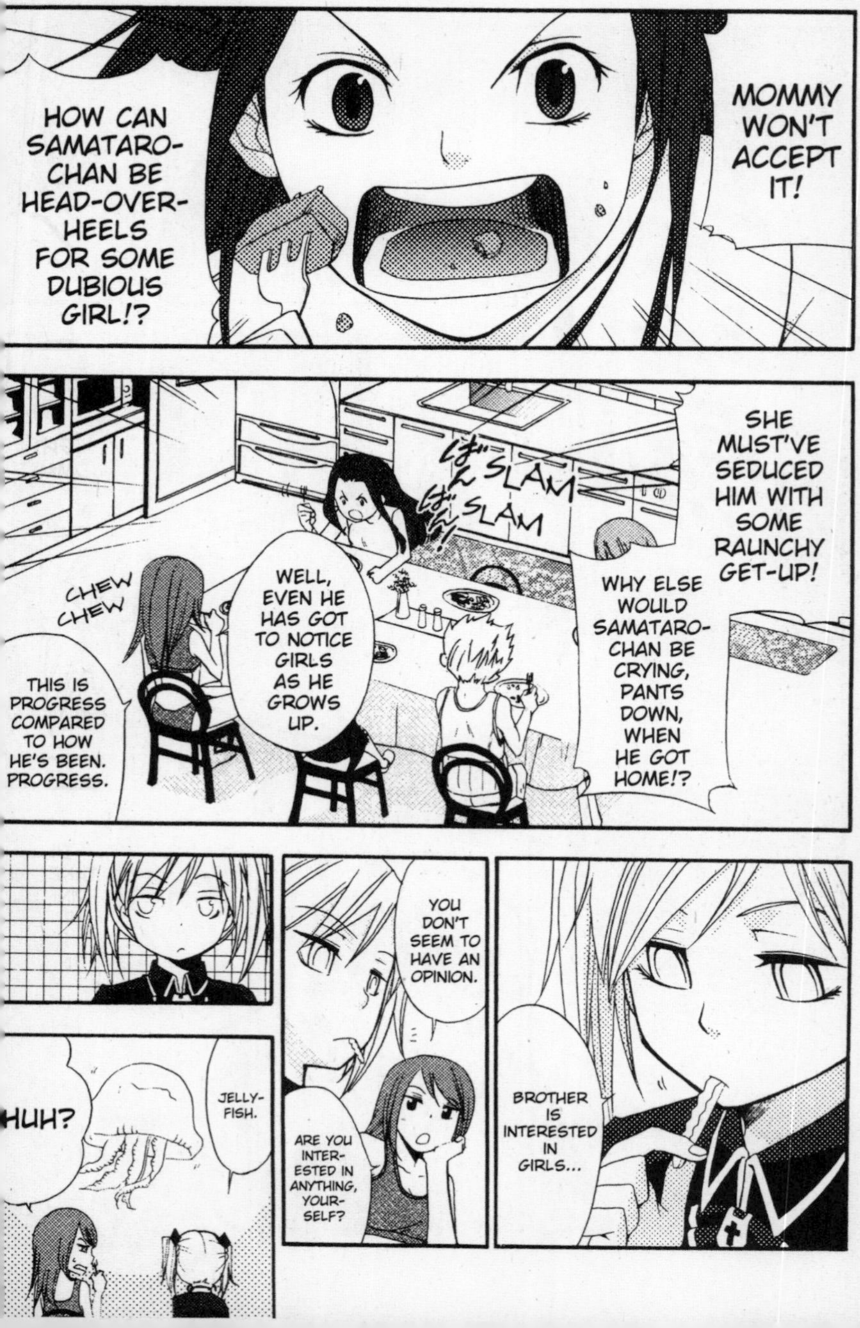
MOMMY WON'T ACCEPT IT!
HOW CAN SAMATARO-CHAN BE HEAD-OVER-HEELS FOR SOME DUBIOUS GIRL!?
SHE MUST'VE SEDUCED HIM WITH SOME RAUNCHY GET-UP!
WHY ELSE WOULD SAMATARO-CHAN BE CRYING, PANTS DOWN, WHEN HE GOT HOME!?
ばんばん
SLAM SLAM
WELL, EVEN HE HAS GOT TO NOTICE GIRLS AS HE GROWS UP.
CHEW CHEW
THIS IS PROGRESS COMPARED TO HOW HE'S BEEN. PROGRESS.
BROTHER IS INTERESTED IN GIRLS...
YOU DON'T SEEM TO HAVE AN OPINION.
ARE YOU INTER-ESTED IN ANYTHING, YOUR-SELF?
JELLY-FISH.
HUH?

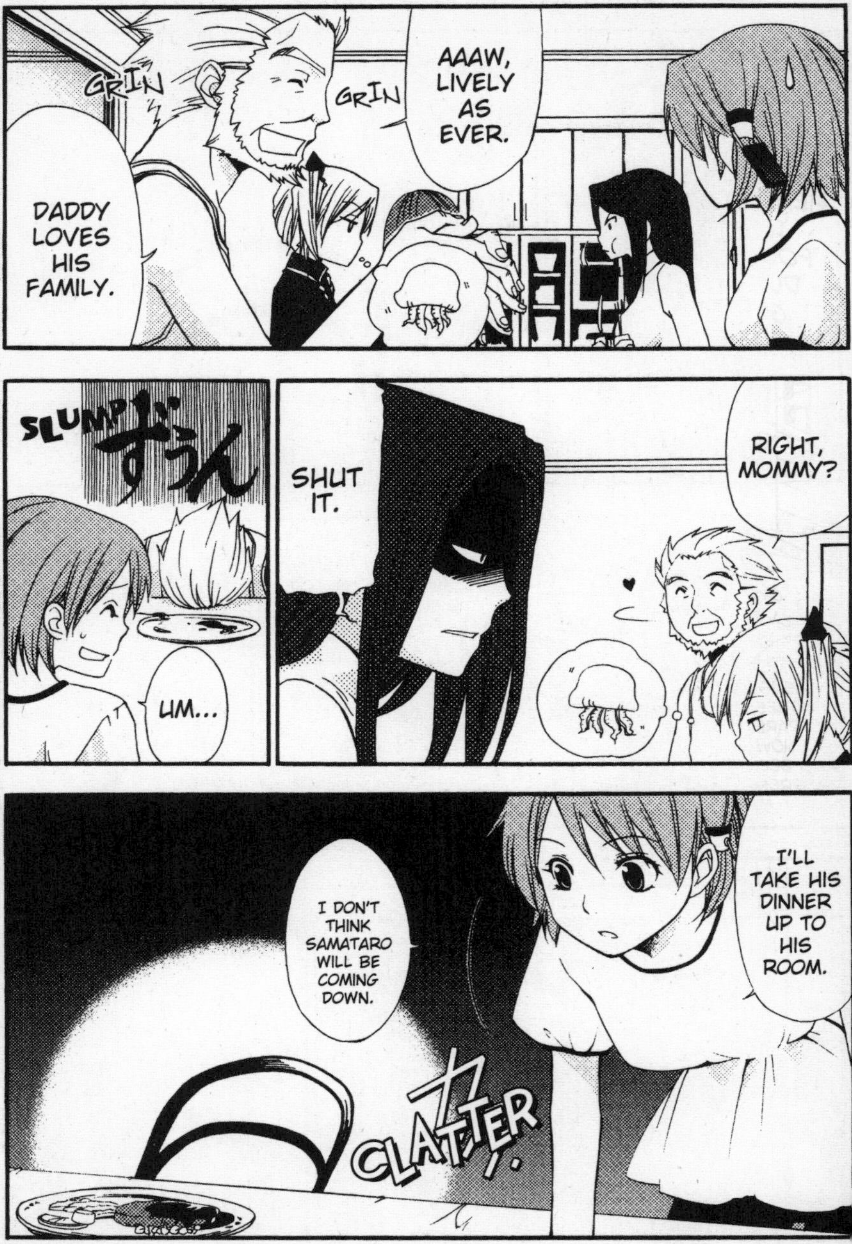
AAAW, LIVELY AS EVER.
GRIN
GRIN
DADDY LOVES HIS FAMILY.
RIGHT, MOMMY?
SHUT IT.
SLUMP
ずうん
UM...
I'LL TAKE HIS DINNER UP TO HIS ROOM.
I DON'T THINK SAMATARO WILL BE COMING DOWN.
CLATTER.

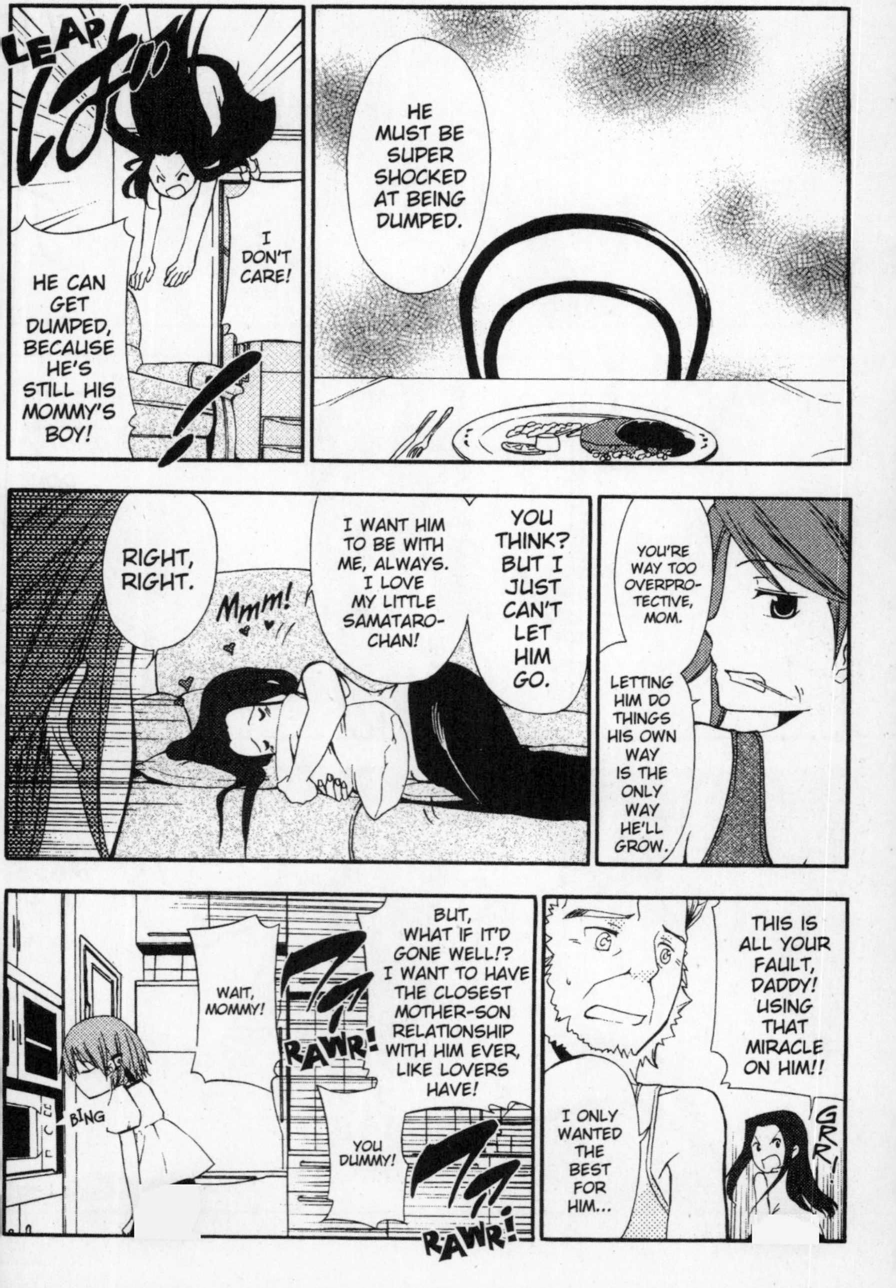
HE MUST BE SUPER SHOCKED AT BEING DUMPED.
LEAP
I DON'T CARE!
HE CAN GET DUMPED, BECAUSE HE'S STILL HIS MOMMY'S BOY!
YOU'RE WAY TOO OVERPROTECTIVE, MOM.
LETTING HIM DO THINGS HIS OWN WAY IS THE ONLY WAY HE'LL GROW.
YOU THINK? BUT I JUST CAN'T LET HIM GO.
I WANT HIM TO BE WITH ME, ALWAYS. I LOVE MY LITTLE SAMATARO-CHAN!
Mmm!
RIGHT, RIGHT.
THIS IS ALL YOUR FAULT, DADDY! USING THAT MIRACLE ON HIM!!
GRR!
I ONLY WANTED THE BEST FOR HIM...
BUT, WHAT IF IT'D GONE WELL!? I WANT TO HAVE THE CLOSEST MOTHER-SON RELATIONSHIP WITH HIM EVER, LIKE LOVERS HAVE!
RAWR!
WAIT, MOMMY!
YOU DUMMY!
RAWR!
BING

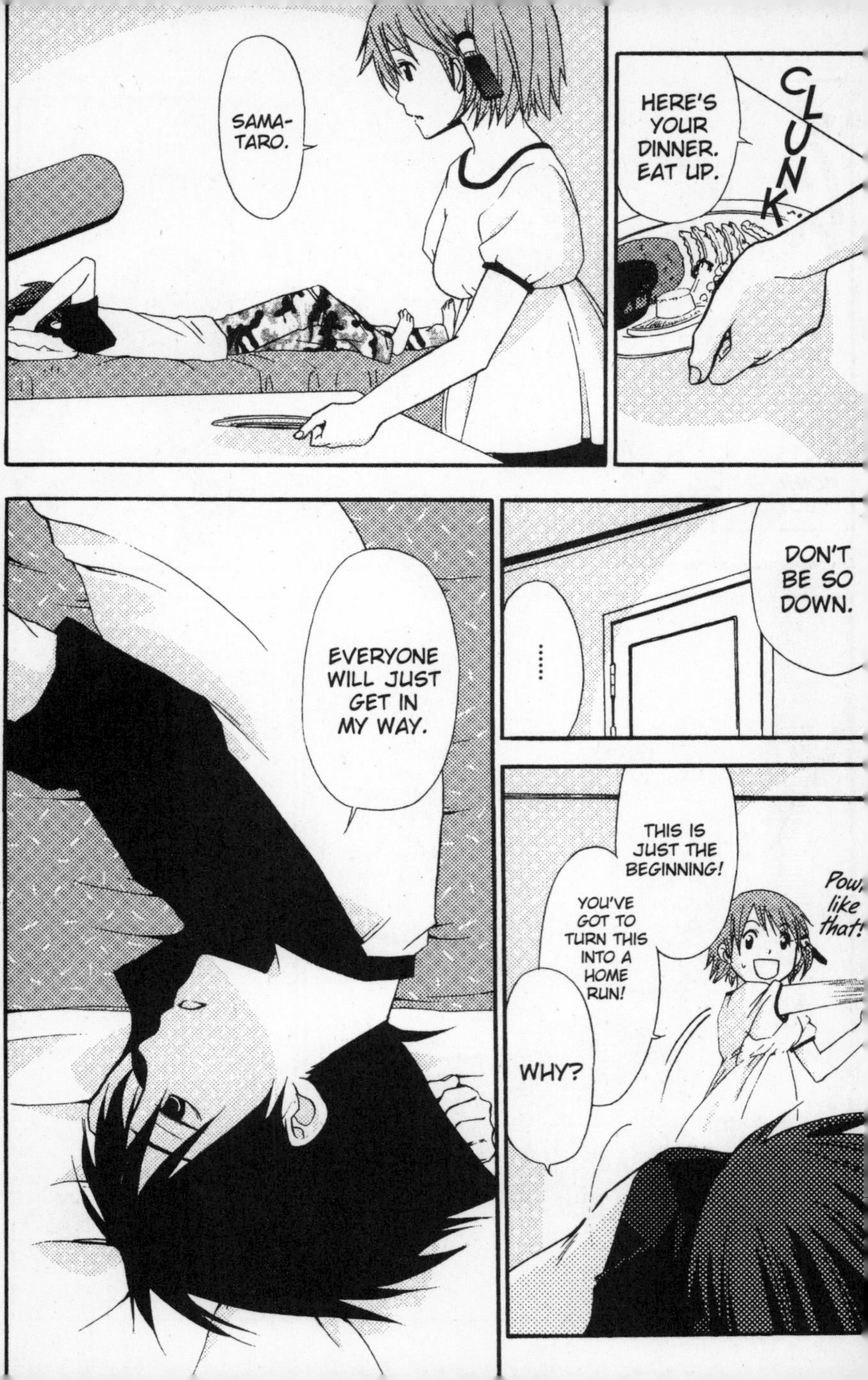
HERE'S YOUR DINNER. EAT UP.
CLUNK
SAMA-TARO.
DON'T BE SO DOWN.
......
THIS IS JUST THE BEGINNING!
YOU'VE GOT TO TURN THIS INTO A HOME RUN!
Pow, like that!
WHY?
EVERYONE WILL JUST GET IN MY WAY.

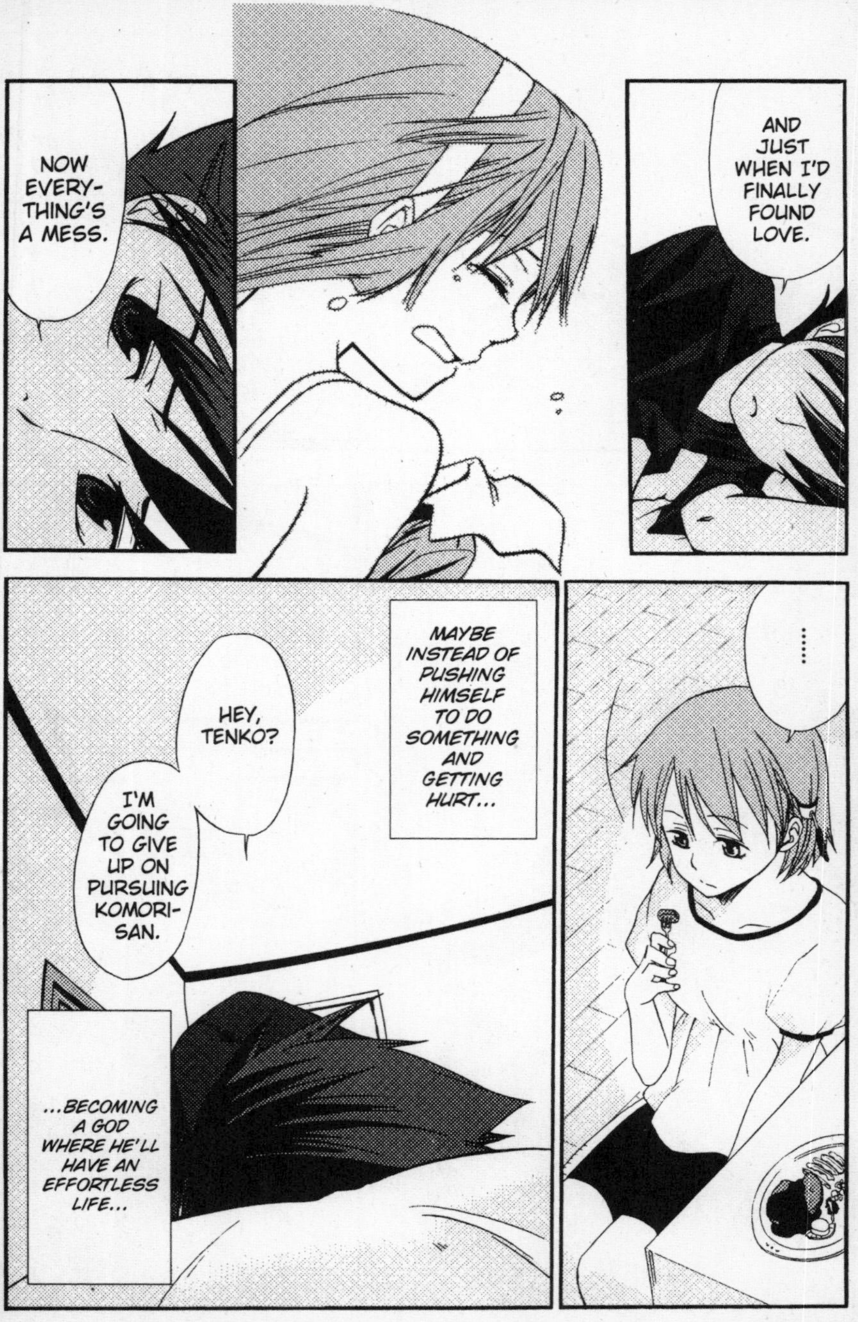
AND JUST WHEN I'D FINALLY FOUND LOVE.
NOW EVERY-THING'S A MESS.
......
MAYBE INSTEAD OF PUSHING HIMSELF TO DO SOMETHING AND GETTING HURT...
HEY, TENKO?
I'M GOING TO GIVE UP ON PURSUING KOMORI-SAN.
...BECOMING A GOD WHERE HE'LL HAVE AN EFFORTLESS LIFE...

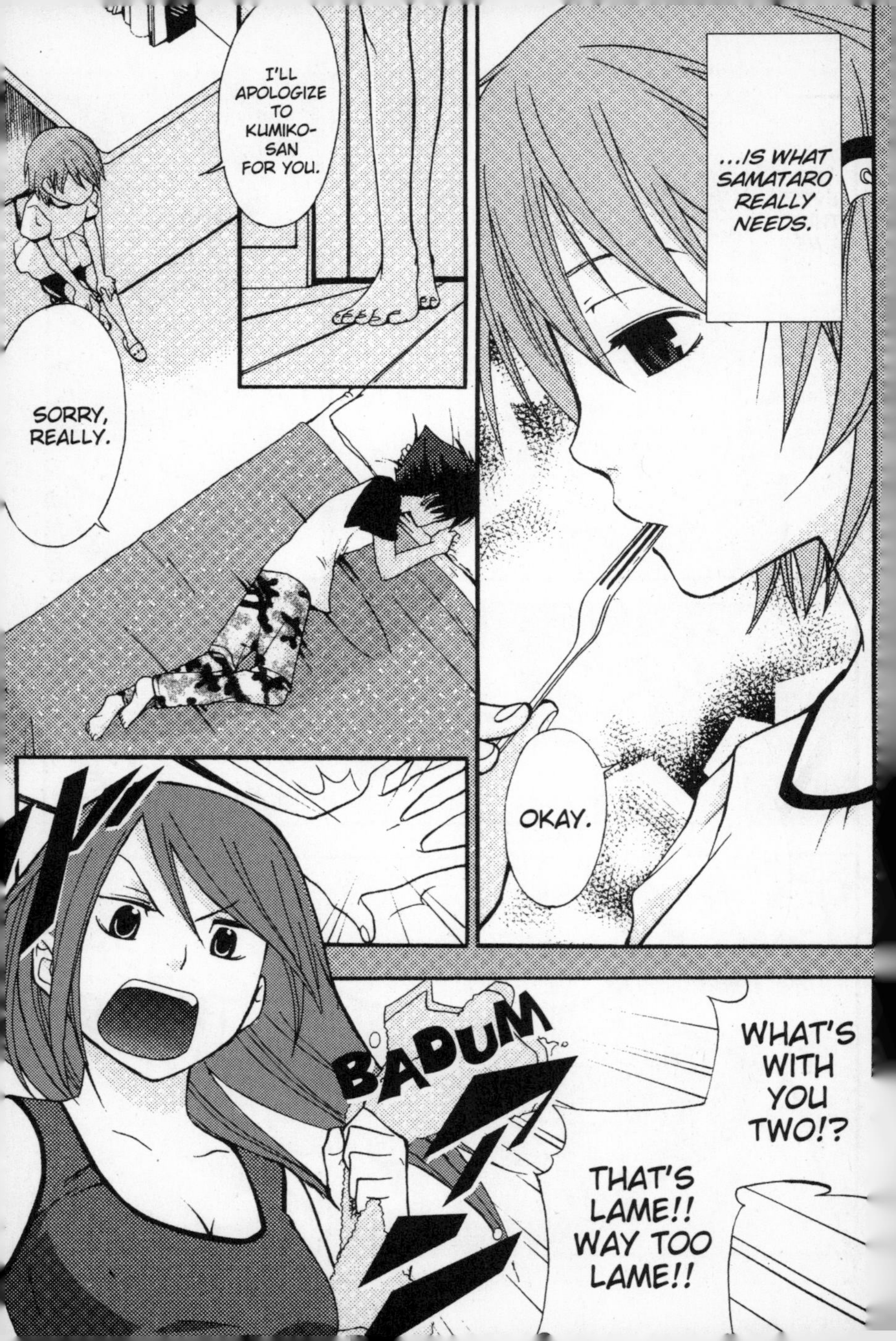

...IS WHAT SAMATARO REALLY NEEDS.
OKAY.
I'LL APOLOGIZE TO KUMIKO-SAN FOR YOU.
SORRY, REALLY.
BADUM
WHAT'S WITH YOU TWO!?
THAT'S LAME!! WAY TOO LAME!!

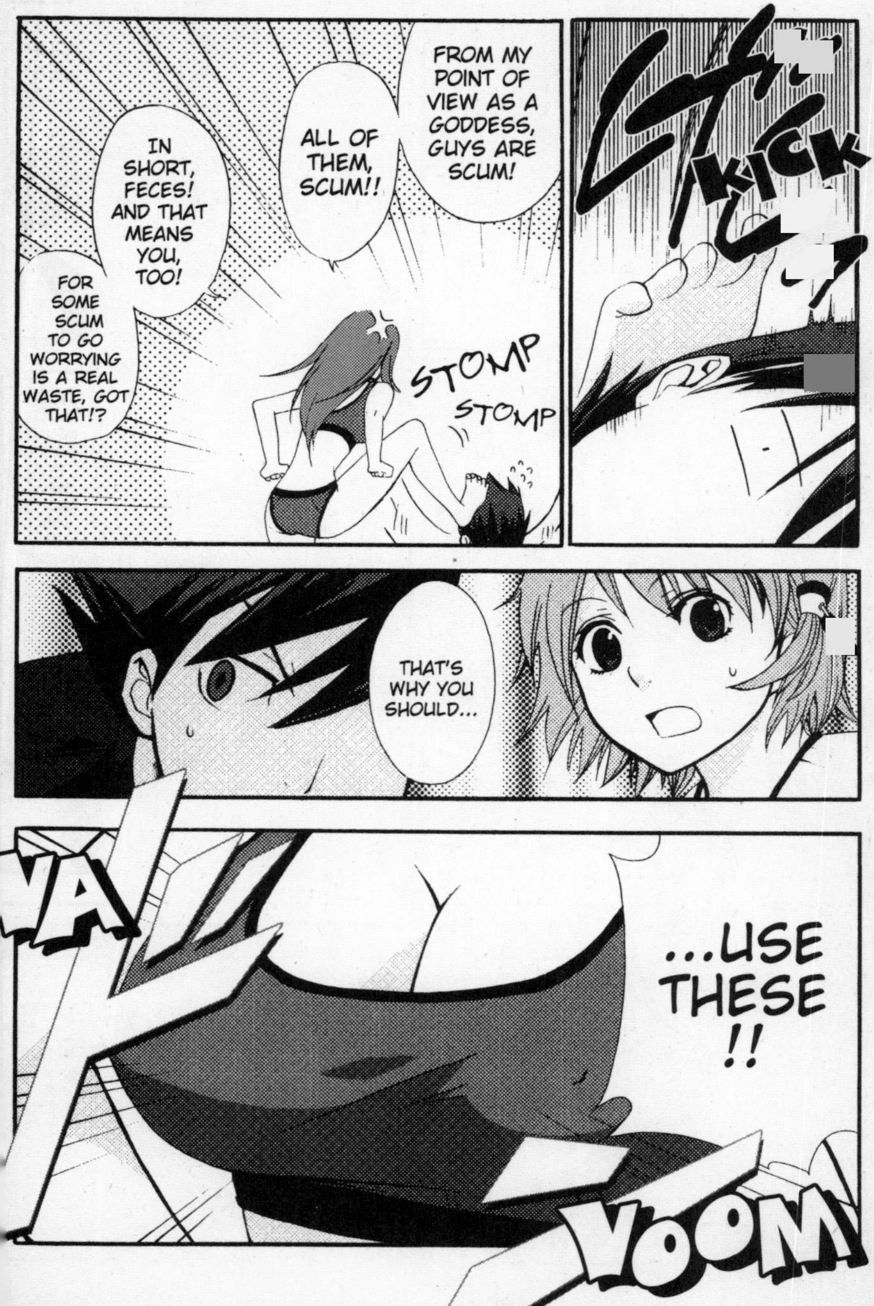
KICK
FROM MY POINT OF VIEW AS A GODDESS, GUYS ARE SCUM!
ALL OF THEM, SCUM!!
IN SHORT, FECES! AND THAT MEANS YOU, TOO!
FOR SOME SCUM TO GO WORRYING IS A REAL WASTE, GOT THAT!?
STOMP
STOMP
THAT'S WHY YOU SHOULD...
...USE THESE!!
VOOM

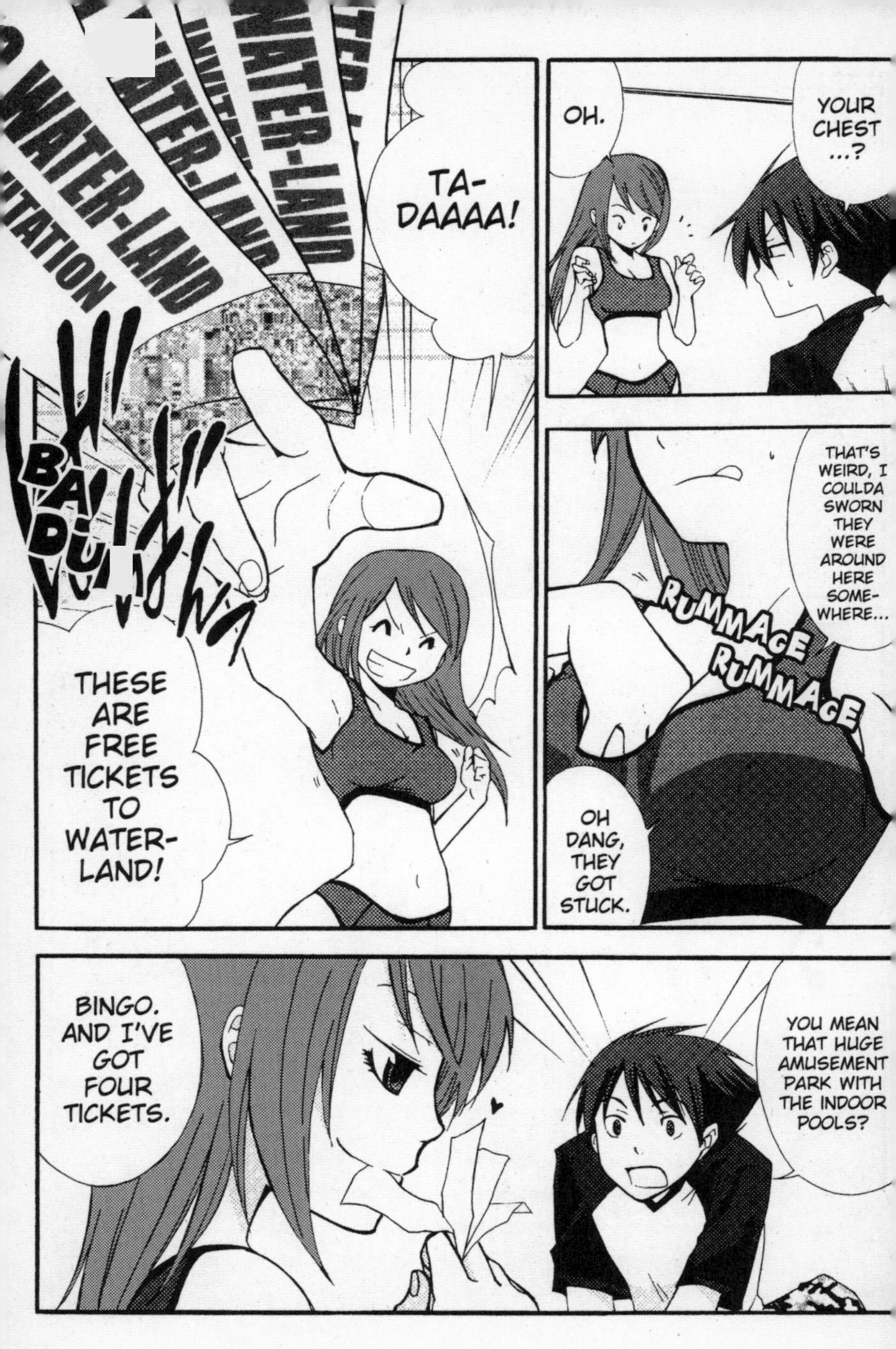
YOUR CHEST ...?
OH.
THAT'S WEIRD, I COULDA SWORN THEY WERE AROUND HERE SOME-WHERE...
RUMMAGE RUMMAGE
OH DANG, THEY GOT STUCK.
TA-DAAAA!
WATER-LAND
WATER-LAND
WATER-LAND
BADUM
THESE ARE FREE TICKETS TO WATER-LAND!
YOU MEAN THAT HUGE AMUSEMENT PARK WITH THE INDOOR POOLS?
BINGO. AND I'VE GOT FOUR TICKETS.

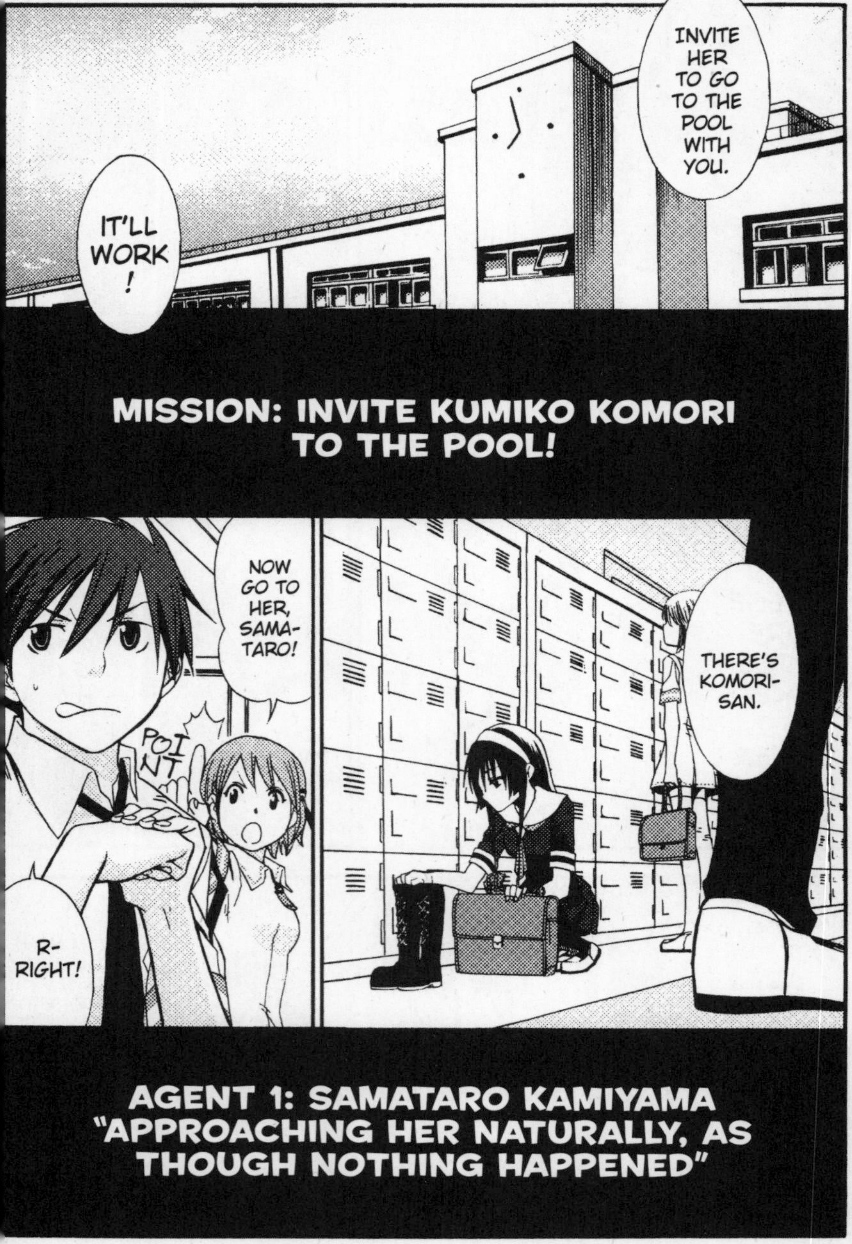
INVITE HER TO GO TO THE POOL WITH YOU.
IT'LL WORK!
MISSION: INVITE KUMIKO KOMORI TO THE POOL!
THERE'S KOMORI-SAN.
NOW GO TO HER, SAMATARO!
POINT
R-RIGHT!
AGENT 1: SAMATARO KAMIYAMA "APPROACHING HER NATURALLY, AS THOUGH NOTHING HAPPENED"

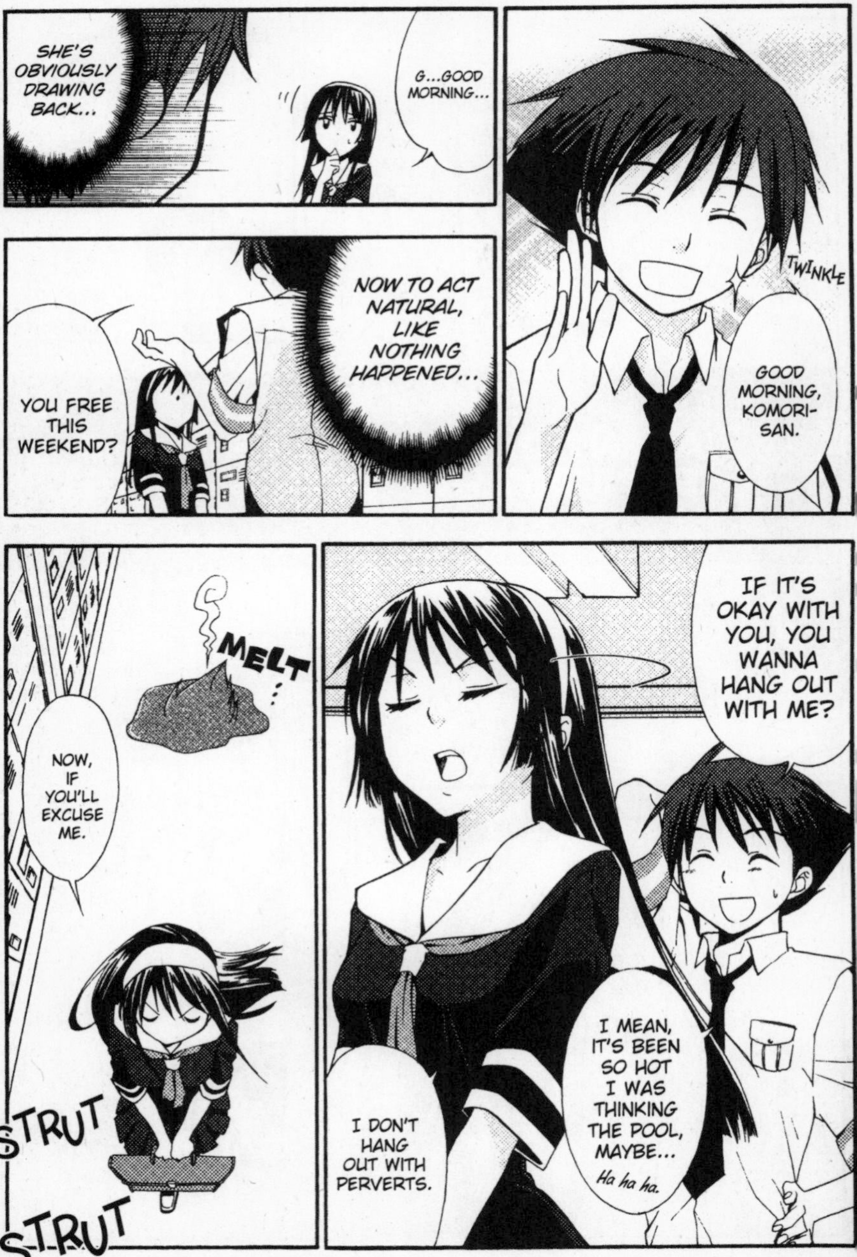
TWINKLE
GOOD MORNING, KOMORI-SAN.
G...GOOD MORNING...
SHE'S OBVIOUSLY DRAWING BACK...
NOW TO ACT NATURAL, LIKE NOTHING HAPPENED...
YOU FREE THIS WEEKEND?
IF IT'S OKAY WITH YOU, YOU WANNA HANG OUT WITH ME?
I MEAN, IT'S BEEN SO HOT I WAS THINKING THE POOL, MAYBE... Ha ha ha.
I DON'T HANG OUT WITH PERVERTS.
MELT
NOW, IF YOU'LL EXCUSE ME.
STRUT
STRUT

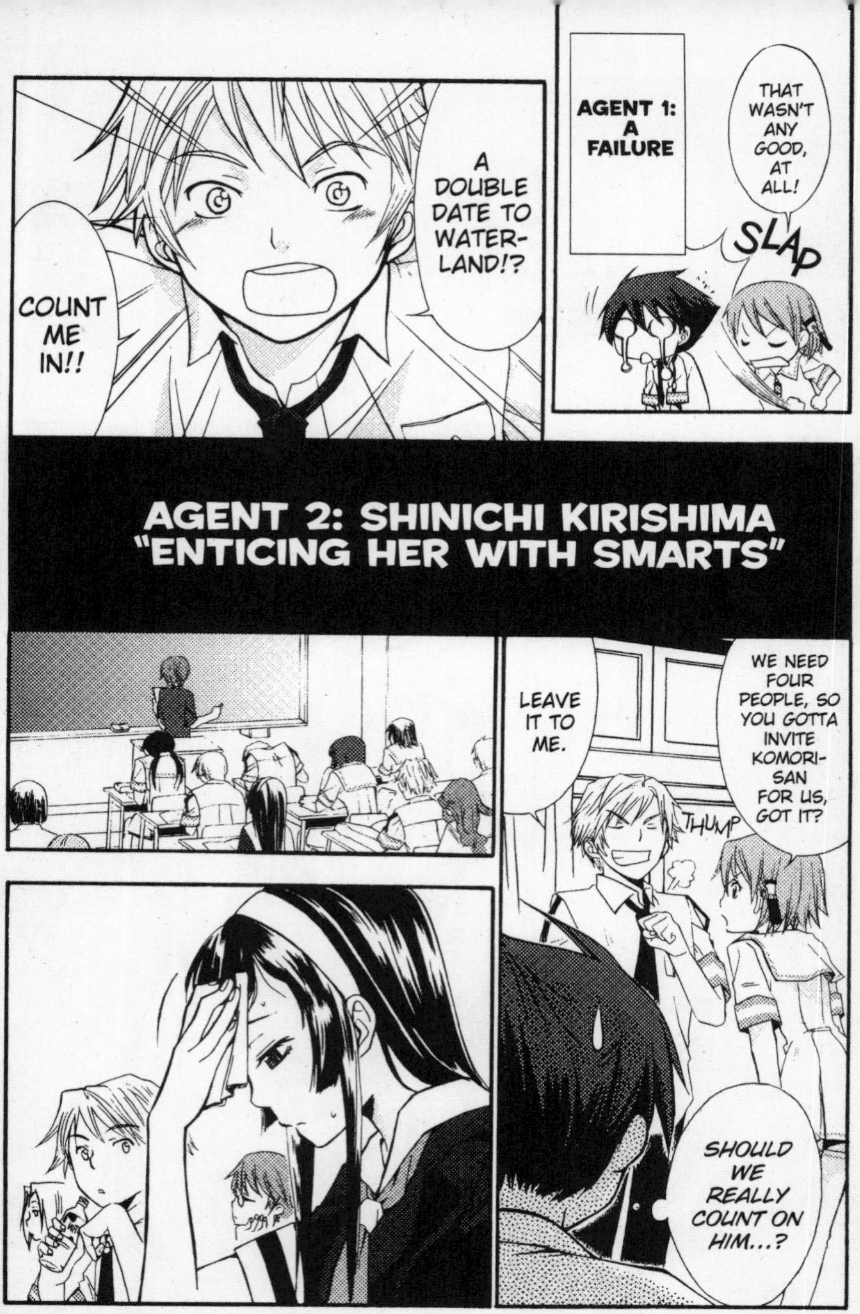
AGENT 1: A FAILURE
THAT WASN'T ANY GOOD, AT ALL!
SLAP
A DOUBLE DATE TO WATER-LAND!?
COUNT ME IN!!
AGENT 2: SHINICHI KIRISHIMA "ENTICING HER WITH SMARTS"
WE NEED FOUR PEOPLE, SO YOU GOTTA INVITE KOMORI-SAN FOR US, GOT IT?
LEAVE IT TO ME.
THUMP
SHOULD WE REALLY COUNT ON HIM...?

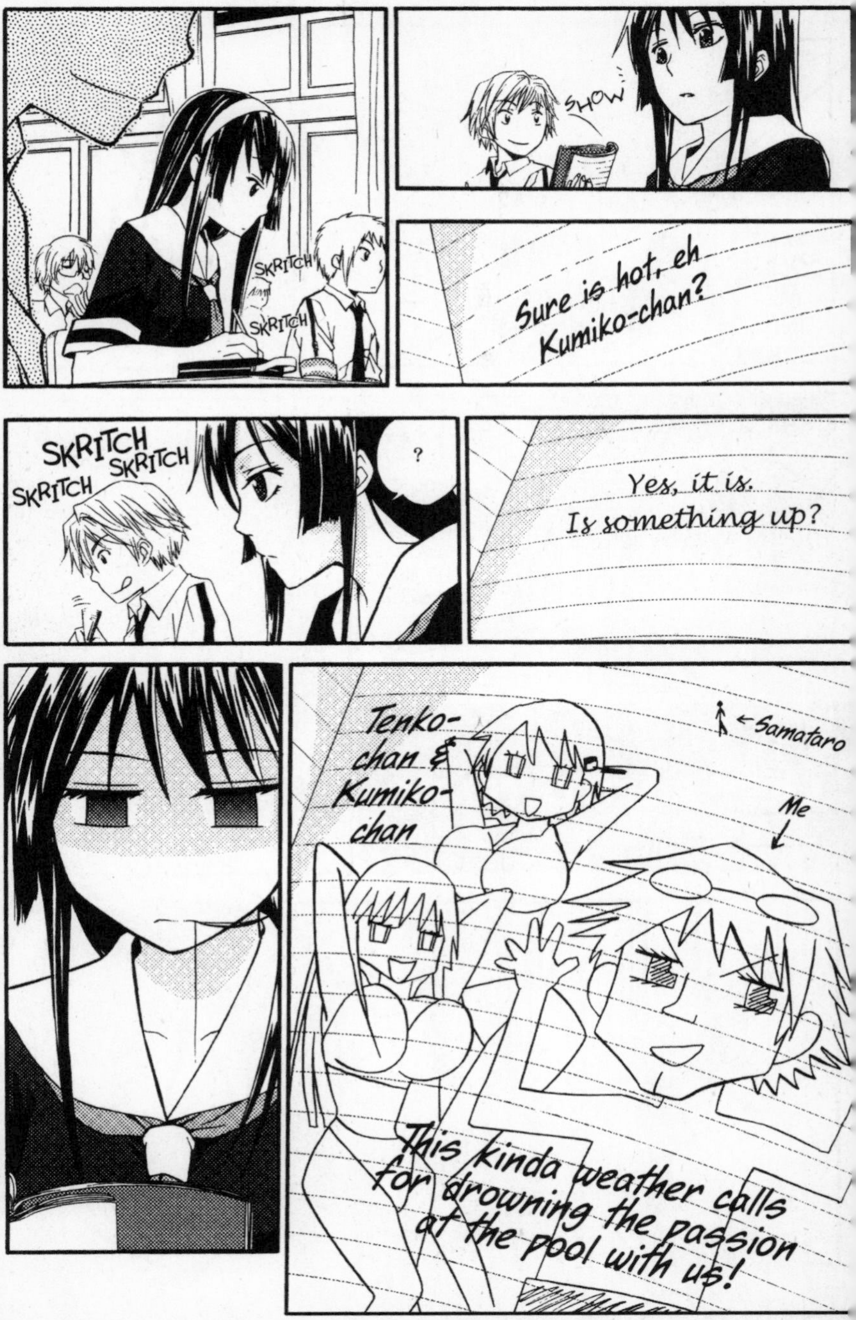
SHOW
Sure is hot, eh Kumiko-chan?
SKRITCH
SKRITCH
Yes, it is. Is something up?
?
SKRITCH
SKRITCH
SKRITCH
Tenko-chan & Kumiko-chan
←Samataro
Me
This kinda weather calls for drowning the passion at the pool with us!

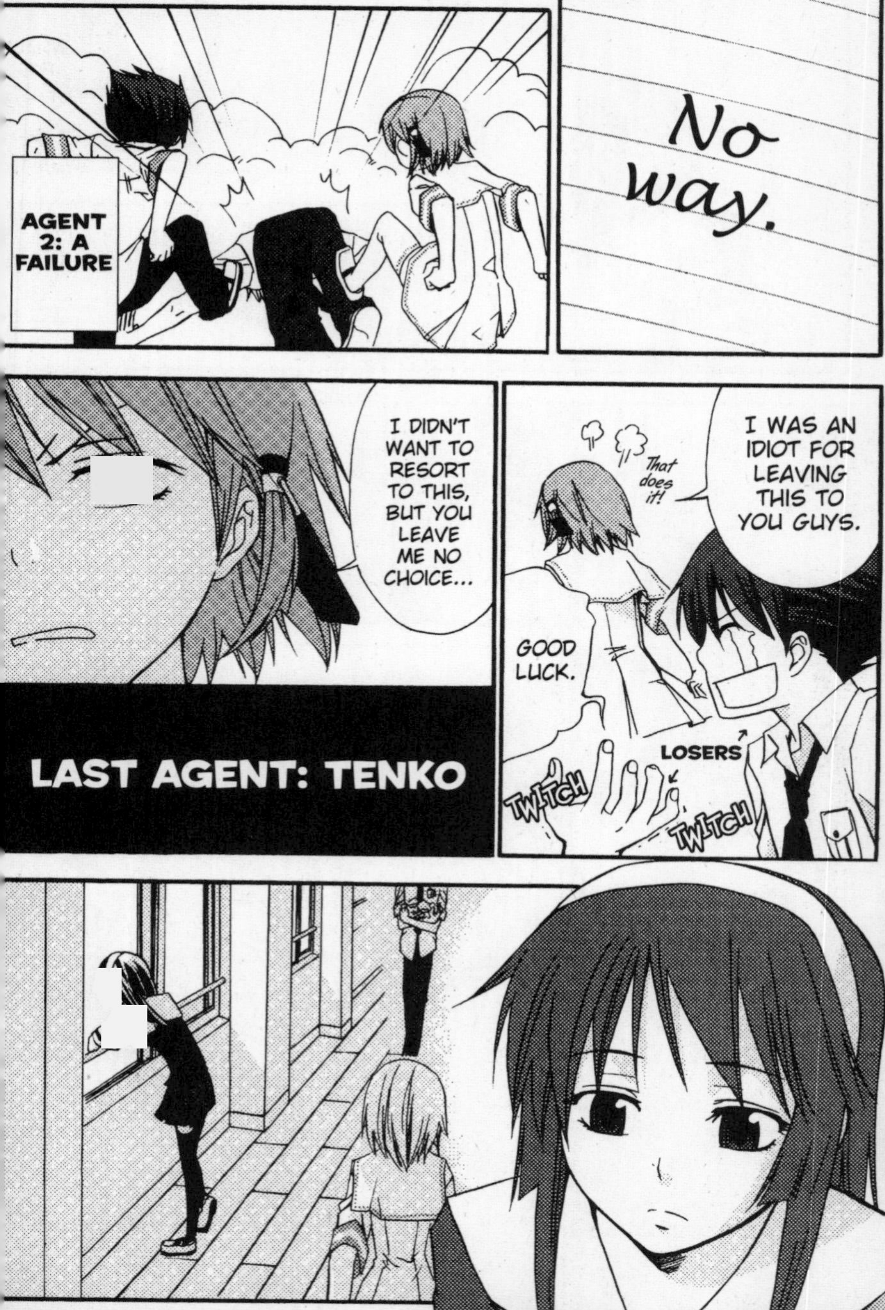
No way.
AGENT 2: A FAILURE
I WAS AN IDIOT FOR LEAVING THIS TO YOU GUYS.
That does it!
GOOD LUCK.
LOSERS
TWITCH
TWITCH
I DIDN'T WANT TO RESORT TO THIS, BUT YOU LEAVE ME NO CHOICE...
LAST AGENT: TENKO

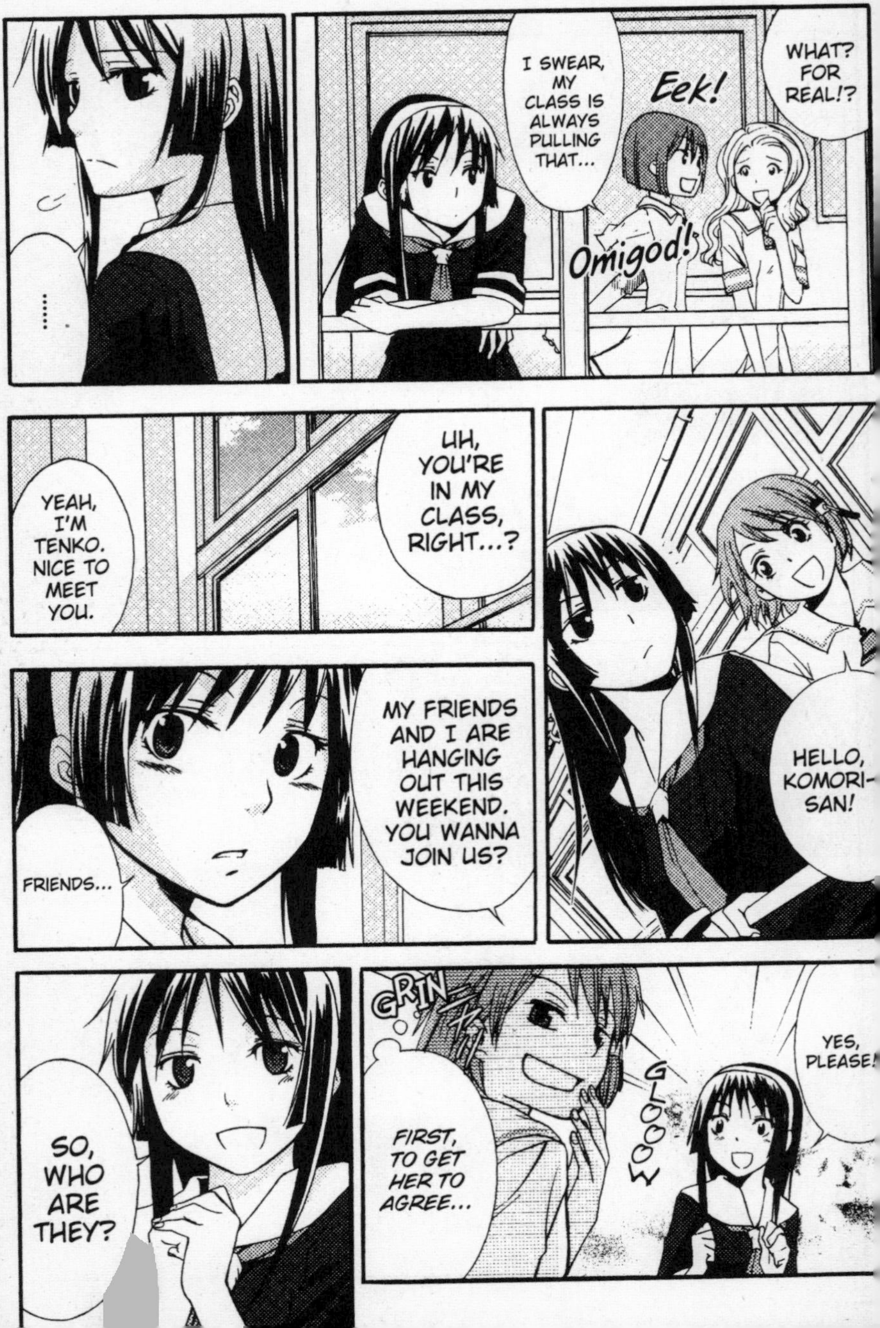
WHAT? FOR REAL!?
Eek!
I SWEAR, MY CLASS IS ALWAYS PULLING THAT...
Omigod!
......
HELLO, KOMORI-SAN!
UH, YOU'RE IN MY CLASS, RIGHT...?
YEAH, I'M TENKO. NICE TO MEET YOU.
MY FRIENDS AND I ARE HANGING OUT THIS WEEKEND. YOU WANNA JOIN US?
FRIENDS...
YES, PLEASE!
GLOOOOW
GRIN
FIRST, TO GET HER TO AGREE...
SO, WHO ARE THEY?

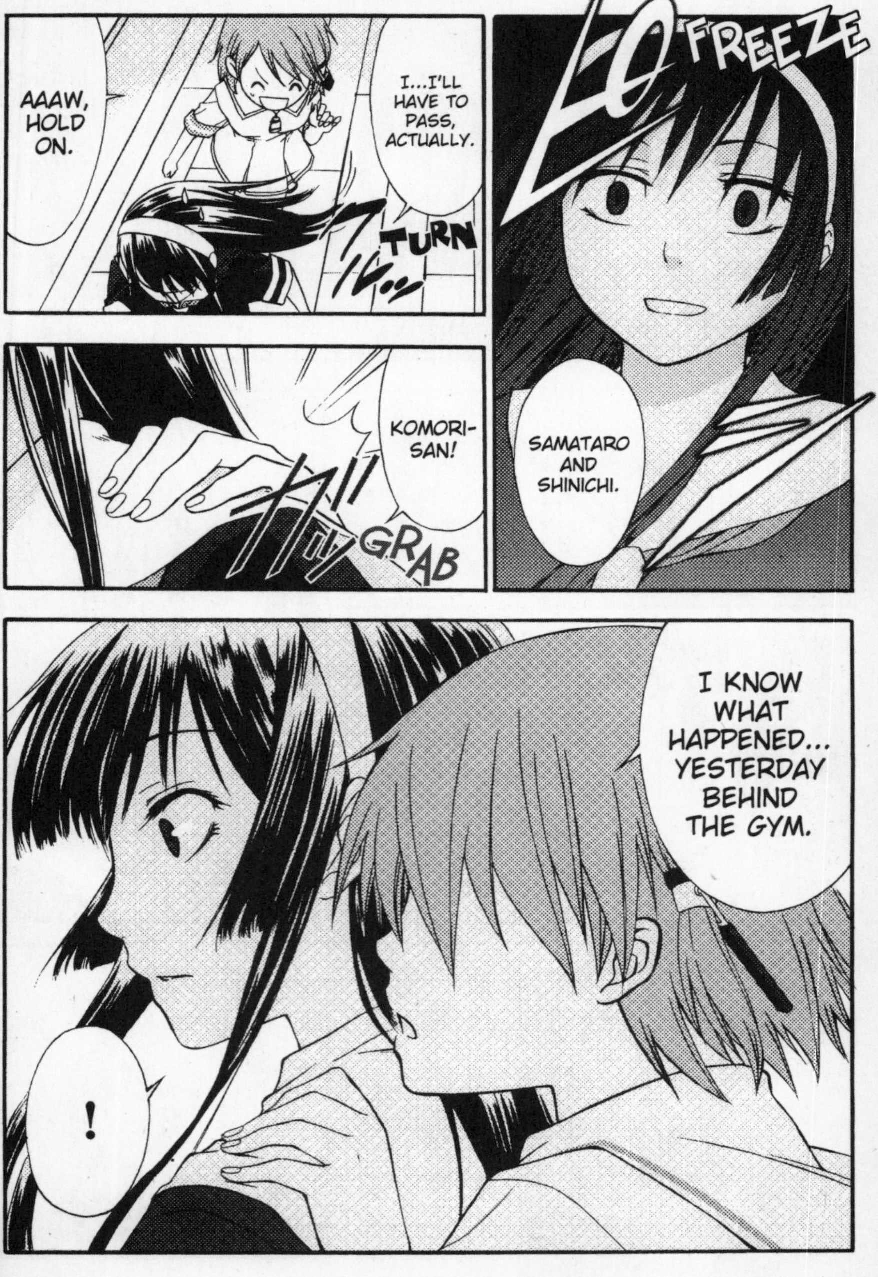
FREEZE
SAMATARO AND SHINICHI.
I...I'LL HAVE TO PASS, ACTUALLY.
AAAW, HOLD ON.
TURN
KOMORI-SAN!
GRAB
I KNOW WHAT HAPPENED... YESTERDAY BEHIND THE GYM.
!

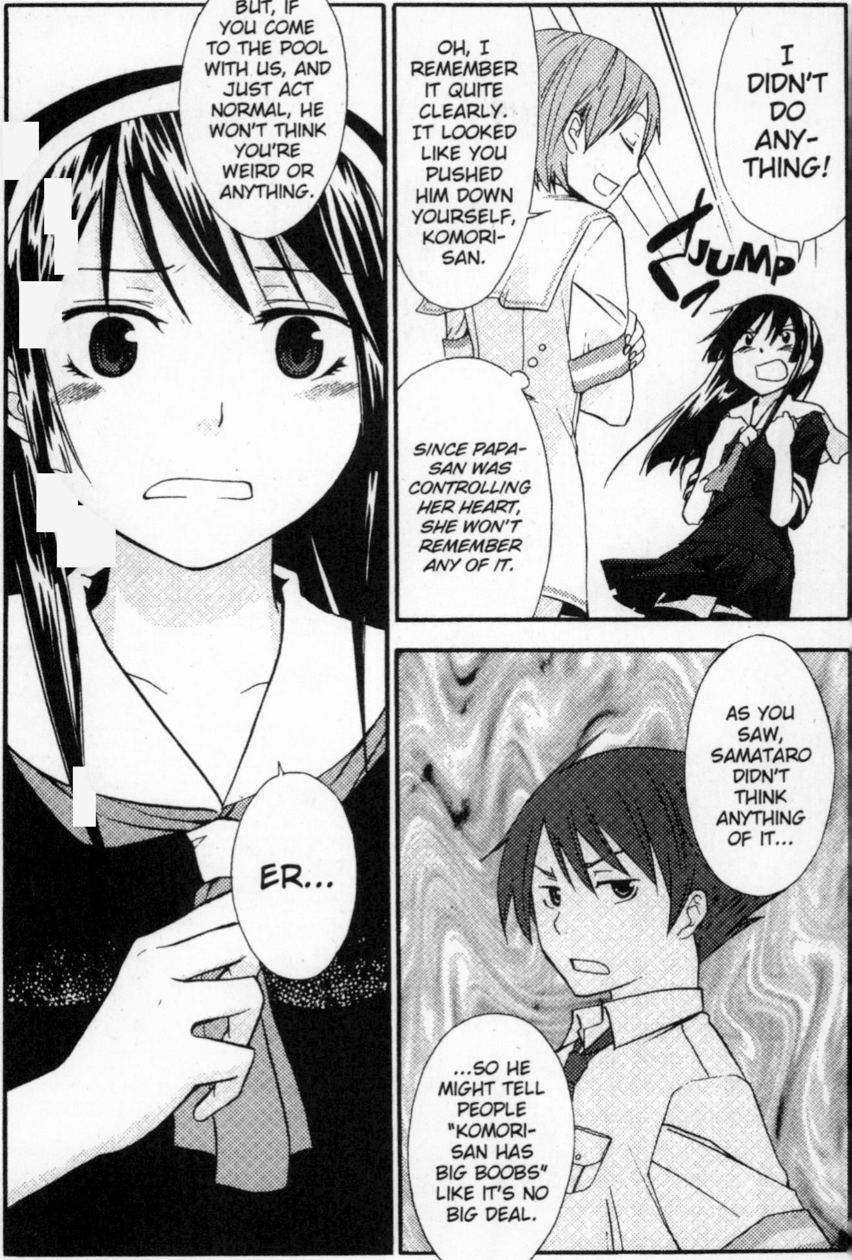
I DIDN'T DO ANY-THING!
JUMP
OH, I REMEMBER IT QUITE CLEARLY. IT LOOKED LIKE YOU PUSHED HIM DOWN YOURSELF, KOMORI-SAN.
SINCE PAPA-SAN WAS CONTROLLING HER HEART, SHE WON'T REMEMBER ANY OF IT.
AS YOU SAW, SAMATARO DIDN'T THINK ANYTHING OF IT...
...SO HE MIGHT TELL PEOPLE "KOMORI-SAN HAS BIG BOOBS" LIKE IT'S NO BIG DEAL.
BUT, IF YOU COME TO THE POOL WITH US, AND JUST ACT NORMAL, HE WON'T THINK YOU'RE WEIRD OR ANYTHING.
ER...

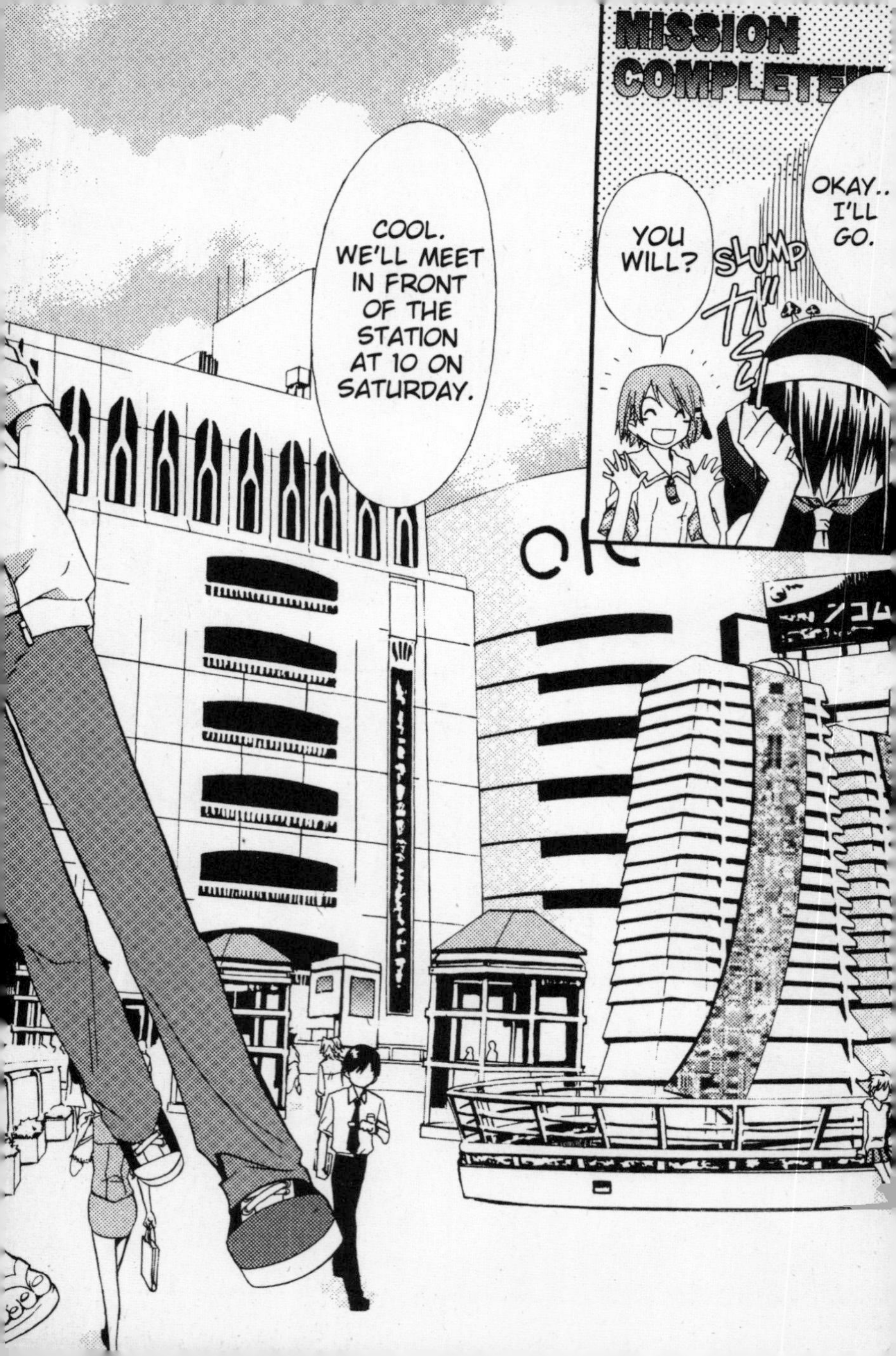
MISSION COMPLETE
OKAY.. I'LL GO.
SLUMP
YOU WILL?
COOL. WE'LL MEET IN FRONT OF THE STATION AT 10 ON SATURDAY.

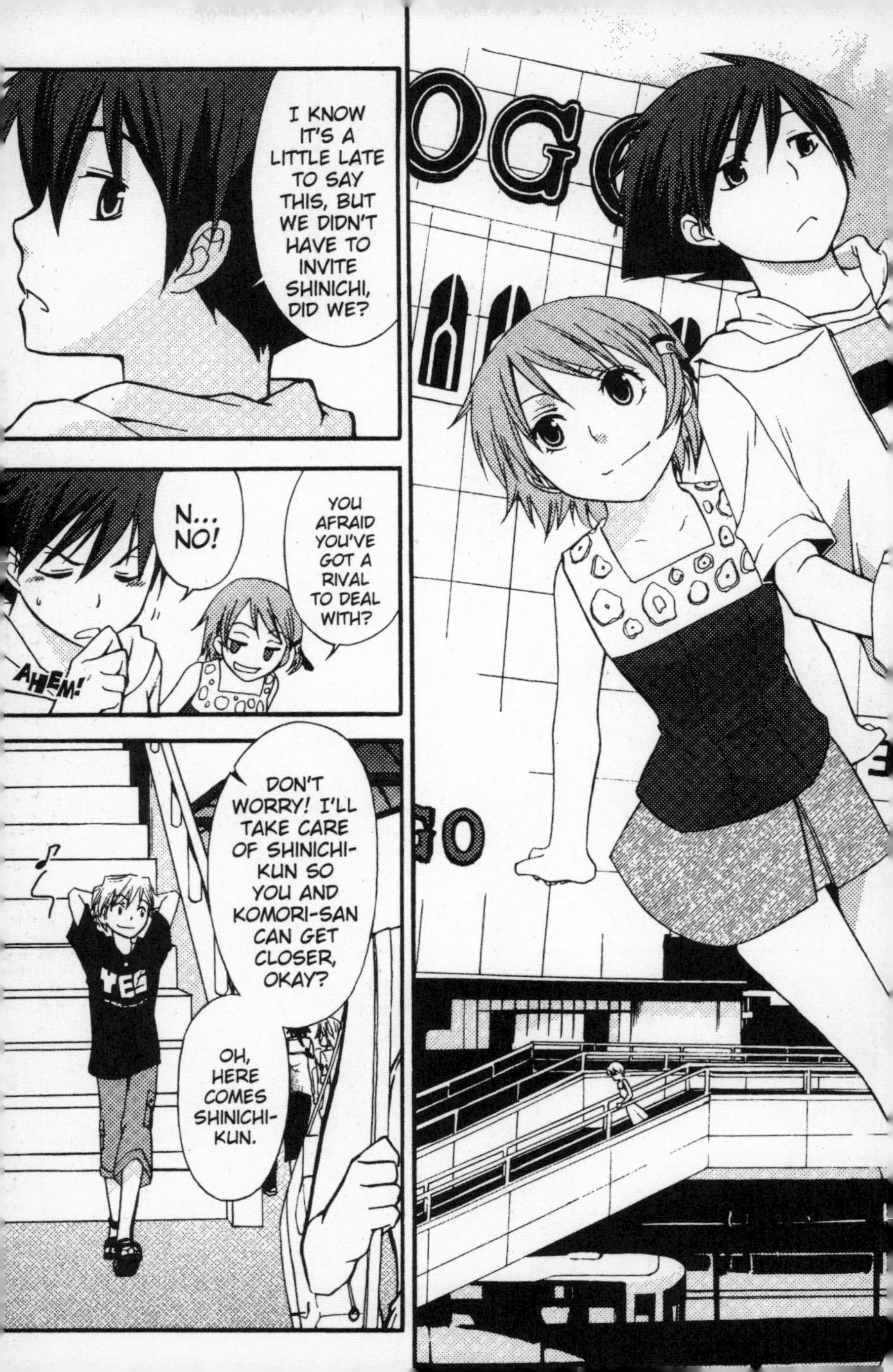
I KNOW IT'S A LITTLE LATE TO SAY THIS, BUT WE DIDN'T HAVE TO INVITE SHINICHI, DID WE?
YOU AFRAID YOU'VE GOT A RIVAL TO DEAL WITH?
N... NO!
AHEM!
DON'T WORRY! I'LL TAKE CARE OF SHINICHI-KUN SO YOU AND KOMORI-SAN CAN GET CLOSER, OKAY?
OH, HERE COMES SHINICHI-KUN.

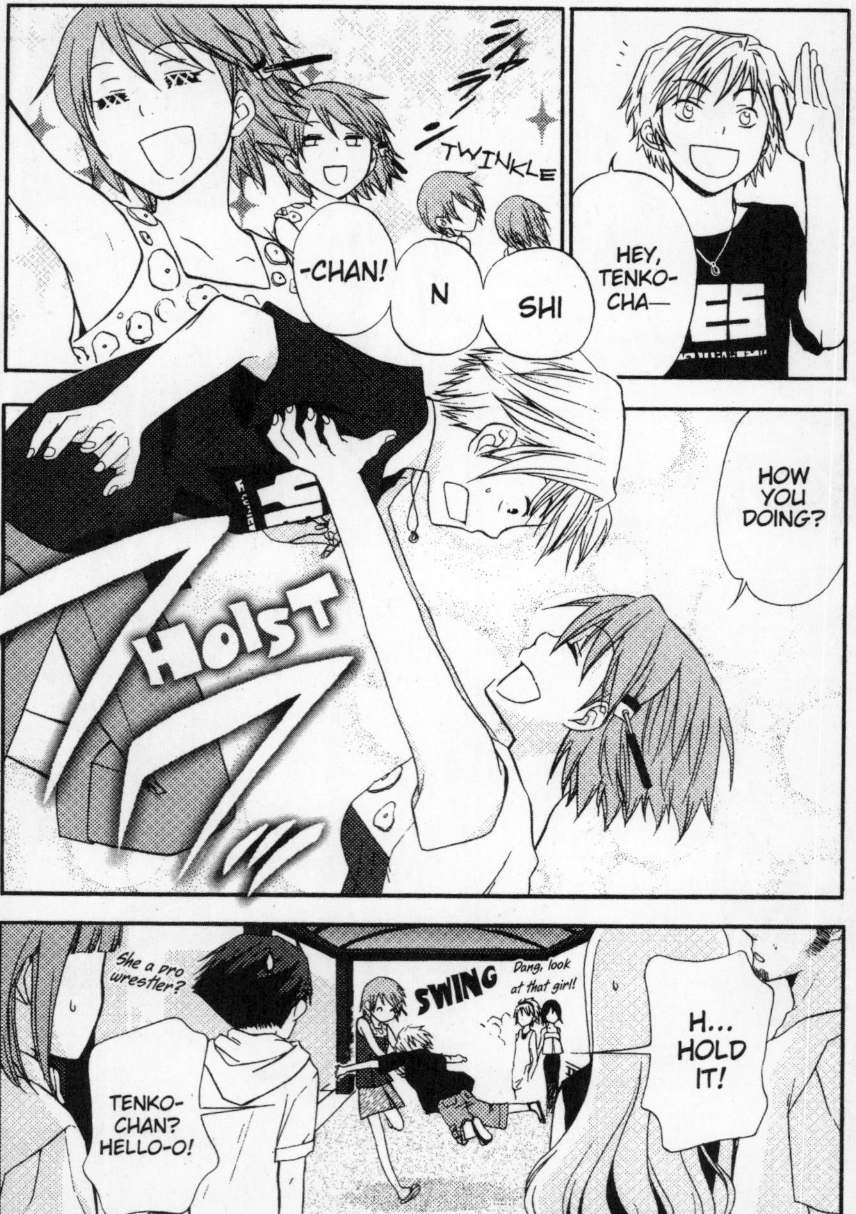
HEY, TENKO-CHA—
SHI
N
-CHAN!
TWINKLE
HOW YOU DOING?
HOIST
H... HOLD IT!
Dang, look at that girl!
SWING
She a pro wrestler?
TENKO-CHAN? HELLO-O!

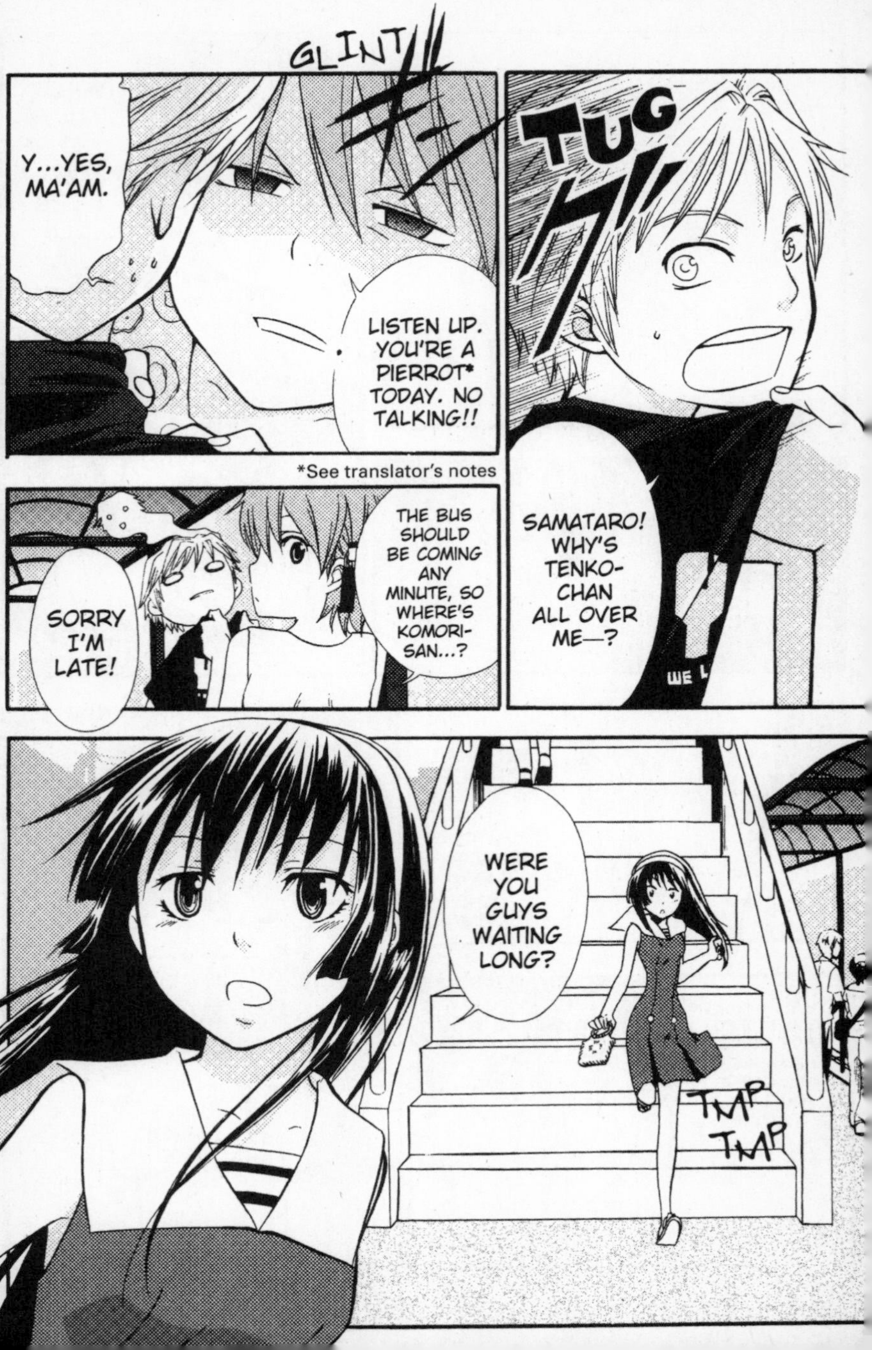
TUG
SAMATARO! WHY'S TENKO-CHAN ALL OVER ME—?
GLINT
LISTEN UP. YOU'RE A PIERROT* TODAY. NO TALKING!!
Y...YES, MA'AM.
*See translator's notes
THE BUS SHOULD BE COMING ANY MINUTE, SO WHERE'S KOMORI-SAN...?
SORRY I'M LATE!
WERE YOU GUYS WAITING LONG?
TMP TMP

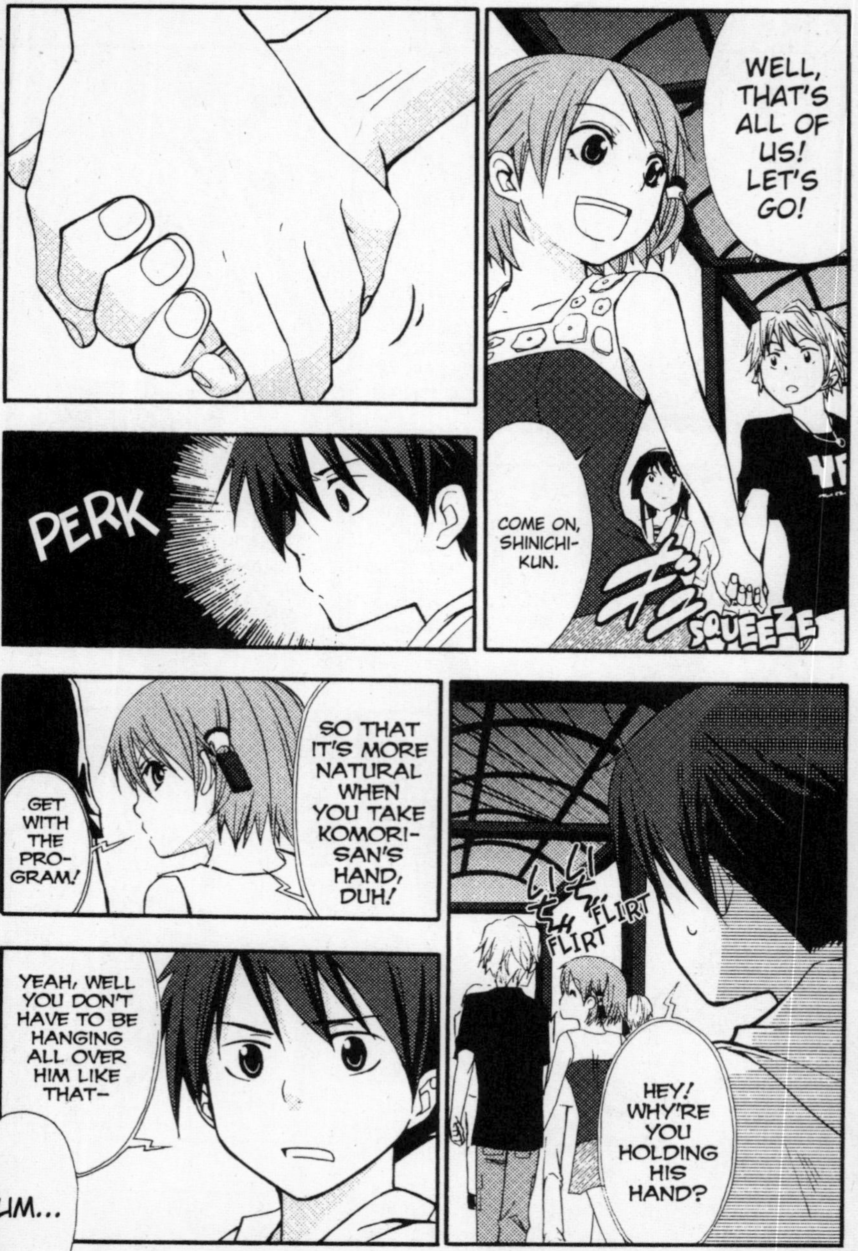
WELL, THAT'S ALL OF US! LET'S GO!
COME ON, SHINICHI-KUN.
SQUEEZE
PERK
FLIRT FLIRT
HEY! WHY'RE YOU HOLDING HIS HAND?
SO THAT IT'S MORE NATURAL WHEN YOU TAKE KOMORI-SAN'S HAND, DUH!
GET WITH THE PRO-GRAM!
YEAH, WELL YOU DON'T HAVE TO BE HANGING ALL OVER HIM LIKE THAT–
UM...

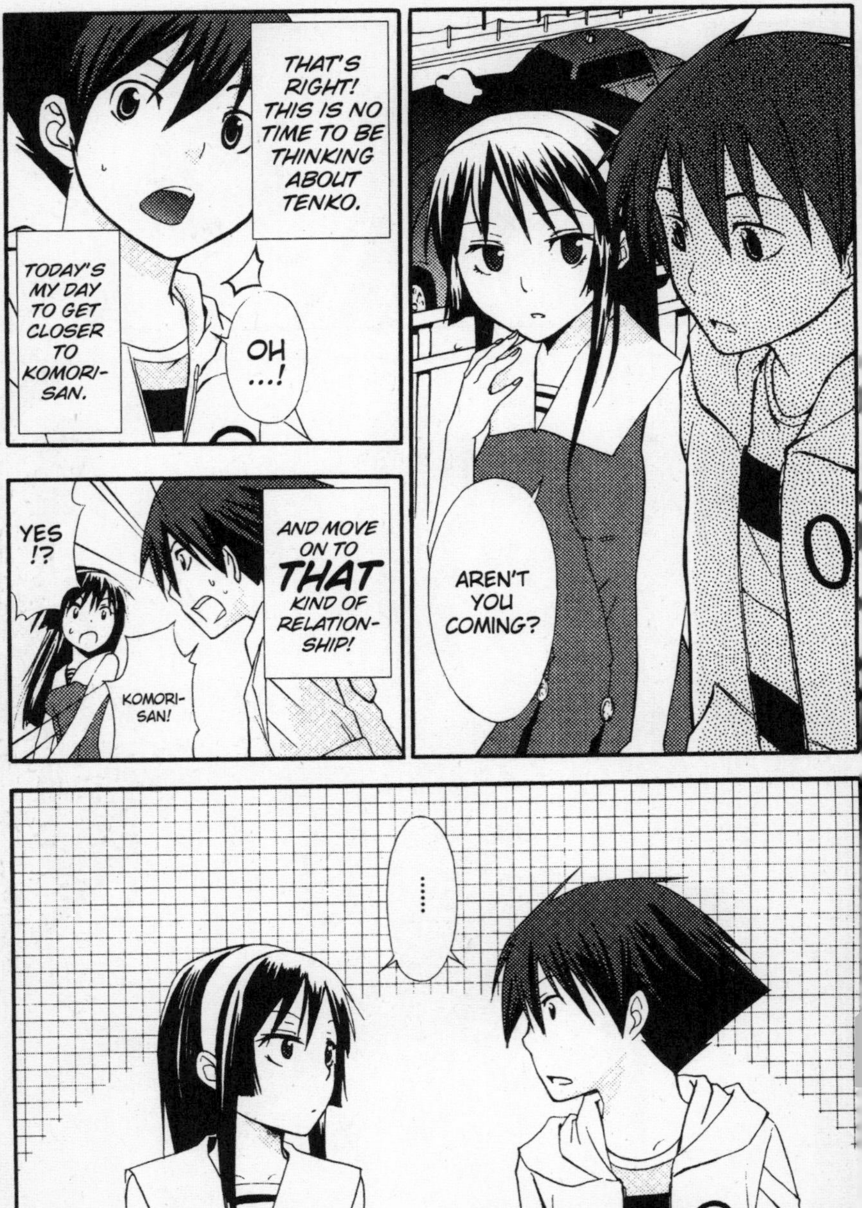
AREN'T YOU COMING?
OH ...!
THAT'S RIGHT! THIS IS NO TIME TO BE THINKING ABOUT TENKO.
TODAY'S MY DAY TO GET CLOSER TO KOMORI-SAN.
AND MOVE ON TO THAT KIND OF RELATIONSHIP!
YES !?
KOMORI-SAN!
......

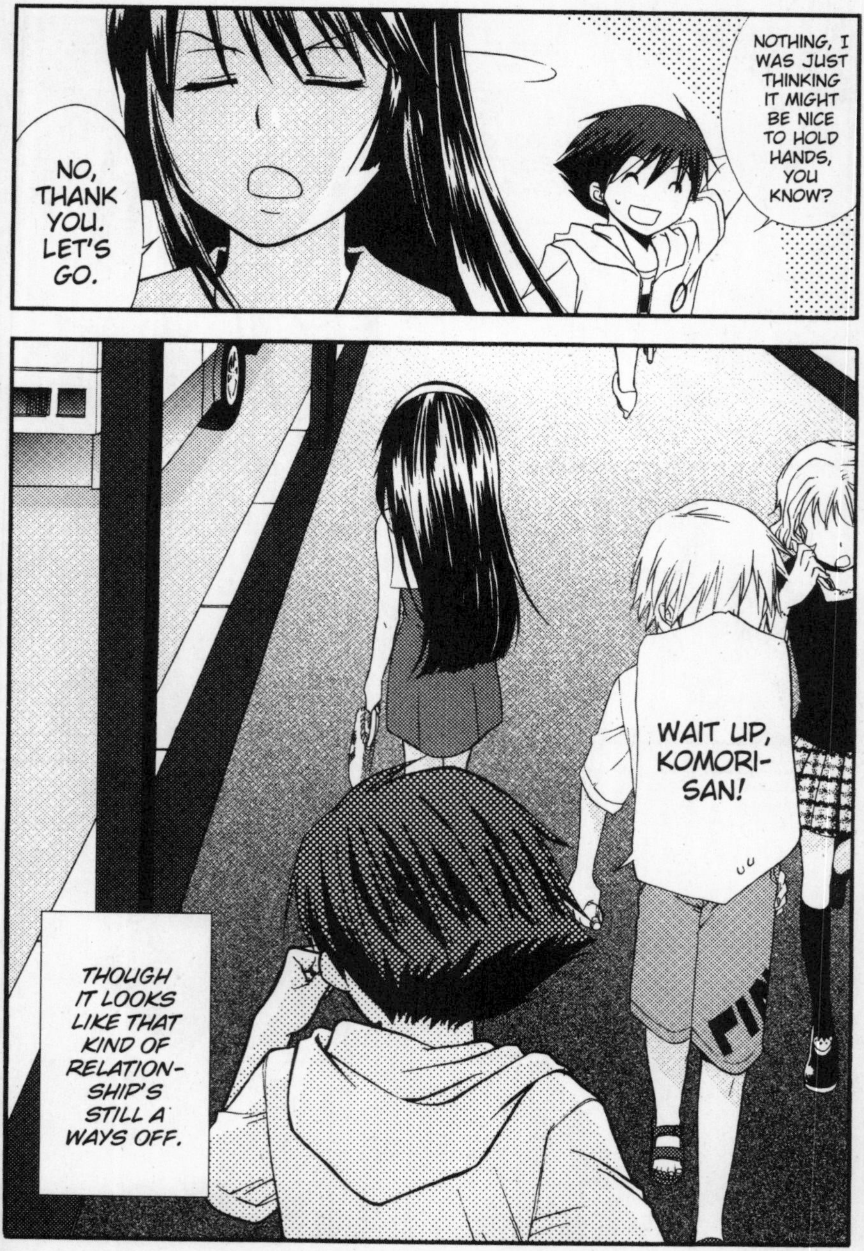
NOTHING, I WAS JUST THINKING IT MIGHT BE NICE TO HOLD HANDS, YOU KNOW?
NO, THANK YOU. LET'S GO.
WAIT UP, KOMORI-SAN!
THOUGH IT LOOKS LIKE THAT KIND OF RELATION-SHIP'S STILL A WAYS OFF.

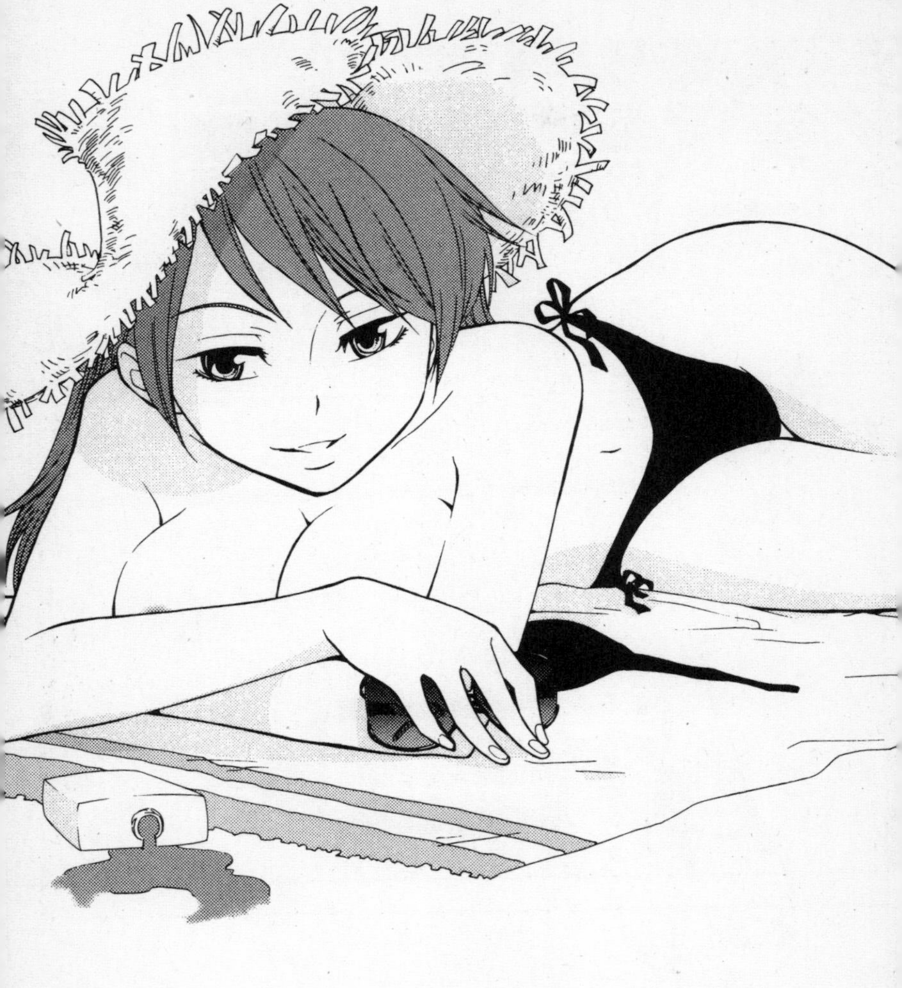

When a Goddess Blows her Breath

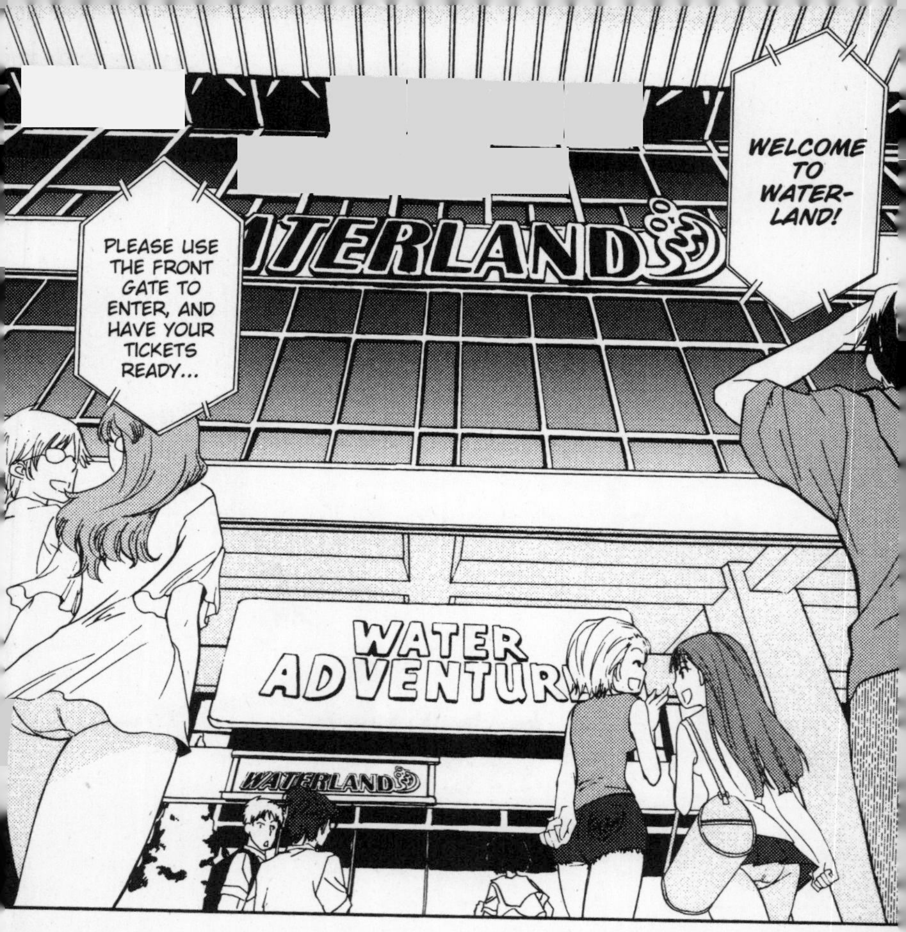
WELCOME TO WATER-LAND!
PLEASE USE THE FRONT GATE TO ENTER, AND HAVE YOUR TICKETS READY...
WATER ADVENTUR
WATERLAND

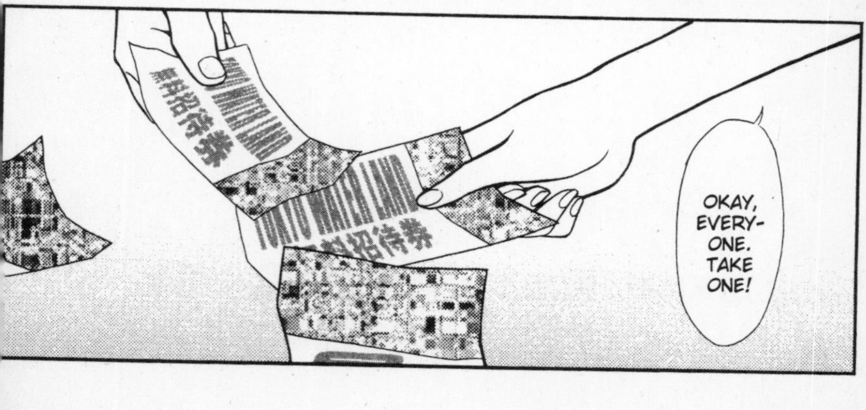
TOKYO WATER LAND
無料招待券
OKAY, EVERY-ONE. TAKE ONE!

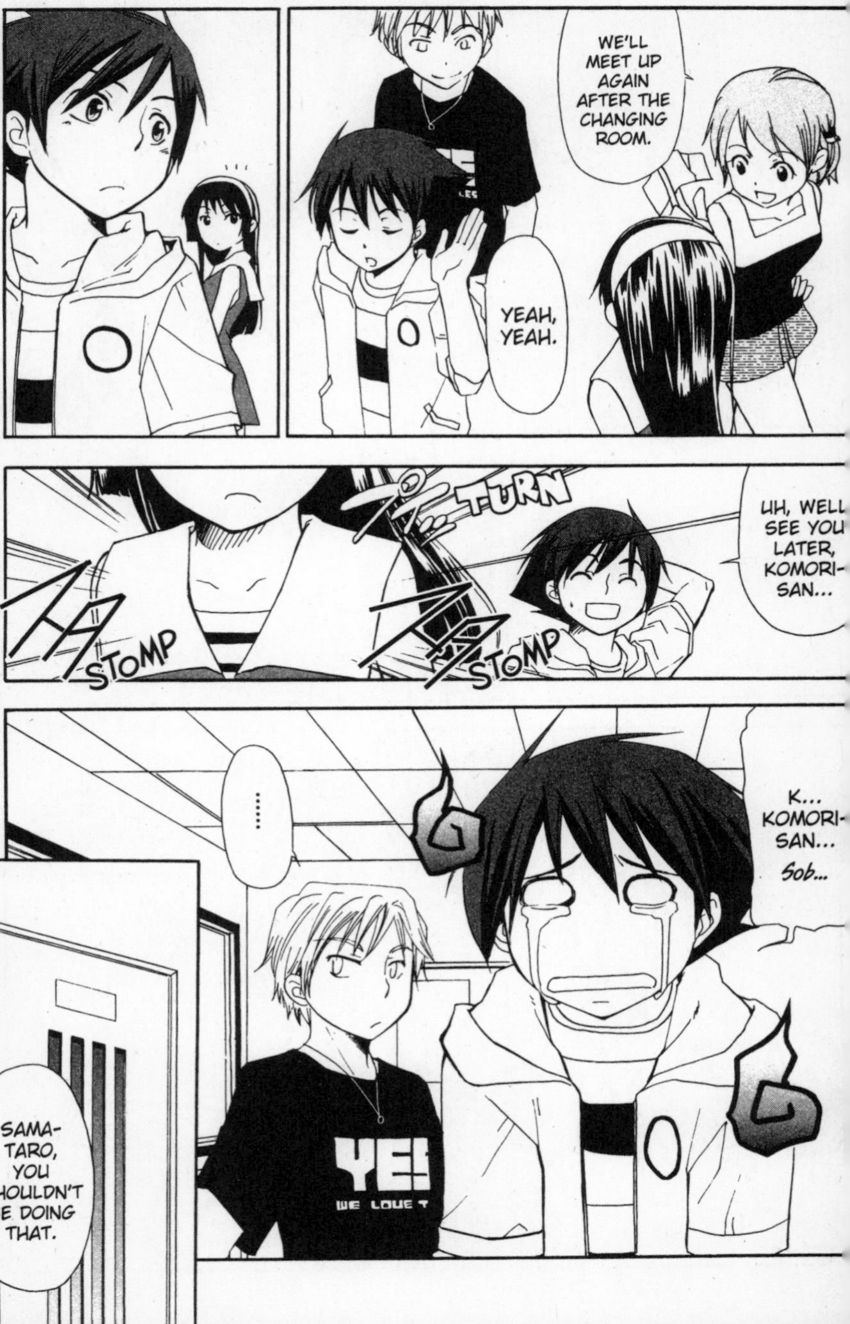
WE'LL MEET UP AGAIN AFTER THE CHANGING ROOM.
YEAH, YEAH.
UH, WELL SEE YOU LATER, KOMORI-SAN...
TURN
STOMP
STOMP
K... KOMORI-SAN...
Sob...
......
SAMATARO, YOU SHOULDN'T BE DOING THAT.

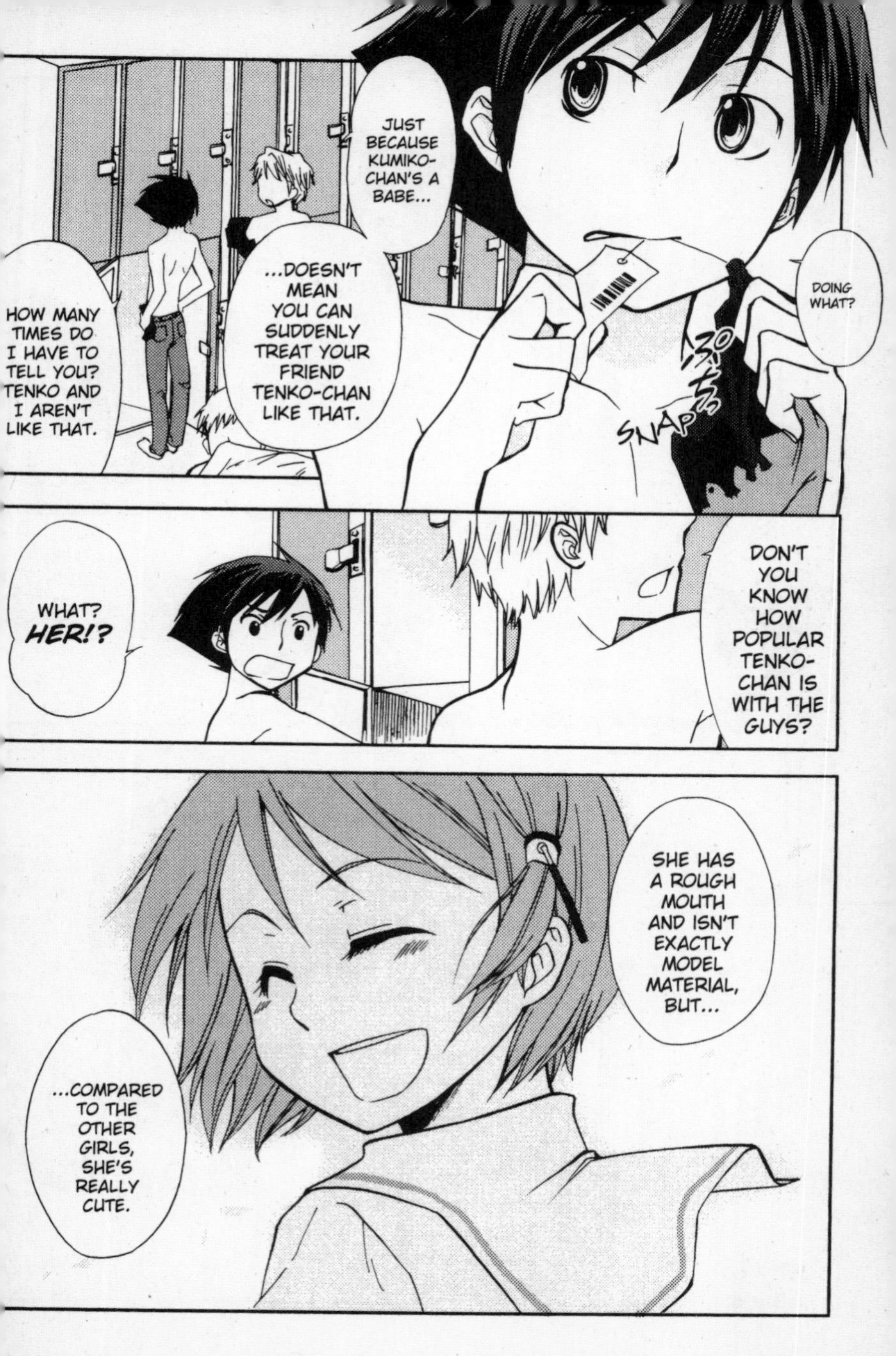
JUST BECAUSE KUMIKO-CHAN'S A BABE...
...DOESN'T MEAN YOU CAN SUDDENLY TREAT YOUR FRIEND TENKO-CHAN LIKE THAT.
DOING WHAT?
SNAP
HOW MANY TIMES DO I HAVE TO TELL YOU? TENKO AND I AREN'T LIKE THAT.
DON'T YOU KNOW HOW POPULAR TENKO-CHAN IS WITH THE GUYS?
WHAT? ***HER!?***
SHE HAS A ROUGH MOUTH AND ISN'T EXACTLY MODEL MATERIAL, BUT...
...COMPARED TO THE OTHER GIRLS, SHE'S REALLY CUTE.

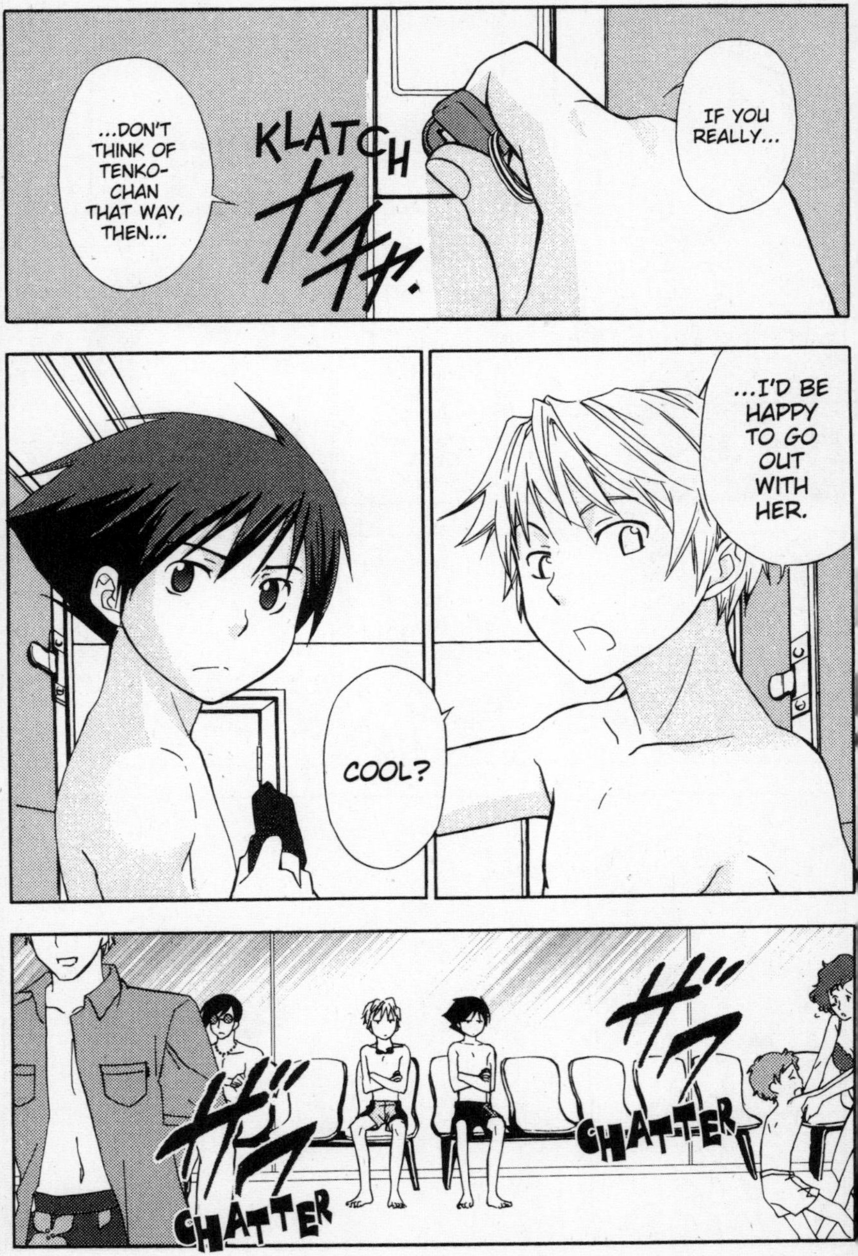
IF YOU REALLY...
KLATCH
カチャ.
...DON'T THINK OF TENKO-CHAN THAT WAY, THEN...
...I'D BE HAPPY TO GO OUT WITH HER.
COOL?
ザワ
CHATTER
ザワ
CHATTER

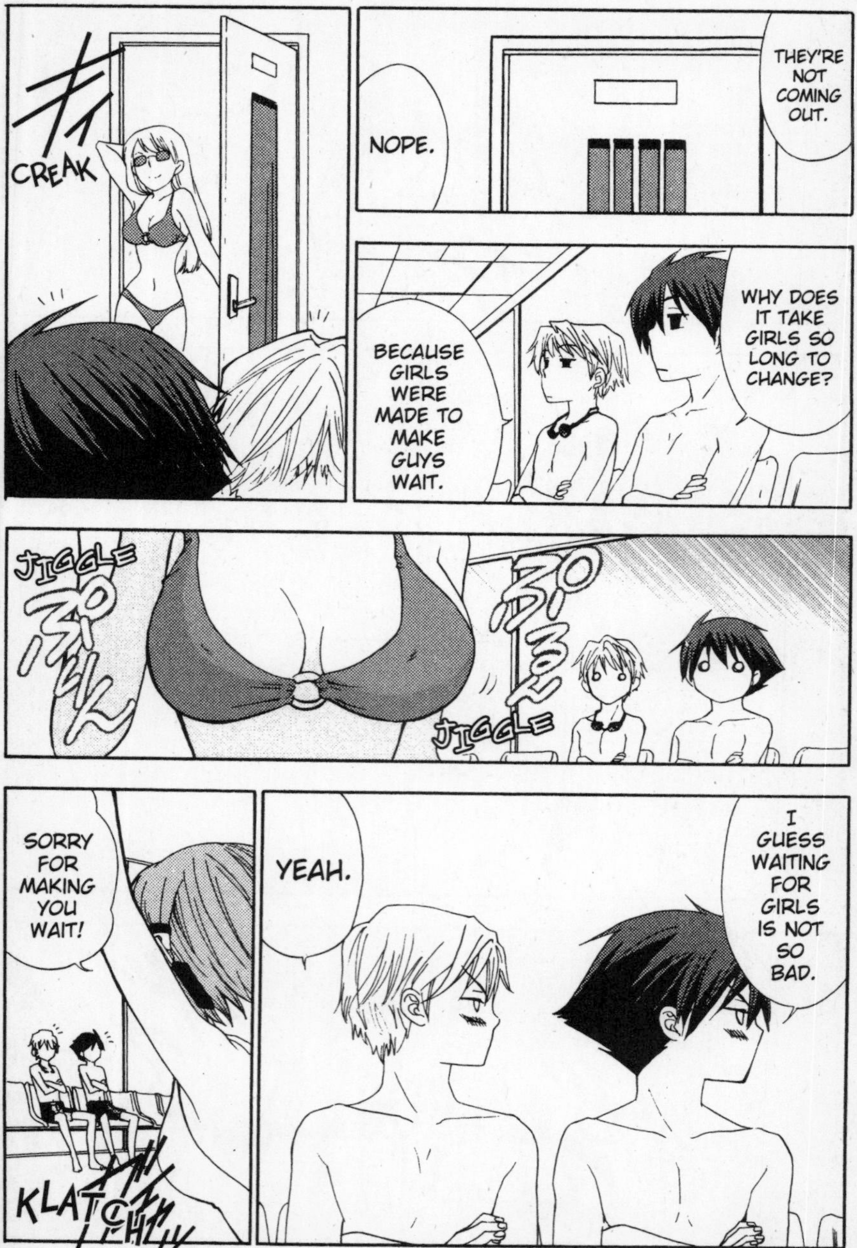
THEY'RE NOT COMING OUT.
NOPE.
WHY DOES IT TAKE GIRLS SO LONG TO CHANGE?
BECAUSE GIRLS WERE MADE TO MAKE GUYS WAIT.
CREAK
JIGGLE
JIGGLE
I GUESS WAITING FOR GIRLS IS NOT SO BAD.
YEAH.
SORRY FOR MAKING YOU WAIT!
KLATCH

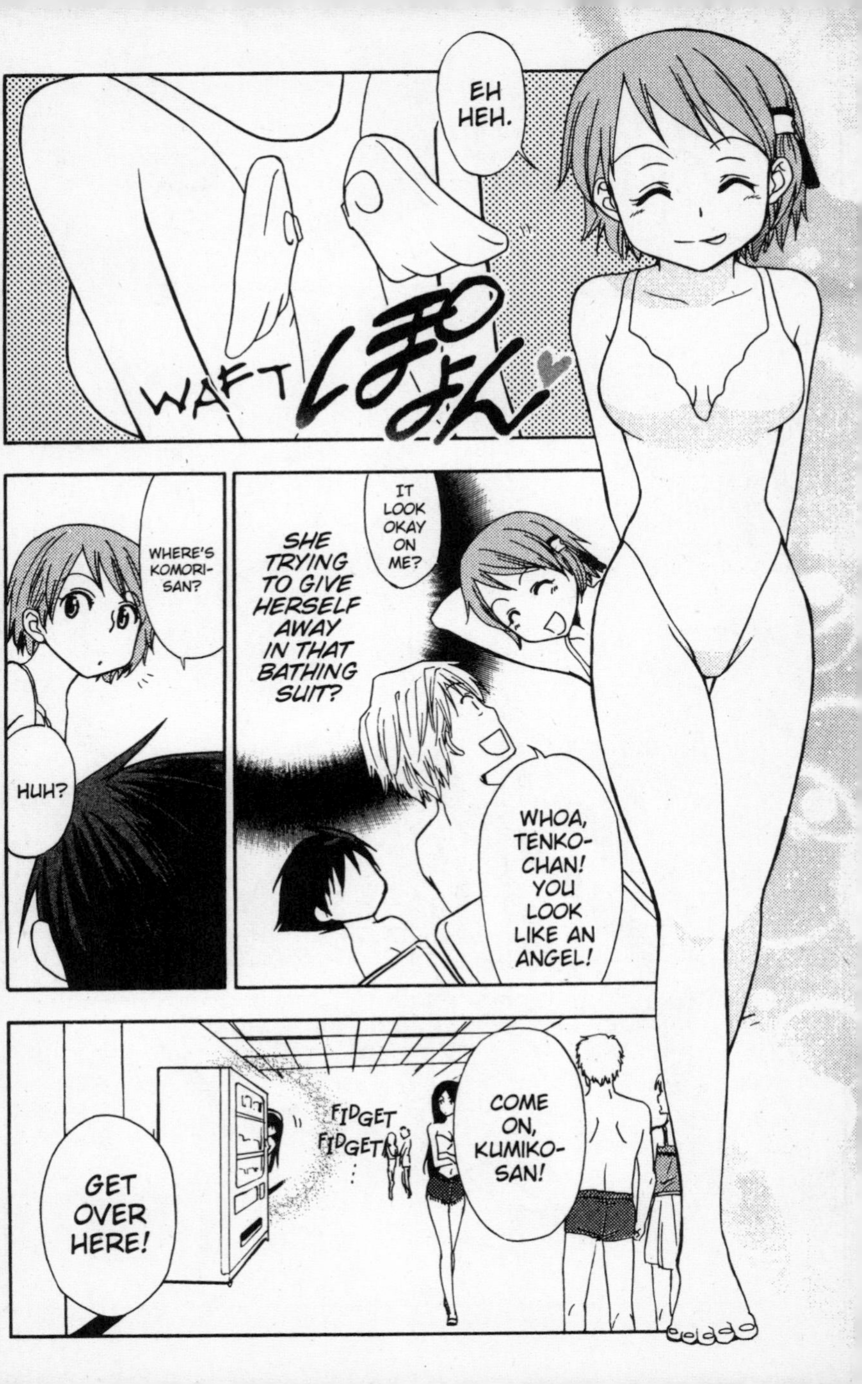

EH HEH.
WAFT
IT LOOK OKAY ON ME?
SHE TRYING TO GIVE HERSELF AWAY IN THAT BATHING SUIT?
WHOA, TENKO-CHAN! YOU LOOK LIKE AN ANGEL!
WHERE'S KOMORI-SAN?
HUH?
COME ON, KUMIKO-SAN!
FIDGET FIDGET
GET OVER HERE!

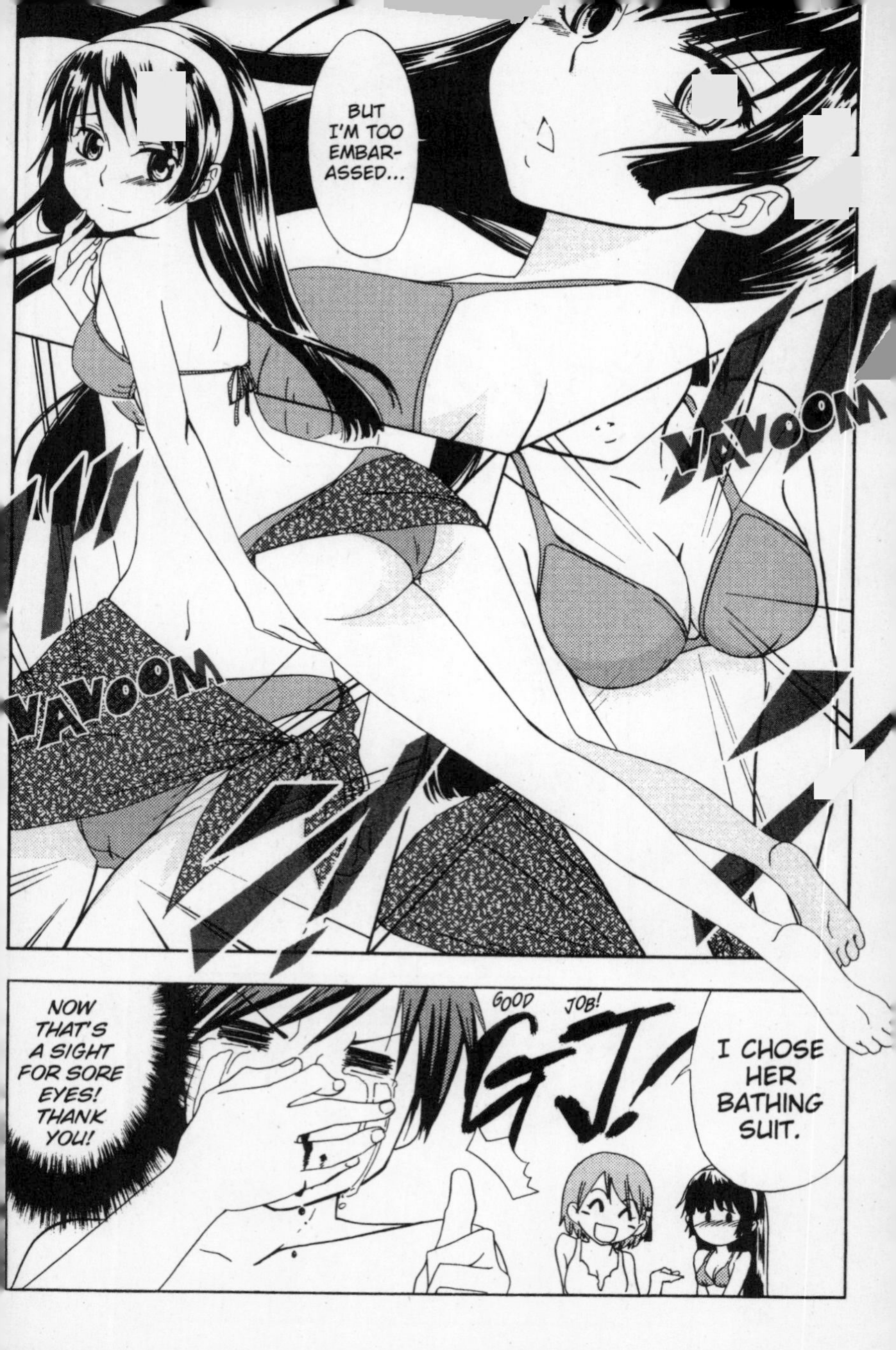
BUT I'M TOO EMBAR-ASSED...
VAVOOM
VAVOOM
I CHOSE HER BATHING SUIT.
GOOD JOB!
GJ!
NOW THAT'S A SIGHT FOR SORE EYES! THANK YOU!

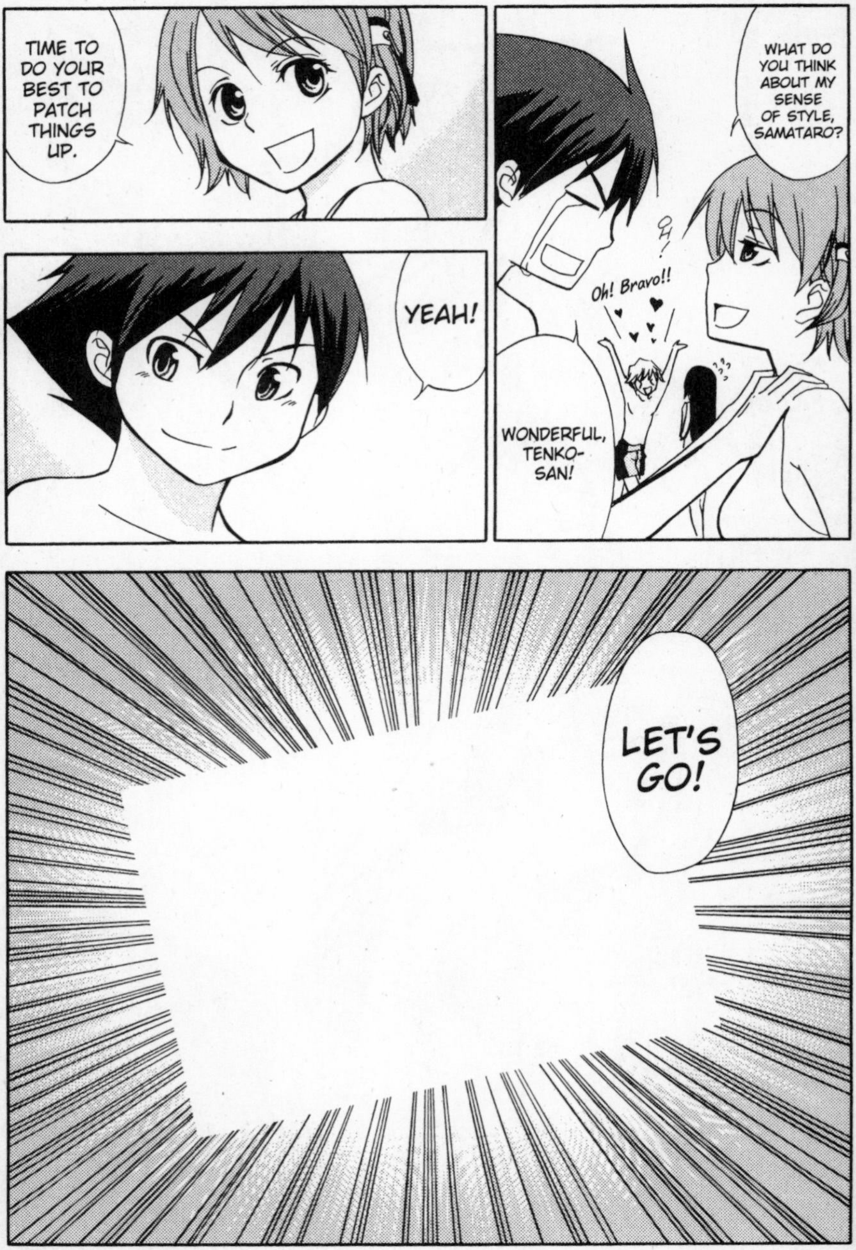
WHAT DO YOU THINK ABOUT MY SENSE OF STYLE, SAMATARO?
OH!
Oh! Bravo!!
WONDERFUL, TENKO-SAN!
TIME TO DO YOUR BEST TO PATCH THINGS UP.
YEAH!
LET'S GO!

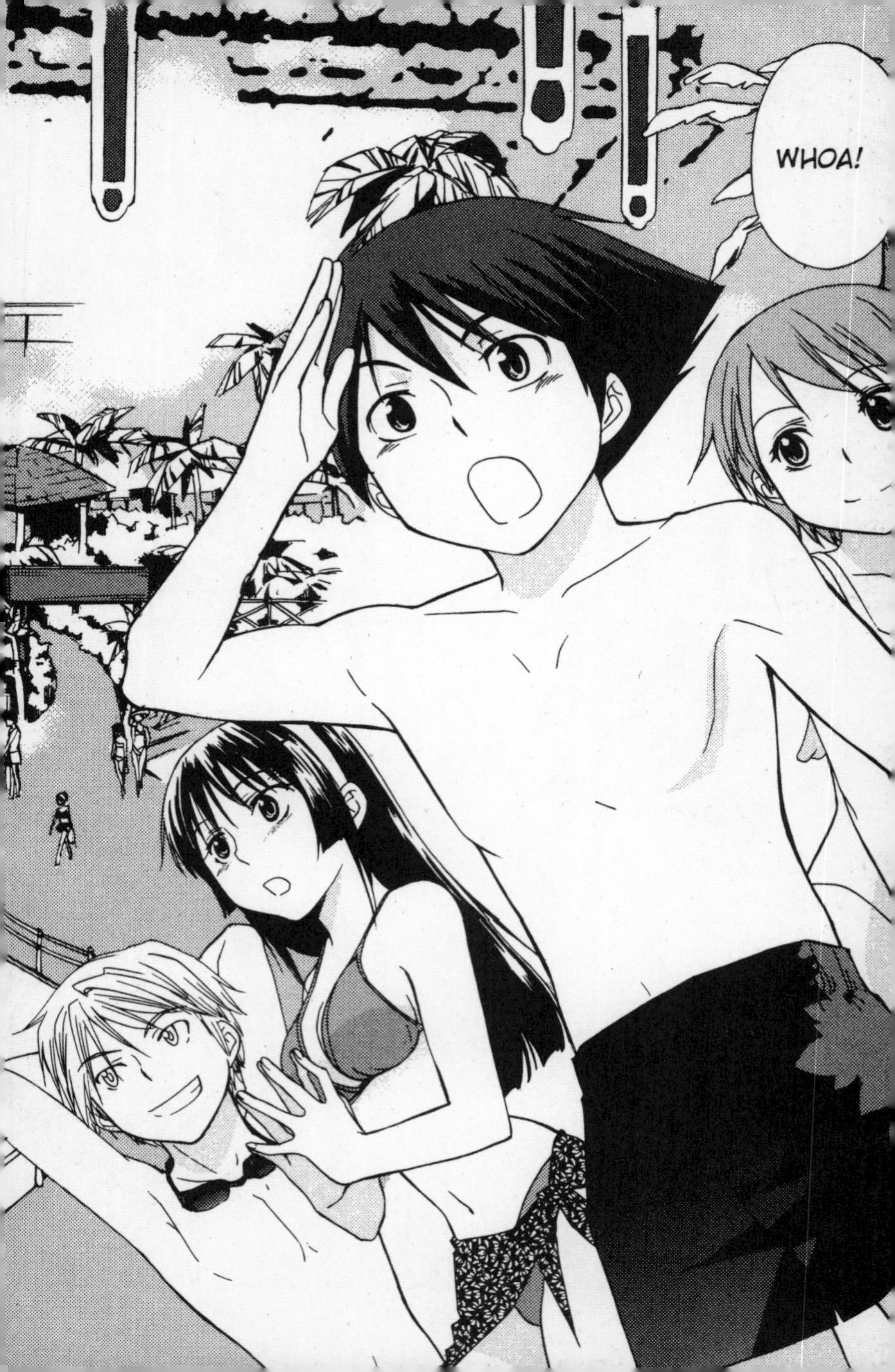
WHOA!

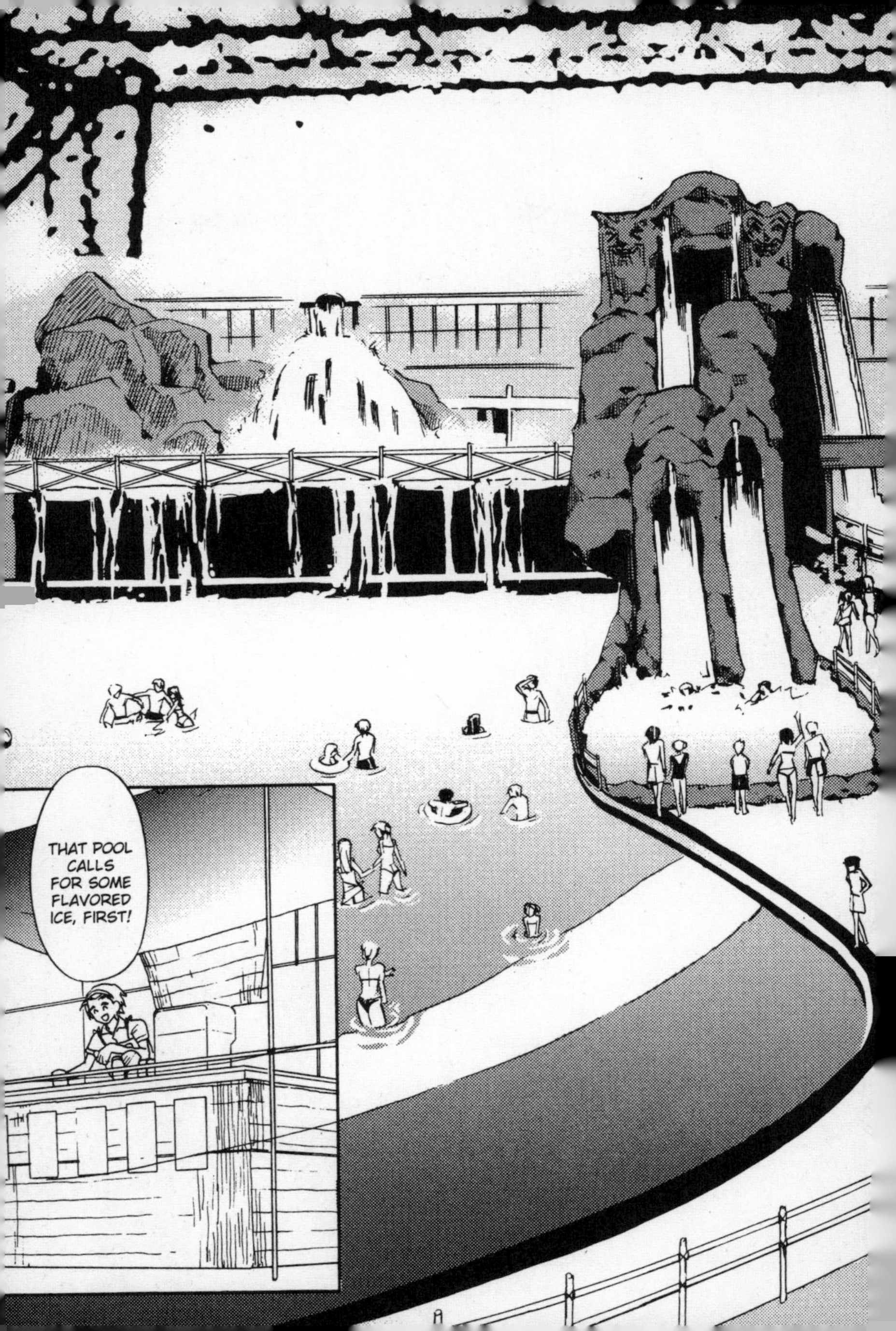
THAT POOL CALLS FOR SOME FLAVORED ICE, FIRST!

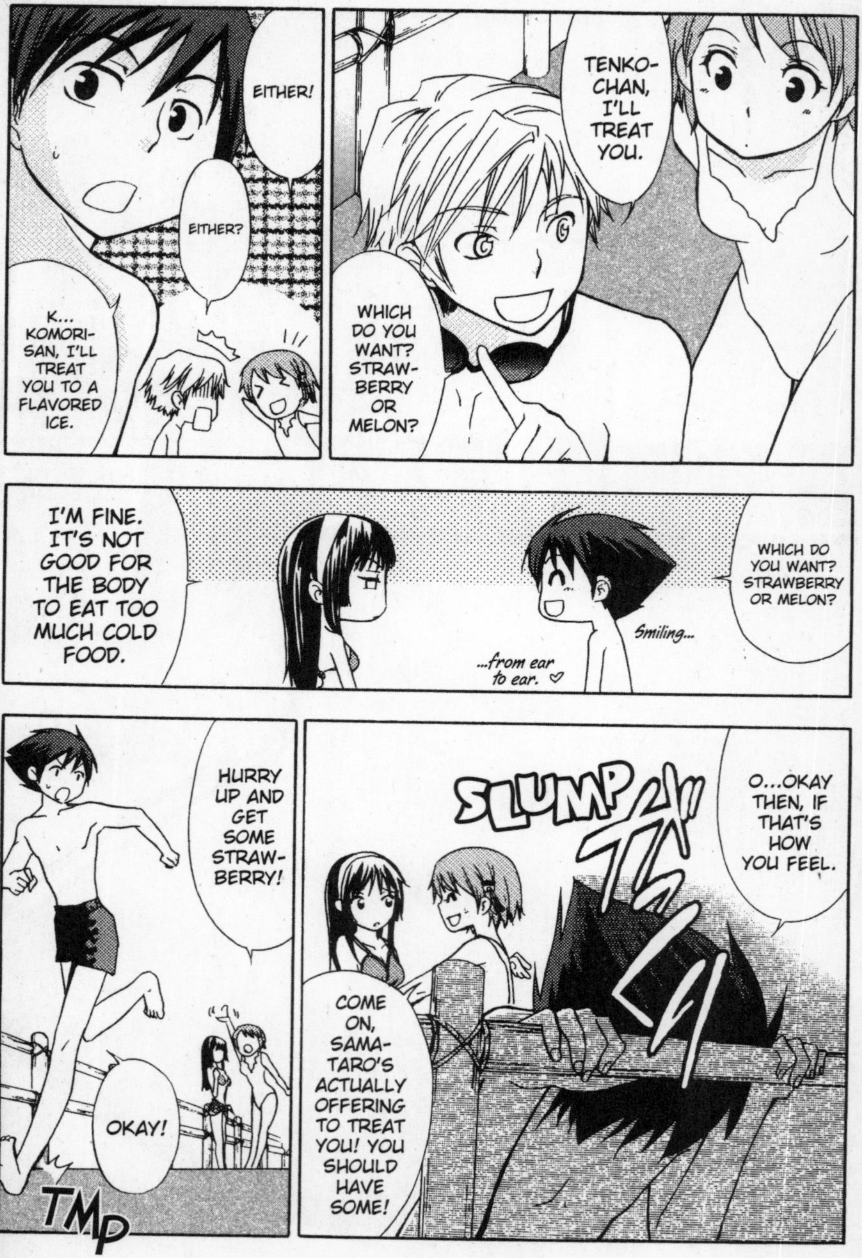
TENKO-CHAN, I'LL TREAT YOU.
WHICH DO YOU WANT? STRAWBERRY OR MELON?
EITHER!
EITHER?
K... KOMORI-SAN, I'LL TREAT YOU TO A FLAVORED ICE.
WHICH DO YOU WANT? STRAWBERRY OR MELON?
Smiling...
...from ear to ear.
I'M FINE. IT'S NOT GOOD FOR THE BODY TO EAT TOO MUCH COLD FOOD.
O...OKAY THEN, IF THAT'S HOW YOU FEEL.
SLUMP
COME ON, SAMATARO'S ACTUALLY OFFERING TO TREAT YOU! YOU SHOULD HAVE SOME!
HURRY UP AND GET SOME STRAWBERRY!
OKAY!
TMP

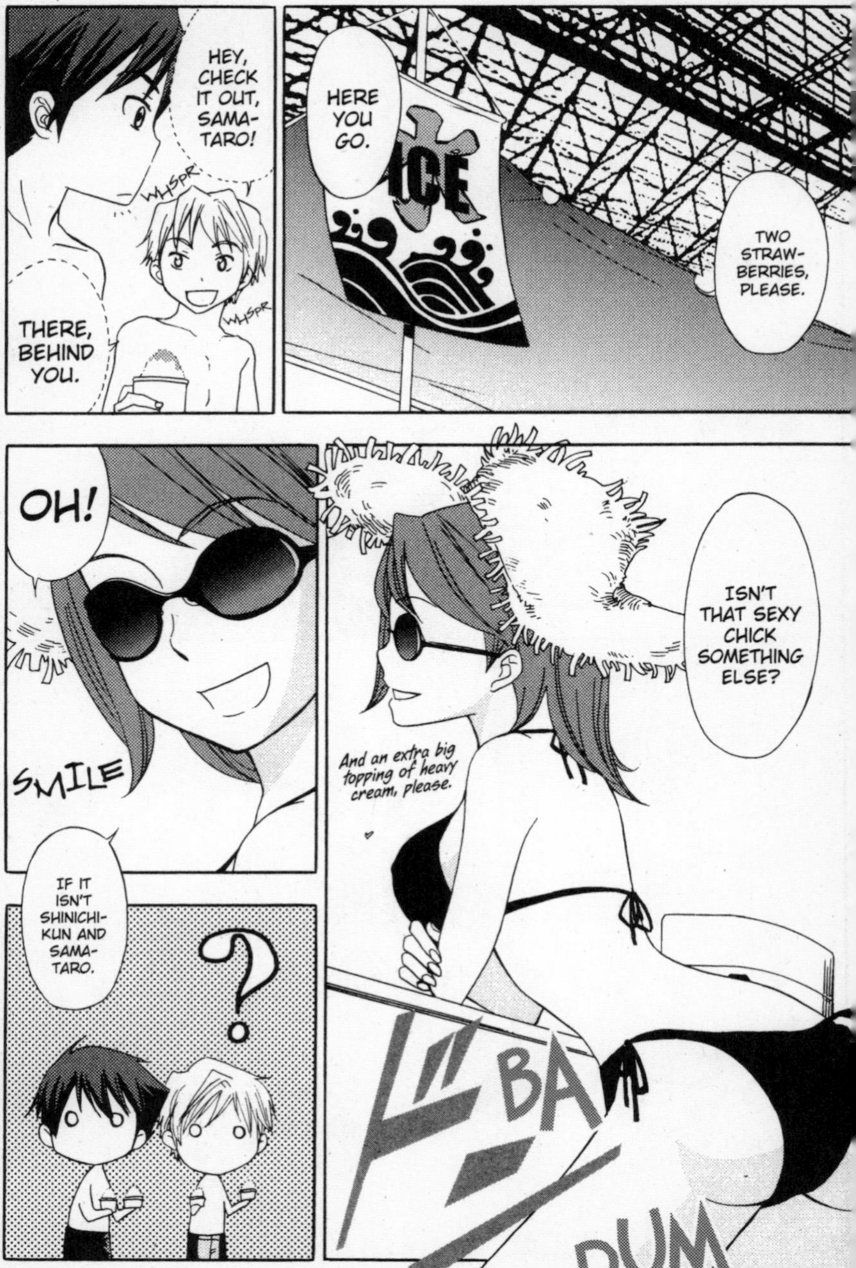
TWO STRAW-BERRIES, PLEASE.
HERE YOU GO.
ICE
HEY, CHECK IT OUT, SAMA-TARO!
WHSPR
THERE, BEHIND YOU.
WHSPR
ISN'T THAT SEXY CHICK SOMETHING ELSE?
And an extra big topping of heavy cream, please.
BA
DUM
OH!
SMILE
IF IT ISN'T SHINICHI-KUN AND SAMA-TARO.
?

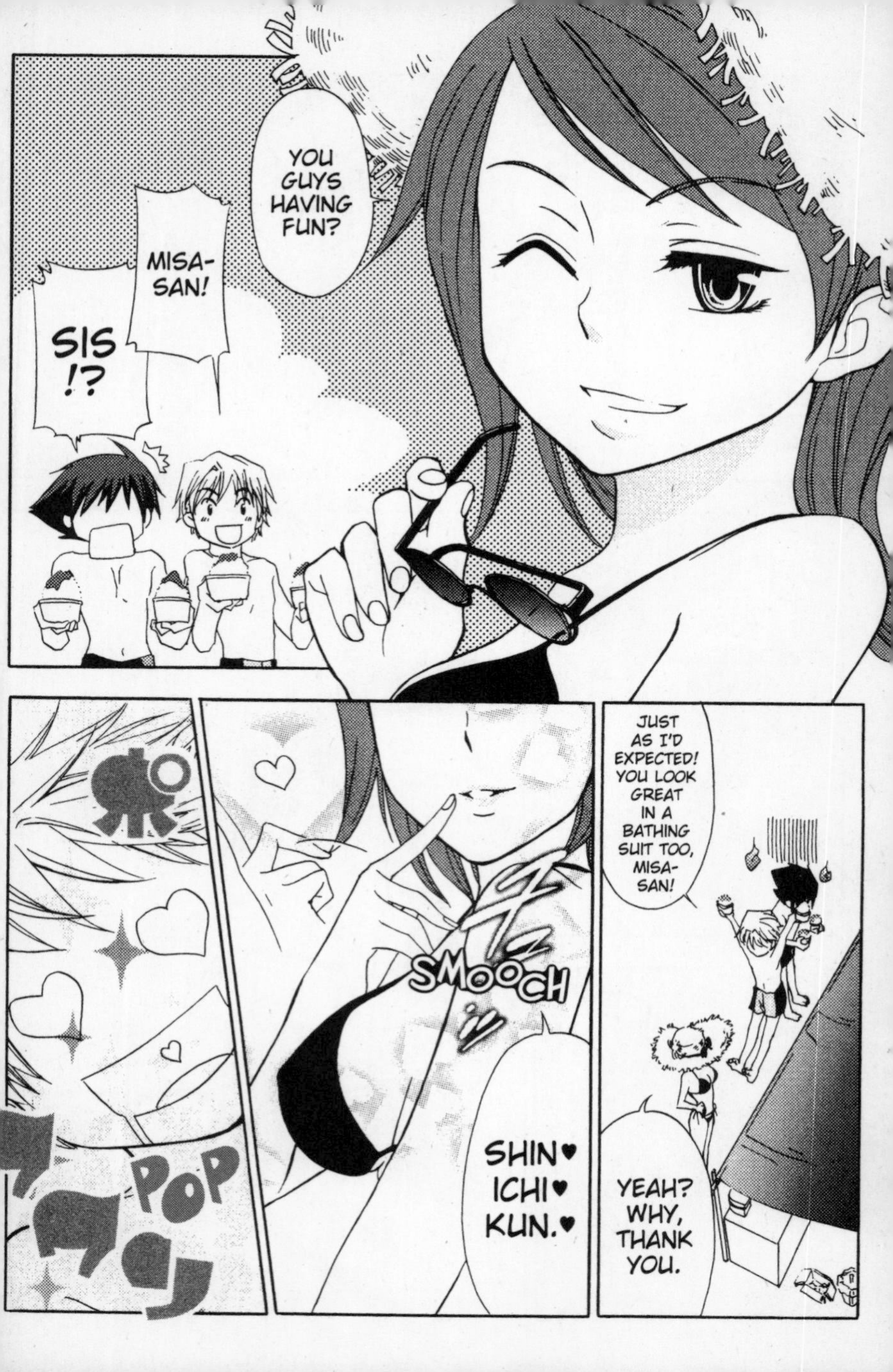
YOU GUYS HAVING FUN?
MISA-SAN!
SIS!?
JUST AS I'D EXPECTED! YOU LOOK GREAT IN A BATHING SUIT TOO, MISA-SAN!
YEAH? WHY, THANK YOU.
SMOOCH
SHIN♥ ICHI♥ KUN.♥
POP

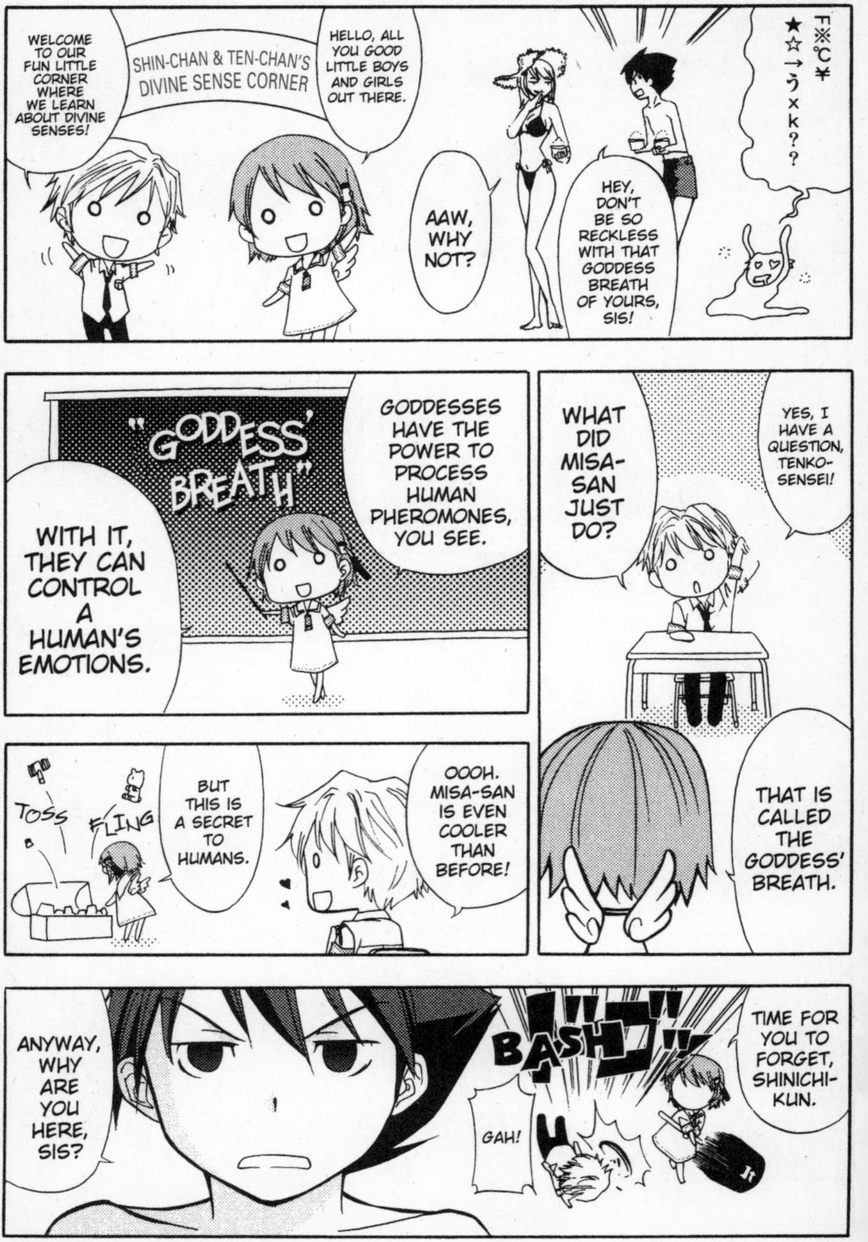
F※℃¥★☆→う×k??
HEY, DON'T BE SO RECKLESS WITH THAT GODDESS BREATH OF YOURS, SIS!
AAW, WHY NOT?
HELLO, ALL YOU GOOD LITTLE BOYS AND GIRLS OUT THERE.
SHIN-CHAN & TEN-CHAN'S DIVINE SENSE CORNER
WELCOME TO OUR FUN LITTLE CORNER WHERE WE LEARN ABOUT DIVINE SENSES!
YES, I HAVE A QUESTION, TENKO-SENSEI!
WHAT DID MISA-SAN JUST DO?
THAT IS CALLED THE GODDESS' BREATH.
"GODDESS' BREATH"
GODDESSES HAVE THE POWER TO PROCESS HUMAN PHEROMONES, YOU SEE.
WITH IT, THEY CAN CONTROL A HUMAN'S EMOTIONS.
OOOH. MISA-SAN IS EVEN COOLER THAN BEFORE!
BUT THIS IS A SECRET TO HUMANS.
FLING
TOSS
TIME FOR YOU TO FORGET, SHINICHI-KUN.
BASH!!
GAH!
ANYWAY, WHY ARE YOU HERE, SIS?

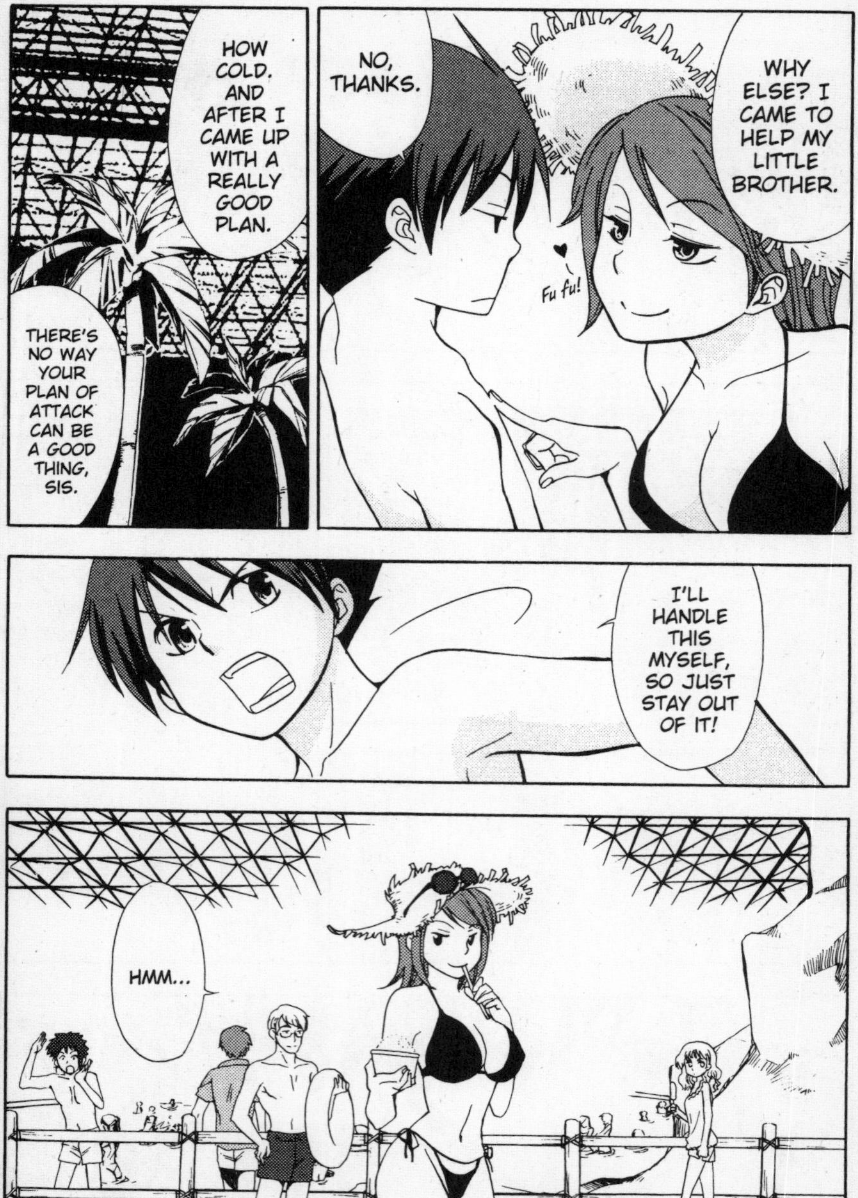
WHY ELSE? I CAME TO HELP MY LITTLE BROTHER.
Fu fu!
NO, THANKS.
HOW COLD. AND AFTER I CAME UP WITH A REALLY GOOD PLAN.
THERE'S NO WAY YOUR PLAN OF ATTACK CAN BE A GOOD THING, SIS.
I'LL HANDLE THIS MYSELF, SO JUST STAY OUT OF IT!
HMM...

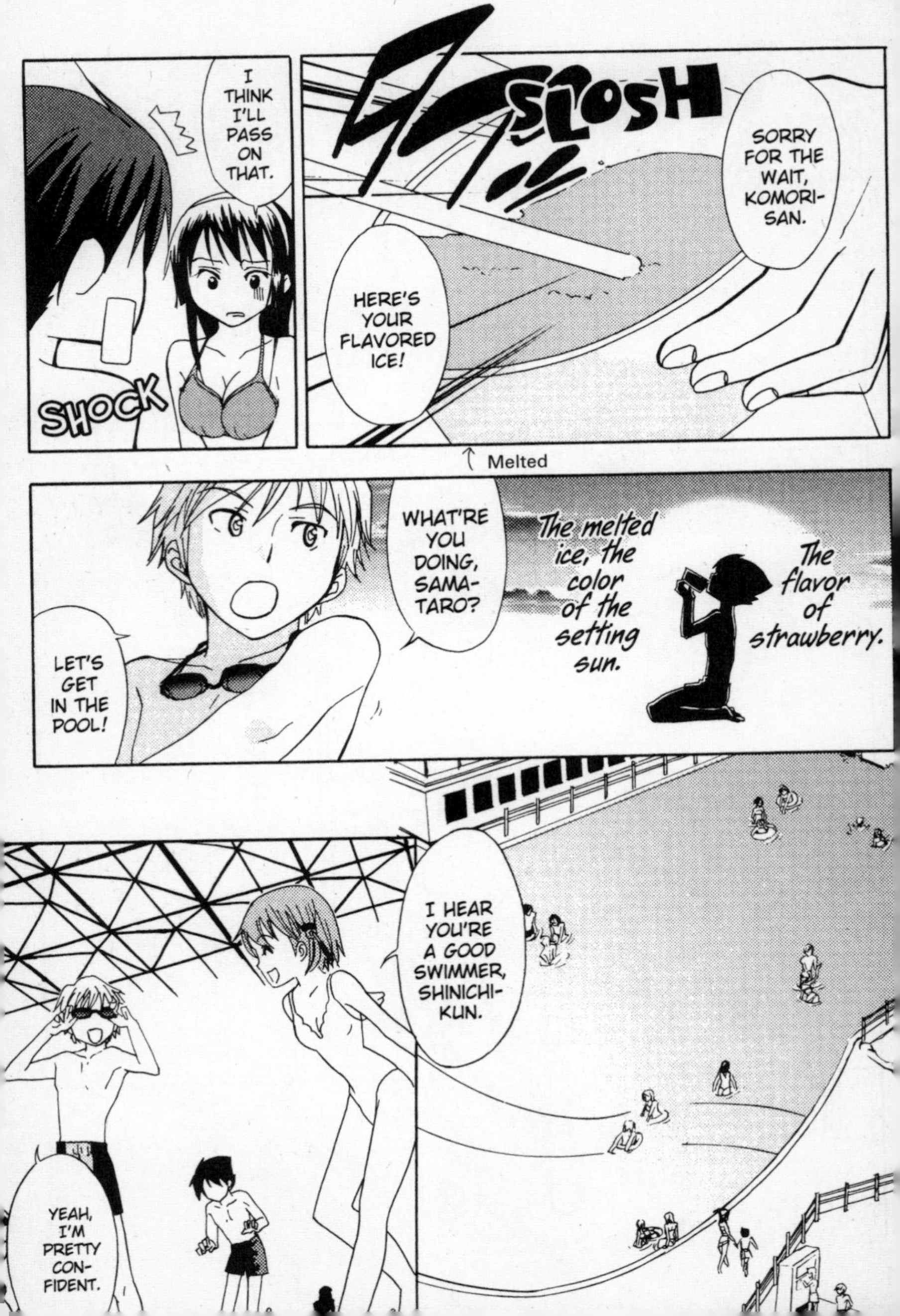
SLOSH
SORRY FOR THE WAIT, KOMORI-SAN.
HERE'S YOUR FLAVORED ICE!
I THINK I'LL PASS ON THAT.
SHOCK
↑ Melted
The flavor of strawberry.
The melted ice, the color of the setting sun.
WHAT'RE YOU DOING, SAMATARO?
LET'S GET IN THE POOL!
I HEAR YOU'RE A GOOD SWIMMER, SHINICHI-KUN.
YEAH, I'M PRETTY CONFIDENT.

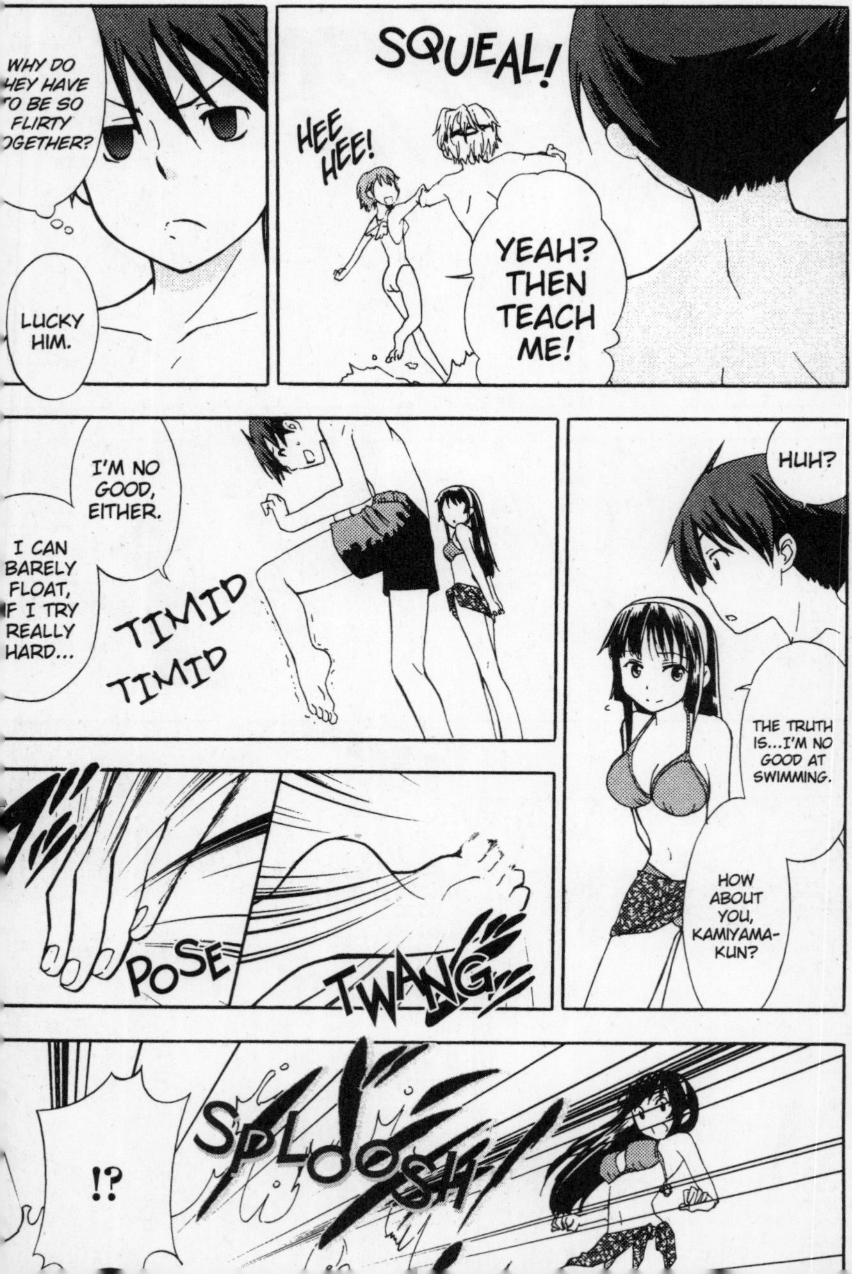
SQUEAL!
HEE HEE!
YEAH? THEN TEACH ME!
WHY DO HEY HAVE TO BE SO FLIRTY OGETHER?
LUCKY HIM.
HUH?
THE TRUTH IS...I'M NO GOOD AT SWIMMING.
HOW ABOUT YOU, KAMIYAMA-KUN?
I'M NO GOOD, EITHER.
I CAN BARELY FLOAT, F I TRY REALLY HARD...
TIMID TIMID
TWANG
POSE
SPLOOSH!
!?

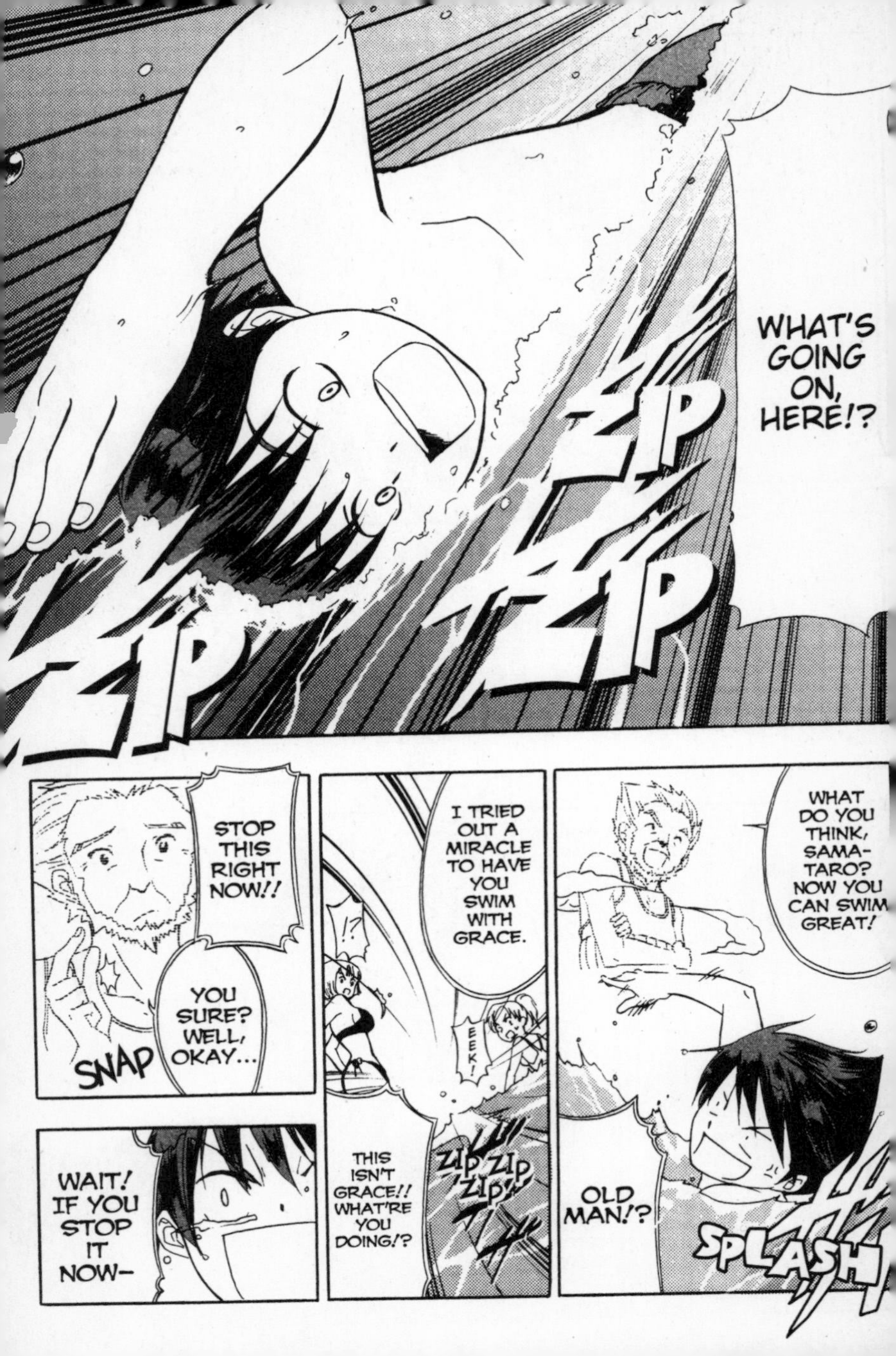
WHAT'S GOING ON, HERE!?
ZIP
ZIP
ZIP
WHAT DO YOU THINK, SAMA-TARO? NOW YOU CAN SWIM GREAT!
SPLASH
OLD MAN!?
I TRIED OUT A MIRACLE TO HAVE YOU SWIM WITH GRACE.
!?
EEK!
ZIP ZIP ZIP
THIS ISN'T GRACE!! WHAT'RE YOU DOING!?
STOP THIS RIGHT NOW!!
YOU SURE? WELL, OKAY...
SNAP
WAIT! IF YOU STOP IT NOW-

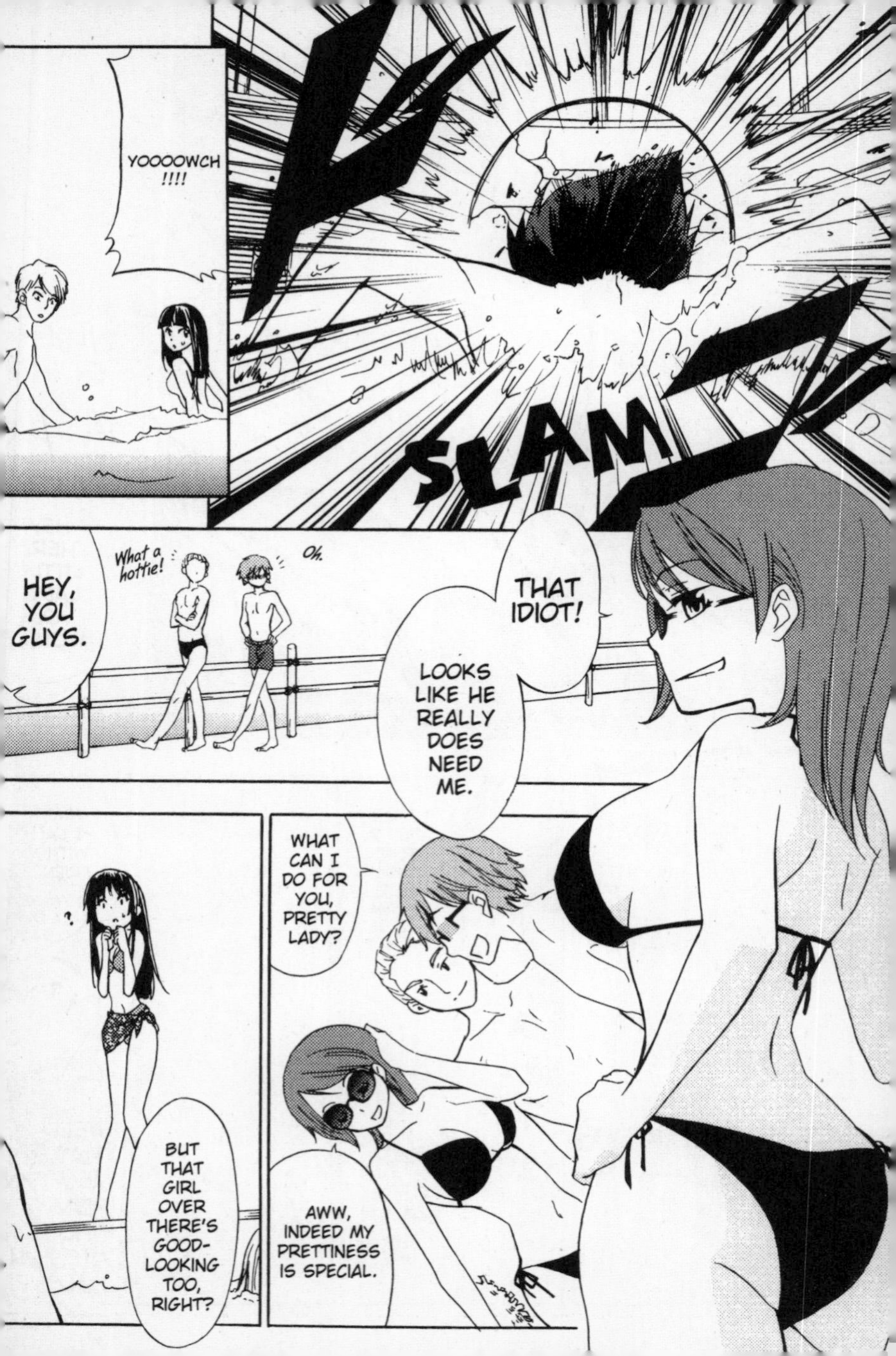
SLAM
YOOOOWCH !!!!
THAT IDIOT!
LOOKS LIKE HE REALLY DOES NEED ME.
Oh.
What a hottie!
HEY, YOU GUYS.
WHAT CAN I DO FOR YOU, PRETTY LADY?
AWW, INDEED MY PRETTINESS IS SPECIAL.
BUT THAT GIRL OVER THERE'S GOOD-LOOKING TOO, RIGHT?

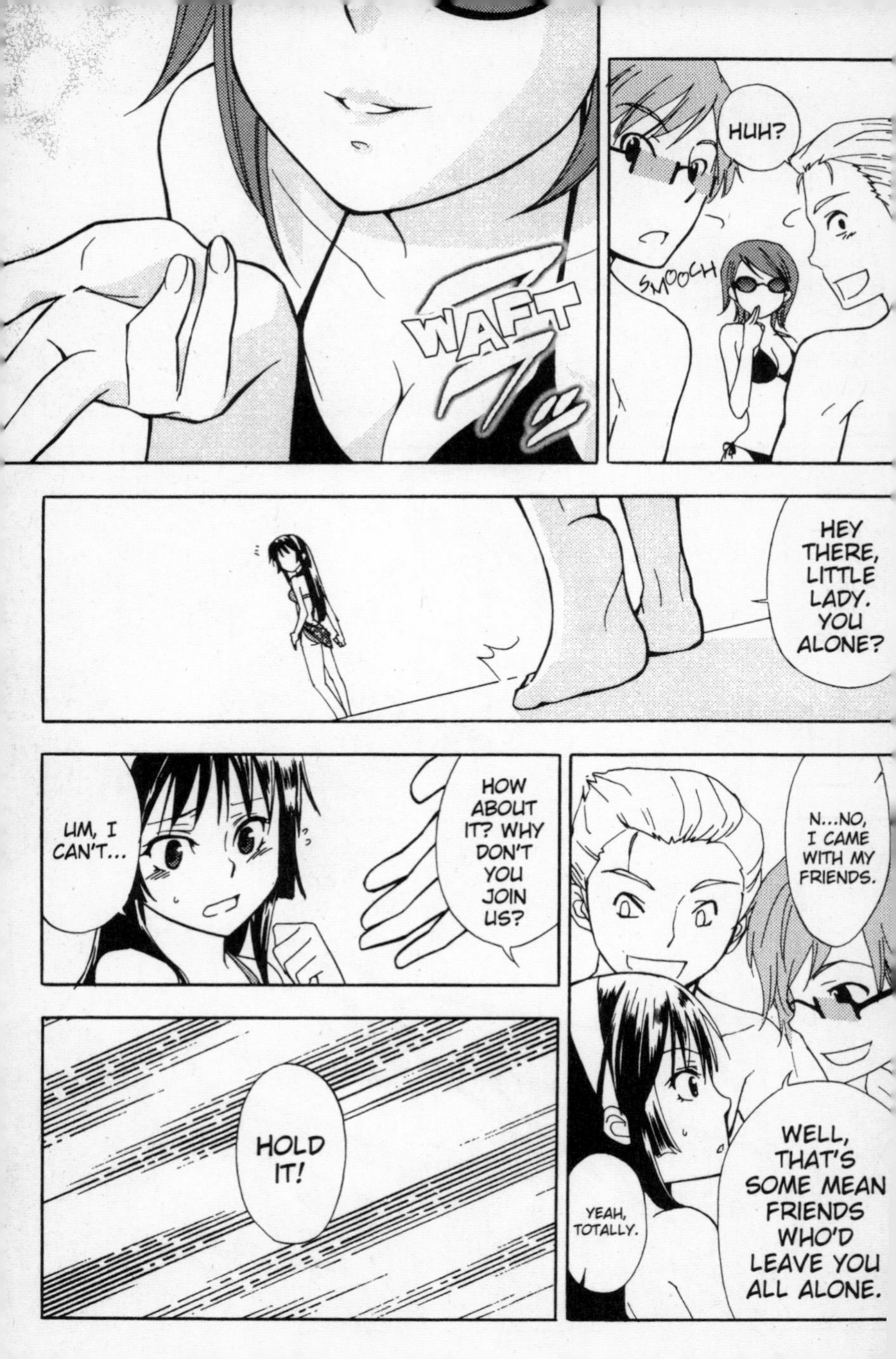
HUH?
SMOOCH
WAFT
HEY THERE, LITTLE LADY. YOU ALONE?
N...NO, I CAME WITH MY FRIENDS.
WELL, THAT'S SOME MEAN FRIENDS WHO'D LEAVE YOU ALL ALONE.
YEAH, TOTALLY.
HOW ABOUT IT? WHY DON'T YOU JOIN US?
UM, I CAN'T...
HOLD IT!

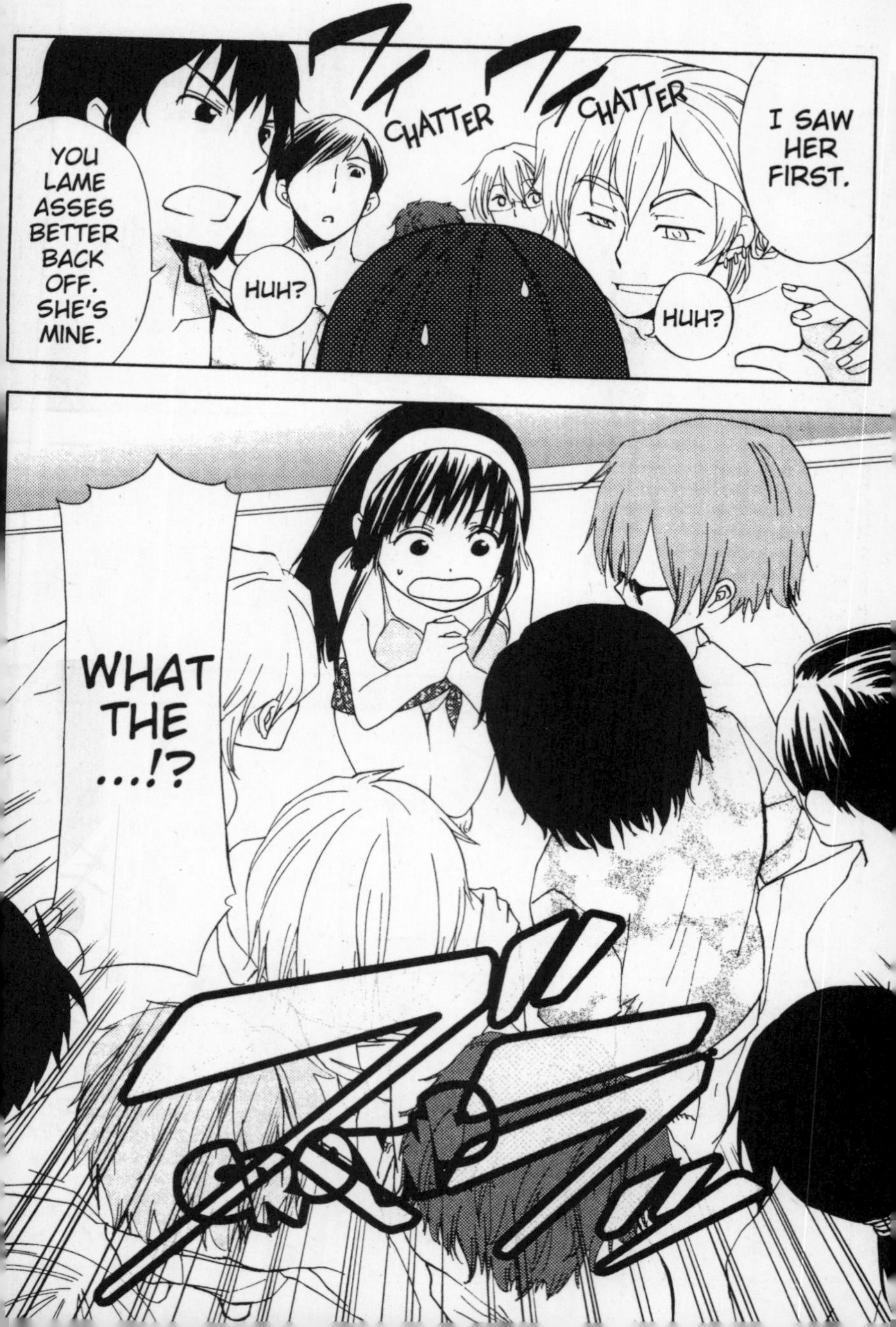

I SAW HER FIRST.
HUH?
CHATTER
CHATTER
HUH?
YOU LAME ASSES BETTER BACK OFF. SHE'S MINE.
WHAT THE ...!?

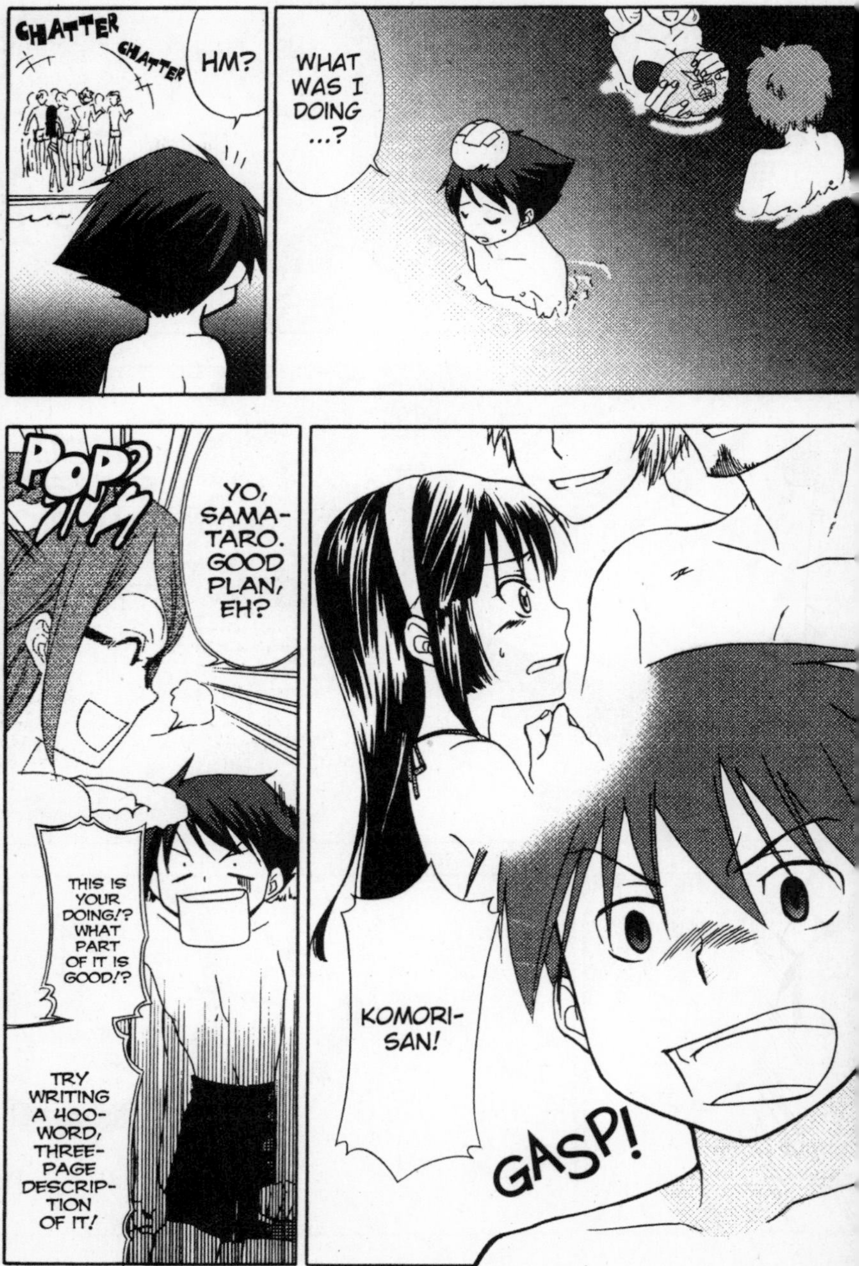
WHAT WAS I DOING ...?
CHATTER
CHATTER
HM?
KOMORI-SAN!
GASP!
POP
YO, SAMATARO. GOOD PLAN, EH?
THIS IS YOUR DOING!? WHAT PART OF IT IS GOOD!?
TRY WRITING A 400-WORD, THREE-PAGE DESCRIPTION OF IT!

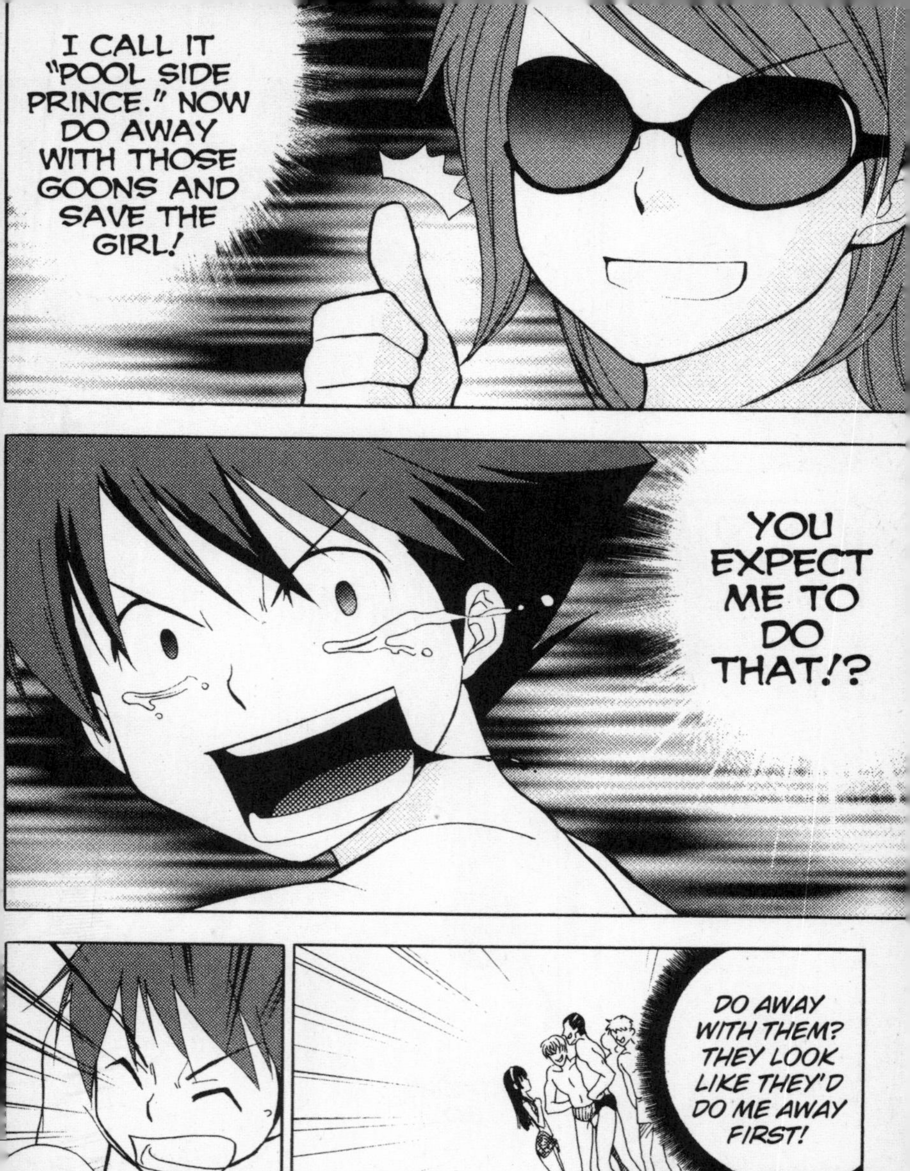
I CALL IT "POOL SIDE PRINCE." NOW DO AWAY WITH THOSE GOONS AND SAVE THE GIRL!
YOU EXPECT ME TO DO THAT!?
DO AWAY WITH THEM? THEY LOOK LIKE THEY'D DO ME AWAY FIRST!
FINE, HERE GOES!

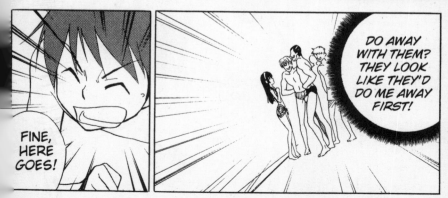

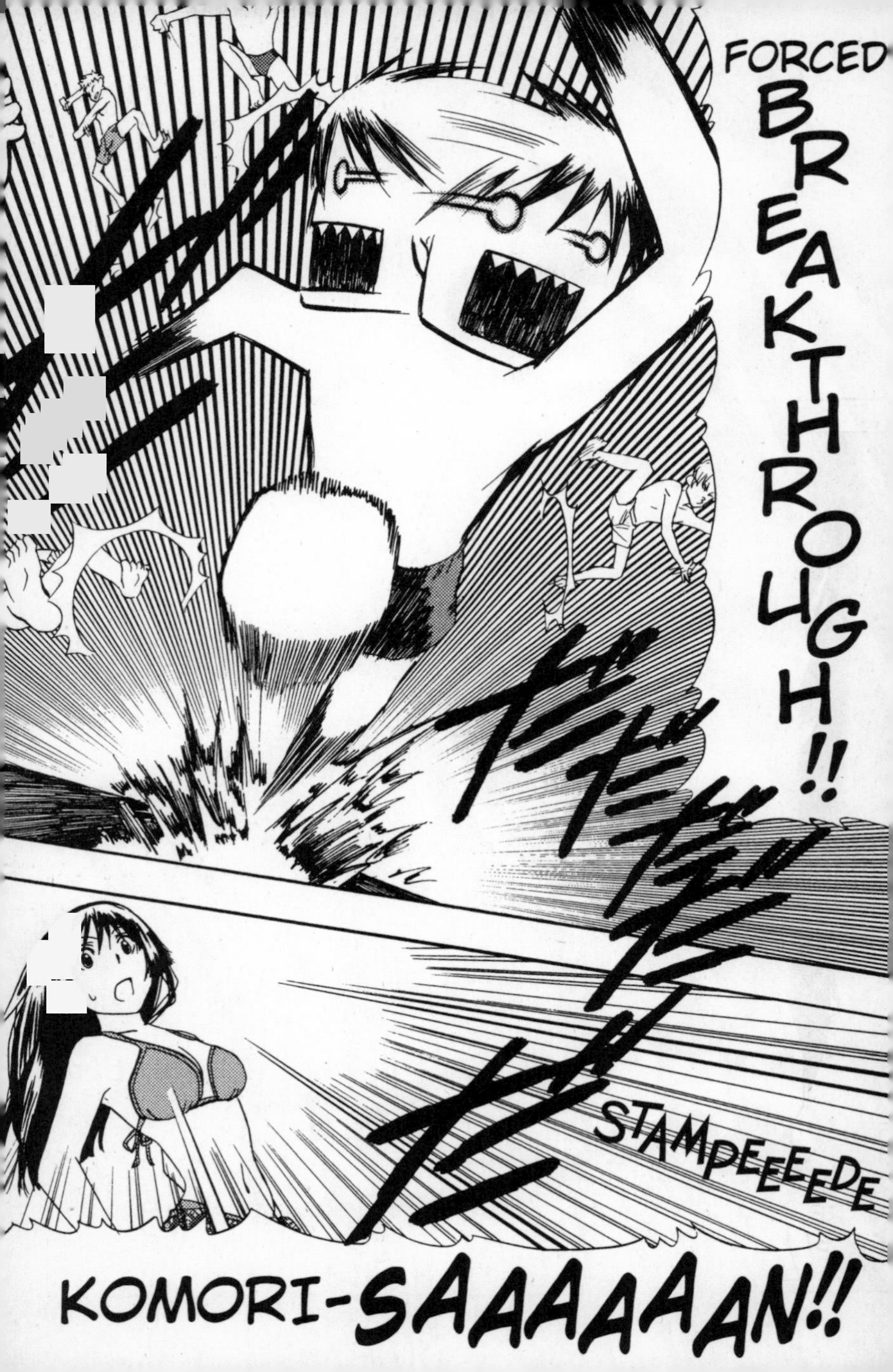
FORCED BREAKTHROUGH!!
STAMPEEEEDE
KOMORI-SAAAAAAN!!

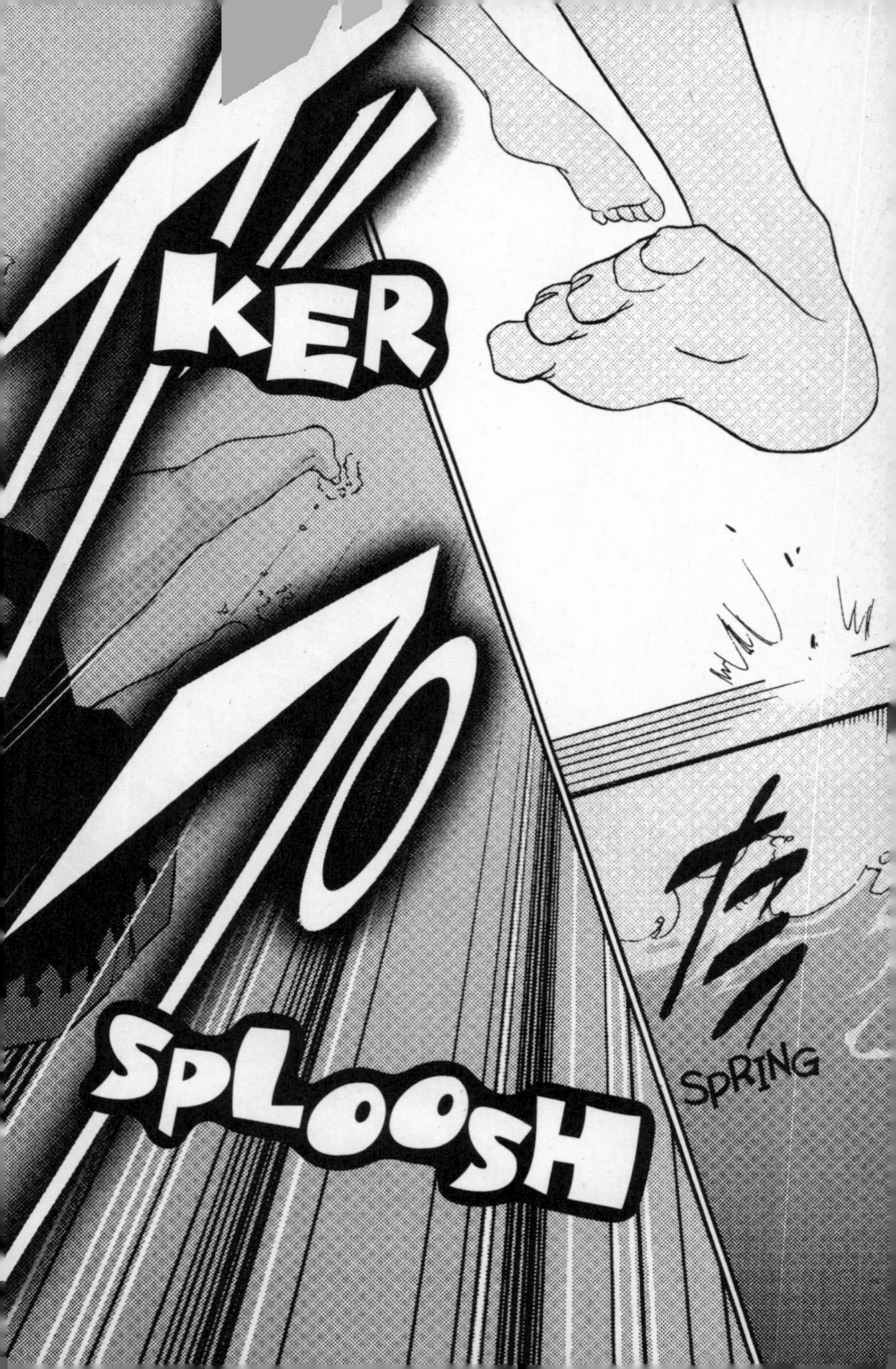
SPRING
KER
SPLOOSH

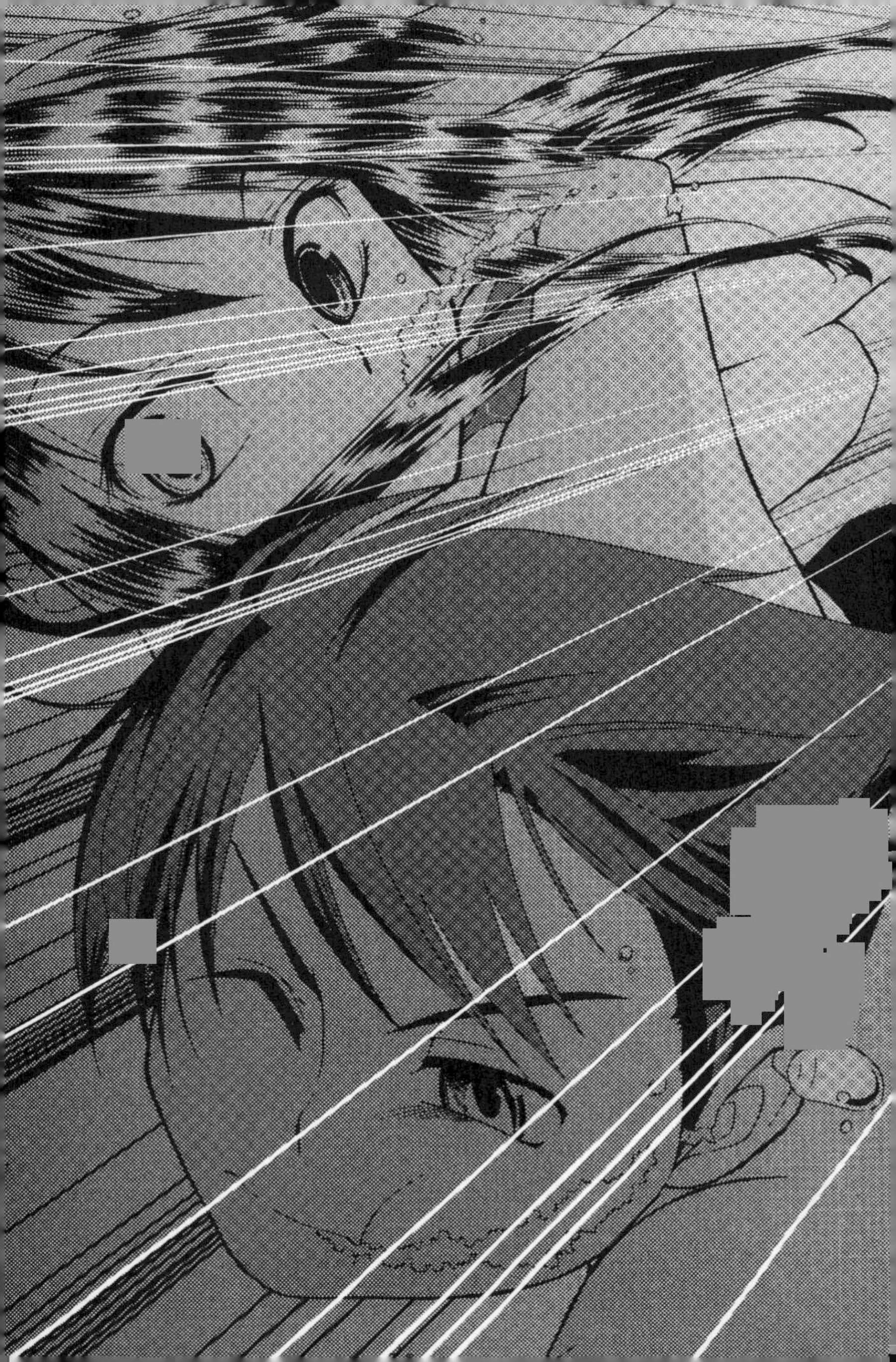

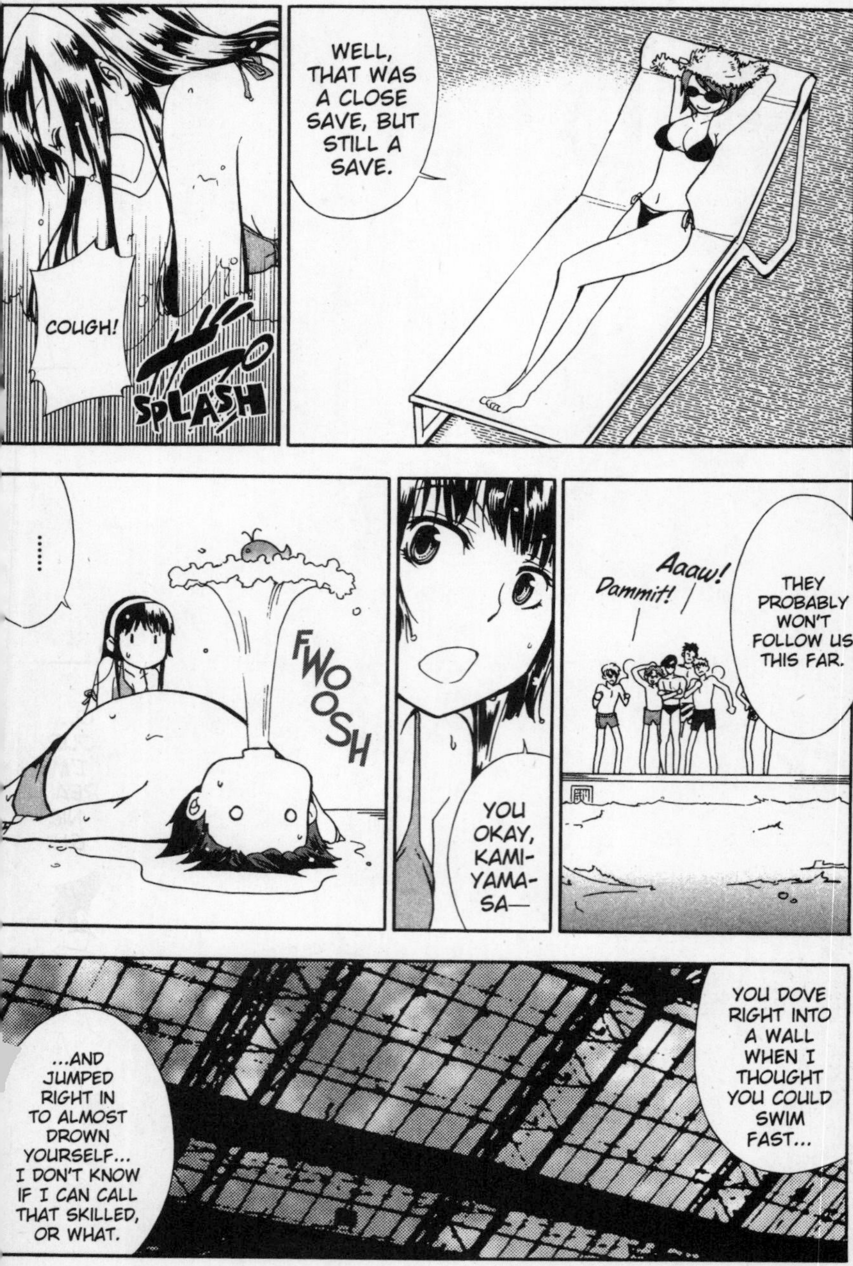
WELL, THAT WAS A CLOSE SAVE, BUT STILL A SAVE.
COUGH!
SPLASH
THEY PROBABLY WON'T FOLLOW US THIS FAR.
Aaaw!
Dammit!
YOU OKAY, KAMI-YAMA-SA—
FWOOSH
......
YOU DOVE RIGHT INTO A WALL WHEN I THOUGHT YOU COULD SWIM FAST...
...AND JUMPED RIGHT IN TO ALMOST DROWN YOURSELF... I DON'T KNOW IF I CAN CALL THAT SKILLED, OR WHAT.

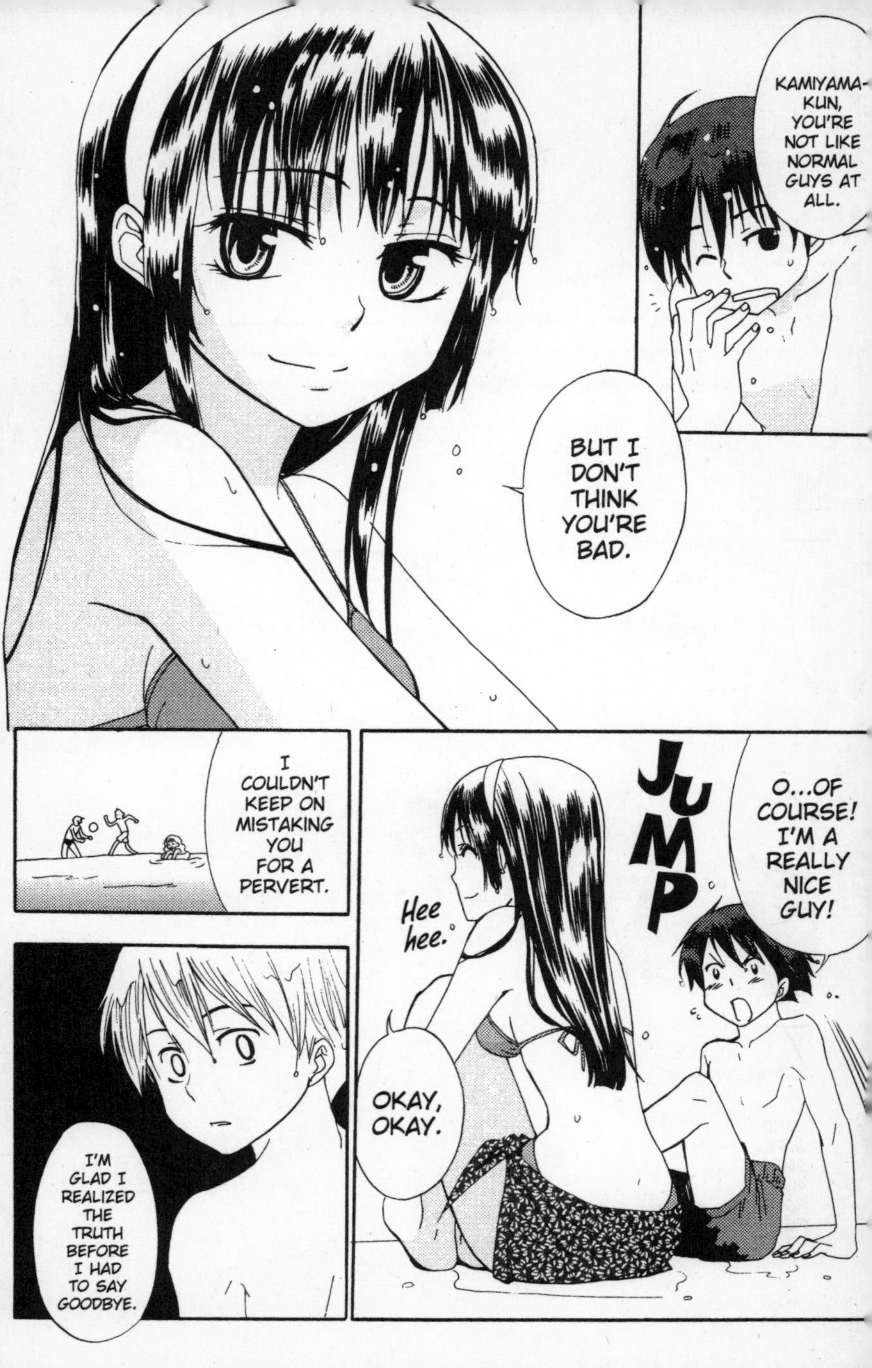
KAMIYAMA-KUN, YOU'RE NOT LIKE NORMAL GUYS AT ALL.
BUT I DON'T THINK YOU'RE BAD.
O...OF COURSE! I'M A REALLY NICE GUY!
JUMP
Hee hee.
OKAY, OKAY.
I COULDN'T KEEP ON MISTAKING YOU FOR A PERVERT.
I'M GLAD I REALIZED THE TRUTH BEFORE I HAD TO SAY GOODBYE.

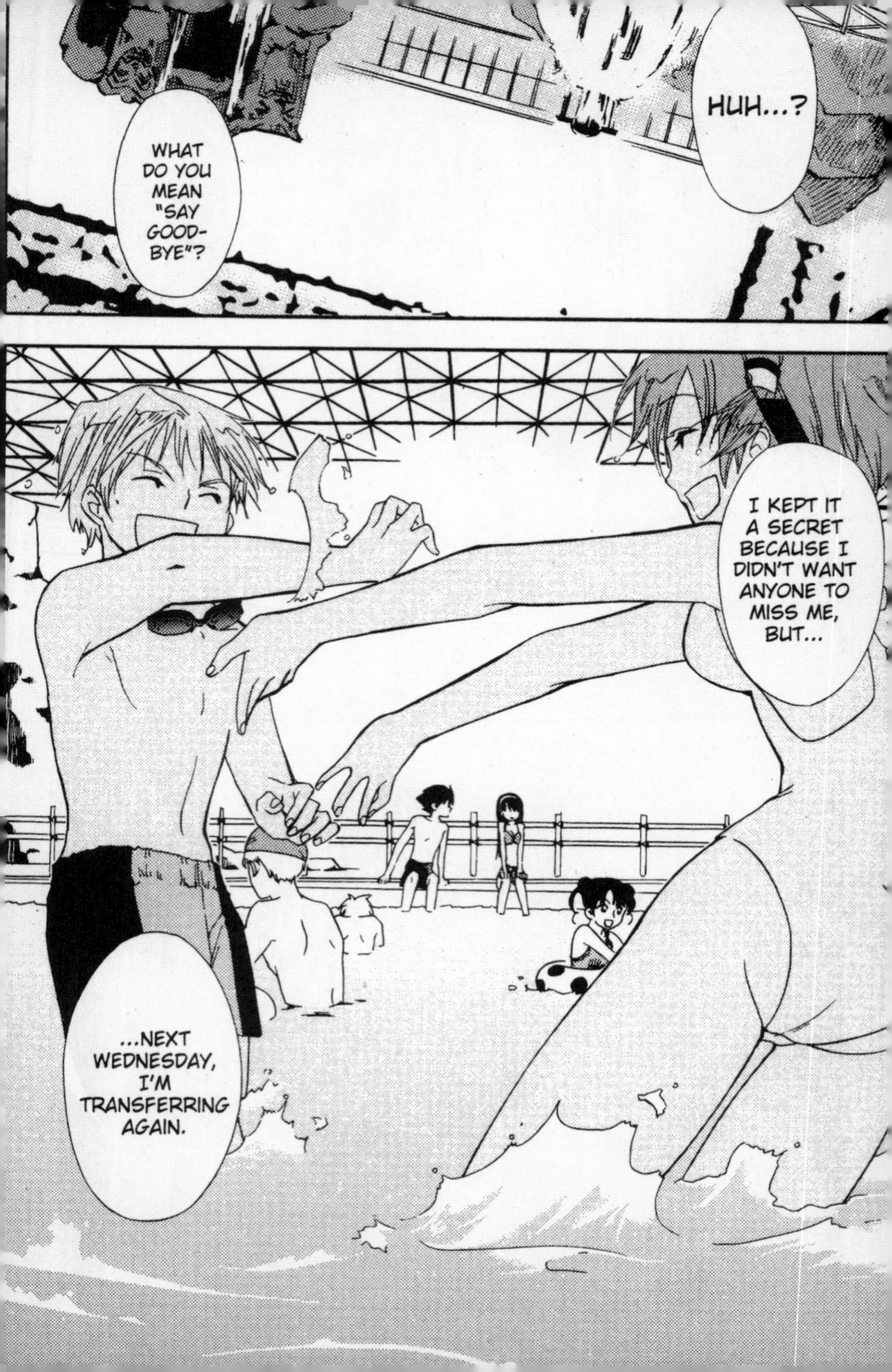
HUH...?
WHAT DO YOU MEAN "SAY GOOD-BYE"?
I KEPT IT A SECRET BECAUSE I DIDN'T WANT ANYONE TO MISS ME, BUT...
...NEXT WEDNESDAY, I'M TRANSFERRING AGAIN.

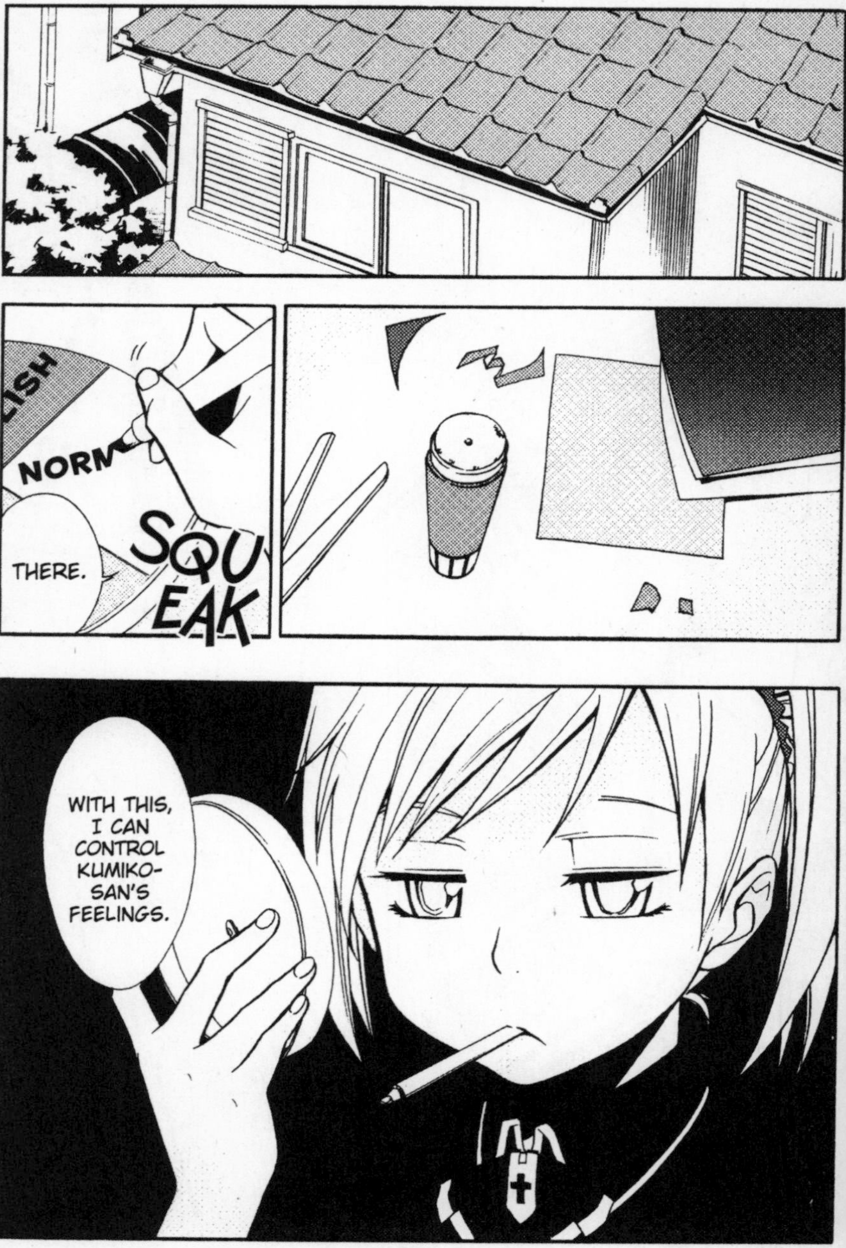
LISH
NORM
SQUEAK
THERE.
WITH THIS, I CAN CONTROL KUMIKO-SAN'S FEELINGS.

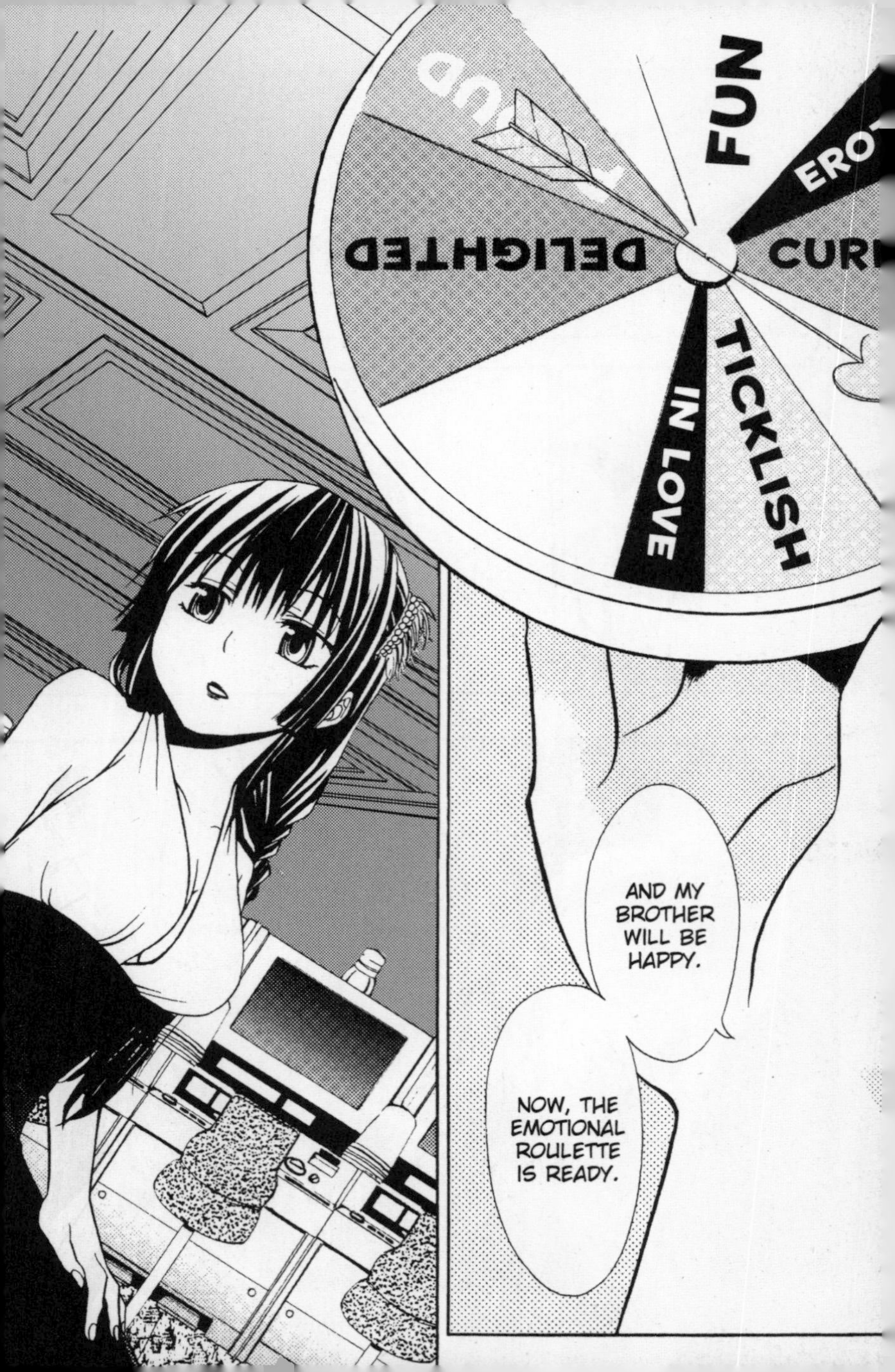
AND MY BROTHER WILL BE HAPPY.
NOW, THE EMOTIONAL ROULETTE IS READY.
FUN
DELIGHTED
TICKLISH
IN LOVE

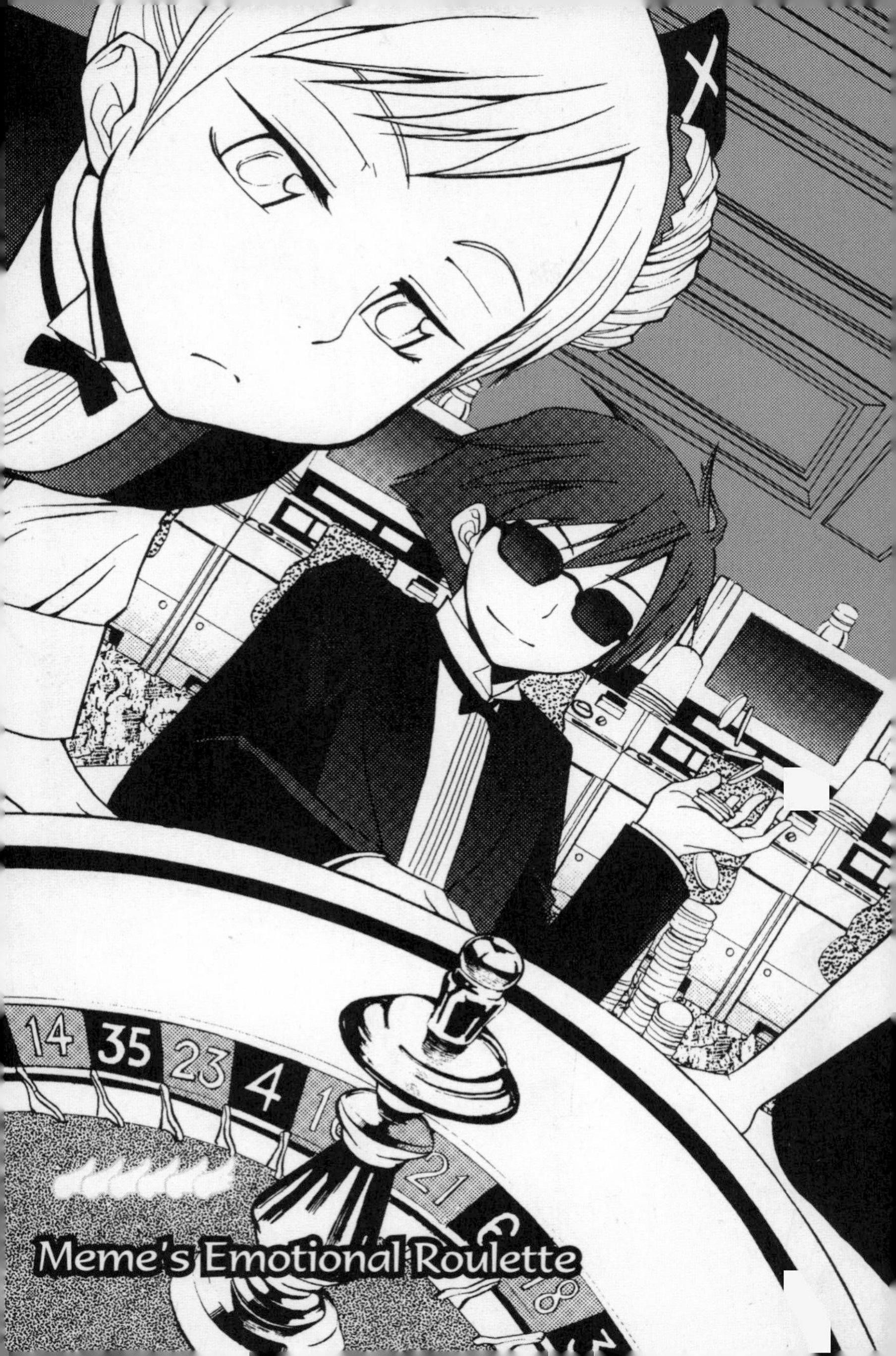
14 35 23 4 21
Meme's Emotional Roulette

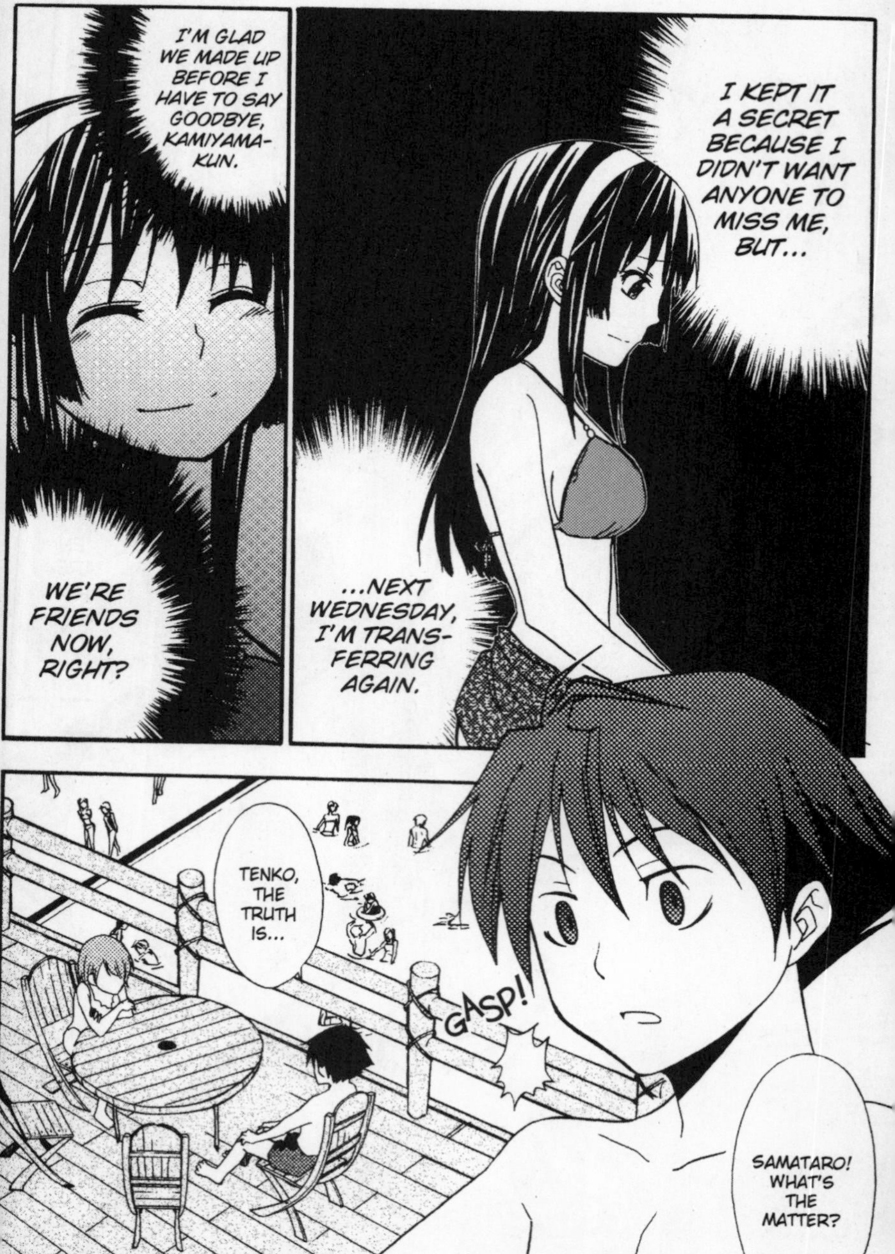
I KEPT IT A SECRET BECAUSE I DIDN'T WANT ANYONE TO MISS ME, BUT...
...NEXT WEDNESDAY, I'M TRANS-FERRING AGAIN.
I'M GLAD WE MADE UP BEFORE I HAVE TO SAY GOODBYE, KAMIYAMA-KUN.
WE'RE FRIENDS NOW, RIGHT?
GASP!
TENKO, THE TRUTH IS...
SAMATARO! WHAT'S THE MATTER?

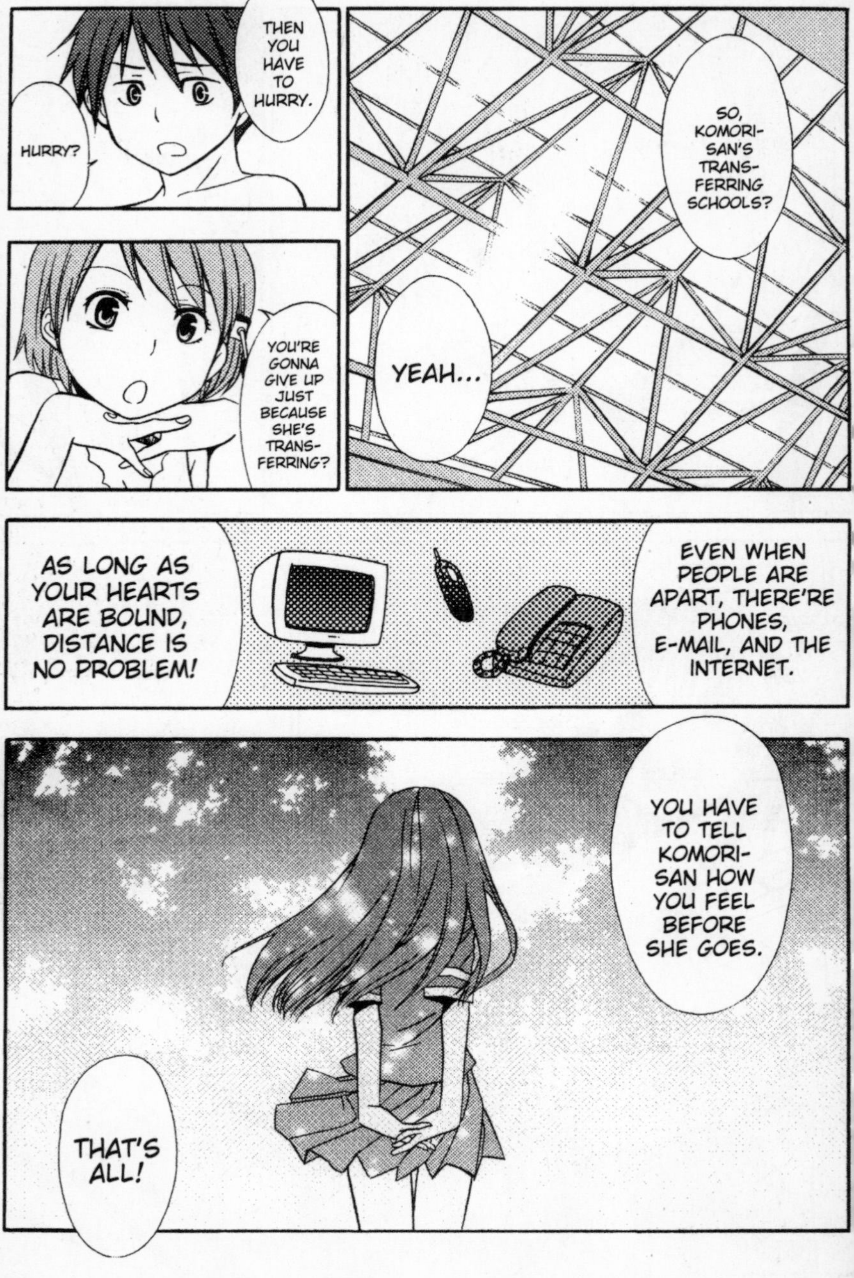
SO, KOMORI-SAN'S TRANS-FERRING SCHOOLS?
YEAH...
THEN YOU HAVE TO HURRY.
HURRY?
YOU'RE GONNA GIVE UP JUST BECAUSE SHE'S TRANS-FERRING?
EVEN WHEN PEOPLE ARE APART, THERE'RE PHONES, E-MAIL, AND THE INTERNET.
AS LONG AS YOUR HEARTS ARE BOUND, DISTANCE IS NO PROBLEM!
YOU HAVE TO TELL KOMORI-SAN HOW YOU FEEL BEFORE SHE GOES.
THAT'S ALL!

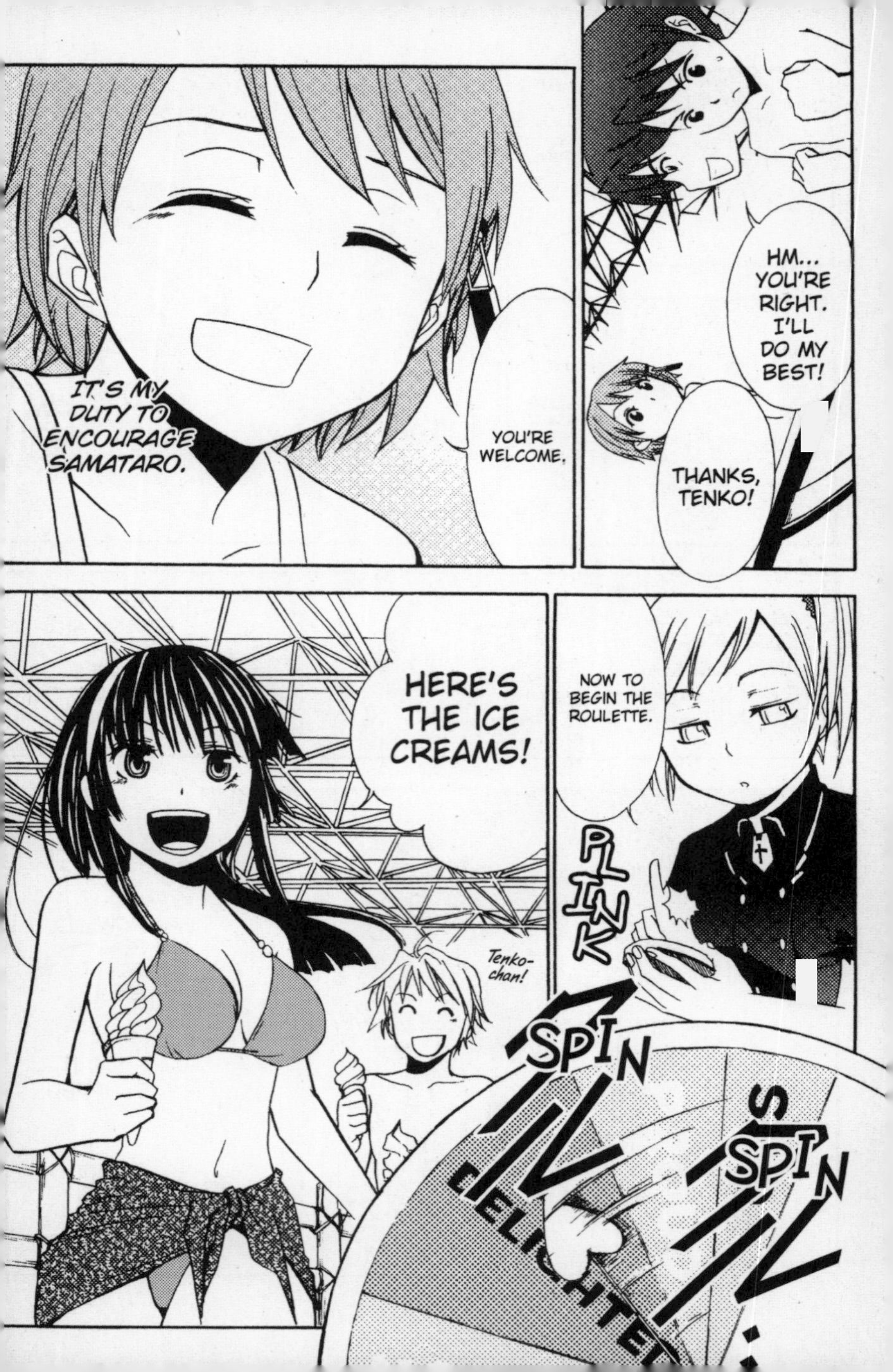
HM... YOU'RE RIGHT. I'LL DO MY BEST!
THANKS, TENKO!
YOU'RE WELCOME.
IT'S MY DUTY TO ENCOURAGE SAMATARO.
NOW TO BEGIN THE ROULETTE.
PLINK
SPIN
SPIN
HERE'S THE ICE CREAMS!
Tenko-chan!

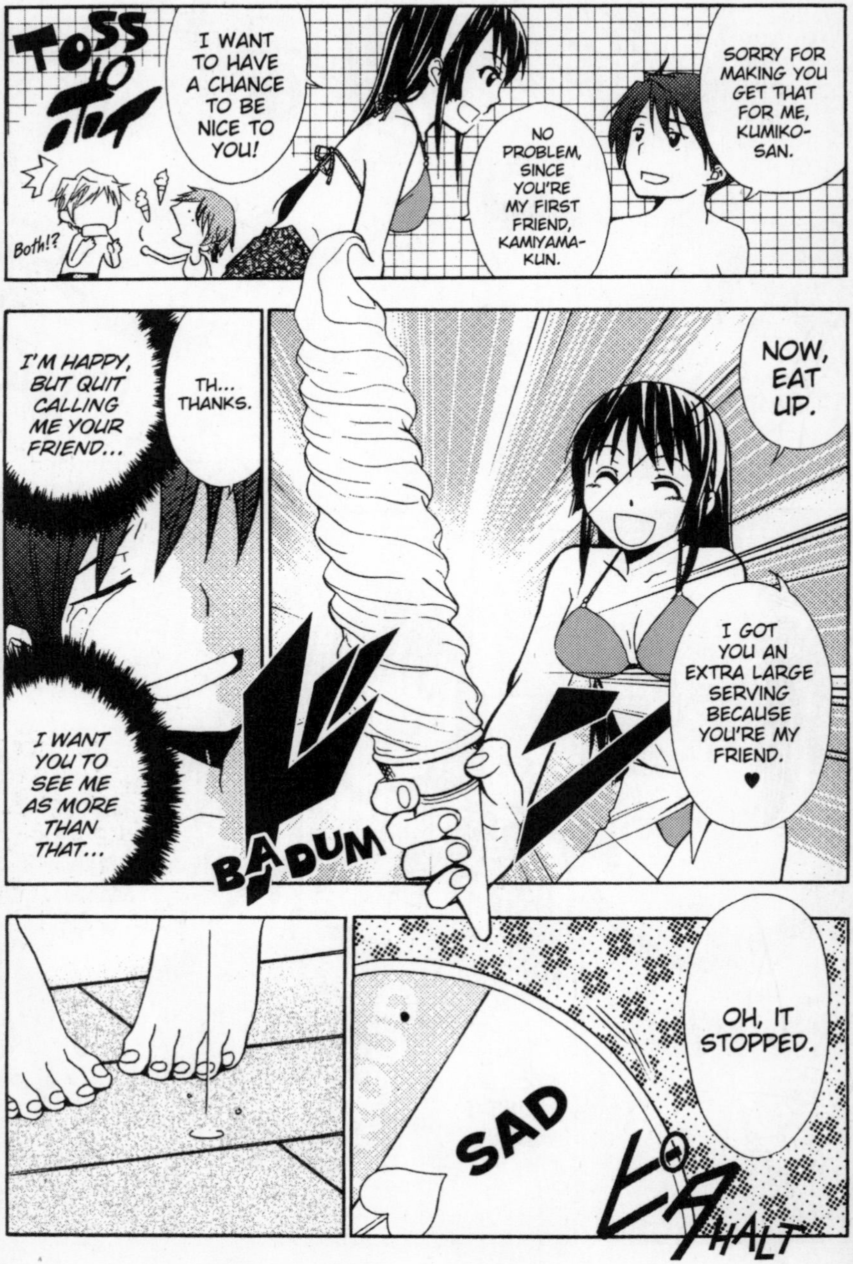
SORRY FOR MAKING YOU GET THAT FOR ME, KUMIKO-SAN.
NO PROBLEM, SINCE YOU'RE MY FIRST FRIEND, KAMIYAMA-KUN.
I WANT TO HAVE A CHANCE TO BE NICE TO YOU!
TOSS
Both!?
NOW, EAT UP.
I GOT YOU AN EXTRA LARGE SERVING BECAUSE YOU'RE MY FRIEND. ♥
BADUM
TH... THANKS.
I'M HAPPY, BUT QUIT CALLING ME YOUR FRIEND...
I WANT YOU TO SEE ME AS MORE THAN THAT...
OH, IT STOPPED.
SAD
HALT

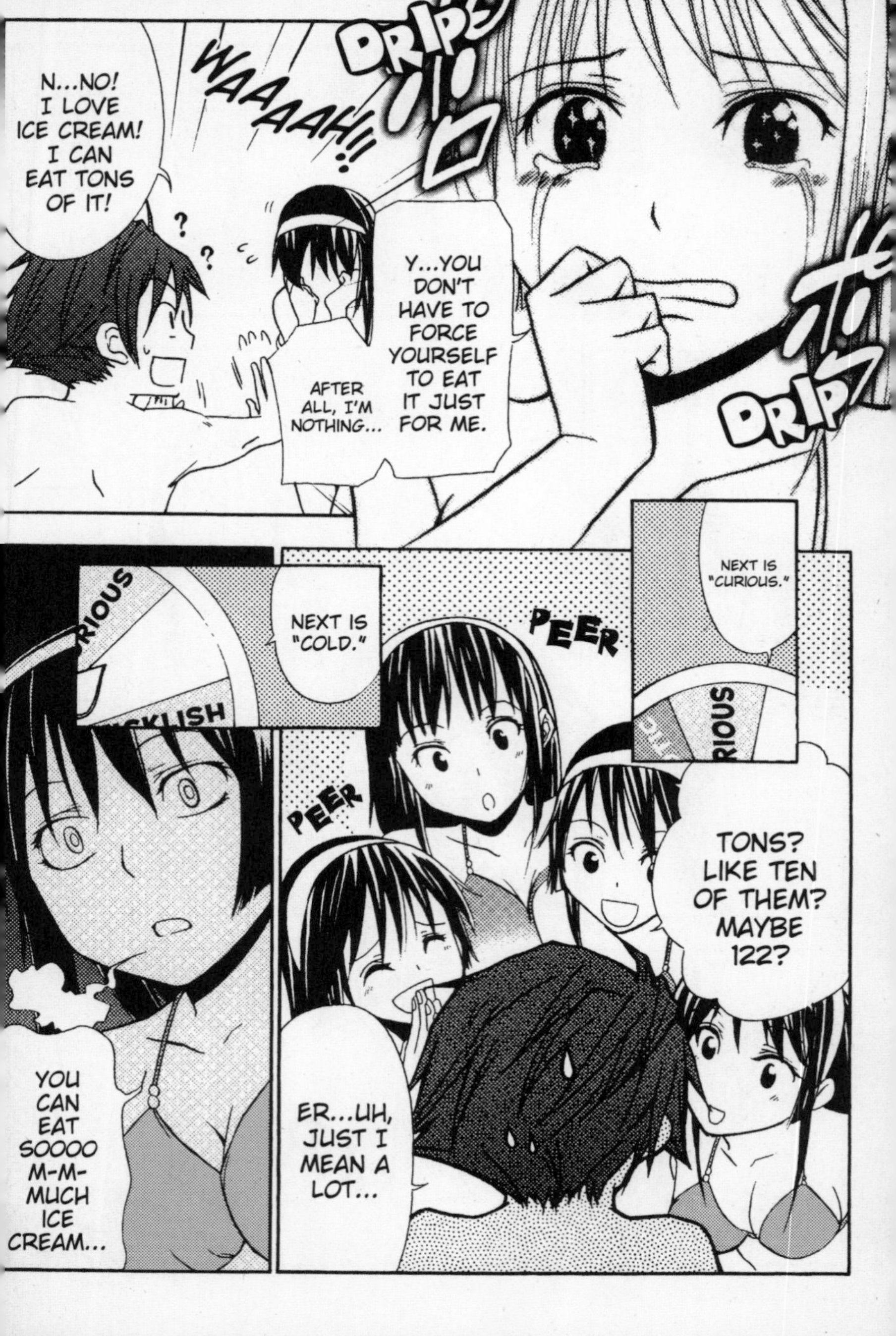
DRIPS
WAAAAH!!
Y...YOU DON'T HAVE TO FORCE YOURSELF TO EAT IT JUST FOR ME.
AFTER ALL, I'M NOTHING...
DRIP
N...NO! I LOVE ICE CREAM! I CAN EAT TONS OF IT!
NEXT IS "CURIOUS."
RIOUS
PEER
PEER
TONS? LIKE TEN OF THEM? MAYBE 122?
ER...UH, JUST I MEAN A LOT...
NEXT IS "COLD."
RIOUS
YOU CAN EAT SOOOO M-M-MUCH ICE CREAM...

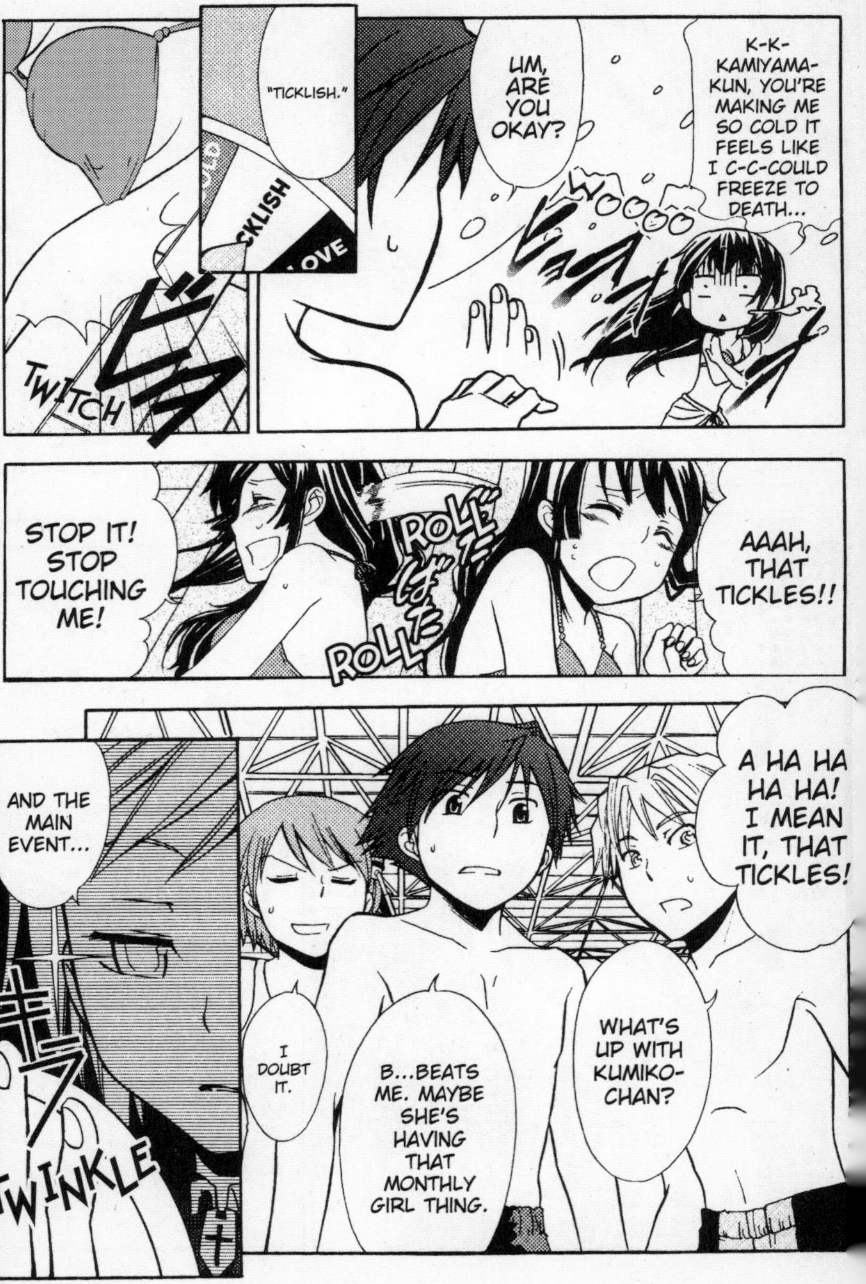
K-K-KAMIYAMA-KUN, YOU'RE MAKING ME SO COLD IT FEELS LIKE I C-C-COULD FREEZE TO DEATH...
WOOOO
UM, ARE YOU OKAY?
"TICKLISH."
LOVE
TWITCH
AAAH, THAT TICKLES!!
ROLL
ROLL
STOP IT! STOP TOUCHING ME!
A HA HA HA HA! I MEAN IT, THAT TICKLES!
WHAT'S UP WITH KUMIKO-CHAN?
B...BEATS ME. MAYBE SHE'S HAVING THAT MONTHLY GIRL THING.
I DOUBT IT.
AND THE MAIN EVENT...
TWINKLE

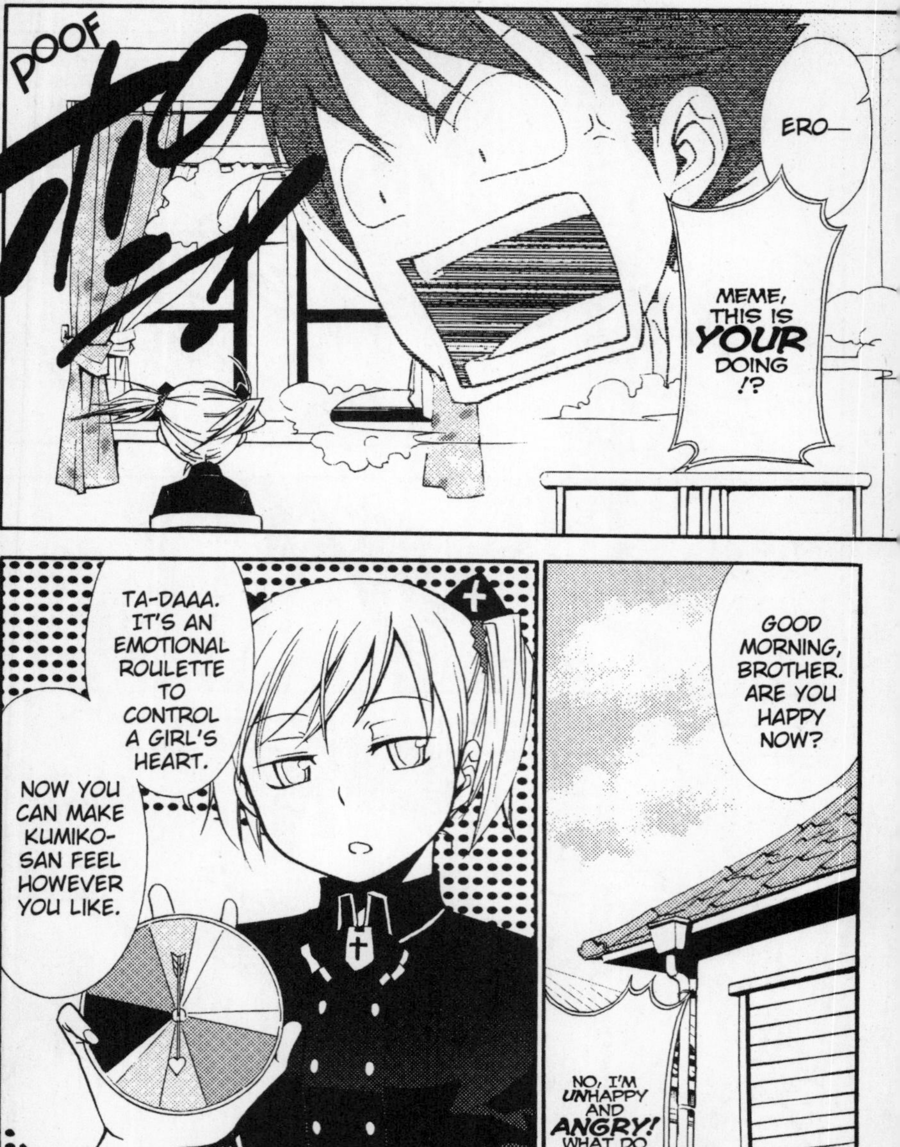
ERO—
MEME, THIS IS YOUR DOING!?
POOF
GOOD MORNING, BROTHER. ARE YOU HAPPY NOW?
NO, I'M UNHAPPY AND ANGRY! WHAT DO YOU THINK YOU'RE DOING!?
TA-DAAA. IT'S AN EMOTIONAL ROULETTE TO CONTROL A GIRL'S HEART.
NOW YOU CAN MAKE KUMIKO-SAN FEEL HOWEVER YOU LIKE.

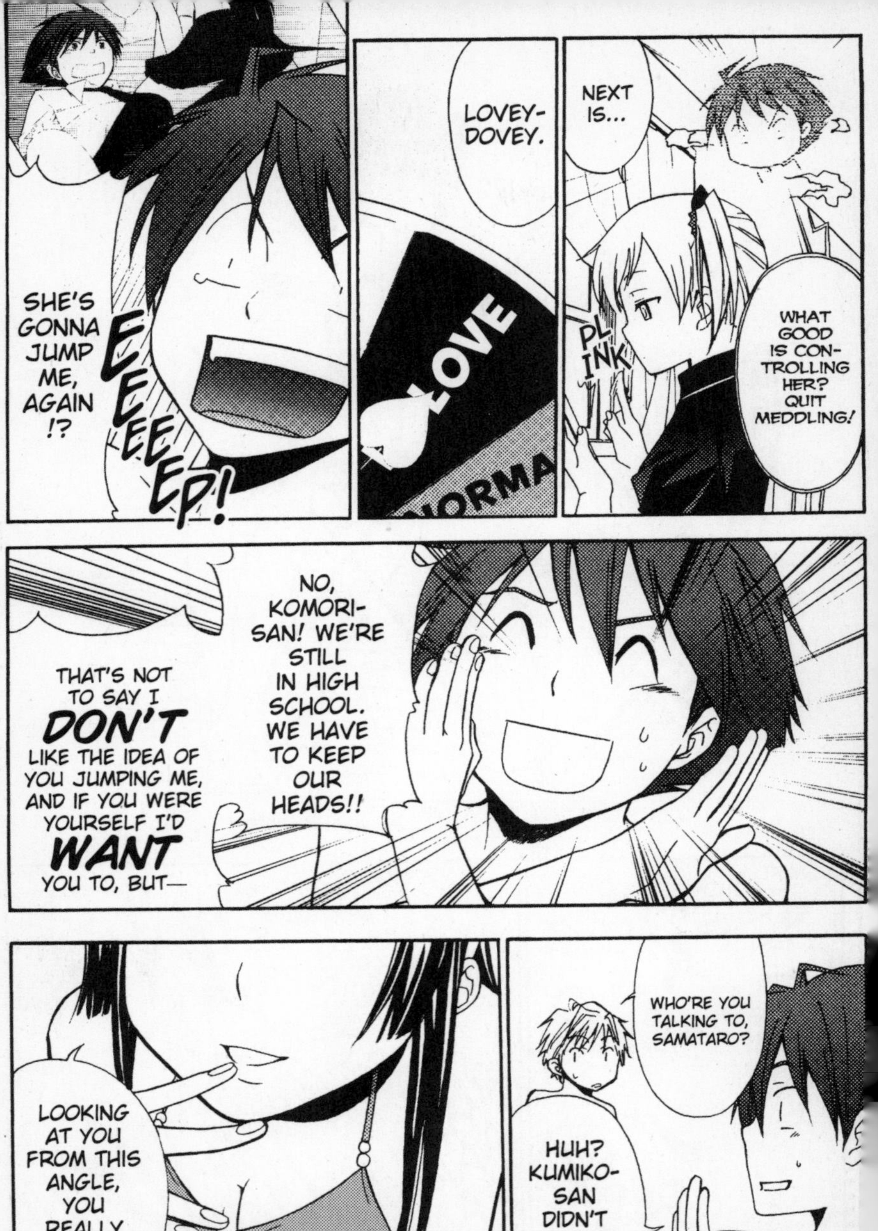
NEXT IS...
WHAT GOOD IS CONTROLLING HER? QUIT MEDDLING!
PLINK
LOVEY-DOVEY.
LOVE
NORMA
SHE'S GONNA JUMP ME, AGAIN!?
EEEEEP!
NO, KOMORI-SAN! WE'RE STILL IN HIGH SCHOOL. WE HAVE TO KEEP OUR HEADS!!
THAT'S NOT TO SAY I DON'T LIKE THE IDEA OF YOU JUMPING ME, AND IF YOU WERE YOURSELF I'D WANT YOU TO, BUT—
WHO'RE YOU TALKING TO, SAMATARO?
HUH? KUMIKO-SAN DIDN'T FALL IN LOVE?
LOOKING AT YOU FROM THIS ANGLE, YOU REALLY ARE CUTE...

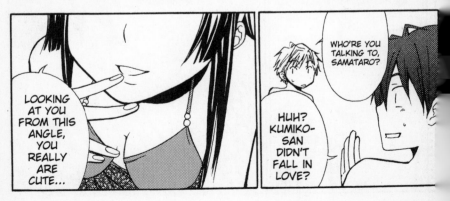

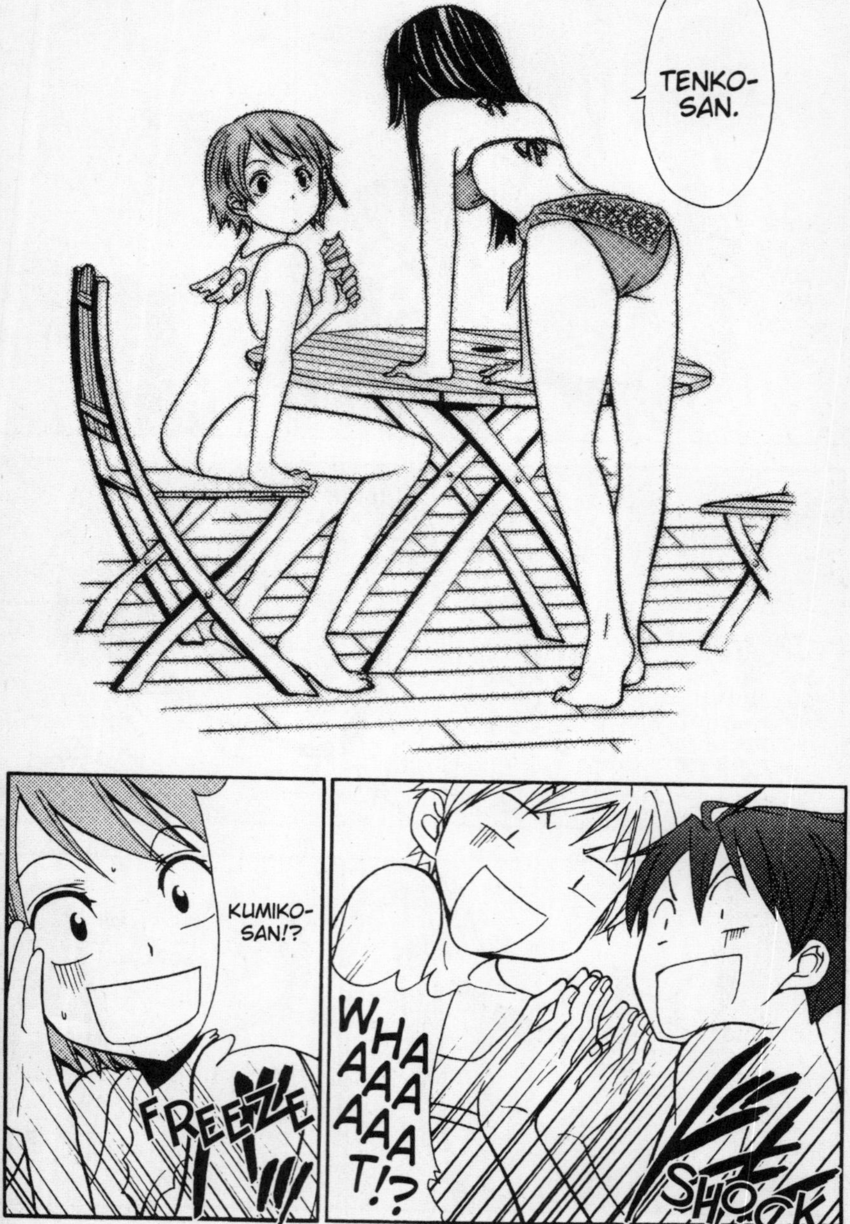
TENKO-SAN.
WHAAAAAAAAT!?
SHOCK
KUMIKO-SAN!?
FREEZE

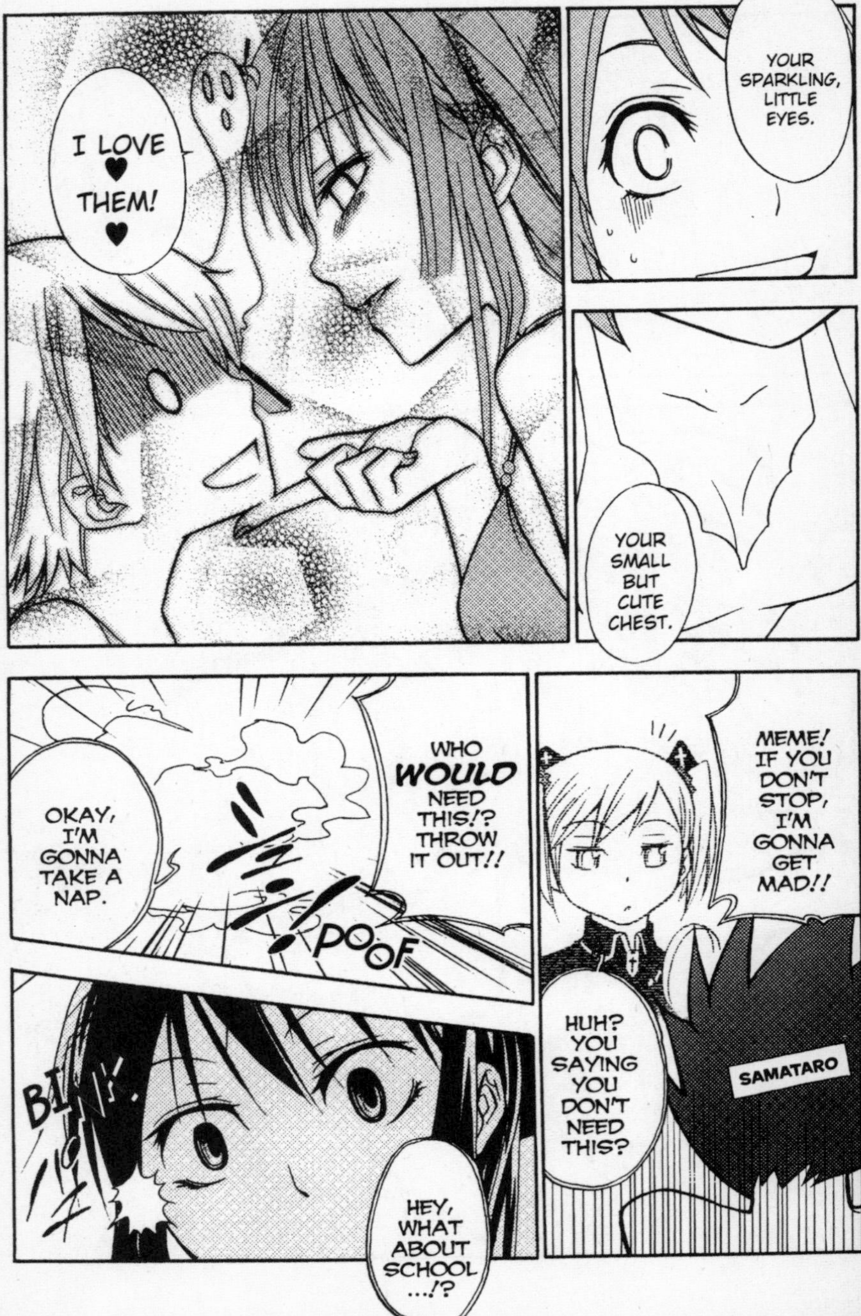
YOUR SPARKLING, LITTLE EYES.
YOUR SMALL BUT CUTE CHEST.
I LOVE ♥ THEM! ♥
MEME! IF YOU DON'T STOP, I'M GONNA GET MAD!!
WHO WOULD NEED THIS!? THROW IT OUT!!
POOF
OKAY, I'M GONNA TAKE A NAP.
SAMATARO
HUH? YOU SAYING YOU DON'T NEED THIS?
HEY, WHAT ABOUT SCHOOL ...!?

HUH? WHAT'S THE MATTER, TENKO-SAN?
TWITCH
TWITCH
IT'S N-N-N-N-NOTHING! SHE'S FINE!
LET'S GO ON THE WATER SLIDES, 'KAY?
TWIN SLIDERS
CHEER
SQUEAL

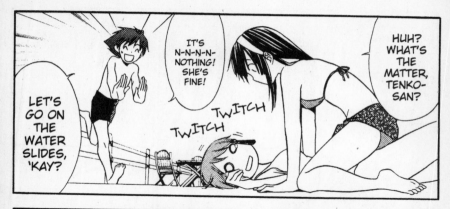

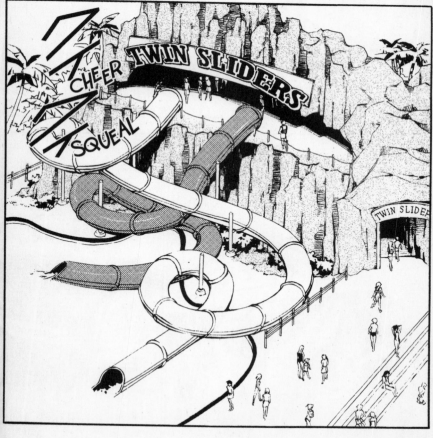

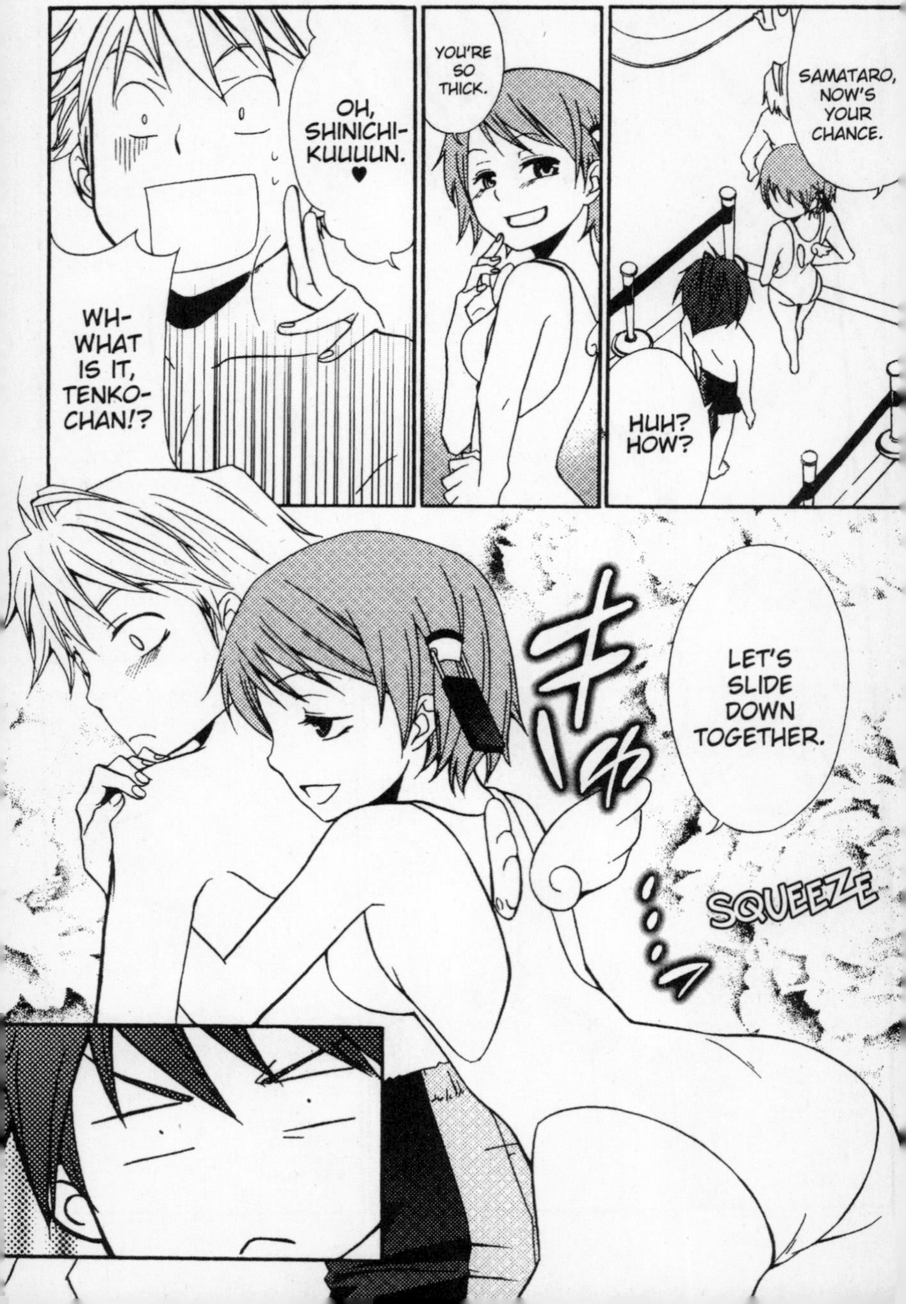
SAMATARO, NOW'S YOUR CHANCE.
HUH? HOW?
YOU'RE SO THICK.
OH, SHINICHI-KUUUUN. ♥
WH-WHAT IS IT, TENKO-CHAN!?
LET'S SLIDE DOWN TOGETHER.
SQUEEZE

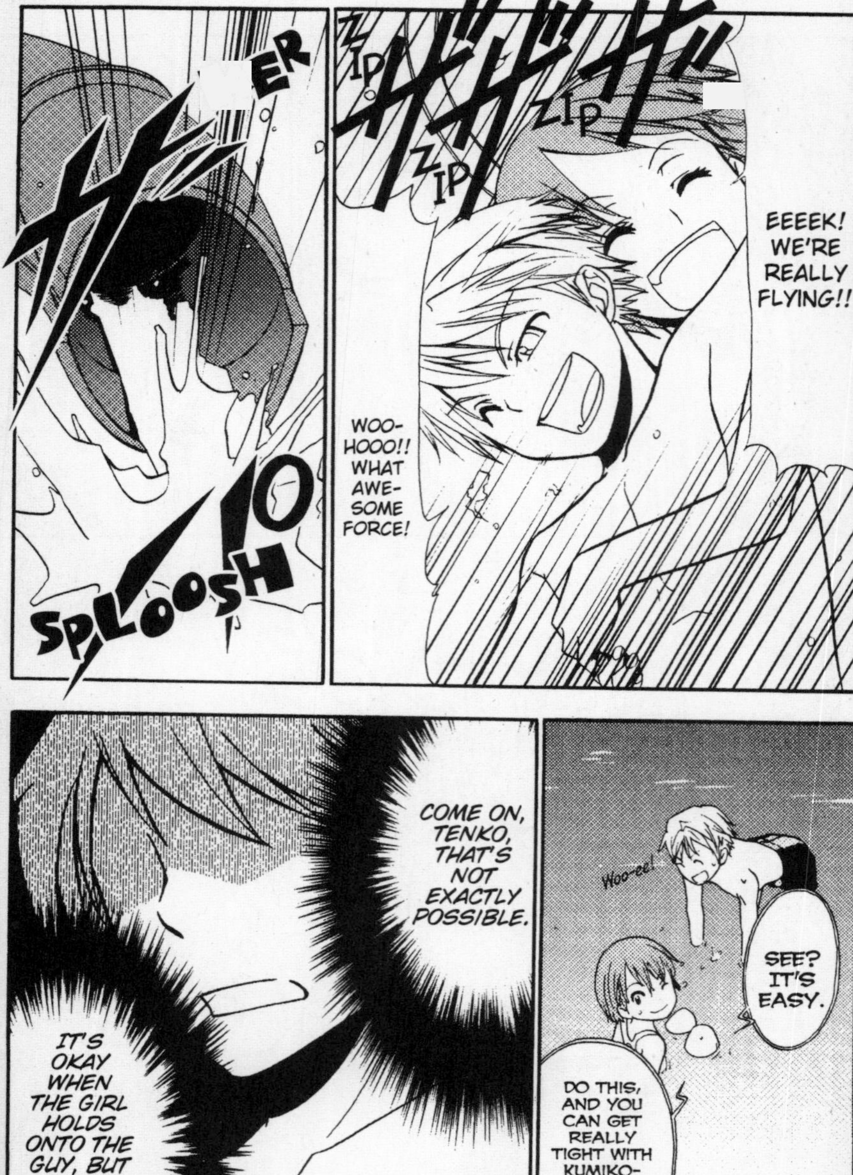

ZIP
ZIP
ZIP
EEEEK! WE'RE REALLY FLYING!!
WOO-HOOO!! WHAT AWE-SOME FORCE!
ER
SPLOOSH
Woo-ee!
SEE? IT'S EASY.
DO THIS, AND YOU CAN GET REALLY TIGHT WITH KUMIKO-SAN, NO PROBLEM.
COME ON, TENKO, THAT'S NOT EXACTLY POSSIBLE.
IT'S OKAY WHEN THE GIRL HOLDS ONTO THE GUY, BUT VICE-VERSA...

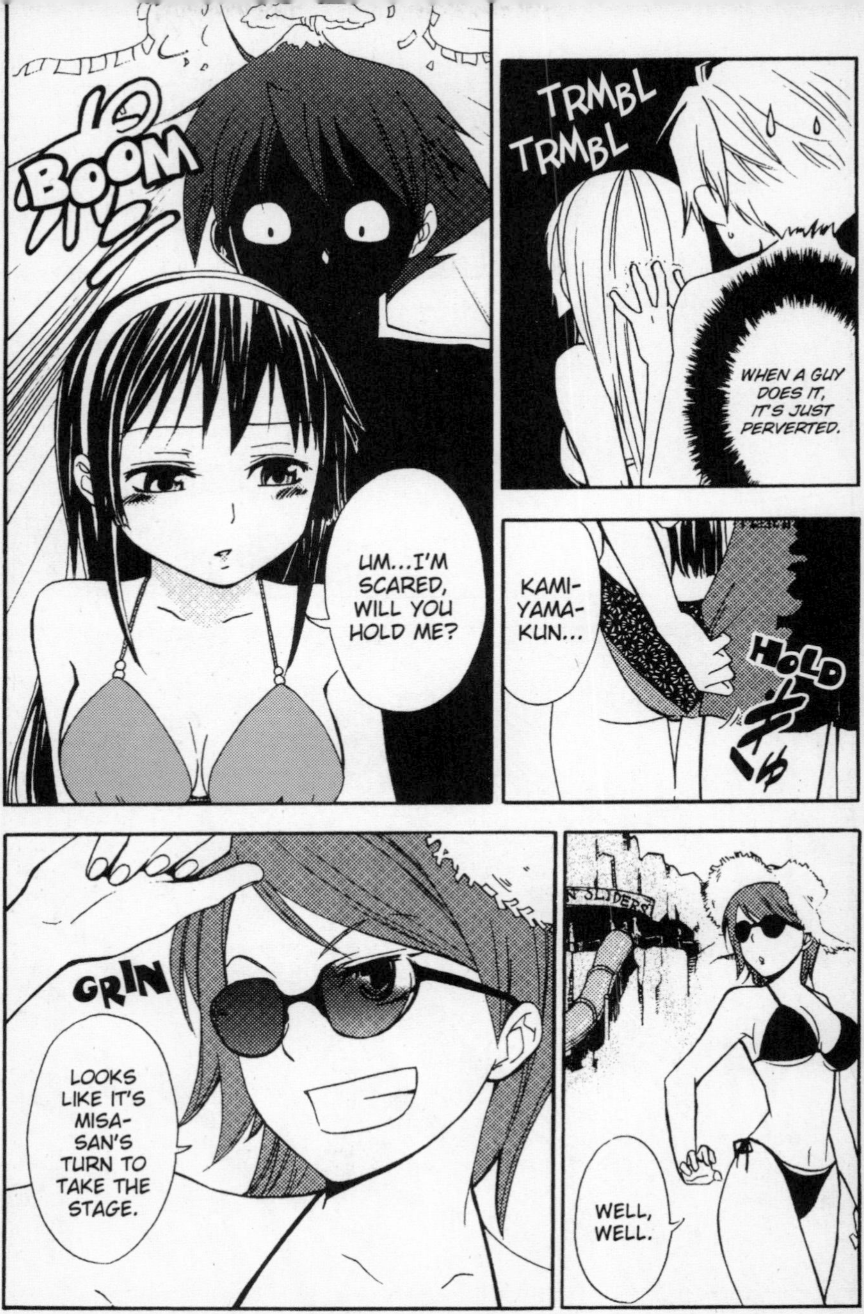
TRMBL TRMBL
WHEN A GUY DOES IT, IT'S JUST PERVERTED.
KAMI-YAMA-KUN...
HOLD
BOOM
UM...I'M SCARED, WILL YOU HOLD ME?
N SLIDERS
WELL, WELL.
GRIN
LOOKS LIKE IT'S MISA-SAN'S TURN TO TAKE THE STAGE.

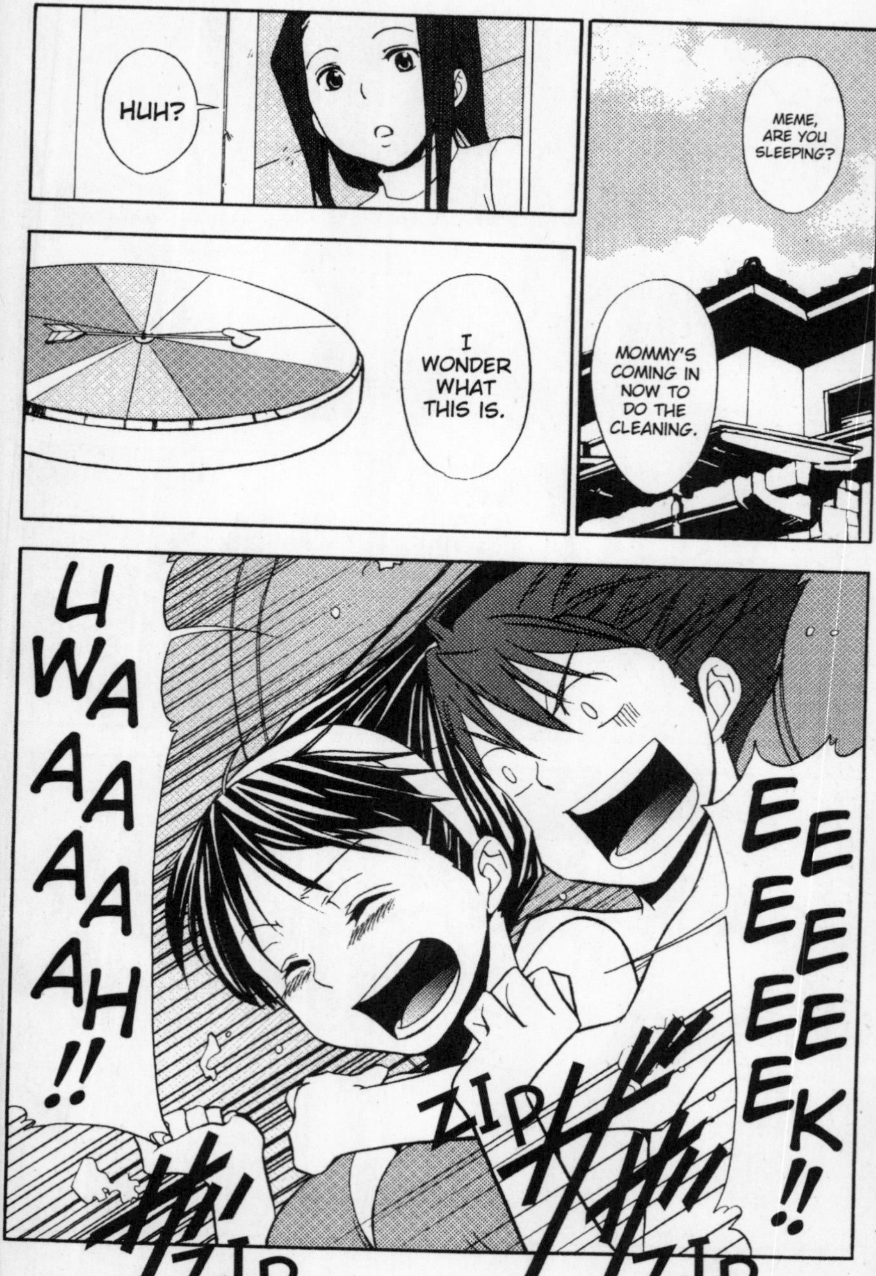
MEME, ARE YOU SLEEPING?
MOMMY'S COMING IN NOW TO DO THE CLEANING.
HUH?
I WONDER WHAT THIS IS.
EEEEEEEK!!
ZIP
ZIP
UWAAAAAAH!!
ZIP

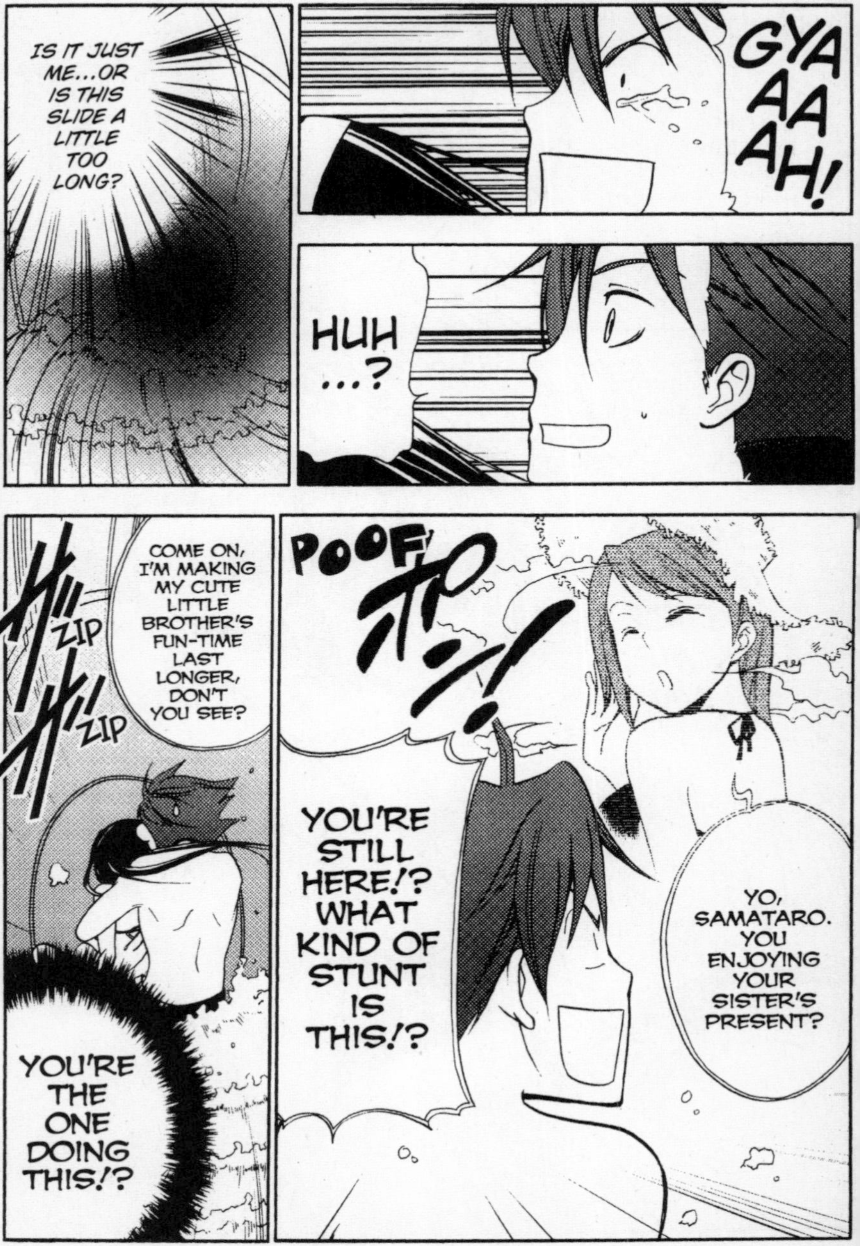

GYAAAAH!
HUH...?
IS IT JUST ME...OR IS THIS SLIDE A LITTLE TOO LONG?
POOF
ポン!
YO, SAMATARO. YOU ENJOYING YOUR SISTER'S PRESENT?
YOU'RE STILL HERE!? WHAT KIND OF STUNT IS THIS!?
ZIP
ZIP
COME ON, I'M MAKING MY CUTE LITTLE BROTHER'S FUN-TIME LAST LONGER, DON'T YOU SEE?
YOU'RE THE ONE DOING THIS!?

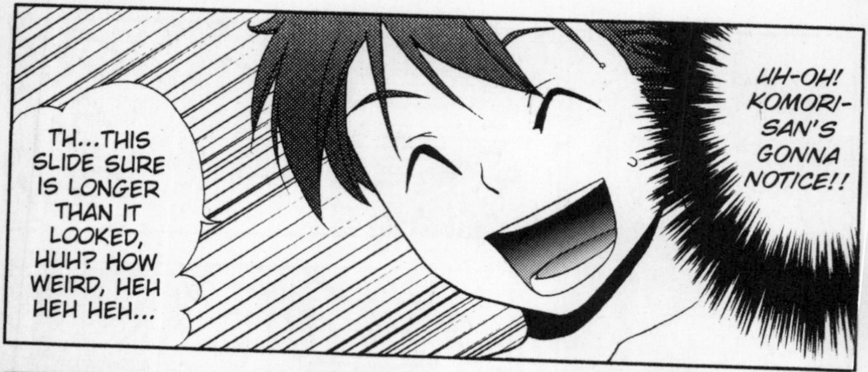
UH-OH! KOMORI-SAN'S GONNA NOTICE!!
TH...THIS SLIDE SURE IS LONGER THAN IT LOOKED, HUH? HOW WEIRD, HEH HEH HEH...

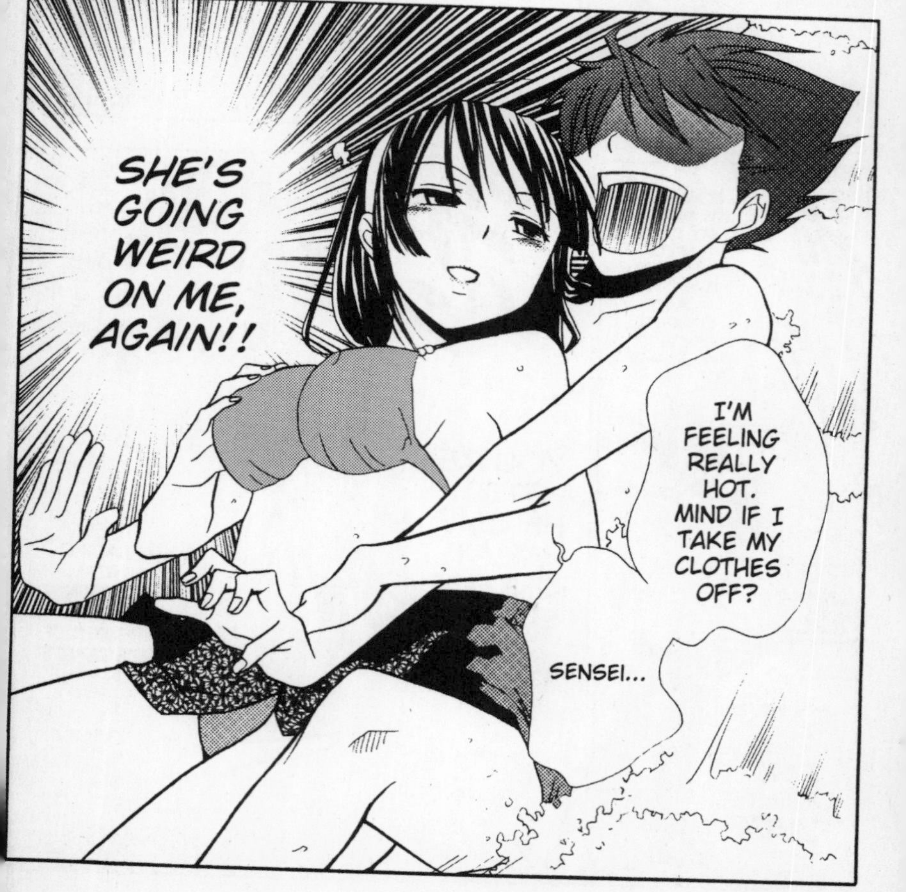
I'M FEELING REALLY HOT. MIND IF I TAKE MY CLOTHES OFF?
SENSEI...
SHE'S GOING WEIRD ON ME, AGAIN!!

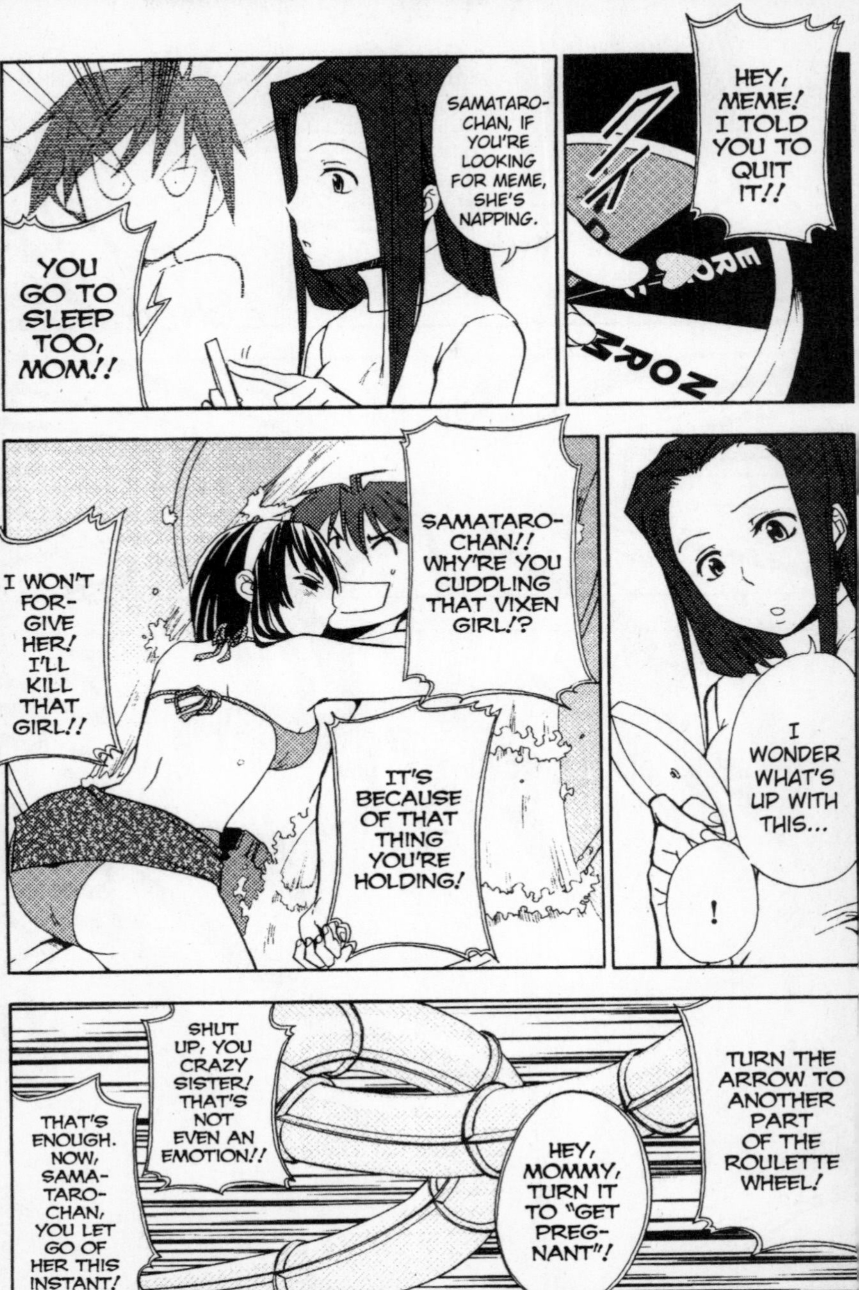
HEY, MEME! I TOLD YOU TO QUIT IT!!
SAMATARO-CHAN, IF YOU'RE LOOKING FOR MEME, SHE'S NAPPING.
YOU GO TO SLEEP TOO, MOM!!
I WONDER WHAT'S UP WITH THIS...
!
SAMATARO-CHAN!! WHY'RE YOU CUDDLING THAT VIXEN GIRL!?
IT'S BECAUSE OF THAT THING YOU'RE HOLDING!
I WON'T FOR-GIVE HER! I'LL KILL THAT GIRL!!
TURN THE ARROW TO ANOTHER PART OF THE ROULETTE WHEEL!
HEY, MOMMY, TURN IT TO "GET PREG-NANT"!
SHUT UP, YOU CRAZY SISTER! THAT'S NOT EVEN AN EMOTION!!
THAT'S ENOUGH. NOW, SAMA-TARO-CHAN, YOU LET GO OF HER THIS INSTANT!

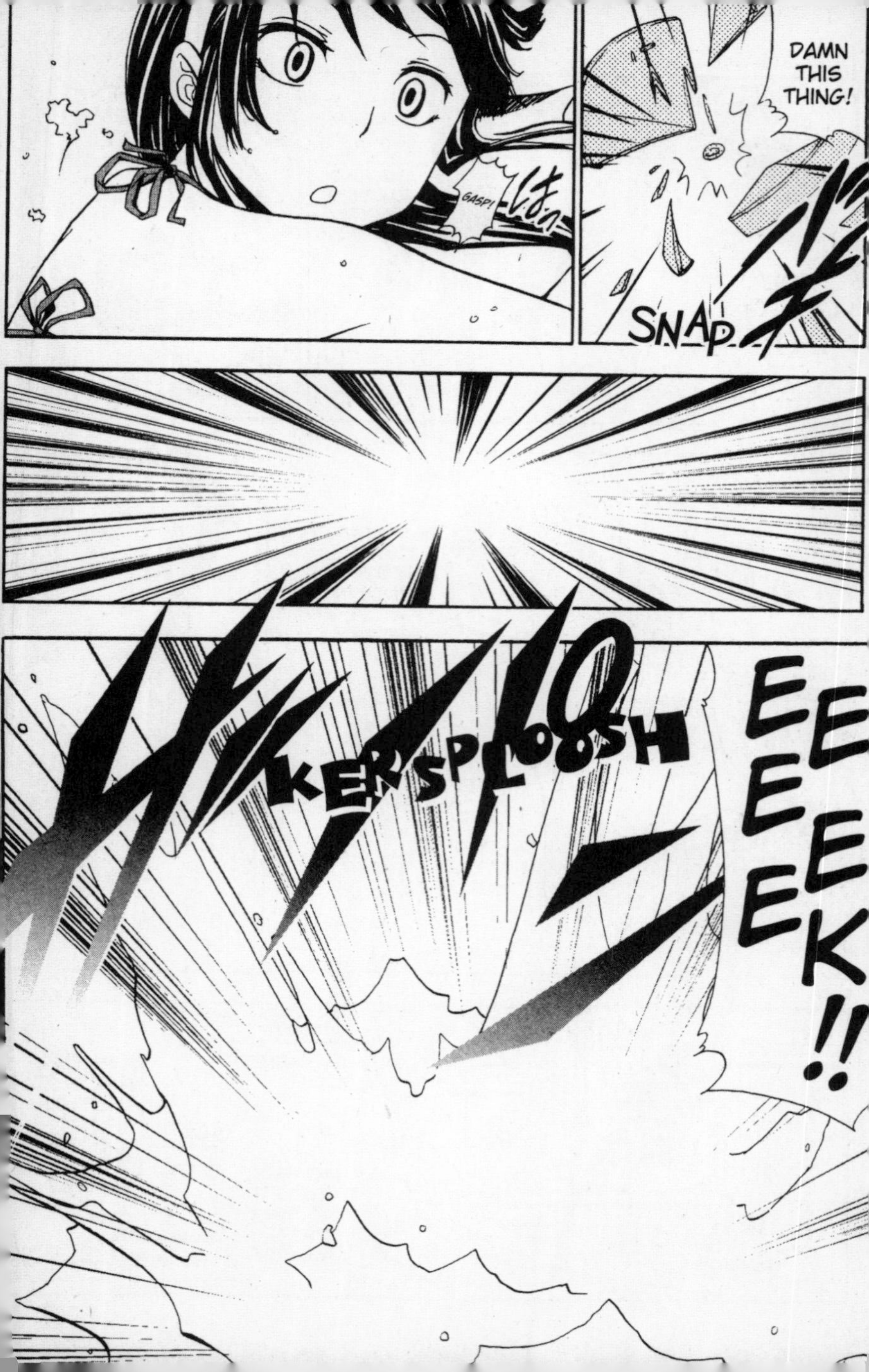
DAMN THIS THING!
SNAP
GASP!
はっ
EEEEEEK!!
KERSPLOOSH

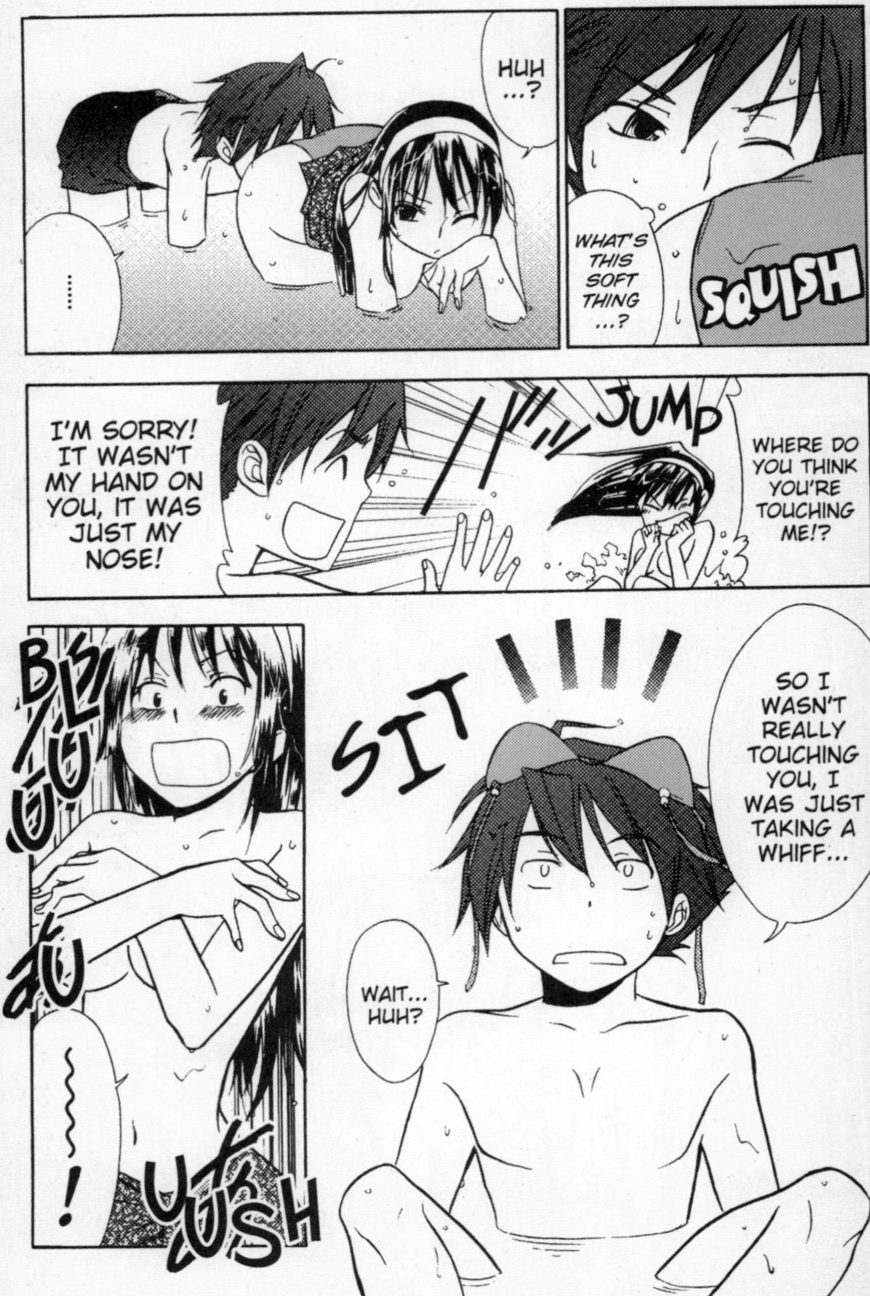
WHAT'S THIS SOFT THING ...?
SQUISH
HUH ...?
......
WHERE DO YOU THINK YOU'RE TOUCHING ME!?
JUMP
I'M SORRY! IT WASN'T MY HAND ON YOU, IT WAS JUST MY NOSE!
SO I WASN'T REALLY TOUCHING YOU, I WAS JUST TAKING A WHIFF...
SIT
WAIT... HUH?

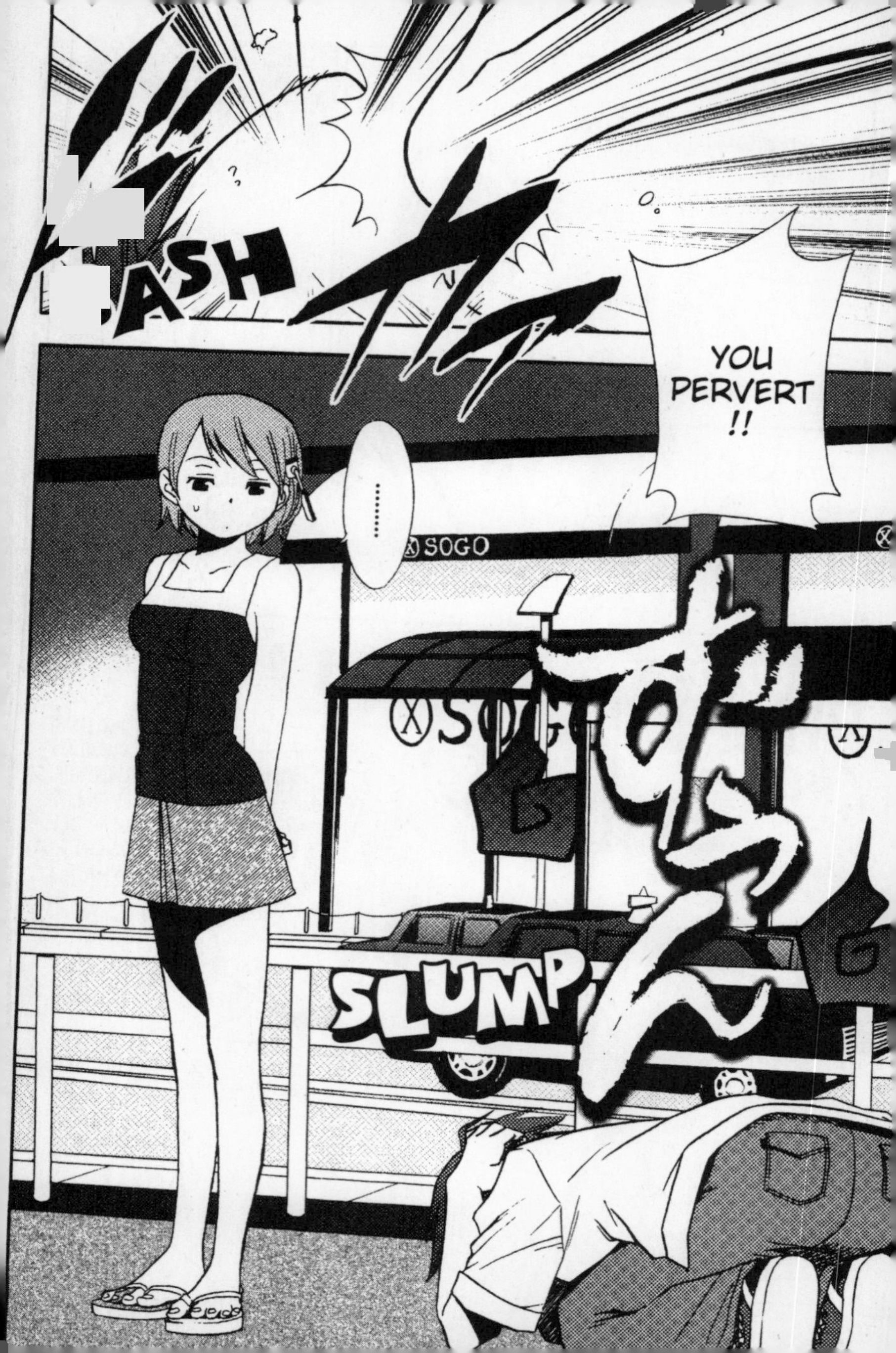
ASH
YOU PERVERT !!
......
SOGO
SLUMP

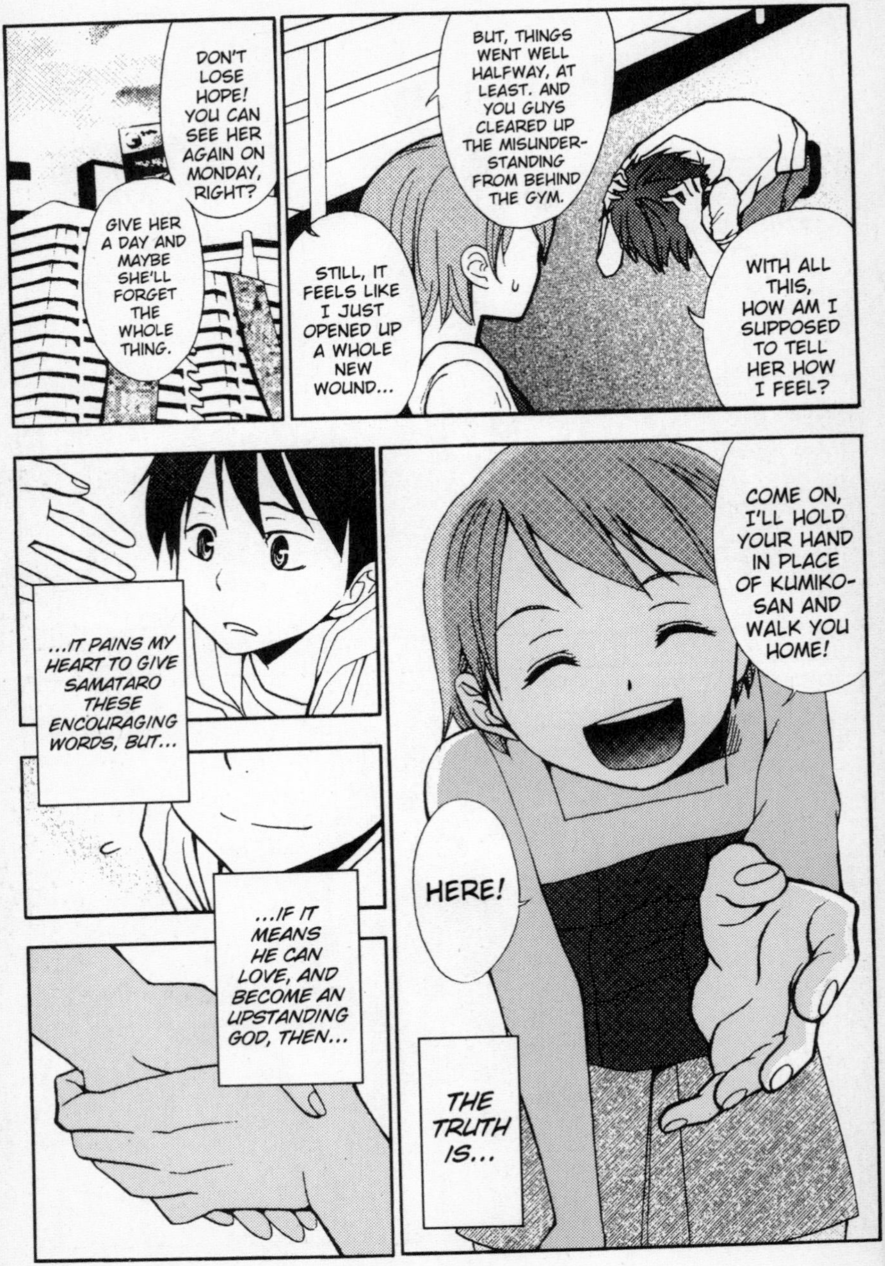
BUT, THINGS WENT WELL HALFWAY, AT LEAST. AND YOU GUYS CLEARED UP THE MISUNDER-STANDING FROM BEHIND THE GYM.
WITH ALL THIS, HOW AM I SUPPOSED TO TELL HER HOW I FEEL?
STILL, IT FEELS LIKE I JUST OPENED UP A WHOLE NEW WOUND...
DON'T LOSE HOPE! YOU CAN SEE HER AGAIN ON MONDAY, RIGHT?
GIVE HER A DAY AND MAYBE SHE'LL FORGET THE WHOLE THING.
COME ON, I'LL HOLD YOUR HAND IN PLACE OF KUMIKO-SAN AND WALK YOU HOME!
HERE!
THE TRUTH IS...
...IT PAINS MY HEART TO GIVE SAMATARO THESE ENCOURAGING WORDS, BUT...
...IF IT MEANS HE CAN LOVE, AND BECOME AN UPSTANDING GOD, THEN...

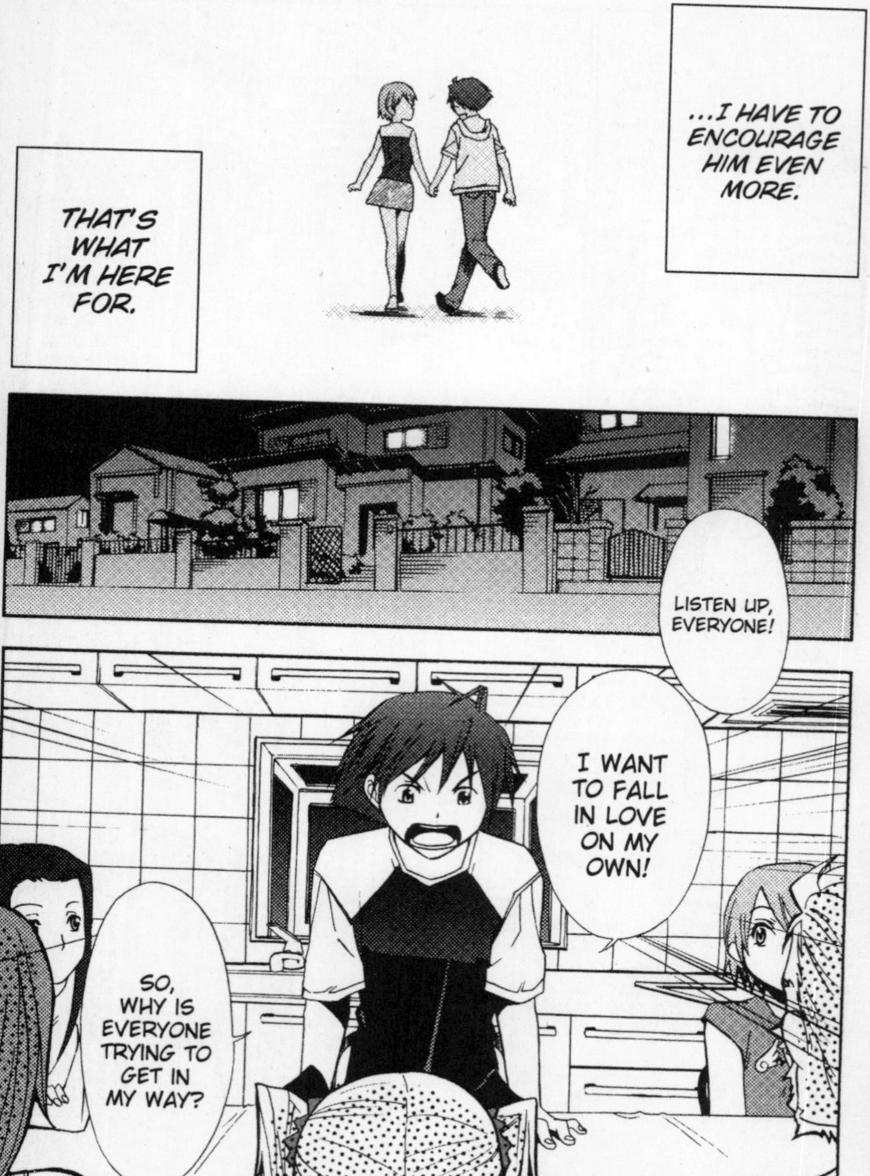
...I HAVE TO ENCOURAGE HIM EVEN MORE.
THAT'S WHAT I'M HERE FOR.
LISTEN UP, EVERYONE!
I WANT TO FALL IN LOVE ON MY OWN!
SO, WHY IS EVERYONE TRYING TO GET IN MY WAY?

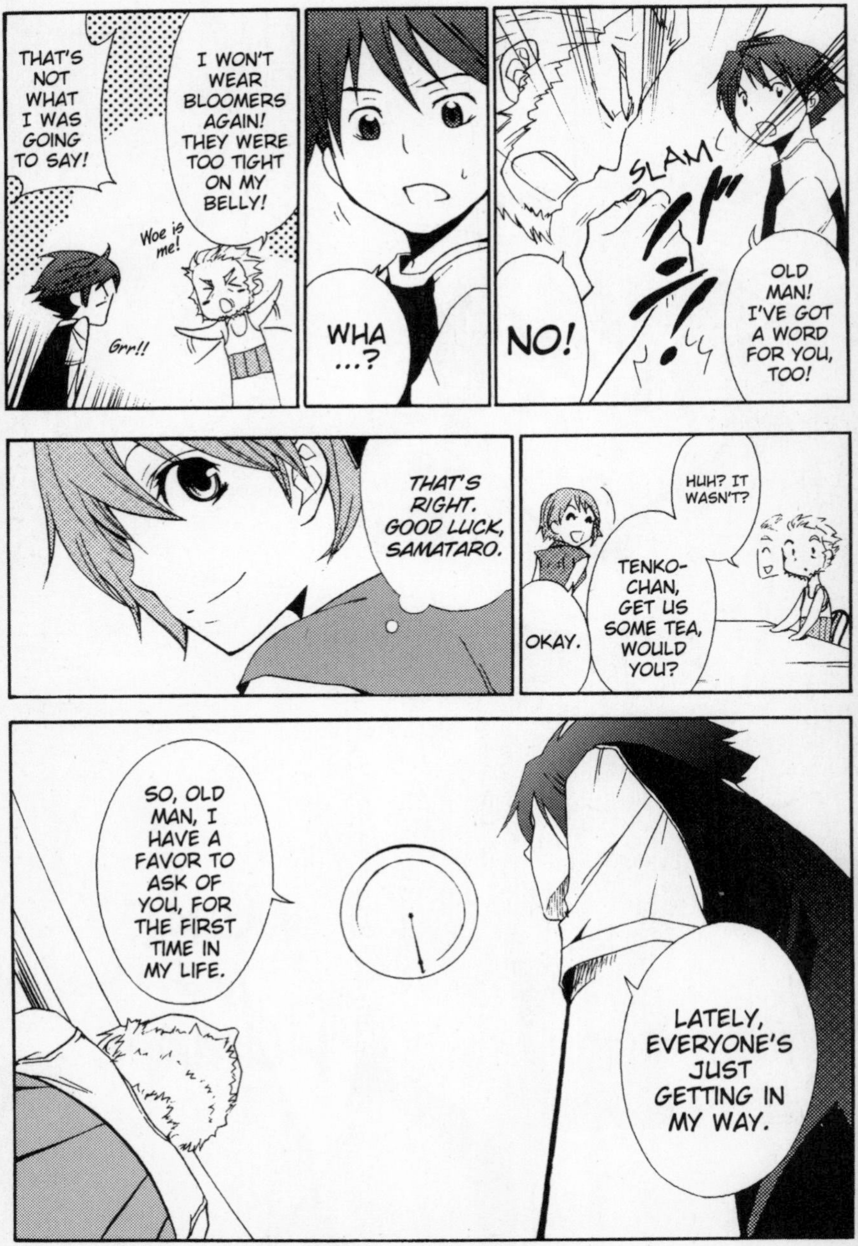
OLD MAN! I'VE GOT A WORD FOR YOU, TOO!
SLAM
NO!
WHA ...?
I WON'T WEAR BLOOMERS AGAIN! THEY WERE TOO TIGHT ON MY BELLY!
THAT'S NOT WHAT I WAS GOING TO SAY!
Woe is me!
Grr!!
HUH? IT WASN'T?
TENKO-CHAN, GET US SOME TEA, WOULD YOU?
OKAY.
THAT'S RIGHT. GOOD LUCK, SAMATARO.
SO, OLD MAN, I HAVE A FAVOR TO ASK OF YOU, FOR THE FIRST TIME IN MY LIFE.
LATELY, EVERYONE'S JUST GETTING IN MY WAY.

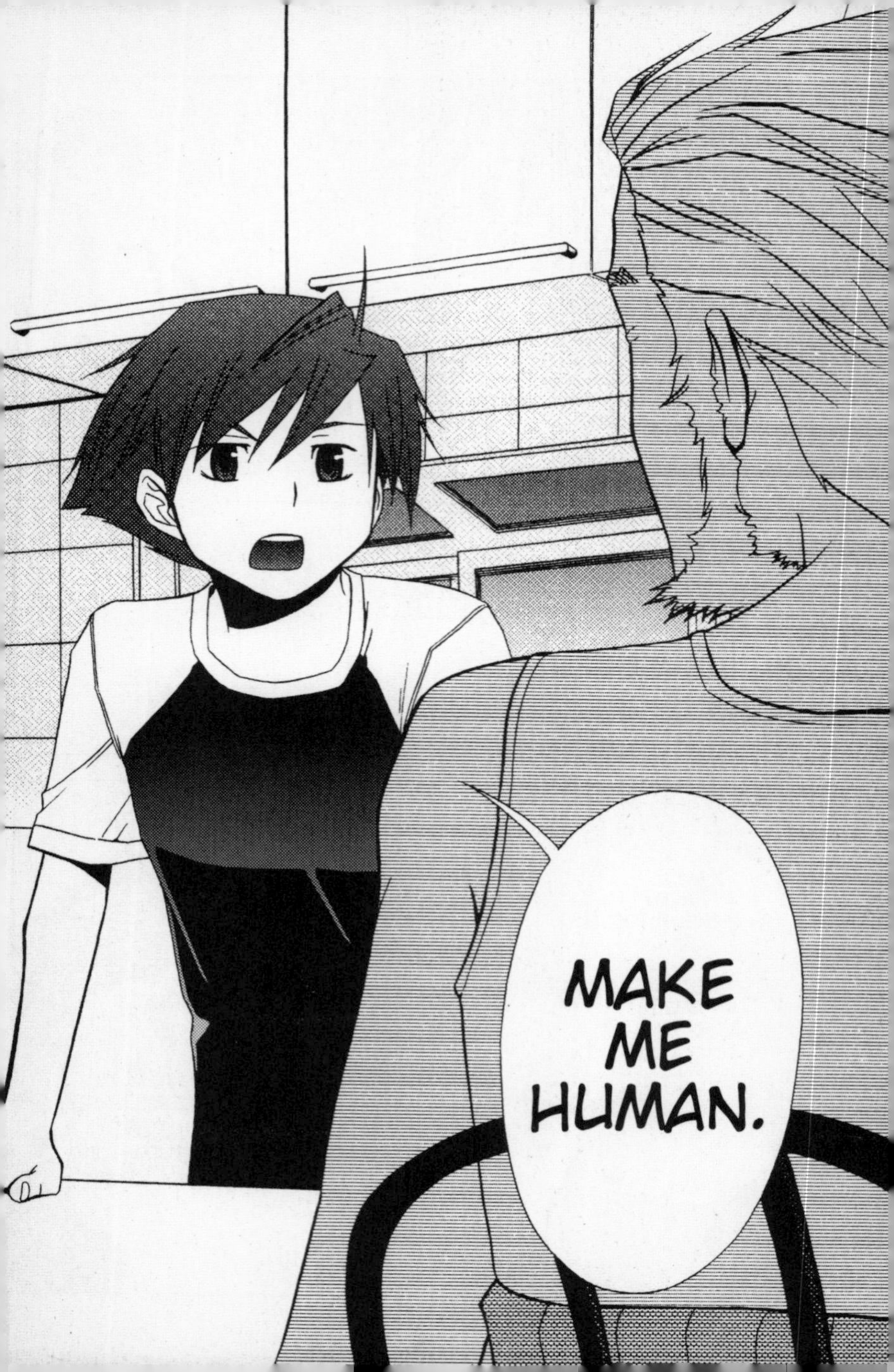
MAKE ME HUMAN.

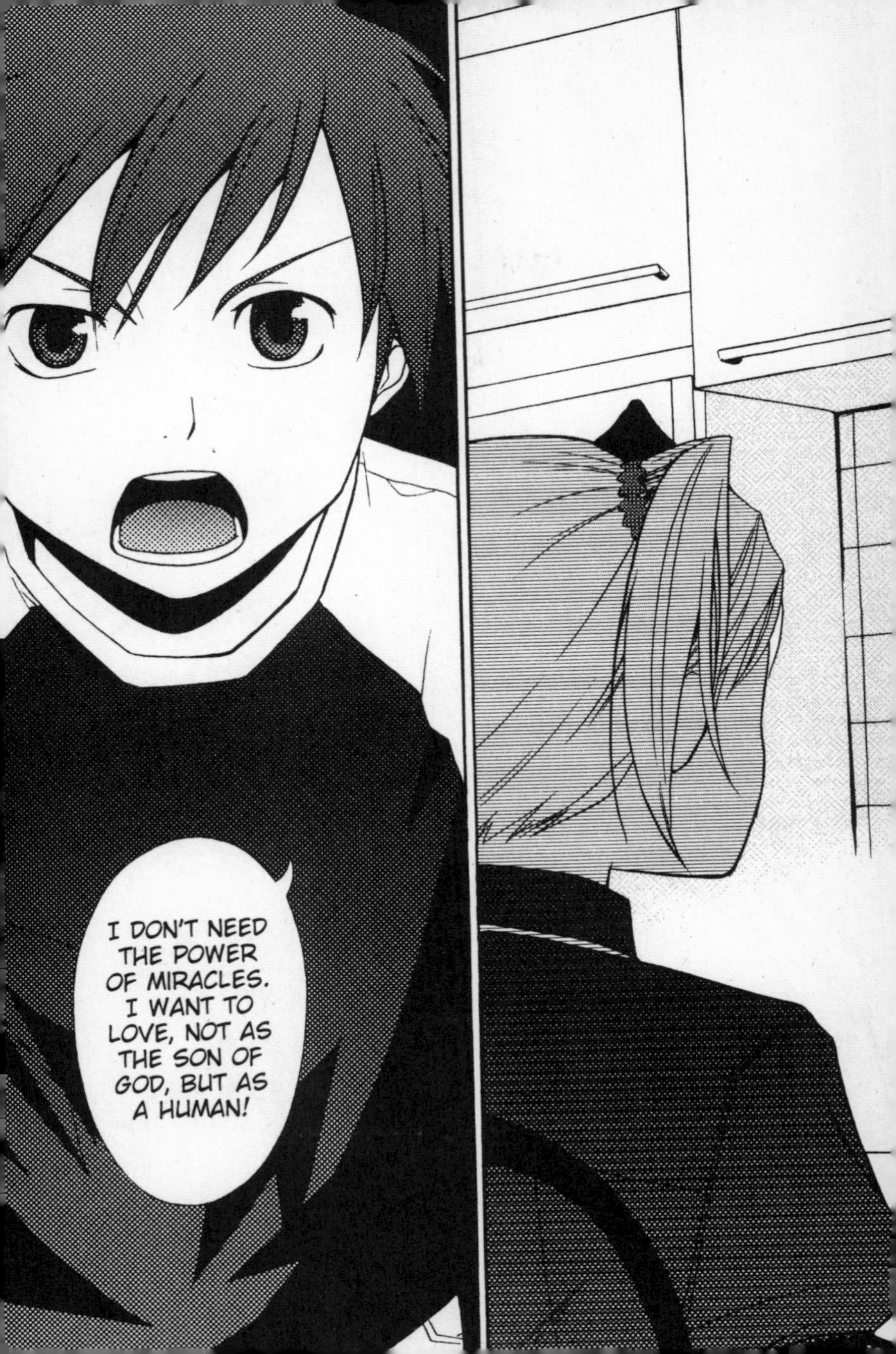
I DON'T NEED THE POWER OF MIRACLES. I WANT TO LOVE, NOT AS THE SON OF GOD, BUT AS A HUMAN!

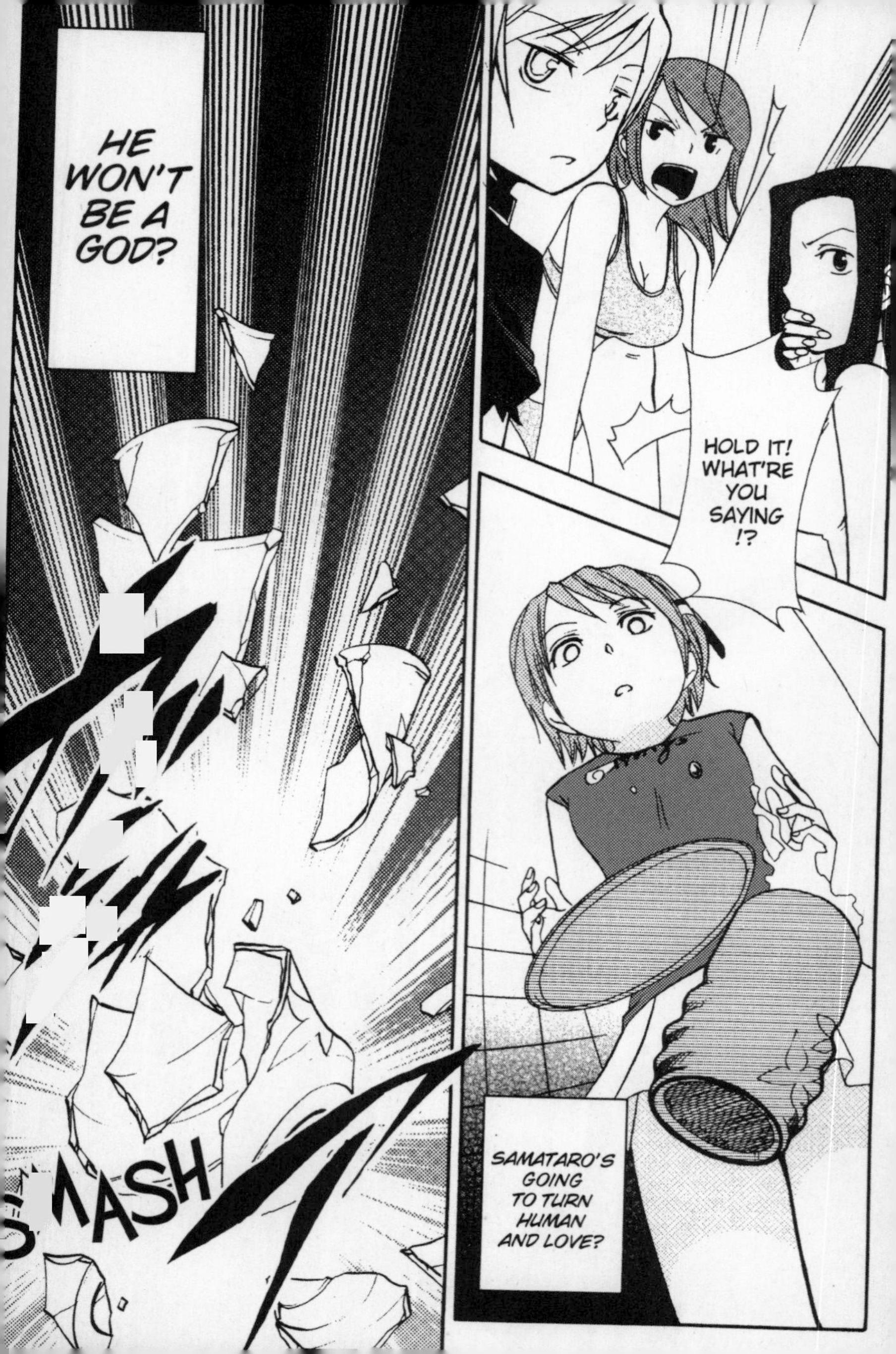
HOLD IT! WHAT'RE YOU SAYING!?
SAMATARO'S GOING TO TURN HUMAN AND LOVE?
HE WON'T BE A GOD?
MASH

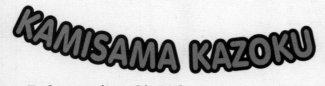

To be continued in Volume 2

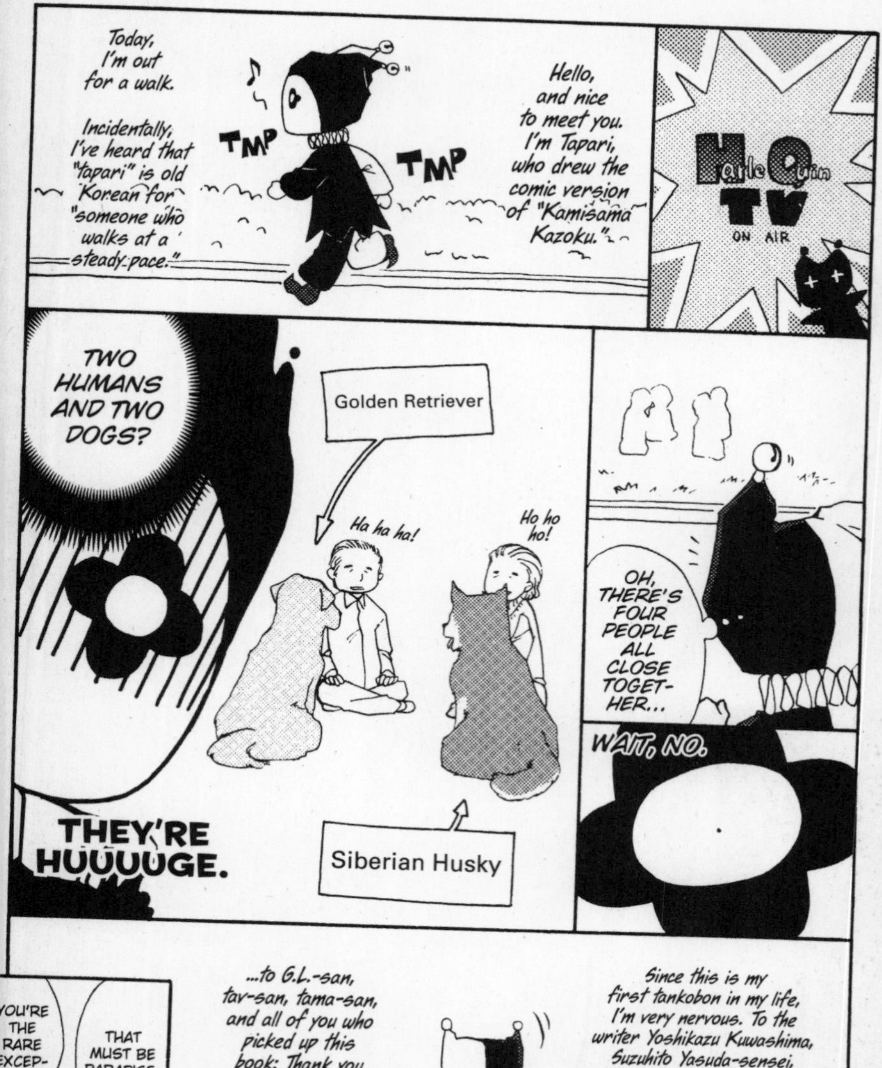
HarleQuin TV
ON AIR
Hello, and nice to meet you. I'm Tapari, who drew the comic version of "Kamisama Kazoku."
TMP
TMP
Today, I'm out for a walk.
Incidentally, I've heard that "tapari" is old Korean for "someone who walks at a steady pace."
OH, THERE'S FOUR PEOPLE ALL CLOSE TOGET-HER...
WAIT, NO.
TWO HUMANS AND TWO DOGS?
Golden Retriever
Ho ho ho!
Ha ha ha!
Siberian Husky
THEY'RE HUUUUGE.
Since this is my first tankobon in my life, I'm very nervous. To the writer Yoshikazu Kuwashima, Suzuhito Yasuda-sensei, editor Matsuoka, my manager Fujiwara, and my Korean manager Kim-san and Park-san from the international relations department...
...to G.L.-san, tav-san, tama-san, and all of you who picked up this book: Thank you very much! I hope you tag along for the second volume, too!
THAT MUST BE PARADISE.
YOU'RE THE RARE EXCEP-TION.
Friend who loves dogs.

In the next volume of

KAMISAMA KAZOKU

Samataro was willing to give up divinity for love...

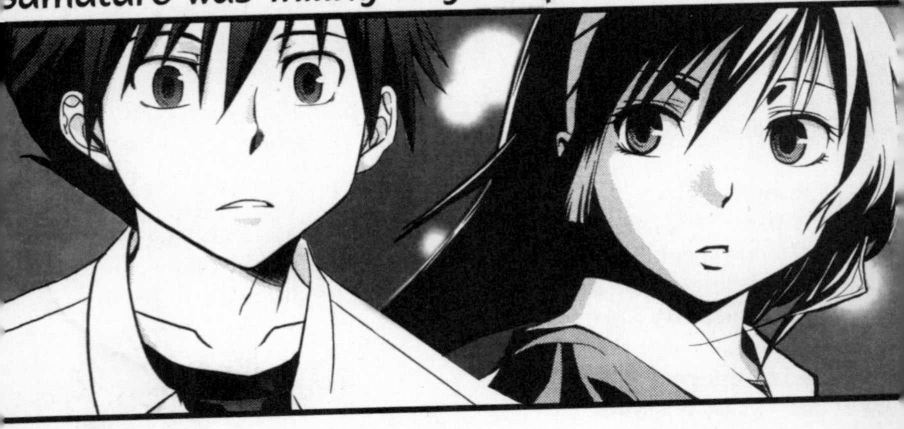

...but what about friendship?

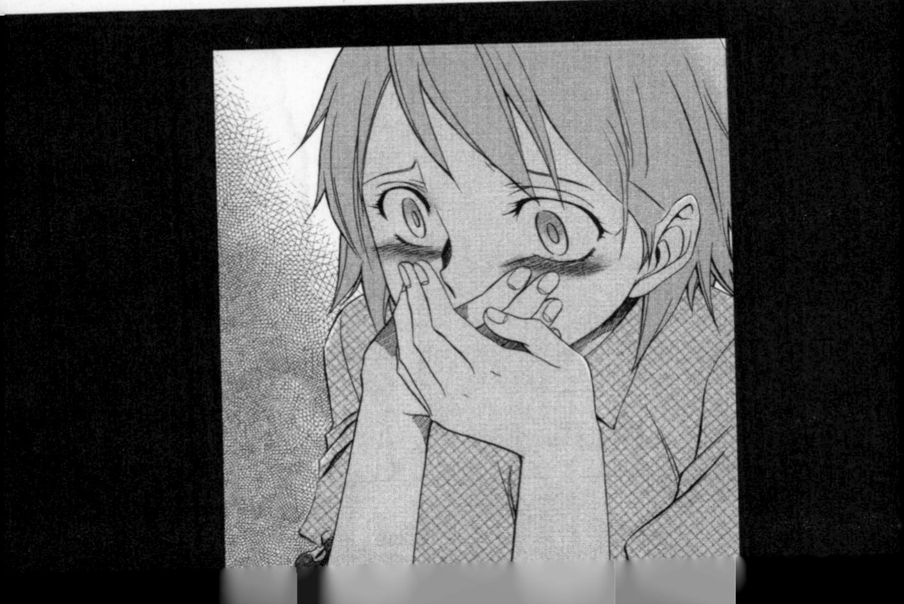

Translator's Notes

Pg. 6 – Kamiyama
Samataro's last name "Kamiyama" 神山 is a pun. Phonetically, it's a common name, though in his case the "kami" uses the symbol for "God."

Pg. 11 – heart voice
Literally the "voice of the heart", this is when Samataro and his divine family/friends speak "telepathically" in a way so that only they can hear each other. It might be a reference to, or variation of *tashintsuu*, which is one of the fabled Six Superhuman Powers.

Pg. 14 – bloomers
These are basically shorts with elastic at the legs. They were often used in the gym uniforms of Japanese girls, but are becoming much less common.

Pg. 123 – *pierrot*
One of the most popular characters in Commedia dell-Arte and mime. This character is a sad clown, though Tenko's obviously referring to the fact that he is silent.

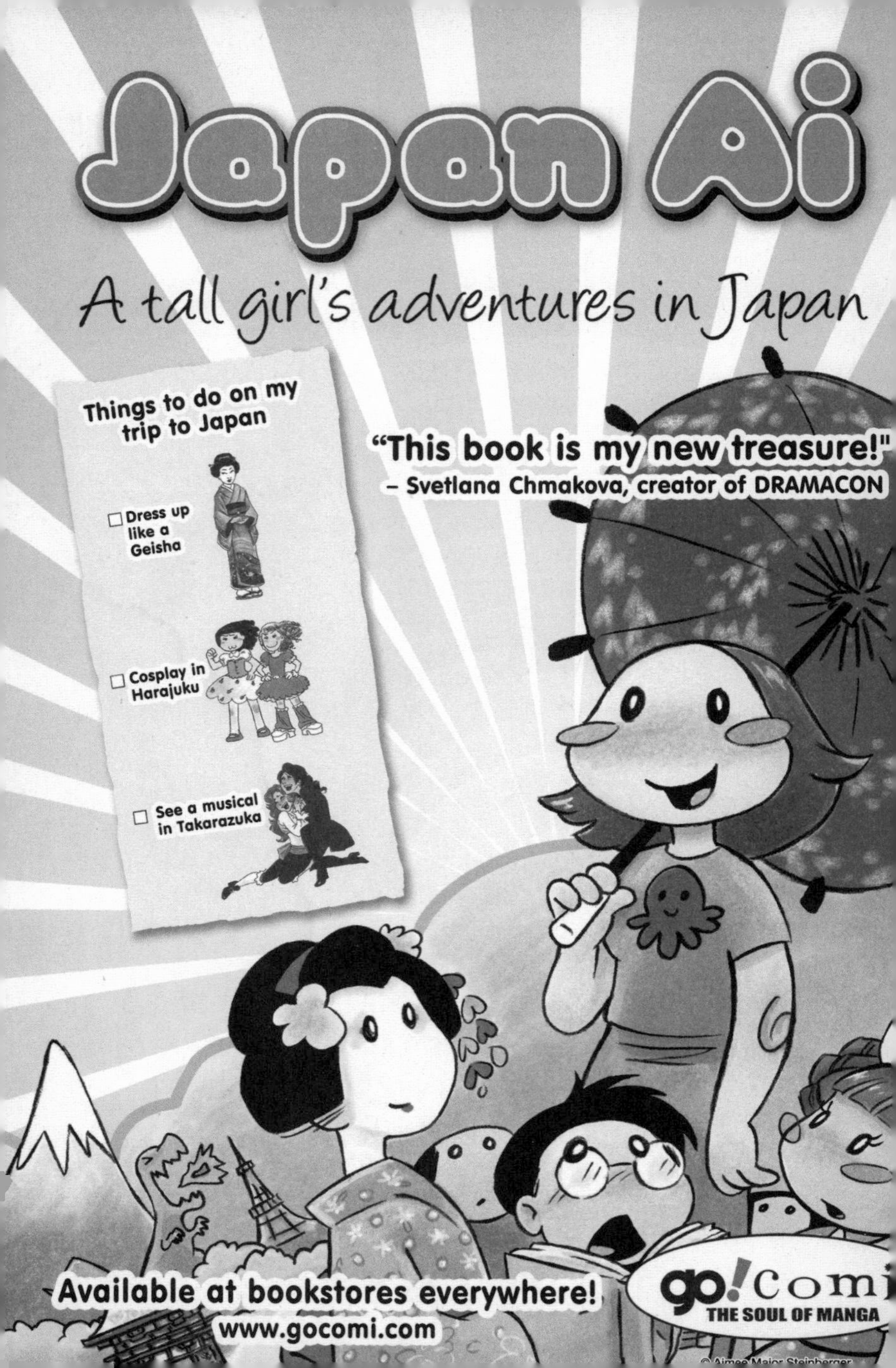
Japan Ai
A tall girl's adventures in Japan
Things to do on my trip to Japan
Dress up like a Geisha
Cosplay in Harajuku
See a musical in Takarazuka
"This book is my new treasure!"
– Svetlana Chmakova, creator of DRAMACON
Available at bookstores everywhere!
www.gocomi.com
go!comi
THE SOUL OF MANGA
© Aimee Major Steinberger

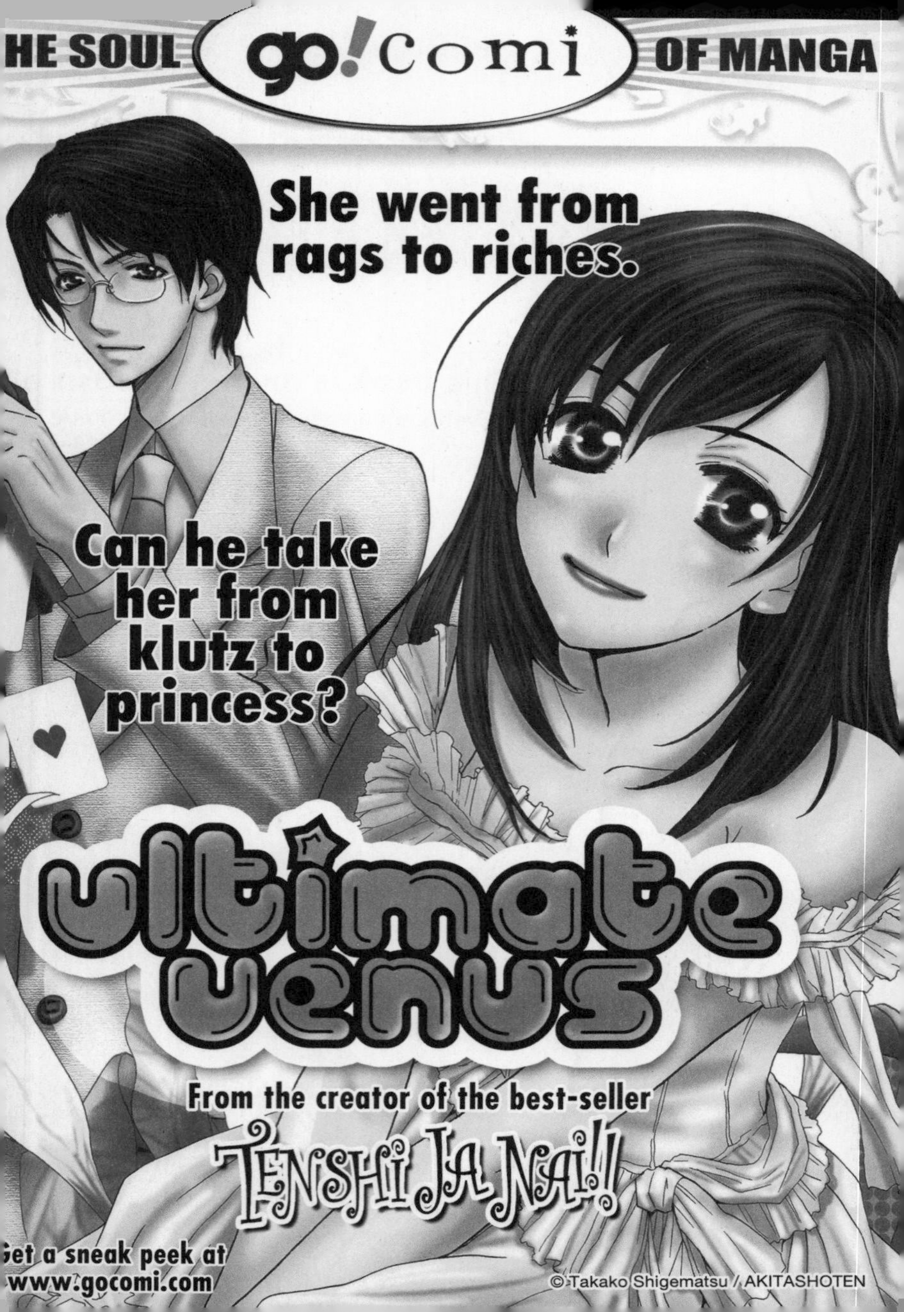
HE SOUL go!comi OF MANGA
She went from rags to riches.
Can he take her from klutz to princess?
ultimate venus
From the creator of the best-seller
TENSHI JA NAI!!
Get a sneak peek at www.gocomi.com
© Takako Shigematsu / AKITASHOTEN